# The Challenges of Orpheus

# The Challenges of Orpheus

*Lyric Poetry and Early Modern England*

HEATHER DUBROW

The Johns Hopkins University Press

*Baltimore*

The Johns Hopkins University Press
2715 North Charles Street
Baltimore, Maryland 21218-4363
www.press.jhu.edu

Library of Congress Cataloging-in-Publication Data

Dubrow, Heather
The challenges of Orpheus : lyric poetry and early modern England /
Heather Dubrow.
    p.   cm.
Includes bibliographical references (p.   ) and index.
ISBN-13: 978-0-8018-8704-8 (hardcover : alk. paper)
ISBN-10: 0-8018-8704-6 (hardcover : alk. paper)
1. English poetry—Early modern, 1500–1700—History and
criticism—Theory, etc. 2. Literature and society—England—History.
3. Poetics—History. 4. Literary form—History. I. Title.
    PR549.L8D83   2007
    821'.0409—dc22        2007018748


A catalog record for this book is available from
the British Library.

*Special discounts are available for bulk purchases of this book. For more
information, please contact Special Sales at 410-516-6936 or
specialsales@press.jhu.edu.*

*For my students*

# Contents

# Acknowledgments

The norms of lyric often—though, I will argue, not invariably—generate short poems. The debts I incurred while writing about lyric generate a long list. My work on this book has been supported by the Guggenheim Foundation, the National Endowment for the Humanities, and the Graduate School Research Committee of the University of Wisconsin–Madison. I am grateful for the efficiency, judiciousness, and encouragement of Michael Lonegro, my editor at the Johns Hopkins University Press. I am delighted to have the opportunity to acknowledge my indebtedness to the following colleagues for useful information and suggestions: Stephen Buhler, Ronald Bush, Jonathan Culler, the late Gwynne Blakemore Evans, David Fleming, Cecilia Ford, Sara Guyer, Hannibal Hamlin, Jonathan Hart, Jane Hedley, Richard Helgerson, Jean Howard, Wendy Hyman, Robert Kaufman, Lynn Keller, Theresa Kelley, Richard Knowles, Barbara Lewalski, Jennifer Lewin, David Loewenstein, Harold Love, Carole Newlands, Jack Niles, Marcy North, James Phelan, Anne Lake Prescott, Patricia Rosenmeyer, David Schalkwyk, Henry Turner, William Waters, Neil Whitehead, Helen Wilcox, Susanne Wofford, Linda Woodbridge, and Carla Zecher. Special thanks to those who also read and offered valuable advice about chapters of the manuscript: Marshall Brown, Colin Burrow, Bonnie Costello, Mary Crane, Roland Greene, Jack Niles, James Phelan, Thomas Schaub, and the members of my department's Draft Group. By fostering my own career as a poet, the creative writers in my department fostered my work on this book; I am grateful to Ronald Wallace in particular. A series of conscientious research assistants worked energetically and meticulously on the manuscript: Sarah Armstrong, Patricia Frank, Kimberly Huth, David Plastrik, Jason Siegel, and Aaron Spooner. It is a pleasure as well to acknowledge the indirect but nonetheless powerful contributions of the two undergraduate teachers who developed my interest in lyric poetry: the late David Kalstone and Neil Rudenstine. Some thirty years ago Sandy Mack became both a mentor to me and a model for me of generous and judicious professionalism; his helpfulness on innumerable occasions in the intervening years has deepened my debt. By incorporating the names of two elementary school teachers, Mary and Patricia Tighe, into the title of my endowed chair, I emphasized the significance of K–12 teachers, and I want to acknowledge it here as well. My debts to—and delight in—my own students, ranging from undergraduates to dissertators, are enumerated in the endnotes and celebrated in the dedication. Over the past six years, Donald Rowe has enriched this book in many ways; over the past sixteen years, he has enriched the life of its author in even more ways.

Part of Chapter 4 was published in different form in *Tulsa Studies in Women's Literature* 22 (2003), published by the University of Tulsa. Sections of Chapter 5 have also appeared in earlier form elsewhere and are reprinted with the permission of the publishers: "The Interplay of Narrative and Lyric: Competition, Cooperation, and the Case of the Anticipatory Amalgam," *Narrative* 14 (2006), 254–271; " 'He had the dialect and different skill': Authorizers in *Henry V*, 'A Lover's Complaint,' and *Othello*," in *Critical Essays on Shakespeare's "A Lover's Complaint": Suffering Ecstasy*, ed. Shirley Sharon-Zisser (Burlington, VT: Ashgate, 2006, pp. 121–136).

*Note to the Reader*

With one exception, my citations of Renaissance texts retain the original spelling, but I have regularized u/v and i/j, as well as the capitalization in titles, and ampersands have been replaced; in the instance of Spenser, however, orthography is not regularized.

# Introduction

Despite the problems posed by defining and describing lyric, the term appears with telling frequency in contexts ranging from the scholarship of many disciplines to the seductions of Madison Avenue to the stanzas of lyric poets themselves. Northrop Frye, characteristically no less acerbic than acute, remarks that "there is a popular tendency to call anything in verse a lyric that is not actually divided into twelve books."[1] The word in question and its cognates are indeed used at best liberally and variously, and at worst merely loosely, in numerous academic fields. Deployed broadly by film critics, "lyric" is also applied more specifically to the work of Stan Brakhage; his own writings on his films and those of his critics draw attention to characteristics frequently though not uncontroversially attributed to lyric poetry, such as intensity, a disruption of linear chronology, and an emphasis on the emotions of the artist.[2] A placard in the San Diego Art Museum observes of Edouard Vuillard, who, like other members of the late-nineteenth-century Nabi movement, created highly decorative surfaces: "his paintings are lyrical, poetic visions." One study attributes to the modern Dutch architect and designer W. R. Dudock "a lyricism which had a close affinity with the Amsterdam School."[3]

Positioned by John Stuart Mill, Theodor W. Adorno, and many others as an antithesis and even potentially an antidote to the commodified marketplace, lyric has nonetheless repeatedly been impressed into the service of commodification.[4] An advertisement from the Crate and Barrel chain of stores celebrates the "lyrical patterning in luxurious, frosty silver" of a tablecloth.[5] A type of wine glass from the same company has been graced with the name "Lyric Stemware," either because it has the delicacy sometimes attributed to that mode or because it will contain the drink supposed to inspire it. A bar in Madison, Wisconsin, perhaps playing on that same ambiguity, sports the name "Liquid Lyric Lounge," presumably encouraging its more sober patrons to debate whether the adjective applies to poetic or potable fare.

Poets too have attempted to deploy the resonances of the term present in both scholarly discussions and advertisements. When Robert Herrick declares in "An Ode to Sir Clipsebie Crew" that "A Goblet, to the brim, / Of Lyrick Wine" (15–16) will be quaffed, he is referring not only to the wine's capacity to inspire poetry and its association with Anacreon but also to the energy and sensuous pleasure that it, like poetry, can evoke.[6] In our own era, the Irish poet Eavan Boland writes of an illness:

> I re-construct the soaked through midnights;
> vigils; the histories I never learned
> to predict the lyric of
>
> ("Fever," 25–27)[7]

In the context of a poem where fever is associated with desire, loss, and irrationality and where disease also arguably gestures towards the presence of all three in Irish politics, lyric here seems to represent both the beauty and the meaning that are lost when temperatures rise. By linking that mode to "histories" (26), Boland also alerts her readers to the frequency with which it can be the companion and culmination of narrative rather than a temporary impediment, a point explored in Chapter 5.

A more cynical view of lyric is adumbrated by the twentieth-century Australian poet and librettist Gwen Harwood, whose own work in that mode is extraordinary in its range and complexity—no less extraordinary than the widespread neglect of it in both Great Britain and the United States. In a poem about the many ways communication breaks down when a marriage does, she declares, "Master writes a lyric poem / So his pain is manifest" ("Fido's Paw is Bleeding," 21–22), thus ironically gesturing towards yet another way the expository functions of language can really be an instrument for misleading oneself, others, or both.[8] Langston Hughes's "Little Lyric (Of Great Importance)," which reads in its entirety, "I wish the rent / Was heaven sent," deploys its title to play the idealization associated with lyric, ironically signaled as well by the noun in its second line, against the practical exigencies of quotidian life.[9] In addition to these stars of the poetic playing fields, players indubitably on minor league teams have also utilized "lyric" as a trope; for example, I too engaged with the complexities of the word when I compared the remission of a cancer patient to "the new-born curls that lyric across a baby's head" ("Remission and Revision," 19), associating her temporary reprise and the hair that signaled and symbolized it at once with fragility, energy, and delight.[10]

In responding to these conflicting definitions and descriptions of lyric, I choose to explore a range of its attributes without crisply positing a single characteristic, such as a trope, that could categorize all lyric poetry, or even all its versions in a particular period. Indeed, at several junctures this book demonstrates the problems arising from attempts to attribute a signature characteristic to the mode; such an enterprise is more foolhardy than brave (in the study as in the kitchen, aiming for crispness risks brittleness or even conflagration). Similarly, rather than developing a single overarching thesis, the book pursues a series of interlocking arguments. This introduction specifies why and how I have adopted these and related approaches and adumbrates some of their results.

_c, ᘀ_

The range of historical periods and of putatively lyric creations within even the handful of examples on which this chapter has opened gestures towards three of the principal questions, interrelated but separable, confronting the author of a study of lyric. Should it be defined transhistorically? What other problems complicate defining and describing it? And, however that first query is resolved, should a study of this mode focus primarily on a given historical period? This introduction argues for the real though limited value of transhistorical definitions if inflected—and hence sometimes destabilized—historically; at the same time, I defend the decision to concentrate on a single era as one of several viable responses to the complexities variously manifest in those definitions and in, for example, the poetry of Herrick and the platitudes of Crate and Barrel.

In considering the first of my three questions, the viability of transhistorical definitions, it is immediately clear that to deny significant generic affinities between, say, Anacreon and Herrick would be merely tendentious, not least because Herrick himself emphasizes those connections in a poem explored at the end of Chapter 1. And surely one needs to ask why, for example, stanzas recur in the lyrics of many different eras. Yet what might be categorized as the same characteristic may serve different functions and elicit different responses in different eras—variations that are no less significant than the apparent similarities. For example, whereas lyric is indeed associated with stanzas in many periods, the cultural coding of form varies from period to period and within a given era or a given text. The decision to write a sonnet in particular is typically an advertisement of one's virtuosity and genealogy in the early modern period and of a determined, in some circles even defiant, interest in form in our own day.

Unnuanced transhistorical generalizations court further dangers: the history of the criticism of lyric offers all too many examples of the perils of positing as normative a characteristic that dominates in a given period or author. Marjorie Perloff frequently attacks the celebration of Romantic poetry as the norm for its mode.[11] Cogently and characteristically, Earl Miner emphasizes that apostrophe and its companion prosopopoeia, though heralded as the signature trope of the mode in large part because of their centrality to the work of Romantic poets, in fact appear rarely in much of the world's literature.[12] Indeed, as my own study stresses, they are relatively rare even in English early modern texts.

Despite caveats like Perloff's and Miner's, generalizations about lyric rendered dubious by the absence of historical inflection continue to flourish. The dismissal of the mode as the last refuge of a scandal—that is, of the positing of an idealized, individuated subjectivity—flourishes in many quarters and includes pronouncements by some experimental poets eager to distinguish their own work (in both senses of that verb), an agenda to which I will return. One study declares that the dialogic propensities of the Song of Solomon distinguish it from "the lyrical tradition as we know it in the West"; yet that tradition in fact includes numerous dialogic poems, and pastoral in particular has a propensity for the dialogic.[13] Similarly, although his emphasis on the social interactions in classical lyric is a valuable counterweight to commonplaces about the isolated speaker, W. R. Johnson's establishment of those interactions as normative leads him to condemn the alternative meditative form as "an essentially unsatisfactory genre."[14]

Divided on so many other issues, those who discuss definitions of lyric often unite in despairing of that task. Daniel Albright's attempt to anatomize the form opens with, "In one sense there is no such thing as a lyric."[15] René Wellek, lamenting the impact of German theories of *Erlebnis*, despairs of transhistorical definitions: "One must abandon attempts to define the general nature of the lyric or the lyrical."[16] Other students of lyric, however, defend traditional descriptions of it with the unqualified intensity often associated with the mode itself. Helen Vendler firmly announces that while lyric may refer to social events, it "directs its *mimesis* toward the performance of the mind in *solitary* speech. Because lyric is intended to be voiceable by anyone reading it, in its normative form it deliberately strips away most social specification. . . . A social reading is better directed at a novel or a play."[17] The many German scholars who have anatomized the form are often equally firm in their judgments; Emil Staiger insists that we do have a clear sense of lyric, though in arguing that it is a quality that may be represented by, for example, a landscape, he blurs the distinction between lyric and lyricality that, as I have indicated, other critics of the form attempt to establish.[18]

Despite the assurance of Vendler and the assurances of Staiger, virtually all the qualities on which the category of lyric is based have been challenged, as even a brief catalogue of issues and scholarly debates will indicate. Is it the product of a single sensibility, as the highly influential German concept of *Erlebnis* would suggest, or is it dialogic—or are both those readings symptomatic of an undue emphasis on the issue of personality, a position explored by students of lyric ranging from Jonathan Culler to those opponents of the mode as they conceive it, the Language Poets?[19] The choral performance of many classical lyrics confounds these questions.[20] And is lyric unmediated expression or, as so many critics have insisted, the representation of such expression? Behind that debate lies a particularly fraught conundrum: is lyric expression as trustworthy as Paul Celan famously implies when he compares poems to a handshake or pressing of hands (a statement to which I will return in Chapter 3), or is it tainted with rhetoricity? Is it immediate or do its titles, authorial and otherwise, create effects of distance, as Anne Ferry has asserted?[21] Similarly, is a type of present tense a presupposition of lyric, or should one second Sharon Cameron's argument that Dickinson and other lyric poets struggle to achieve timelessness while often dovetailing several temporalities, or is neither position correct?[22] Is lyric hermetic meditation, or is it social in its direction of address, as its putative roots in communal chants and, later, ceremonial odes might suggest?[23] And might it even be social in its authorship, as those connections with choral performance could again indicate?

That last problem is but one of many issues arising from the links between lyric and music. C. Day Lewis asserts, "A lyric is a poem written for music—for an existing tune, or in collaboration with a composer, or in an idiom demanded by contemporary song-writers, or simply with music at the back of the poet's mind. Lyrical poetry is a much looser thing, but it has not quite forgotten its origin in music and has not lost the singing line."[24] More recently, Marshall Brown has commented acutely on the relationship of the modes in certain texts: "Song converts logic into mood, negation into hesitation, and hence dialectic into an existential skepticism."[25]

Song and lyric are, then, certainly closely allied; yet the interdisciplinary linkage Day Lewis posits is, as we will see throughout this book, fraught and sometimes debatable, challenged by critics as distinguished as Paul de Man, among others.[26] It is not easy to discern songlike characteristics in, say, Donne's "Flea"; conversely, an important study of song emphasizes its distinction from many written lyrics.[27] Nor is it safe to collapse distinctions among various types of song and singing: the presence or absence of musical accompaniment and the possibility of the audience joining in are among the many important variations.[28] Moreover, not song but chant lies behind the Greek conception of lyric, insists no less an authority than Northrop Frye.[29] And even at this juncture one can observe that the term "song" and associated labels are used in loose and often confusing ways in the early modern as well as other periods. How literally is one to interpret the references to the Muse "sweetly warbling" (7) her "melodious notes" (9) in "Alli Veri Figlioli delle Muse," the introductory poem of the anonymous sequence *Zepheria*? (And for that matter, how is the reader to respond when the same poem pulls the Donnean move of calling apparently secular lyrics "hymns" [11]?)[30]

Negotiating such problems in relation to the systemic workings of genre, Alastair Fowler cogently argues for definitions based on Wittgensteinian family resemblances. Fowler adduces that philosopher's analogy between language games and other games ("'These phenomena have no one thing in common which makes us use the same word for all—but they are *related* to one another in many different ways'" [italics in original]) and demonstrates its relevance: "Literary genre seems just the sort of concept with blurred edges that is suited to such an approach. Representatives of a genre may then be regarded as making up a family whose septs [clans] and individual members are related in various ways, without necessarily having any single feature shared in common by all. . . . Genres appear to be much more like families than classes." He proceeds to formulate useful models for tracing how such potentialities are modified in particular periods.[31] The chapters that succeed this one will both exemplify and justify my debt to such approaches. For example, rather than simply noting the relative scarcity of prosopopoeia in early modern poetry, I employ arguments developed by Jonathan Culler, among others, about the roles that figure can serve, especially his trenchant suggestion that it permits poetic agency, however limited; thus at a couple of junctures I posit a "prosopopoeia function"—that is, comparable devices that serve comparable functions, such as implicit allusions to earlier poets. In other words, not the least reason for drawing attention to the transhistorical potentialities of lyric is that doing so alerts one to how they may be translated or traduced in response to specific cultural pressures.

The issue of whether or not lyric should be defined transhistorically is related to but separable from other choices that necessarily antedate and shape a book like this. Should one write a transhistorical study or one that concentrates on a particular period? Does the current emphasis on globalization call into question a study that focuses on a single country? Some of the most acute and influential volumes on genre and genres, notably Paul Alpers's *What Is Pastoral?*, have been transhistorical books, many of which engage with history precisely by playing constant characteristics of the type in question against changing ones; similarly, Michael McKeon's *Origins of the English Novel, 1600–1740* in fact adduces evidence from a broader time period than its title suggests.[32] More immediately relevant here, the same breadth enriches recent studies of lyric and other poetry by Timothy Bahti, Susan Stewart, and William Waters, volumes that are not only transhistorical but comparatist in their orientation.[33]

In return for the often stimulating and sometimes brilliant insights of studies like the ones enumerated above, however, their authors necessarily comment very selectively on any particular historical moment. In part because I am particularly interested in tracing in some detail the influences on lyric distinctive of or even unique to a given period and country, such as the interaction among writer, printer, and publisher in English early modern print culture, I have chosen to concentrate on a single—and singular—era, the one extending roughly between 1500 and 1660, though with the awareness that those boundaries, like so much else about periodization, are now being redefined. (So too is the terminology; this study uses both "English Renaissance" and "early modern period" for the specified years, though with the awareness that both terms are problematical, the second in particular sometimes referring to a longer era.)

This is not to say that I intend to limit the audience of a book that emphasizes the multiple audiences of lyric to students of early modern England. Quite the contrary. The issues about lyric analyzed herein—How is it defined and discussed? Who are its audiences? How valid is the conventional wisdom about its immediacy? In what senses is it indeed short? What are its relationships with narrative?— occur in lyric poetry written in other historical periods and other countries. In the subtitle, "Lyric Poetry and Early Modern England," I try to gesture towards the relevance of this book to studies of lyrics composed in other eras. Thus, as I suggest, my discussion of the reinterpretations of prosopopoeia in the sixteenth and seventeenth centuries might well cast new light on the more mainstream versions of that trope in other periods. Similarly, in response to the current emphasis on the global, my analysis of how the songs in Shakespearean drama empower the disempowered could fruitfully be read in relation to, for example, the *ghinnāwa*, a type of popular Bedouin song that is associated with the disadvantaged members of the society and often expresses sentiments challenging cultural norms.[34] But these are the sort of investigations this book aims to encourage and enable, not enact.

One advantage of delimitation of historical and geographical scope is the opportunity to be capacious in the choice of poems from within that period and country. Among the principal aims of this book is to offer new perspectives on some of the most familiar canonical texts while also drawing attention to relatively neglected writings. I discuss Robert Sidney as well as his better-known brother and daughter; I include both Samuel Daniel's *Delia* and Richard Lynche's *Diella*; and, although I concentrate largely on the print tradition, I allude to texts from manuscripts as well at several junctures.

Focusing closely on one chronological period and one country has also allowed me to identify and explore in some detail many characteristics that, though not necessarily unique to England in the early modern era, occurred with particular frequency or intensity or assumed distinctive contours there and then. I argue, for example, that a major change in ecclesiastical practice, the congregational singing of psalms, affected both subject positions and the use of framing devices even in secular poems. I trace the consequences of the vogue for poetry of praise in the early modern era, ranging from the guilt engendered by lauding a mistress or patron to its assuagement through celebrating God. I demonstrate certain forms that such guilt and other anxieties about lyric assumed, such as connections between lyric and the contagion of the plague, and trace how the period finessed some of these concerns. Conversely, responding to Miner's and Perloff's warnings about imposing transhistorical definitions, I devote less space than would otherwise be necessary to some issues that are central in lyric poetry of other periods but relatively minor in the English Renaissance, notably anthropomorphism. In his discerning study of Catullus, William Fitzgerald laments the fact that the influence of de Man and the resulting emphasis on Romantic and modernist lyric has rendered unduly prominent issues less significant in Latin poetry, such as presence and voice: "A large part of my project in this book is to read the positional structures of the lyric through Roman concerns and relations; I argue that an alternative set of issues about the lyric can be elaborated from Catullus' poetry and its Roman cultural context, in which questions of performance, positionality, and power are more central."[35] *The Challenges of Orpheus* similarly concentrates on issues about lyric that are central to early modern "concerns and relations." Thus, as noted above, this book aims not to resolve the problems of defining lyric with a stable transcultural and transhistorical encapsulation of its characteristics, let alone the privileging of a single attribute, but rather to explore how and why multiple characteristics assumed the form they did, or lay dormant, or were superseded by other predilections in that era. (Because so many distinctions between lyric and narrative occur transhistorically, my discussion of those modes devotes proportionately less space than the other chapters to what is historically specific, but even there the analyses are rooted in the potentialities and problems of early modern England.)

If studies that bridge many centuries risk overlooking nuances within apparent similarities and positing the local as normative, those that largely concentrate on a specific period obviously must acknowledge and accommodate, if not finesse, their own temptations. Some dangers result from the slipperiness of periodization itself. Recent challenges to it remind us that some of John Milton's lyrics might fruitfully be read in relation to Dryden's or to the literature of the Revolution, rather than as the culmination of that hypostasized English Renaissance. Sir Thomas Wyatt is in some important senses and in some important lyrics a late medieval poet. Moreover, critics focusing on a given period need to eschew the common temptation to oversimplify its predecessors in order to celebrate it or establish its distinctiveness; for example, many of the indeterminacies attributed by some to post-Enlightenment lyric could have been lifted from a description of Petrarch's poetry, while attempts to distinguish the Victorian dramatic monologue from the work of Donne are often unsuccessful.

A study of a particular era must of course address historical shifts within it; for example, the flowering of religious poetry in the seventeenth century countered, though it did not erase, anxieties about the triviality of its mode, and Nigel Smith persuasively traces changes in the social functions of lyric and the gendering of its authorship to events associated with the Civil War.[36] No less important is the coexistence of conflicting styles of writing and representing lyric. Charles Bernstein's observation about poetry in general applies to early modern lyric in particular: "There is of course no state of American poetry, but states, moods, agitations, dissipations . . . no music to our verse but vastly incompatible musics; no single sentiment but clashes of sentience."[37] Although Bernstein's commitment to conflictual models may explain some of the severity of this pronouncement, it aptly glosses the range even within a chronologically circumscribed group of lyrics.

Possibly the most useful monitory example of Bernstein's contention comes from the visual arts. Less acute or more polemically driven art historians sometimes merely describe Christopher Dresser, who lived between 1834 and 1904, as a precursor of modernism, yet some of his best work develops conceptions of decoration antithetical to many modern aesthetic principles. Dresser's career also exemplifies the coexistence of a range of styles at a given moment. Much of Edmund Spenser's *Faerie Queene* and many of Donne's love lyrics were probably written during the 1590s, in close conjunction temporally though not stylistically, and so too Dresser did indeed craft objects that appear to be prototypes of modern design as well as ones that violate its principles. Consisting as it does of two conjoined hexagonal shapes, clean and handsome in their lines, one of his toast racks could be mistaken for something Frank Lloyd Wright created for his own paean to the hexagon, Hanna House. Early modern lyric, like Dresser's designs, complicates and even on occasion mocks labels like "modern" and "proto-modern."

The student of historical shifts within an era, or between eras, also needs to be alert to the risks involved in drafting predication into the service of narration, especially teleological storytelling—in other words, using a statement like "lyric is x and y" to establish its superiority over preceding forms or its prefiguration of later ones. Celebrating Dresser as a modernist is a case in point, as is the predilection for seeing the dramatic monologue as a welcome rejection of the Romantic lyric and a no less happy anticipation of its modernist successor. The agendas—political in many senses—that may underwrite that form of narrative are nowhere more apparent than in an otherwise valuable study of the English sonnet initially published, arguably not by chance, only about ten years after the end of World War II: "When therefore Petrarch begins a sonnet to Laura by describing her as the joint handiwork of nature and heaven . . . he is voicing . . . the primeval convictions of Mediterranean peoples. But convictions such as these were essentially alien to the English mind. . . . The Tudor poets were indeed true pioneers both in form and content, breaking a virgin soil on which, in the fullness of days, the great Elizabethans were to raise their golden harvest."[38]

_⌒᷇ ᷆⌒_

In addition to the challenges variously resolved and posed by the decision to focus on a single historical era and a single national tradition, studying the mode on which this book focuses poses further methodological problems. Writing about lyric, no less than writing lyric, is inevitably an art of omission, compression, and elision, and even a book that devotes itself to a relatively narrow time frame must omit potentially valuable material. The state of the field, the strengths and limitations of my own expertise, and the stringencies of publishers' budgets have all shaped my decisions, especially those about the foci of my principal chapters. For example, given the plethora of excellent studies on the relationship of music and poetry and my own lack of training in musicology, that issue, while pervasive, is a passing concern in these chapters rather than the subject of one of them. My original plan to devote a chapter to the lyric speaker was superseded by an awareness that this subject really requires a book in its own right, not least because the very act of positing and focusing on such a figure would be controversial; so again I include many observations on the issue, thus suggesting directions for future study, rather than pretending to definitive treatment.

Other challenges stem from the difficulties of classification, especially when addressing an era whose usages of terms associated with lyric are varied and inconsistent. Whereas many early modern statements about song, for example, have evident implications for lyric, the two are obviously not synonymous. If evocations of the Orpheus myth are clearly germane to lyric, that pied piper is also the patron saint of poetry in general and of eloquence. Moreover, many poems that critics of the English Renaissance regularly label lyric, such as dialogic pastorals or sonnets addressing the mistress, would not be accepted as such according to the norms associated with texts in other periods.

Similar complexities attend the usage of the related term "ode" both in the early modern period and other eras. One may employ it as precisely as Ben Jonson does or as broadly as many eighteenth-century writers do, turning the word into an all-purpose label for poetry; one eighteenth-century treatise classifies "Lycidas" as an "irregular ode."[39] The association between lyric and the ode in the more limited senses of twentieth- and twenty-first-century critics, though prominent in that period, arises in the early modern era as well; for example, the manuscript of an unpublished commonplace book now in the Newberry Library, Case MS A. 15.179, enumerates genres and lists the writers associated with each of them. Next to "Lyrique" appears "Pindarus, Anacreon, Callimachus, Horace, Catullus," a catalogue that emphasizes the connections between lyric and ode and also tells us for the first of many times that the former was often associated not with meditation but with public poetry.[40] Such problems are further complicated by the contradictions that Paul H. Fry has trenchantly pointed out within the ode, especially its propensity for undermining its ostensible public and celebratory mission.[41]

The best approach to these classificatory dilemmas, like many other problems about genre, is an informed and cautious engagement with them; hence I recur to such issues when they are particularly relevant to the argument. Although this study necessarily encompasses many texts labeled lyric according to some but not all of the many criteria of their age and our own, in choosing texts to illustrate central arguments, I have attempted to include at least some whose claim to be lyrics is virtually indisputable.

It is tempting and sometimes appropriate to resolve such problems by asserting that even texts that resist the label "lyric" may be lyrical, much as one talks of dramatic elements in texts that are clearly not drama. Fair enough in many instances, yet such adjectives are often used too loosely, as David Lindley among others has argued.[42] Moreover, in the instance of lyric in particular, the relationship between the noun and adjective proves paradoxical, the first of many paradoxes encountered in defining and describing the mode. For lyricality in the sense of a timeless state, dreamlike or visionary in its intensity, often is not inherent in lyric but rather functions as the goal towards which lyric strives—and which lyric often criticizes or ironizes even as it is achieved. Witness John Milton's Nativity Ode.

That poem both celebrates and questions the association of lyric with spiritual enlightenment, a widespread linkage that exemplifies another challenge in studying the mode—recognizing and negotiating the investments of critics from many different eras.[43] For example, if the doctrine of American exceptionalism has complicated politics in a range of respects, a commitment to lyric as an atypical, even deviant form of discourse that contrasts with ordinary language and in so doing fulfills a special mission has shaped and misshaped analyses. The adjectives critics use to distinguish this alternative from the everyday vary, but usually they suggest something magical, almost supernatural. As George T. Wright puts it, "This sublimity, this sense of enchantment, seems to me essentially a quality of the lyric poem. . . . it is a new light on the experience of human beings in a world full of feelings and troubles."[44] That sense, he argues, is expressed grammatically through a special type of present tense: "Deliberately bypassing all the modifiers that normal speech requires, the lyric present appears to offer as actual, conditions that we normally accept only as possible, special, figurative, provisional."[45] Reflecting the survival of Romantic and symbolist conceptions of lyric, these representations of it as something extraordinary, atypical, even holy, draw attention to the cultural work it does for many movements and cultures; lyric often becomes the repository of what the ostensibly dispassionate analyst of it sees as precious but imperiled in the current climate. At the same time, in many instances lyric is imbued with profound anxieties, represented as symbol, and perhaps source as well, of what the author or the entire culture fears. Given how often it takes the form of love poetry, it is hardly surprising that lyric is frequently associated with the irrationality of desire, the triviality of love games, or both. The poem that concludes Chapter 1, Herrick's "Vision" ("Me thought I saw"), exemplifies commonly made connections between that mode and female temptation, as well as the temptation of effeminization. Hence the late-twentieth- and twenty-first-century critics who in effect conflate lyric with New Criticism and see the genre itself as synecdochic for a mystified concept of individualism and an adulation of the aesthetic may rightly be interpreted as part a trend that predates them of conscripting lyric into preexisting battles.

Another challenge that a study of a topic as broad as lyric confronts is structural: how should the argument be organized, and, in particular, does the book require or profit from a single overarching thesis? I maintain that in the instance of early modern lyric, the search for a single claim that would unite the issues explored below, like the cognate search for a single defining characteristic, would be compromised by how variously that mode was written, read, and represented in the early modern period. Indeed, the variety and lability of lyric are among my principal arguments. (Of course, whereas *The Challenges of Orpheus* resists distillation into a single thesis, many chapters pivot on a thesis specific to their own topic, and the study as a whole does pursue interlocking methodological and substantive arguments, such as the case about myths and tropes adumbrated below.) This book further maintains that we need to reexamine fundamental assumptions about lyric that are too often treated as presuppositions behind the critical analysis of other issues rather than as problems necessitating analysis in their own right. Hence, although I do focus in detail on numerous texts, I have organized the book in terms of the workings of lyric rather than the works of specific lyric poets: instead of scrutinizing a series of writers seriatim, I devote one chapter to each of four sites of commonplaces about lyric, that is, its audiences, its putative immediacy, its length, and its relationship to narrative.

Another methodological argument behind *The Challenges of Orpheus* is that to examine lyric, we need not only to round up the usual suspects—explicit statements on it by poets of the era, passages in texts, and so on—but also to examine evidence sometimes neglected, notably the witness of trope and myth. And, as I have asserted in many other venues, we need to recognize the compatibility of studying language and form and examining the workings of culture.[46] The renewed interest in form in many reaches of literary and cultural studies is one of the most promising developments of the first decade of the twenty-first century.

Such approaches generate several revisionist interpretations of the mode, crystallized by in the paradoxes that Chapter 1 enumerates and subsequently traced throughout the study. For example, the story of Orpheus proves paradigmatic of lyric in its Mobius strip of turnings and re-turnings and of gendered success and failure.[47] These shifts alert us as well to the many ways in which the mode associated etymologically with *versus*, the Latin word whose principal denotations include "turning," involves process and lability.[48] To cite just a few cases, the positionalities of both lyric speaker and audience involve many turns; rather than impeding narrative, lyric often turns to it or turns into it. I argue also that the immediacy commonly associated with lyric participates in a complex dynamic with strategies for distancing the text and that scribal culture allows certain types of authorial agency that have been neglected. As these instances suggest, each chapter challenges some widespread assumptions clinging to its subject.

My first chapter introduces such issues by exploring how lyric is described and defined in the early modern period; in so doing, it analyzes the agendas that so often compromise pronouncements about the mode delivered then, no less than assertions about it by critics today. "The Rhetoric of Lyric," the title of this chapter, thus refers not only to the language used in lyric poetry but also to the language chosen by both early modern poets and commentators and our own contemporaries when talking about the workings of that mode in the English Renaissance. Such commentaries are not infrequently rhetorical in that they aim to persuade—and thus to convince their readers of positions beyond those ostensibly presented.

# CHAPTER 1

# The Rhetoric of Lyric

## *Definitions, Descriptions, Disputations*

Annotated exhaustively, imitated widely, disseminated in editions that not co-incidentally look very like Bibles, Francesco Petrarch's *Rime sparse* is prototype and progenitor of the English early modern lyric, and, indeed, it might offer a credible model for those who attempt a transhistorical definition of that mode. But the confession of transgression that is its opening poem repeatedly trans-gresses characteristics commonly proposed as the norms of lyric. If this literary type represents the poet talking to himself, as numerous critics have assumed, the *Canzoniere*, like many English sonnet cycles, nevertheless begins on a poem to and about an audience. If the mode in question comprises an immediate out-pouring of emotion, this text instead scrutinizes prior outpourings. And if a lyric is a discrete, short text, how does one explicate the threads that link the putatively individual lyrics in the *Rime sparse* to each other, tying them in patterns as elu-sive yet ineluctable as the bonds between Petrarch and Laura?

I open my analysis of the problems of defining and describing lyric in the En-glish Renaissance with a brief reference to an Italian text in part because it offers so apt a specimen of the dilemmas about audience, immediacy, and structure dis-cussed seriatim in the chapters following this one. More to my purposes now, given its virtually iconic status in the early modern period, the *Rime sparse* pro-vided the English poets who read and re-read it with a particularly potent and memorable instance of definitional and classificatory challenges. When Petrarch bequeaths to his English progeny a paradigm for the sonnet, he leaves to them as well a model not of clearly defined lyric characteristics but of problems in study-ing that mode. Petrarch's heirs and assigns in the English Renaissance, this chapter argues, address such problems in many venues, but above all in two overlapping ones, the mythological narratives and the figurative language associated with poesy in general and lyric in particular.

This is not to say that these or other sources reveal a widely accepted definition of lyric. Many English Renaissance writers and readers were cognizant of the category, and assays at description and definition do appear; but the period in question certainly did not have an uncontroversial formula for categorizing poems as lyric, and many commentaries are inconsistent with each other or even within themselves. Such contradictions are especially evident in the myth—or, more to the point, the conflicting myths—associated with Orpheus. The aim of this chapter is not to resolve inconsistencies by attributing to the early modern era more common ground on this subject than actually existed; on the contrary, I demonstrate below that the term "lyric" was used in a range of ways in the period. Hence I will explore what the very tensions and contradictions in question reveal about early modern lyrics and the processes of writing them and writing about them.

The alternatives to focusing on myth and figure prove limited in more senses than one. Commentaries by Michael Drayton, George Puttenham, John Milton, and above all Philip Sidney are indubitably revealing, not least because they demonstrate some ways the term "lyric" was actually used in the early modern period, but these discussions are brief. Adducing the relative paucity of analyses like these as evidence, critics in our own period sometimes claim that the problem of discussing lyric was generally handled simply by being avoided. Not so, if one examines implicit commentaries as well as explicit ones. "In many ways the most acute poetics of the early modern lyric," Roland Greene has argued about one version of such commentaries, "is written out in poems themselves."[1] Acute, yes, and an example of the significance of implicit observations, but not necessarily the most acute poetics. In fact, it is instead the allusions embedded in myth and trope that provide the most extensive and intriguing evidence of how the early modern period saw lyric.

Admittedly, mining those two sources is complicated inasmuch as some such allusions involve types of verse besides lyric; and Orpheus himself, the subject of the most significant myths, wears many hats besides the beret of lyric poet. The data bases of myth and figure, however, remain invaluable for analyses of early modern lyric. At the very least, when the usages in question apply to other types of poetry as well as lyric, they remain resonant as descriptions, if not as definitions. Moreover, often, especially in the case of gendered anxieties, other cultural associations with lyric activate or intensify the application of these words to that mode in particular.

This chapter, then, develops two closely related lines of argument. The first is methodological: it is through the indirections of metaphoric language and of mythological narrative that readers can best understand the directions, in the several senses of the word, of early modern discussions of lyric. It is not surprising that a culture that might well join Chaucer in claiming Ovid as its "owne auctor" thinks about lyric, like so much, through myth. No less surprising, though less often recognized and analyzed, is the fact that an age that delights in troping discusses genre and so many other issues through figuration.

And second, when one approaches early modern lyric from these and other perspectives, certain interrelated characteristics and practices clearly emerge. To begin with, one repeatedly encounters texts that represent lyric paradoxically and writers and commentators who approach it divisively. Some of these paradoxes are predictable, but others challenge the conventional wisdom about the form. In many texts from the English Renaissance, this chapter demonstrates, lyric is variously and at times simultaneously represented as source and symptom of disease and as medicinal; as masculine, feminine, and cross-dressed; as public, private, and the denizen of territories that cannot readily be classified as either. Often associated with the insubstantial and ephemeral, lyric is also seen as a material object; often considered static, it is also repeatedly described as both an embodiment of motion and an incitement to it; often read in terms of the isolation of both poet and poem, it is also represented as communal and public. Conceptions of lyric as an artisanal material product coexist with representations of it as the result of Platonic *furor*. Whereas lyric delights in process, typically expressed in terms of turning and twisting, it may culminate in an apparently stable kernel of truth, on occasion both expressed in and troped by a couplet. Especially central, however, are two paradoxes in particular: early modern lyric is represented as the site of both extraordinary power and helpless passivity, and as the source of both glorious achievements, especially in military and spiritual spheres, and of perilously seductive threats.

More significant than the mere presence of these paradoxes and outright contradictions, however, is their impact on the practices of reading, writing, and representing early modern lyric. They help to explain responses that range from intense guilt to ambivalence to celebration. To express and negotiate such divergent responses, I argue, early modern texts rely on numerous strategies, traced in this chapter and throughout *The Challenges of Orpheus*. For example, Renaissance writers insistently distinguish Good Lyric and Evil Lyric; firm distinctions between a putatively beneficent form of lyric and its Othered twin are often posited and deployed, though sometimes subsequently undermined, in attempts to finesse apparent contradictions. Perhaps one might initially be tempted to read this divide between two versions of the mode not as a fraught and strategic response to unresolved ambivalences but rather as a dispassionate and judicious description of differences inherent in lyric. But the examples from musicology adduced below, demonstrating as they do the breakdown of such differences, encourage one to explore the more complex functions the putative distinction in fact serves. And similarly, as I will demonstrate throughout this study, even the apparently admirable versions of lyric, religious poetry and public poems of praise, are on many occasions viewed suspiciously by their writers and readers, thus suggesting that contrasts between two forms of lyric often respond not to objective classificatory data but rather to anxieties about the mode, not least the fear that its versions cannot in fact be clearly distinguished.[2]

Tensions about lyric encourage many other strategies as well. At times the mode operates reactively and dialogically, a putative or realized modal characteristic generating the assertion of its antithesis. For example, if lyric blocks normative sexualities, as I will suggest it can also impel them, in part in response to previous or potential transgressions; fears that this mode is deviant in these and many other ways lead Sir Philip Sidney and many others to insist on its connections to masculinity. Early modern lyric also responds to—and intensifies—the contradictions associated with it by gendering and re-gendering texts, their authors, and their readers; those re-genderings are among the many respects in which the mode involves process and movement.

In short, this chapter argues that in early modern England lyric is represented as Dr. Jekyll and Mr.—or, more often and more to the point, Ms.—Hyde. The valences of the form, linked to turning themselves, turn and twist paradoxically and on occasion collide, and the shifts between success and failure and power and impotency are especially telling. Many strategies, such as the imputed distinction between types of lyric and the genderings of that mode, variously and sometimes simultaneously resolve and intensify these ontological skirmishes and even battles. Examining the myths and figures through which the early modern period knows and makes known lyric can demonstrate why these are the primary arenas in which the struggles about its workings are waged and in which the treaties that sometimes ensue are signed.

_co co_

The varied representations of lyric emerge in the differences between one myth and another and in the diverse versions a given myth may assume; distinctions connected with its potency and its morality are strikingly recurrent. Often those distinctions are expressed through stories that sedulously distinguish good and bad alter egos of the lyric poet, and often, too, that contrast is expressed through contrasting musical instruments. But if studying these myths thus supports and extends the preliminary answers about defining and describing lyric adumbrated above, such an analysis also insistently poses another question. Although multiple narratives involve or gesture towards lyric poetry, Orpheus clearly has a much better press agent than either Arion or Amphion. The obvious explanations for the striking popularity of this tale, such as the prominence of Orpheus in the *Metamorphoses* and in medieval sources, are only part of the story. Why, then, does this particular legend become so popular a repository and source of conceptions of lyric—and of so much else—in early modern England? The answers can also explicate the attraction of cognate myths such as that of the sirens.

Lyric can be associated with rocks and stones (as discussed later in this chapter), and it is associated as well with one of the principal legendary figure who could move them, thus again recalling the linkage between lyric and motion. The tale of Orpheus is alive and well in our own culture: witness the modern poems referring to him by John Ashbery, Jorie Graham, Edward Hirsch, Muriel Rukeyser, Mark Strand and many others.[3] Witness, too, the decision of the upscale S. T. Dupont company to entitle a group of pens "the Orphéo Collection," thus presumably attempting to sell their writing instruments by connecting them with not only the singer's liquid words but also his putative power. An advertisement tellingly heralds these pens as "a new generation of writing instruments." Much as French architecture veers back to neoclassicism despite and even during its flirtation with Art Nouveau, so in this instance distinction is pursued by borrowing status from a classical past even while celebrating that new generation.

In the early modern period, no mythological link is more firm and pervasive than the one between poetry and Orpheus, which encompasses but is not exclusive to lyric; he appears prominently at the beginning of Spenser's "Epithalamion," Shakespeare refers to him by name four times, Milton alludes to him in "Lycidas," while "L'Allegro" culminates on a description of a song that, the reader is told, would move even Orpheus. These better-known allusions coexist with a host of others, whether they be overt, as in Herrick's poem "Orpheus," Jonson's *Masque of Augurs*, and numerous emblems, or, alternatively, subterranean, as in the putative mention in the April eclogue posited by Spenser's editors.[4] On the one hand, these discussions share many preoccupations with those by later writers (for example, the work of our contemporary poet Edward Hirsch, like some early modern examinations of the myth, draws attention to Orpheus's same-sex relationships); on the other hand, Renaissance poets are, predictably, more preoccupied with the spiritual dimensions of the myth than many of their successors.

The early modern preoccupation with Orpheus is notoriously difficult to explicate, for a range of narratives, often as contradictory or paradoxical as lyric itself, swirl around this figure.[5] The Renaissance inherited from classical mythology and iconography, as well as from extensive medieval commentaries, a series of discordant legends, some the product of evolution and some participants in an uneasy coexistence. The paternity of the keynote speaker of Renaissance lyric is contested; in versions that claim he is the son of the wine god, the associations of abandonment and orgiastic festivity are stressed, while as the son of Apollo he is instead sired by rationality. This tension recurs in many aspects of his legends. Orpheus is variously portrayed as Apollonian and Dionysiac, as the exemplar of rationality and of its opposite, and, indeed, in some versions he abandons his earlier role as devotee of Bacchus to join the cult of Apollo. These divergences generate conflicting glosses on his relationship to Eurydice: she is variously presented as his concupiscent side, drawing him to Hell, and as the Good that he cannot achieve. In the analysis by William of Conches, for example, Orpheus represents wisdom and eloquence and Eurydice the concupiscence that tempts him. The explanations for his death similarly vary from version to version, with some claiming that he is being punished for revealing the secrets of the gods, others that Venus incited those who killed him, while Hellenic accounts often assert that those women were angry because he was not interested in any females after Eurydice died. A more thorough survey of mythological versions like these might well have encouraged the executives of S. T. Dupont to think twice.

Renaissance poets also inherited and developed a series of linkages between Orpheus and other figures: he was seen as a prefiguration of Christ, he was associated with Pan, he was represented as a medieval knight. Particularly germane to my purposes here is the parallel sometimes made with David. The connection, indeed conflation, of the two becomes recurrent in the Renaissance; Anthony Cope's 1547 treatise refers to the psalmist as "our celestial Orpheus."[6] This phrase gestures towards one of the principal arguments of this study, the centrality of psalms in the development of even secular lyric. Like so many other responses to lyric, this connection with David also works to check anxieties associated with that mode: if poetry is tainted with seductiveness, triviality, and many other dangers, if some of those threats are prominent in versions of the Orpheus legend itself, the pairing of that figure with David can sanctify the mode (although, as I argue in Chapter 2, David's own reputation is ambiguous, which further complicates the connection of the two narratives). The relationship between Good Lyric and Evil Lyric, like so much else about the mode, is at times dynamic; it generally involves sedulously posited distinctions but may instead include conflations or a move from one to the other. Especially relevant to Renaissance commentaries on lyric is one reason for the pairing, even twinning, of Orpheus and David: their ability as healers links these figures, with David curing Saul and Orpheus, granted magical powers in some forms of the legend, curing snakebite. The makers of this version of the Orpheus myth had read their Derrida, for lyric is established as a *pharmakon*: contributing to the rabid disease of love sickness and other forms of melancholy, it also can physic illness, thereby testifying that it is not a trivial toy but a potent weapon with significant material effects. David's status as a monarch is also germane, for Orpheus is sometimes associated with judicious government, thus again connecting Pindar's mode to the public sphere.

The potentialities of the legend are realized in telling ways in certain texts of especial interest to early modern writers. To begin with, Quintilian's commentary in I.x.9–12 of *Institutio Oratoria* provides a textbook example of some recurrent patterns in versions of the story. Comparing Orpheus and the writer Linus, Quintilian observes that they united the roles of musician, poet, and philosopher; he proceeds to insist that, related as it is to the study of wisdom, music is necessary for an orator. Thus Orpheus provides yet another model for the connections among poetry, song, and eloquence that is so central to early modern representations of lyric. In particular, Quintilian's account, again like many other statements about Orpheus, links suasive force and artistic pleasure, reminding us of the long history of connections between rhetorical ploys and aesthetic pleasure, the cornerstone of many materialist pronouncements on art.

Widely read in both the original Latin and Golding's famous translation, Ovid's *Metamorphoses* offers what was probably the most influential version of the Orpheus legend in the Renaissance, in so doing emphasizing two nexuses of intertwined issues particularly germane to early modern lyric. First, it restructures the relationship between success and failure that centrally but variously recurs in the period.[7] In the narrative in question, poetry is the site neither of unqualified power nor of impotence but rather of a dynamic in which extraordinary, indeed magical, power repeatedly confronts a threatened or realized blockage or truncation of itself, recalling Northrop Frye's connection between lyric and blocking.[8] In gendered terms, that mode is eventually emasculated or, in a related but different pattern, destroyed by the feminine. Success and failure are twinned and twined, as inextricably embracing each other as destruction and creation do in the legend of the god Shiva. And second, process is central in another sense as well: poetic achievement is one stage in a continuing saga of rivalry that involves battles between different writers, different instruments, and their differing views of art. Through forms of blockage the battles between rivals are staged.

Both elements emerge in the story of the wedding. Hymen is successfully summoned by Orpheus, but his presence does not ensure good fortune: the poet's achievement is limited, blocked, thus anticipating the movement from initial success to heartrending failure when he attempts to call Eurydice back from the dead—from the world tellingly evoked by the Australian poet Judith Wright as "clay corridors / below the reach of song" ("Eurydice in Hades," 6–7).[9] If Eurydice's death is replicated ("gemina nece" ["double death"], X.64), so too is the poet's failure: during his subsequent gig in the underworld, the man who moves stones succeeds in moving the spirits to tears and making Ixion's wheel stop, but he fails to follow the directive about not looking at his wife, and so he embraces only air. This slippage between success and failure is, of course, also the signature of the Petrarchan lover, connected with Orpheus in more ways than one.

Ovid's rendition of Orpheus's death also emphasizes both that slippage and its imbrication in three interrelated characteristics repeatedly associated with lyric, blocking, turning, and transgression; all three impel the often contradictory valuations of the mode and the guilt associated with it. Ovid's lines emphasize the blockage of heterosexual desire—

> omnemque refugerat Orpheus
> femineam Venerem
>
> . . . . . . .
>
> ille etiam Thracum populis fuit auctor amorem
> in teneros transferre mares citraque iuventam
> aetatis breve ver et primos carpere flores.
>
> ("and Orpheus had shunned all love of womankind.
> . . . He set the example for the peoples of Thrace
> of giving his love to tender boys, and enjoying the
> springtime and first flower of their youth")
>
> (X.79–80, 83–85)

From one perspective, the death of Eurydice blocks other heterosexual relationships; from another, explored by Mario DiGangi and a few other critics, the homoerotic blocks marital heterosexuality.[10] Tracing the effects of Orpheus's defense of homoerotic desires on the polymorphous sexuality of Elizabethan poetry, Jonathan Bate aptly observes that "Orpheus is the patron saint of homosexuality, or, more specifically, of pederasty."[11] To put it differently, the exemplar of verse performs a turning in sexualities, his loss of Eurydice generating an interest in homoerotic relationships instead. Thus lyric is yet again associated with turning and transforming. This turn is presented as transgressive in Golding's version, which tellingly supplements the pastoral imagery that implicitly justifies Orpheus's choice with a reference to that antipastoral site of corruption and disease the brothels: "He also taught the *Thracian* folke a stewes of Males too make / And of the flowring pryme of boayes the pleasure for to take" (X.90–91). In yet another version of the contagiousness of lyric, that icon of the mode inspires homoerotic love in others.

As with so many other issues concerning sexualities, the responses of commentators and writers of the early modern period to Orpheus's homoeroticism have been varied and inconsistent. George Sandys's version of Ovid, unlike Golding's, flirts with blocking Orpheus's blockage of heterosexuality through an expurgated translation and a marginal note: "Not rendering the Latin fully; of purpose omitted."[12] Might not fears about the poetic expression of heterosexual love, overtly present in the work of Sidney and so many of his compatriots, conceal comparable fears of the relationship of the mode to the love that dare not speak its name?

The contrasting sexualities central to legends about Orpheus's death also involve textbook examples of the putative contrasts between Good Lyric and Evil Lyric, a distinction related in these stories to two other elements germane to lyric in the early modern period: blocked agency and rival music. As we have seen, according to some versions of his murder, including the one in Ovid, Orpheus pays for his shunning of women with his life. Whatever its cause, the attack on him is not successful at first precisely because Orpheus himself is: respecting him as they do, the stones refuse to hit him. And after that the assault would have been harmless ("cunctaque tela forent cantu mollita" ["And all their weapons would have been harmless under the spell of song]" [X.15])—except that his lyre, whose magical song protected him, is drowned by sounds from flutes, lions, drums, and the howlings of the maddened maenads. In other words, the women who resent their rival, Eurydice, are associated with rival instruments—not the stringed lute but wind instruments, a contrast that recurs in various forms throughout the history of lyric. By listing the breastbeating and howlings of the women with the rival instruments, Ovid denigrates the music from them: they seem less musical performances than outpourings of emotion.

Orpheus speaks, Ovid tells his readers, but for the first time in his life his words are not heeded; again, his power, associated with eloquence here as in

Quintilian's text, is tragically impeded. The potency of lyric initially blocks the stones, then is itself blocked. Thus the mode that pivots on loss has as its originary legend the narrative in which its own powers are lost. Here, as in many other texts, lyric is repeatedly associated not only with many types of turning but also with motion that is stirred, though often only to be blocked. From this perspective, it is also telling that the exponent of a mode often seen as in motion itself and exciting motion in others moves through the water even after death.

Although Orpheus and David, who is discussed in Chapter 2, were probably the most significant exemplars of lyric in the early modern period, some other myths deserve more attention than they have received from recent students of the Renaissance, contributing as they did to perceptions of that mode. Husband of the ill-fated Niobe, Amphion shares Orpheus's ability to appeal even to inanimimate objects: according to one legend about the founding of Thebes, the stones used in its construction move of their own accord in response to his music. Thus, as Scott Newstok points out in his study of epitaphs, because of its association with the suasive power of rhetoric, the legend of Amphion gestures as well towards how the epitaphic speech on tombstones moves.[13] This connection anticipates the floral tropes that represent lyric in terms of both evanescent flowers and inscriptions in stone.

Arion was apparently a historical figure, credited with creating the dithyramb, a choric hymn.[14] Transformed into a mythic being, this character again draws attention to the potency so often associated with lyric. Though the narratives about him, like the stories of Orpheus, take significantly different forms, in the version in Herodotus, sailors carrying him home attempt to kill him for his money. They accede, however, to his suggestion that he sing one final song, in his full ceremonial costume. Then he plunges into the sea. His swan song turns out to be a dolphin song, however, for one of those creatures carries him safely to shore, where he is eventually revenged on his would-be assassins. Like the story of Orpheus, then, this tale emphasizes the power of lyric by suggesting that it can woo even the inhabitants of the deep. But, unlike the story of Orpheus, Arion's curriculum vitae is an unqualified success story; it provides a palinode to the darker implications about the Muse's "enchanting son" (Milton, "Lycidas," 59), demonstrating an instance where lyric rescues the singer rather than being blocked in its palliative effects or even contributing to his ruin.

The Prologue of Gower's *Confessio Amantis* culminates in a tribute to Arion, associating him with many powers more commonly attributed to Orpheus, notably the ability to tame beasts and bring accord to human beings as well. Nor were the stories of Amphion and Arion neglected by early modern poets, and the appearance of Arion in the Kenilworth entertainments probably intensified interest in him.[15] Amphion is mentioned in Thomas Campion's *Lord Hay's Masque*, while references to Arion may be found in the published works of Shakespeare, Spenser, and Thomas Watson and in the manuscripts of Robert Sidney and John Ramsey.[16] (That latter-day Spenserian Byron alludes to Arion as well, and he and his dolphin are represented on a ceiling of the Boston Museum of Fine Arts.) Yet the fact remains that Orpheus indubitably appears in far more early modern texts than either of these siblings.

Analogue to or even twin of Orpheus, Pan is another singer who was associated with lyric in the early modern period, and his story is similarly varied in its implications. Within Spenser's *Shepheardes Calender* alone the reader encounters, for example, the "rude *Pan*" of the shepherds (January eclogue, 67), the "great *Pan*" (May eclogue, 54) who is closer to the Christian god than a pastoral deity, and the architect of theological and marital Pandemonium who fathers the Eliza of the April eclogue. Most relevant to my arguments, however, is Pan's relationship to the bifurcation of lyric that I have been tracing. Repeatedly associated with wind instruments, his legend contributes their connection with the erotically and musically unruly, with the destructiveness of the maenads rather than the curative powers of their victim's magical lyre. In an intriguing woodcut by the seventeenth-century Italian Jiulio Bonasone, the sirens are socializing with Circe; in Milton's "At a Solemn Music," they are "Sphere-born harmonious Sisters" (2), who, rather than leading men to their destruction, inspire them to imitate heavenly harmony. Yet another myth, in short, expresses and encourages divided responses to song in ways very germane to lyric. Renaissance poets variously explore each side of the narrative; Herrick's "To Musick. A Song," for example emphasizes the connection between the sirens and the spheres. And in Milton's *Comus*, I will demonstrate in my conclusion, the opposing readings of this choir uneasily coexist. In any event, in all these variants on the myth, it involves a choral union, not a soloist: once again, music is seen as communal and public, not individual.

The more negative versions of the myth of the sirens, emphasized in an emblem in Geoffrey Whitney's 1586 collection, *Choice of Emblems*, and in numerous literary texts, are germane to lyric from several perspectives.[17] First, their song is associated with temptation; its evil is manifest in how it can draw out the potential for evil in the listener, much as Milton represents Comus's ability to build on his audience's propensity for being deceived. That temptation is gendered, as are so many other aspects of lyric.[18] Permitting poets to deflect their own guilt about writing lyric, women tempt men in this myth; they become the singers, allowing that would-be singer the poet to identify through gender with the victims. More specifically, the sirens tempt their listeners into effeminization in the sense that they abandon their roles as warriors for a passive self-indulgence; so, anticipating the connections that I will explore shortly between the lyric mode and the air that transmits plague, this myth in effect enacts a kind of contagion. From another perspective, the linearity of the epic journey is blocked. To put it yet another way, as Stephen Owen points out, the sirens represent a variant of the myth of a stonelike woman who causes men to melt.[19] The ability in effect to turn men into women clearly speaks to the instrumental power encountered throughout this chapter in the ideologies, mythologies, and etymologies of lyric and its kin and invites one to think further about its relationship to gender, an issue that arises in some of the commentaries to which I will turn in the final two sections of this chapter.

More to my purposes now, however, even this brief review of myths directly or indirectly associated with lyric explicates the prominence of Orpheus. Whereas his popularity is overdetermined, two reasons for it relate to the central arguments of this chapter. First, this legend explores gender and masculinity, especially the connections of masculinity with power and impotence and with what we today call sexual preferences, in ways that interested readers in early modern England, as the sonnet tradition and so many plays repeatedly remind us. In so doing, the legend of Orpheus connects writing lyric to assuming multiple and shifting gender positions. And second, that myth both substantiates and explicates the very paradoxes that are, as this chapter is arguing, central to many other representations of lyric in early modern England, notably the slippages between agency and its tragic absence, as well as between success and failure. In this the story of Orpheus resembles the tales of Pan, the sirens, and David the psalmist and thus may help us to understand the popularity of such figures as well, and in this it differs significantly from the narratives associated with those rival poets Arion and Amphion. Whereas narratives about Arion and Amphion generally stress their agency and achievements, the story of Orpheus includes both the celebration of lyric and the doubts about its ethical stance and its efficacy so characteristic of early modern culture.

_๏ ๏_

The paradoxes manifest in the myths associated with lyric recur in its tropes as well; in particular, the valences of turning involve virtuous action and virtuosity on the one hand, deceit and defeat on the other. Lyric once more emerges as both disease and cure and as both substantial and evanescent. A study of those tropes also reveals recurrent responses to those threats, notably the guilt, whether potential or realized, of its writers and readers, as well as the genderings of the text itself that are often either source of or antidote to that guilt. But the diversity of early modern lyric encourages a more capacious study of its tropes, not merely a winnowing designed to focus on a few issues already established in this chapter. Some of the patterns that emerge substantiate longstanding assumptions about lyric, while others are likely to surprise—even startle—students of early modern literature. In particular, this broader analysis reveals a range of additional paradoxes that will reappear in subsequent chapters, such as the association of lyric with divergent social statuses and with both a small unit and a collection.

My recurrent emphasis on the guilt suggested by these tropes is not intended to deny the association of other literary forms with guilt—prose romances were often seen as frivolous, drama was demonized as ungodly in Puritan and other insistently godly tracts, and so on—but in the instance of lyric, such concerns are distinctive in their sources and workings. The connection between lyric and erotic poetry is one source of that distinctiveness, but by no means the only one; for, although versions of lyric celebrating heroes and the divine were generally exempt from the criticisms leveled at verses about love, important exceptions do arise. Moreover, guilt about lyric is more than a commentary on illicit desire, partly because the denigrations of lyric poetry encompass so much besides its raw material (even in its rawest versions, like the erotica of the minor poet Barnabe Barnes).

To begin with, lyric, like other forms of poetry, is frequently figured and configured in the early modern period through the etymological root of verse, *versus*, whose principal meanings include "turning." The term is applied in that era to many types of poetry, but readers were surely especially aware of its relevance to lyric: whether or not stanzas structure a particular text, in the instance of lyric the resonances of *versus* are intensified because the strophe, a word based on the Greek for "turning," is often seen as a fundamental unit of lyric. The etymological link between lyric and that turning thus carries with it a range of important consequences, not least its implications for guilt, for gendering, and for materiality.

Modern critics have repeatedly and richly commented on the implications of *versus*, though they have neglected some of its consequences for materiality in particular. Northrop Frye, for example, relates the turning back he associates with verse to its discontinuity; he establishes a provocatively revisionist rebuttal to notions of the lyric as an organic, perfectly polished unit, although he neglects the early modern connections between stanzas and stability that I will explore in Chapter 4.[20] In effect positing lyric as a version of *fort-da*, his emphasis on turning back helps to explain the paradigmatic status of Petrarch's anniversary poems. Arguably, too, his tantalizingly brief comments on links between the lyric and irony can be explicated through their shared commitment to turning.[21] Implicitly exploring the etymology that impels Frye, Barbara Johnson mimetically observes that "verse . . . is an enactment of the alternative as law and of law as alternative."[22] In comparing lyric to a walk, the poet A. R. Ammons observes that "the turns and returns or implied returns give shape to the walk and to the poem."[23] And another poet, Heather McHugh, whose own lyrics involve splendid turns and twists in tone, demonstrates how in Thomas Wyatt's "They fle from me"—that accusing confession and confessional accusation of all sorts of turning—"a verse is turned."[24] Different though they are in other respects, these comments by twentieth- and twenty-first-century critics crystallize the paradoxical valences of turning for early modern poets.

The connections among lyric, turning, and *versus*, and especially that paradox, were crucial to the development of early modern poetry, as the frequency with which poetry is called "verse" would suggest. Shakespeare uses "poesy" only five times and "poem" once, while "verse" and its cognates appear no fewer than fifty-three times in his canon.[25] Even Herrick, who refers to "lyric" more than some poets do, seems to use the term interchangeably with "verse" in the poem entitled "To the King" that begins, "If when these Lyricks."[26]

Some early modern poems make their identification with certain meanings of *versus* explicit. From the translation of the Latin into anglicized headings of "turn" and "counter-turn" to the shifts between addressees to the many types of turning enacted verbally ("Alas, but *Morison* fell young: / Hee never fell, thou fall'st, my tongue" [43–44]), Ben Jonson's "To the Immortall Memorie, and Friendship of that Noble Paire, Sir Lucius Cary, and Sir H. Morison" in effect rings the changes on the word in question.[27] In so doing, Jonson establishes several types of dialogue—between stanzas, between divergent opinions, between sides of the observer—that call into question the association of lyric with the monological, an issue explored in Chapter 2 below. More to the point here, reading Jonson suggests that the linkage between lyric and turning is among the many reasons the Pindaric ode achieves exemplary status in the early modern period.

But in Latin *versus* can also suggest the turning of a plow, an association that may be reinforced by the visual effect of lines, notably in Puttenham's *Arte of English Poesie*, where semicircles link rhyming lines. Might not Ovid's reference to the abandonment of agriculture that accompanied Orpheus's death ("vacuousque iacent dispersa per agros / sarculaque rastrique graves longique ligones" ["Scattered through the deserted fields lay hoes, long mattocks and heavy grubbing-tools"], *Metamorphoses* XI.35–36) hint at these connections between poetry and agriculture?[28] To be sure, this georgic analogue is relevant to epic as well as lyric, as Spenser demonstrates through his punning agricultural metaphors—reminding us again that some usages examined in this chapter do not belong to lyric to the exclusion of other poetry. The canto that traces Calidore's flirtation with pastoral opens on a love affair with georgic expressed through a series of rhetorical turns that are again mimetic:

> Now turne againe my teme thou iolly swayne,
> Backe to the furrow which I lately left;
> I lately left a furrow, one or twayne
> Vnplough'd.

(VI.ix.1)[29]

But given how lyric poetry relies on repetitive patternings such as the rhyme schemes of, say, sestinas or rondeaux, the association of turning with that mode in particular would also have been powerful.

In addition to these overt engagements with the meanings of *versus*, early modern poets were, I maintain, preoccupied with an etymological tension that intensifies and is itself activated and intensified by the guilt one encounters in a range of guises when examining the figurative language describing lyric.[30] On the one hand, the *Oxford English Dictionary* records several contemporary meanings of "turn" that involve trickery and malformation: "to give a curved or crooked form to; to bend or twist" and, more specifically, "to bend back (the edge of a sharp instrument) so as to make it useless for cutting."[31] Again, these troubling associations could adhere to other forms of poetry; but they were particularly resonant to readers and writers of lyric poetry, given their intense anxieties about the powerful dangers of that siren song—a melody whose suasive force could turn a ship from its course and twist the values of both listener and speaker, proving its power by destroying theirs. Moreover, in sonnets whose *volta* introduces a movement towards or intensification of a morally or intellectually dubious position, such as *Astrophil and Stella* 76, among a host of other examples, the dangers of turning are enacted semantically and signaled structurally. Thus this trope, like so many others, signals the potential guilt of the poet—and hints at connections between turning and queering.

Yet the terminology in question itself involves a turning that mimes literary critics' turn towards the material: early modern poets, unlike most of their twentieth- and twenty-first-century critics, were no less aware of a second series of resonances, which variously intensified and counterbalanced the negative associations of *versus*. Lathe work was often described as turning, and Jacobean furniture in particular is proudly festooned with its results—low relief turned columns on chests, chairs with turned backs and struts, and so on. Such work obviously testifies to the agency of the maker, but that agency could be used towards beneficent or evil ends. On the one hand, this type of turning suggests not crookedness but graceful roundness, not deformation but skilled formation, not suspect craftiness but appealing craft. Hence it might recall the well-wrought plot of a sustained narrative; and, given the preoccupation with the craft of rhyme and meter in lyric, these connotations were surely also resonant to those crafting or reading the well-wrought rhyme scheme of, say, a crown of sonnets or a sestina. Yet on the other hand, influenced in particular by Flemish craftsmen, English furniture makers often used the lathe to fashion grotesque figures, distorted bodies that might recall the fear that, if lyric could calm beasts as myths of Orpheus suggest, it could also, Circe-like, turn readers and writers into them.

Moreover, as Henry Turner has cogently pointed out, certain meanings of "turn" link the creation of verse, that pursuit of the gentleman-amateur, with artisanal activities.[32] This introduces another paradox into that kaleidoscope of paradox gender. On the one hand, the allusion to artisans implicitly connects poetry with a largely masculine sphere. But on the other, transgressions of gender and of status may be closely related, as students of Shakespeare's sonnets know well, and arguably the possibility that writing poetry renders one déclassé activates the fear, to which I will return shortly, that it also renders one effeminate or even female. These putative links between turning out lyric poetry and turning the struts of chairs are subterranean, with no overt allusions supporting them. They are, however, buttressed by the other connections between art and artisanal practices that Turner has demonstrated and by those encountered in my discussion of stanzas in Chapter 4. Might these traces of a connection between verse and the pursuits of artisans have been activated by the social connotations of publication, hence further intensifying the distrust of print?

Another implication of the connection between poetic and artisanal turning is that the text is a product created through the execution of an activity. The poet becomes a Maker in a very literal and mundane sense. This emphasis on the materialist status of lyric supports an argument I will examine in more detail in Chapter 3, Mary Thomas Crane's revisionist interpretation of theatrical performance as a kind of execution or making that did not necessarily imply deceit.[33] Associating lyric with artisanal practices like crafting furniture thus signals yet another tension: the very activity that Platonism links to the uncontrolled seizures of *furor* is connected instead to conscious and deliberate activity, in a sense replicating and extending the conflict between certain Platonic and Aristotelian models of art. In short, the paradoxical resonances of turning gloss lyric as both an achievement that may generate respect and delight and as a trick that may generate fear and guilt, as a powerful aesthetic endeavor and as a material and artisanal activity cognate to such quotidian pursuits as plowing fields or making chairs, and as the site of process and movement.

These associations of turning emerge from other tropes as well; many further resonances of *versus*, such as the linkage of lyric to both the insubstantial and the material, are also significant in those figures. In deploying them, early modern texts and their readers sometimes simply draw on preexisting connotations and denotations but sometimes more actively participate in definitions and descriptions of lyric through the terms they associate with it. Such processes are interactive and dynamic, the meanings of those terms shaping the conceptions of those who deploy them while that deployment also encourages the poets in question, other poets, and their readers to meditate on the associations of these resonant terms.

On the most obvious level, calling a poem an "air" differs from the figurative practices discussed elsewhere in this section in that it literally establishes the text as a song, sometimes, though not invariably, a light one. Presumed and pursued by critics of lyric, the connections between the two arts of music and literature have informed numerous analyses of poetry, such as the suggestion that the eighteen lines of George Herbert's "Easter" are a hieroglyph for the double strings of a nine-course lute and the hypothesis that Wyatt wrote his psalms to be sung.[34]

Yet, as my Introduction suggested, the process of tracing the connections between poetry and music suggested by the usage of "air" involves many ambiguities and controversies, even tempests. Musicologists disagree on whether these links are typically analogies or more concrete connections.[35] Some posit direct influences, citing Petrarchism as a source for a growing expressiveness and metaphysical complexity as an incentive to the development of recitative. Other scholars, however, issue caveats about these and similar links; in one of the most judicious discussions of the issue, David Lindley seconds John Hollander's emphasis on the separation between the two in the early modern period and declares that "the two systems are independent and distinct."[36] Debates also surround arguments about the relationship within particular poems, such as whether the monody or madrigal is the principal musical influence on "Lycidas." John Stevens cogently reminds us that for all our assertions of connections between music and poetry, it is hard to be sure which poems were actually written for music.[37]

Despite these and many other uncertainties about how music and poetry were related in the early modern period, however, it is clear that poets and other members of their culture, including those who often assigned titles to poets' writings, want to emphasize that relationship and that they do so in part through linguistic usages. "Song" and "hymn" often appear in the titles of poems that may or may not have been sung. In his magisterial study of music in the period, John Hollander points out that Herbert often uses "sing" for "pray"; and Patrick Cheney has cogently demonstrated how often Shakespeare associated song and lyric, citing particularly compelling evidence of their visual similarity in books.[38] The myths of Orpheus, Arion, and the sirens, analyzed above, also recur with telling frequency. To the reasons for and effects of this putative linkage between these arts I will return at several points during this study, but at this juncture a few can be sketched. Emphasized by the movement of musical humanism, the expressive powers of music become tied to those of poetry, intensifying the sense of its potency. As Thomas Ravenscroft puts it in his 1614 treatise, music can provide "both a *relish*, and a *beauty*" to poetry.[39] Similarly, the curative power of music, celebrated by Plato, among many others, adheres to poetry as well.

At the same time, however, the status of music in the early modern period both intensified the guilt adhering to lyric and provided opportunities for negotiating it.[40] To begin with, comparable dangers, especially seduction, were associated with both arts; prostitutes, Linda Phyllis Austern has demonstrated, were often being described in musical terms by the middle of the seventeenth century.[41] Yet music offered analogues to and evidence for a recurrent drive to counter reservations about poesy by sharply distinguishing Good and Evil Lyric. Renaissance poets were aware that, much as Sidney so sedulously distinguishes moral lyric from its evil twin, so classical texts repeatedly contrast the music of stringed instruments with that of wind instruments, a pattern traced with particular acuity by John Hollander.[42] Indeed, in classical Greece the flute in particular was often associated with slave girls; Othered through this and other means, it was seen as not-male and not-Greek. In vase paintings, the faces and mouths of those female slaves are often distorted.[43] As we have seen, a similar contrast impels the narrative of Orpheus's death at the hands—and through the musical instruments—of the maenads. Such contrasts were to recur in the many texts of the English and continental Renaissance that represented the lute, lyre, and harp as virtuous instruments. And the distinction in question was also intensified and updated by an analogous contemporary one: the putative divide between the chastity of homophonic settings and the sensuality and unintelligibility of polyphonic Bad Girls.

Like so many other dichotomies related to lyric, however, this one would break down. On the one hand, even types of music subject to moral disapprobation were, under other circumstances, respected and celebrated; the father of John Milton, after all, composed polyphony. And, on the other hand, types and instruments generally classified as virtuous were sometimes represented as more dubious. The musicologist Matthew Spring comments tellingly on the broken string in Holbein's "Ambassadors"; Carla Zecher catalogues the French texts that link the lute to prostitutes; while in England, Spring reminds us, lutes were associated both with erotic poetry and with the psalms.[44] Conversely, although wind instruments were often disdained, even demonized, some were associated with the glories of royal music, thus again demonstrating the instabilities that were both source and symptom of the divide between Good and Evil Lyric.

Although I have been focusing mainly on how "air" may signal literal, direct connections with music, it is no accident that I am exploring that usage in a section on tropes: often, rather than suggesting that a lyric is an actual song, the term invites attention to the consequences of seeing lyric as related to song, as song-like. Discussing Catullus's preoccupation with talk, William Fitzgerald demonstrates that the poet is not merely concerned to elevate that practice into something more serious but also to investigate speech, showing how it works in general.[45] As a number of passages in subsequent chapters, such as my commentary on Donne's "Triple Foole," demonstrate, the usage of "air" raises similarly broad questions about song and its sibling lyric.

In addition to introducing all these musical associations, however, the word "air" puns on one of the four elements, thus bringing to bear an additional series of suggestive connotations no less contradictory than those attached to "turn." To begin with, "air" may suggest something insubstantial, without agency, tying in with the notion of lyric as the purview of women and children and recalling from another perspective its link to passively received inspiration. Herrick hints at this reading when, in "The Argument of his Book," he promises, "I sing of Dewes . . . I sing / The court of Mab" (7, 11–12); other lines in that extraordinary poem, of course, represent the succeeding lyrics very differently. Mutable and moveable, "air" also draws attention to the transformative qualities of lyric.

The linkage of poetry in general or lyric itself with air in its several forms is not, of course, unique to the early modern period. Troubadour poets refer to breath; their Romantic counterparts often connect inspiration to the wind. Generalizing about poetry rather than lyric in particular, Wallace Stevens's lines "Poetry is a finikin thing of air / That lives uncertainly and not for long / Yet radiantly beyond much lustier blurs" ("Like Decorations in a Nigger Cemetery," 68–70) show no less ambivalence than the Renaissance texts I have been exploring.[46] In his suggestive though controversial study *Toy Medium*, Daniel Tiffany adduces this and many other passages to argue for transhistorical connections among toys, meteors, weather, and poetry.[47] Those connections, like so much else about lyric, are best, indeed brilliantly, explicated by Susan Stewart, who observes, "wind and water are the great forces of wearing away and wearing down, but as they are eroding elements they are also inspiring elements," thus adding further ambivalences and paradoxes to those catalogued above.[48]

But those ambivalences and many other implications of associating lyric and air also assume forms that are culturally specific, though not unique to early modern England. The destructive impact of wind on stone would have been more evident to inhabitants of that culture than to twentieth- and twenty-first-century Americans living in milieux where buildings are more likely to be torn down than worn down and where many cemeteries, like the towns that house them, are too recent to manifest those effects. Above all, in a culture repeatedly threatened by that terrorist the plague, widely believed to be disseminated through the atmosphere, air could suggest not insubstantiality and insignificance but rather a medium with active, threatening power. Thus lyric is again associated with both agency and its absence. Stressing the extraordinary potency of air, the seventeenth-century Scottish doctor John Makluire observes:

> it passeth so quickly through the body, that it printeth presently the qualities wherewith it is indued in the parts of the same, and therefore there is nothing able to change more shortly the body than it. . . . A good air . . . revives the spirits, purifieth the blood, procureth appetite. . . . A contaminate aire with filthy exhalations, arysing from standing waters, dead carcases, middings, gutters, closets, and the filth of the streets, (all which if any where are to bee found heere, which argueth a great oversight of the magistrats, bringeth a great hurt to the inhabitants, and a great good to the Physicians, Apothecaries, and bel-man) corrupteth the spirits, and humors, and engendereth often a deadly contagion or pest.[49]

Similarly, in a letter to his friend Henry Goodyer, John Donne attributes his illness to the "raw vapors" from a vault beneath his study.[50] Another aperçu of Wallace Stevens, "Thought is an infection," implies some of the threats that he elsewhere more explicitly associates with poetry, but the links specifically among air, song, and illness were far more characteristic of the early modern than the modern period.[51] In troping drama in terms of disease in general and plague in particular, anti-theatrical tracts remind us that the association of lyric with that dread malady should be seen in terms of the broader fear that art itself involves contamination. At the same time, the unstable meanings of "air" demonstrate that in the instance of lyric in particular, that fear was complicated by distinctive ambivalences.

Many of these suggestions about air were intensified in the seventeenth century by the widespread interest in vitalism. Astutely traced by John Rogers, this movement attributed agency to objects in the physical world.[52] Lyric, then, would be interpreted in relation to the agency of a pneumatic force, an energy that could variously suggest an attractive liveliness or a threatening potency. The association of lyric with persuasion poems substantiates this reading and the perils it potentially involves. At the same time that vitalism emphasizes the power of air, the link between breath and the gendered instability of both male and female voices—a mutability whose attendant anxieties have been powerfully analyzed by Gina Bloom—renders the medium in question threatening in another way as well.[53] In short, as a version of air and its avatars of breath and wind, lyric is at once insignificant, volatile, and potent. Associated with the originary breath of God, it can both create and destroy, thus again inviting the writer or would-be writer to experience both pride and guilt; and in its admixture of creation and destruction, weakness and threatening strength, the term "air" arguably also recalls cultural stereotypes of the feminine.

In addition to the linkages with turning and with air, in the early modern period lyric is repeatedly connected to childhood and childishness. Certain instances, to be sure, exemplify the clichéd troping of artistic works as progeny, or the commonplace condescension towards writers, or both, and thus are specific to neither lyric nor the English Renaissance. But in relation to lyric in particular the image acquires many additional resonances, some of which I scrutinized above. It embeds the paradoxical swerve between seeing writing as source of and threat to agency: the parent literally brings the child into being, and yet any parent knows that this hardly guarantees obedience. Similarly, whereas other eras also connect lyric and childhood (the eighteenth-century writer Joseph Trapp feels obliged to attack those "who look upon it as a trifling Amusement, an Exercise for Boys," and Margaret Atwood reports that her brother denigrated the publication of her first significant collection of poetry by saying it was the sort of thing he used to do when he was younger), certain implications are more common in the Renaissance than in later eras.[54] In particular, given the rates of infant and childhood mortality (a plague bill may simply substitute "infant" for the more precise causes of death listed for other decedents, thus demonstrating how unremarkable such losses were seen to be), seeing lyric as a child would thus at once associate it with promise and with a sense of fragility—that is, with the risk of promise truncated, denied. One should recall that Orpheus loses his wife twice, once on their wedding day.

The term "numbers" is frequently, though not exclusively, applied to lyrics; Donne, for example, declares, "Griefe brought to numbers cannot be so fierce" ("The Triple Foole," 10 ), while Herrick opens his "Ode of the Birth of our Saviour," "In Numbers, and but these few, / I sing Thy Birth, Oh JESU!," and his religious verse is entitled, *His Noble Numbers*.[55] This usage also is not, of course, unique to early modern lyric—"Yet I number him in the song" (35) William Butler Yeats writes in "Easter, 1916"—but the astronomical and spiritual associations of the term are more common to the period on which this book focuses than to many others.[56] Compressed within this commonplace usage are a celebration of verse, a more pragmatic vision of it, and yet again implications of distrust. As Plato's *Timaeus* famously reminds us, heavenly harmony was often seen in musical terms. That harmony was more directly related to lyric by the Pythagorean belief, recorded in Quintilian I.x.12, that the principles on which the universe is based were also used in the construction of the lyre.[57] Although John Hollander has demonstrated a movement in the course of the early modern period away from this celestial model, like the movement away from hagiography it was neither consistent nor steady in its trajectory.[58] At the same time, "numbers" suggests the treatises on arithmetic and mathematics that were so popular in the period, again substantiating Turner's emphasis on the debt of early modern aesthetics to artisanal treatises. Although he focuses on drama, what Turner terms "practical knowledge" shapes early modern lyric as well, as subsequent chapters will demonstrate.[59] But if the association with numbers encompasses the heavenly and the artisanal, it also carries with it more disturbing associations, thus again demonstrating the paradoxical valuations of lyric expressed through its tropes. Throughout her recent study *Shakespeare and the Mismeasure of Man*, Paula Blank documents how frequently measurement was seen as unreliable in early modern England; that era, she demonstrates, often represents numerical systems as deceptive, an argument that may once more remind us that, in making chairs and making interpretations, to turn is often to twist.[60]

"Happy ye leaves," the first poem of *Amoretti* opens, thus exemplifying yet another figure for lyric. Spenser has much company in his deployment of this botanical trope, which offers further evidence of the association of lyric with evanescence and fragility, meanings famously invoked when Milton describes the fallen angels as the autumnal detritus of trees. The association of lyric and leaves suggests that the poet creates not a monument more lasting than brass but a fragile and potentially brittle object liable to blowing away or crumbling, and the figure again calls into question the agency and potency of the writer. But if the leaves in question may be transparent, the language used to evoke them is not, for the association between pages and leaves also involves the restoration of power: whoever turns the leaves exercises some control over them; the poem becomes a manageable object, one that can be held within hands. Of course, its writer may turn the leaves, but generally the person who does so is a reader, and so the trope primarily plays down the power of the author even while vesting it in the reader, precisely the maneuver Spenser performs, or at least pretends to perform, in that opening sonnet of *Amoretti,* a poem examined in more detail in my analysis of lyric audiences. This figure anticipates, then, the tensions I will explore in the chapter on the dynamic relationships between writer and audience, especially the contestations for agency created by early modern conditions of production, both scribal and print.

Two related tropes, among the most revealing of all the figures associated with lyric, are also, as it were, rooted in gardening. First, poems are often compared to flowers. Playing on John Bodenham's own title, *Bel-vedere, or The Garden of the Muses,* a poem addressed to him in *England's Helicon,* declares, "in the Muses Garden, gathering flowres, / Thou mad'st a Nosegay, as was never sweeter."[61] That master punster Sidney thus accuses his rivals and alter egos: "And everie floure, not sweet perhaps, which growes / Neare therabout, into your Poesie wring" (*Astrophil and Stella* 15.3–4). Although flowers may of course be perennials (as Herrick reminds us in "To the Lady Crew"), the primary thrust of this trope is again towards the evanescence of beauty, while the *carpe florem* tradition also hints at connections between poetry and the rhetorics of seduction.

Especially revealing, however, are the recurrent images of bouquets, suggested by the poem to Bodenham and so many other instances, and especially the application of the multivalent term "posy" for them. Demonstrating contemporary awareness of this wordplay, George Gascoigne entitled his collection, published in 1573, *A Hundreth Sundrie Flowres,* while the revised version that appeared two years later is called *The Posies of G. Gascoigne.* The first volume establishes Gascoigne as a shape-shifting trickster who delights in assigning the authorship of his texts to others; despite—and more to the point because of—the way the second volume attempts to establish itself as a palinode for the amorality of its predecessor, a substitution of coming clean for posturing, its author's delight in game-playing encourages the speculation that its title puns on "poses."

But the usage in question has resonances relevant to other writers as well: in the sixteenth and seventeenth centuries, "posy" itself could refer to poetry in general, to a bouquet, or to an emblem or inscription.[62] Imputedly a short, discrete poem, lyric is thus associated with a group of poems, a linkage that would have seemed particularly apt to a culture accustomed to the circulation of manuscripts, the juxtaposition of apparently disparate texts in a commonplace book, and, of course, the print publication of groups of poems, most notably sonnet cycles (which could themselves culminate in a complaint, another type of grouping) and pastorals. To the implications of such groupings for the unit of lyric I will return in Chapter 4. One type of grouping in particular intensifies the ambivalences packed into the association of lyric with "air" and exemplifies the paradoxes lyric so often involves: carried to ward off the plague, posies of flowers were hence both an index of and antidote to illness.[63]

"Poesy" also recalls the *carpe florem* tradition, again connecting this usage with lyric in particular and in turn associating lyric with another type of illness—that is, the madness of love—and with the languages of seduction. And with the targets of seduction as well: such references link poesy to female beauty and the possibility of poetic and sexual appropriations of it, as Rachel Blau du Plessis reminds us.[64] In a sense these associations transfer fragility from the poem about her to the lady herself. She is damned if she does and damned if she doesn't, on the one hand liable to wither if she does not yield to her lover's entreaty, but on the other liable to be plucked and thus destroyed if she agrees. (To return to those fallen leaves, Shakespeare's "Lover's Complaint" refers to the "lettice of sear'd age" [14] of its fallen speaker.[65]) Might not anxieties about the frailty of poetry and its creator be transferred here, re-gendered in a reassuring power play?

But any student of Petrarch recalls the swerves between woman as laurel and woman as stone; similarly, in the early modern period the term "poesy" could also suggest an inscription in stone. In yet another paradox, then, the word in question can invoke both the evanescence of flowers and the hardiness of stone. Lady Mary Wroth plays on the connection with the latter in her unduly neglected "Song 1," discussed in Chapter 3. Thus lyric becomes not merely an evanescent moment but also an "endlesse monument," not merely a locus of transformation and change but a possibility for permanence, hence an apt medium for the immortalization promised in love poetry and more reliably inherent in another form lyric may assume, the celebratory ode. But other implications of inscription are more multivalent. What is happening to gendering? Hardness is gendered as male in the most common stereotypes, and yet the *rime pietose* establish its connections with the female as well. At the same time, inscription suggests cutting (an image also used for artistry in many medieval texts, notably the lyrics of the troubadour Bertram de Born). This linkage returns us to artisanal activities and also reintroduces the hints of violence and destruction that are never far off in discussions of lyric. The collection of flowers that is a poesy may have within it thorns sharp enough to pierce even stone.

Closely related to its denotation of inscription is the now-obsolete use of "posey" for an emblem; Thomas Palmer's sixteenth-century collection in that genre, for example, is entitled *Two Hundred Poosees.*[66] The usage links lyric to moral adages, a kinship variously eagerly asserted and cynically denied in more explicit debates about the virtue—in the several senses of that term—of lyric poetry. At the same time, the allusion to emblems gestures towards the kernel of wisdom, whether represented as the couplet of a sonnet or the motto at the end of a pastoral, through which lyrics achieve, or attempt to achieve, closure. "Poesy," in short, emphasizes both the morality and the materiality of lyric, as well as other kinds of verse. But the word, appropriately enough, itself involves yet another paradox, in this instance a turning between two very different images of the material world: the evanescence suggested by wordplay on "leaves" and the solidity suggested by rocks.

_◦ ◦_

Many issues apparent in the realms of trope and myth recur as well in the more explicit discussions of lyric in early modern treatises. The very term "lyric" is used variously. Poets and rhetoricians present that mode as evanescent and trifling yet powerful as a weapon and durable as stone. For these and other reasons, significant contradictions, often associated with gender, are apparent from one treatise to the next and from one passage of the same treatise to the next. The writings in question, like the myths and tropes on which they draw, however, often resolve, or attempt to resolve, those contradictions by the now familiar strategy of distinguishing two versions of lyric.

Intensely aware of the precedent of classical lyric, writers of such treatises frequently turn to it as another avenue towards resolving the problems associated with defining and describing their mode. In lieu of clear-cut definitions, they are prone to proffer classical examples: lyric is what Pindar and Horace write, and so on. One effect of this habit is to establish prototypes for English poets and their readers—in the instance of Pindar, one of the most frequently cited lyric poets, a prototype emphasizing the public, communal workings of the mode. Yet, the use of Greek and Roman approaches to lyric more often introduces further complexities and contradictions into attempts to define and describe lyric.

Authors and other commentators in the English Renaissance inherited and often showed themselves cognizant of the range of terminology in Latin and Greek culture, more cognizant of it than the many critics of our own day who attempt to establish the type of lyric in which they specialize as normative. Classical usages were rendered further complex and even contradictory by changes from one period to another within those cultures; for instance, while archaic Greek lyric was composed orally and performed aloud at events such as weddings, in the Alexandrian period, the mode was often read in anthologies. Nonetheless, in their many forms, classical lyrics warn us against the parochialism of making of one's own little world an everywhere.[67] The Greek use of "melic" for poetry to be sung, mirroring the connection of "lyric" and "lyre," applied to both monodic and choral verse. We are thus reminded how problematical is an unqualified association of lyric with individuated subjectivity, as is the relationship between lyric and internalized meditation: indeed, as far as scholars can tell, all melic poetry in archaic Greece was communal.

Greek practices of naming and defining forms distinguished melic texts, which were associated with stringed instruments, from iambic and elegiac poems, which were accompanied by the flute and allied with distinctive meters (whether the elegy was originally defined in terms of funerary themes as well is, however, disputed).[68] Thus meter and what Frye was to term "radical of presentation" were linked early in the history of poetry, and, more to my purposes here, the distinctions that were to generate models of Good and Evil Lyric were anticipated linguistically. The Greek term describing the poet as a singer antedates the usage establishing him as a maker. In writing about poetry, the Greeks frequently deployed the words referring to song: in Homer, *aoide*, and subsequently *melos*, the poet being called *aoidós* (singer) or, later, *melopoiós* (maker of songs) and *poietés*.[69] But these usages are not clear-cut or consistent. Moreover, lacking a general word for poetry, the Greeks often used "melic" for any text other than drama or epic, including political poetry. In the Alexandrian period, "lyric" was often applied more broadly to any poem intended to be sung, though the period also witnessed an increasing movement towards texts transmitted through writing, not performance.

Roman usages, which draw heavily on their Greek antecedents, are also complex and varied; and they too often involve metrical issues. At the same time, the label "carmina," so tellingly applied to Horace's poetry, signals the continuing link with song. Latin literature, notably the work of Catullus and Horace, of course provided its English imitators with instances of lyric poetry purporting to concern personal experiences, especially the perturbations and tribulations of love and desire. That focus could on occasion call into question the reputation of the genre; warning in his *Institutio Oratoria* (I.viii.6) that licentious poetry risks corrupting the young, Quintilian insists that elegiac and hendecasyllabic verse should be omitted completely from the classroom if possible, or, failing that, shared only with older students. If, however, the authors are carefully selected, he declares in the same passage, lyric can provide intellectual nourishment. Thus he anticipates both the anxieties about lyric found throughout early modern texts and the move of countering them by sharply distinguishing its various manifestations. Renaissance writers also inherited continental discussions of lyric, including the neo-Latin traditions. Roland Greene has drawn our attention to the emphasis on sound and rhythm in the fifteenth-century treatise *Proemio e carta* by the Marquis of Santillana.[70] Particularly well known in the period was Scaliger's *Poetices libri septem*, which has a chapter on lyric poetry and separate chapters on pastoral, hymns, dithyrambs, and other forms.

Traces of all of these usages survive in treatises of the early modern period, as well as in the poetry itself. In particular, the linkage to song recurs repeatedly, as does the association of lyric with public occasions and the agenda, often advanced by that association, of sharply distinguishing valuable and deleterious forms of lyric. But despite their common ground on such issues, discussions of lyric during the English Renaissance, like their antecedents, are typically inconsistent in their definitions of the mode, notably disagreeing with each other on how narrowly they restrict it and how firmly they distinguish it from other forms. And they are profoundly ambivalent in their valuations of it, some treatises privileging it over other genres, others denigrating it, and still others sliding between those positions.

Unresolved contradictions are endemic, I have maintained; to begin with, writers of the period part company on how, if at all, they use the term "lyric." Although some critics have claimed that the word was unfamiliar in England during the sixteenth and earlier seventeenth centuries, Robert Herrick uses it repeatedly throughout *Hesperides*. In addition to the passage from "An Ode to Sir Clipsebie Crew" discussed in the introduction, he appears to deploy the term in the loose and general way common today, as a synonym for short songlike poems, when he declares in "Lyrick for Legacies" that "each Lyrick here shall be / Of my love a Legacie" (4–5). Since the poems in question involve a range of meters, Jonson also seems to be using the word in a general sense, not a precise metrical one, when he fashions his title, "A Celebration of Charis in Ten Lyrick Peeces." Yet the narrower prosodic sense of lyric clearly survived as well; seventeenth-century editions of Donne, for example, acknowledge the metrical distinction between his other love poetry and his elegies by printing them separately. George Puttenham asserts that classical poets termed themselves "*Heroick, Lyrick, Elegiack, Epigrammatist* or otherwise" and adopts that categorization himself when he praises Elizabeth's abilities "in Ode, Elegie, Epigram, or any other kinde of poeme Heroicke or Lyricke."[71]

Although the triadic distinction among modes is often associated primarily with later periods, it is anticipated in a few important documents of the early modern period, though even here it often coexists with other types of categorization. The preface to the Second Book of Milton's *Reason of Church Government*, cited later in this chapter, alludes to the categories of epic, drama, and lyric. An analogue to the triadic division of modes which, for all its fascinating implications, is far less familiar than Milton's, appears in Roger Ascham's *Scholemaster*. Stressing the importance of *genera dicendi*, he posits divisions among poetry, history, philosophy, and oratory. Having noted that each includes further categories, he subdivides poetry into the comic, tragic, epic, and melic. Thus melic again becomes a capacious category with a problematical relationship to song, a category presumably including epigram and elegy as well as texts more frequently classified as lyric in his period. Despite the breadth of the melic category, Ascham expresses optimism about recognizing and replicating the appropriate decorum. Predictably, the method he advocates is studying classical models, and Pindar is once again included in the list; whoever "shall diligently marke the difference they use in proprietie of wordes, in forme of sentence, in handlyng of their matter," Ascham assures us, "shall easelie perceive, what is fitte and *decorum* in everie one."[72]

The characteristics I am identifying in these brief early modern commentaries on lyric—diversity among texts in how broadly the category is conceived and how confidently it is defined, consciousness of classical models with particularly frequent references to Pindaric odes, and ambivalence about the potentialities and perils of the mode—are expanded and explicated in statements by Michael Drayton, John Milton, George Puttenham, and, of course, Sir Philip Sidney. Drayton prefaces the section of odes in his 1619 *Poems* with "To the Reader":

Odes I have called these my few Poems; which how happie soever they prove, yet Criticisme it selfe cannot say, that the Name is wrongfully usurped: For . . . an Ode is knowne to have been properly a Song, moduled to the ancient Harpe, and neither too short-breathed, as hasting to the end, nor composed of the longest Verses, as unfit for the sudden Turnes and loftie Tricks with which *Apollo* used to manage it. They are (as the Learned say) divers: Some transcendently loftie and farre more high then the Epick . . . witnesse those of the inimitable *Pindarus*, consecrated to the glorie and renowne of such as returned in triumph from *Olympus, Elis, Isthmus,* or the like: Others, among the Greekes, are amorous, soft, and made for Chambers, as other for Theaters; as were *Anacreon's*, the very Delicacies of the Grecian *Erato*, which Muse seemed to have beene the Minion of that Teian old Man, which composed them: Of a mixed kinde were *Horace's*.[73]

Drayton echoes several characteristics that recur in other early modern discussions of lyric: it is associated with song, length is a criterion, the public celebratory odes of Pindar are a model, even perhaps the prototype, as Drayton's adoption of the term "ode" might itself hint. His reference to theaters suggests not the triadic divide found in Ascham and Milton but rather an overlapping of modes that can compromise attempts at neat definitions. Drayton also stresses other kinds of variety that may complicate such attempts, noting in particular that lyric encompasses both praise of the great and erotic verse. Thus it encompasses as well subject matter often coded masculine ("the glorie and renowne") and the stereotypically feminine ("soft, made for Chambers"); some anxiety about such gendering may also be present in his description of the muse Erato, where hints of an imperiled masculinity (he writes "soft" verse and is characterized as an "old Man") are countered by hinting through the term "Minion" that he is the lover of a Muse onto whom the eroticism of lyric is deflected.[74] Arguably similar concerns surface in the curious caveat against overly short lyric. Might an attempt to counterbalance the potential transgressiveness of erotic verse lie behind these comments about length, given that they associate lyric with a moderation, even a golden mean, at odds with the irrationality and immoderation of the erotic?

Puttenham provides a textbook example of some of the principal issues I have been tracing. As I pointed out earlier, he notes that classical poets termed themselves "*Heroick, Lyrick, Elegiack, Epigrammatist* or otherwise" (40) and uses similar terminology himself in relation to the queen's writing. When describing lyric poetry, he explains,

> Others who more delighted to write songs or ballads of pleasure, to be song with the voice, and to the harpe, lute, or citheron and such other musical, instruments, they were called melodious Poets [*melici*] or by a more common name *Lirique* poets, of which sort was *Pindarus, Anacreon* and *Callimachus* with others among the Greeks: *Horace* and *Catullus* among the Latins. There were an other sort, . . . *Elegiak*: such among the Latines were *Ovid, Tibullus,* and *Propertius.*

Note the influence of classical usages in his distinguishing another type of love poetry, the elegiac, from lyric and in his category "the melodious." And, like some of his classical sources, he emphasizes what Frye was to term the radical of presentation.

In the section of *The Reason of Church Government* on lyric, after discussing the possibilities for writing various forms of epic and drama, Milton emphasizes the value of scriptural song over classical lyrics:

Or if occasion shall lead to imitate those magnific odes and hymns wherein Pindarus and Callimachus are in most things worthy, some others in their frame judicious, in their matter most an end faulty. But those frequent songs throughout the law and prophets beyond all these, not in their divine argument alone, but in the very critical art of composition, may be easily made appear over all the kinds of lyric poesy to be incomparable. These abilities, wheresoever they be found, are the inspired gift of God rarely bestowed, but yet to some (though most abuse) in every nation; and are of power beside the office of a pulpit, to inbreed and cherish in a great people the seeds of virtue and public civility, to allay the perturbations of the mind and set the affections in right tune, to celebrate in glorious and lofty hymns the throne and equipage of God's almightiness . . . to sing the victorious agonies of martyrs and saints. . . .[75]

Note the creation of a capacious, overarching category ("all the kinds of lyric poesy") that is clearly contrasted with the two other modes. That category, like its Greek antecedents, not only includes but is also closely associated with the celebratory public verse of Pindar, and Milton emphasizes the public responsibilities of the poet while also stressing the potential benefits for "the perturbations of the mind." The parallel with the pulpit reminds us that a focus on the rhetorical instrumentality of lyric is not merely a product of a twentieth- and twenty-first-century reaction against the Romantic lyric, or rather the hypostatized versions of it. (Indeed, as Roland Greene reminds us, rhetorical theory and lyric were closely connected throughout the early modern period.)[76]

Also telling, however, is the ambivalence excited by a mode that encompasses not only hymns, implicitly presented as more worthy than epic and drama, but also odes "in their matter most an end faulty." If, as Milton's reference to the pulpit reminds us, linking lyric with rhetoric potentially glorifies its suasive force, the well-known early modern anxieties about the dangers of eloquence can also taint our mode. Moreover, one encounters here the first of many instances in which the strange bedfellows made by the breadth of the category "lyric" are valued in very different ways. "Though most abuse" reflects a similar anxiety; if the signature trope of lyric is catachresis, the figure of abuse, as Frye has maintained, perhaps one reason is that both writers and critics associate lyric with abuse as Milton does here, hence creating or uncovering catachresis within the text to express and deflect their anxiety about the abusive practices of lyric poets. Observing these ambivalences, the reader may wonder uneasily about the wording "may be easily made appear," with its passing but tantalizing hint that the process of glossing even the most worthy of lyrics is itself potentially abusive.

The most famous early modern allusions to lyric are surely Sidney's discussions in his *Apology for Poetry*. In tracing why and how poesy has been contemned, Sidney lists its subdivisions in terms that suggest that he, unlike Ascham and Milton, is rejecting an all-encompassing class of lyric or melic poetry in favor of subdivisions: "Is it then the Pastoral poem which is misliked? . . . Or is it the lamenting Elegiac? . . . Is it the bitter but wholesome Iambic? . . . Is it the Lyric that most displeaseth?" (116–118). The succeeding commentary on lyric repulses criticisms of it directly by declaring that it serves ethical and spiritual ends: "who with his tuned lyre and well-accorded voice, giveth praise, the reward of virtue, to virtuous acts; . . . who sometimes raiseth up his voice to the height of the heavens, in singing the lauds of the immortal God" (118).

More revealing, however, is the impact of accusations commonly leveled against lyric. Sidney, like Drayton, counters the fear that the mode is deceptive and seductive by associating it with the civilized harmony and control that were often linked to stringed instruments and denied wind ones: "who with his *tuned* lyre and *well-accorded* voice" (118; italics inserted). The gentleman doth protest too much: behind this insistent diacritical drive, like related statements in the passage from Drayton that I just examined, lie fears that all lyric is contaminated by the erotic agendas of love poetry.

Sidney and his readers knew that, as both the writings of George Gascoigne and the research of modern critics such as Ilona Bell and Arthur F. Marotti demonstrate, love poetry was actually used in courtships.[77] (Revealing how criticism sometimes dismissed as traditional may in fact anticipate later insights, some thirty years before such work John Stevens established important cultural contexts for erotic poetry, demonstrating that whether or not it referred to actual romantic relationships, it was part of courtly games connected with love.[78]) Marotti has also shown that in manuscripts, unlike printed texts, many lyrics were not only erotic but actually obscene.[79] And Sidney, who famously ends one lyric, " 'But ah,' Desire still cries, 'give me some food' " (*Astrophil and Stella* 71.14) knew that the verb "to cry" could, not coincidentally, be used both for the laments of lovers and the act of hawking wares, whether they be oranges or poems or seductive compliments and complaints.[80] Arguably implicit in Sidney's verb, and unmistakably explicit in a passage from Herodotus adduced at the end of this chapter, is a link between writing love poetry, ostensibly the preserve of gentlemen, and the commodified pursuits of social inferiors.

Sidney's commentary, I maintain, parlays fears about both gender and social status. Tellingly deploying the masculine pronoun, Sidney proceeds to rebut the possibility that lyric is feminine or effeminizing in a number of other respects as well. It is associated with military activities, he stresses, and it is part of the discourse of "men," a term that appears three times in the same sentence ("when the lusty men . . . would do" [118–119]). This determined gendering is also enacted on a generic level, for the passage describes the ends of lyric in terms that might well be used instead for the next genre to which Sidney turns, the heroical: "most fit to awake the thoughts from the sleep of idleness, to embrace honourable enterprises" (119). Notice how this claim also counteracts the potential association of lyric with the lower social orders, a linkage intensified by the tropes associated with the mode, as this chapter has demonstrated.

When Sidney returns to lyric later in the treatise, however, he deploys syntax that implicitly denigrates the form, arguably reflecting continuing anxieties about gender and indubitably demonstrating the inconsistent valuations of lyric that not only distinguish early modern commentaries on the subject from one another but are on occasions found within the same tract. "Other sorts of Poetry *almost have we none, but* that lyrical kind of songs and sonnets" (137; italics inserted), he tellingly writes. He then proceeds to divide the form, distinguishing poems that praise God from love poetry. His condemnation of the latter pivots not on inherent failings but on the rhetorical failings of their writers ("so coldly they apply fiery speeches" [137]), a witty attack that allows him to express disapproval that stops short of a blanket condemnation of a form in which he wants to write despite his anxieties about the potential triumph of *cupiditas* over *caritas*. Notice that even while condemning the failures of love poetry he stresses its potential rhetorical efficacy—it is capable of moving a mistress when pursued with the principles of the figure *energia* in mind.

In distinguishing virtuous lyric from its demonic brother, or rather sister, Sidney attempts to recuperate and protect the mode through that dichotomy that so frequently recurs in the early modern and other periods, the contrast between dangerous and beneficent versions of it. From one perspective, then, Sidney's writings can stand as the *locus classicus* of the distinctions between Good and Evil Lyric. Yet from another perspective his texts also demonstrate the need to inflect generalizations with the particularities of historical subdivisions. Although the contrast in question is repeated throughout the early modern period, changes within that era reconfigure the pattern Sidney draws; for example, in the seventeenth century a more active tradition of spiritual poetry conveniently exemplified the defenses of virtuous lyric, while at the same time the development of Cavalier lyrics, often more openly erotic than their Petrarchan predecessors, intensified the need for such defenses. In any event, as we will see, much as Sidney blurs the edges of his contrast, so too its analogues in the work of other writers are as often undermined as they are established.

_⟋ ⟍_

So significant are the implications about gender in Sidney's writing and in other passages examined in this chapter that they invite further attention. Anticlosural though these resonances are, they aptly provide a type of closure here: pervasive and protean, the gendering of lyric encapsulates many problems analyzed above, as the frequency with which I have touched on the issue in passing would suggest, while at the same time it anticipates issues arising in subsequent chapters.[81] Of course, the linkage of gender and lyric did not originate in the early modern era, as we are reminded by a revealing passage from the Greek historian Herodotus, who was notably popular in that period. Roger Ascham retells the story in question in *Toxophilus*. In it the character Croesus, concerned about repeated uprisings by enemy warriors, advises his king that their adversaries should be dressed in women's clothes and forced to teach their children to play an instrument and sing; as a result, they will turn into women and never fight again. Or, as Barnabe Riche's Elizabethan translation of Herodotus puts it, "injoyne them to bringe up their children in playing on the cithern, in singing . . . and undoubtedlye thou shalt see that of valiant men and warlike people they will shortely become effeminate and like unto women."[82] (Does Riche modify the statement in the Greek original that they will actually become women in order to modulate the threat in question?[83]) In any event, both the original version of the passage and the translation also indicate that the song will contribute to further Othering of the "warlike people" by transforming them into the socially inferior position of shopkeepers. If clothes unmake the man in Herodotus's tale, so too does song: like its counterpart lyric, it performs both social and gender turnings.

Elsewhere in *Toxophilus*, Ascham also tellingly genders music. "Nice, fine, minikin fingering," he insists, is "farre more fitte for the womannishnesse of it to dwell in the courte among ladies, than . . . to abide in the universitie amonges scholars" (14). In linking "lutes, pipes, harpes" and other instruments requiring that fingering, he again implies the instability of divisions between wind and stringed instruments and the corresponding blurring of Good and Evil Lyric (14), an erosion familiar to students of Othering. More to my purposes here, since "minikin" could refer to both a woman and the string on an instrument, on one level "minikin fingering" effeminizes music, thus draining power from men associated with it, while on another it might gesture towards a powerful male manipulating a woman in more senses that one.[84] These turns within the word again enact the paradoxical shifts between potency and its absence; although we should not unthinkingly apply Ascham's pronouncements to poetry, his commentaries on music carry implications for the mode whose texts are so often entitled "song," as is frequently the case with such musicological analyses.

Many valuable studies have rightly emphasized the effeminization of song, again an argument with unmistakable cognate implications for lyric.[85] Although she concentrates primarily on France, Carla Zecher's demonstration of how the lute was associated with both the male and female bodies is no less useful as a commentary on the gendering of our mode in early modern England. For in the sixteenth and first half of the seventeenth centuries lyric is queered—that is, it is variously and sometimes virtually simultaneously associated with the feminine, the masculine, and with several types of cross-dressed slippages between and combinations of those apparent poles. These slippages, another source of lyric's paradoxes, are a locus of anxiety in their own right as well as tropes for the other types of suspicion associated with lyric mentioned earlier in this chapter—and for other kinds of potency attributed to it.

I have already demonstrated that under many circumstances lyric is indeed linked to spheres and activities traditionally seen as masculine in early modern England, especially the military and civic. Its connection with Pindar, the psalmist David, and Orpheus contribute to this identification; Sidney's *Defense of Poesy* insistently associates the mode with military camps; lyric is also associated with stony inscriptions. Provocative though somewhat problematical is Roland Greene's linkage of lyric to male coercion;[86] from this perspective, the reader, interpellated into the female subject position, may, like the lute, become a minikin manipulated by the masculine and masculinist lyric poet. These and other instances of the masculinizing of lyric demonstrate again how a characteristic shared by many texts in that mode may in fact function differently in different eras: the femininity of lyric, posited by poets and critics in numerous historical periods, works in distinctive ways in the early modern years, in part because it interacts with these types of assertion of masculinity.

As the legend of Orpheus's sexual preferences after losing Eurydice reminds us, however, the very texts that insistently connect lyric with typically, even stereotypically, masculine activities may also complicate that connection by representing a blocked or atypical version of masculinity. The traditions of Petrarchan poetry, the central model for writing about love in the sixteenth century, pivot on failure and loss. Similarly, as John Donne's "Calme" and Sonnet 7 ("The hardy captain") by Philip Sidney's brother Robert remind us, the military in the

late sixteenth and seventeenth century was often associated with abortive endeavors.[87] The entrance into masculinity, then, paradoxically involves exclusion
from some of the activities sometimes—though certainly not always—associated
with it. Might the very insistence on the masculinity of lyric—witness Sidney's
*Apology* and the many seventeenth-century texts it influences—be a reactive
gesture in response to the fear that real men don't write sestinas? Yet another
complication of the linkage between lyric and the masculine stems from the
psalmist David's sexual appetites: the promiscuity of lyric is not only gendered
female.

The association of lyric with blocked masculinity gestures towards the next
point on the spectrum, its connection to the effeminization of men, apparent
both in a lyric to which I will turn shortly and in the closely related issue of music's propensity for ungendering and re-gendering. No less concerned with sexuality in his discussion of music than in his better-known diatribe on theater,
Philip Stubbes, that prototype of the fanatical religious left, returns repeatedly,
indeed obsessively, to that issue. When performed in public and especially when
associated with dancing, he warns us, music "womannisheth y minde . . . cor-
rupteth good minds, maketh them womanish"; fathers are warned to let their son
learn music only "if you wold have [him] softe, womannish, uncleane, smoth
mouthed, affected to bawdrie, scurrilitie, filthie rimes . . . as it weare transna-
tured into a woman, or worse."[88] The recurrence of the linkage of music, eloquence, and verse is telling for our purposes; so too are the final two words in the
passage I quoted, which may gesture towards Orpheus's sexual preferences after
he loses Eurydice.

In "Gascoignes Lullabie," a fascinating and neglected lyric by the sixteenth-
century poet George Gascoigne, he sings "lullabie," an action specifically
glossed within the poem as what "women do" (1).[89] That is, he sings goodnight to
his sexual desires and, according to one interpretation of the lines, to his male
member as well; the act of singing thus at once demasculinizes him while troping and performing effeminizing.[90] One might perhaps be tempted to equate
emasculation and effeminization in texts like Gascoigne's, but the gendering of
lyric, a process of slippages, often resists that particular slippage. One way it does
so is by the association of lyric with childhood, which was sometimes narrowed to
a turning back to boyhood, a linkage encouraged by the now-obsolete usage of
"toy" for a light tune.[91] Exemplified by the first poem of Sidney's *Astrophil and
Stella*, the association of lyric with the substitution of boyhood for adult masculinity is reflected in the frequency with which lyric poems are described as toys, a usage that recurs even in the twentieth century. If one accepts the argument of

Stephen Orgel and other gender critics who have connected boys and women, seeing lyric as boyish does not preclude seeing it as womanish as well, thus uniting it with two overlapping erotic drives.[92] Lyric's predilection for circularity over linearity, manifest above all in its refrains, is, then, a formal analogue to the blocked chronological progression involved in remaining a boy or returning to boyhood. Like the association of lyric with childishness by later poets, that linkage of immaturity to lyric in the early modern period allows one both to acknowledge and to control the enchantment that drives its ability to turn and transform: to parlay such dangers, one is in effect confining its stanzas in a little room, more specifically in a nursery or other domesticated space.

While lyric is sometimes represented in relation to emasculation in these indirect ways, it is often directly described in terms of qualities stereotypically attributed to women both in early modern culture and our own. Indeed, Linda Phyllis Austern has demonstrated how often music, the sibling of lyric, is personified as a woman.[93] The originary purity of lyric itself is often stressed, as my introduction indicated. Yet, paradoxically, offering a neglected analogue to the language of antitheatrical pamphlets, many texts represent lyric as indeed a siren in the negative senses—that is, a frighteningly destructive femininity that recalls sexual stereotypes of the seductive and, yes, promiscuous. These connections emerge especially though not exclusively in discussions of song, which, as John Hollander among others has shown, was often associated with irrationality, a quality traditionally gendered female, though some glosses on the Orpheus myth remind us that it is also associated with men.[94] Even more revealing, however, is the role of the maenads, those revelers who tear Orpheus apart while playing their rival music. On one level, they exemplify the fear of vengeful women that Melissa F. Zeiger's study of elegy acutely associates with the Orpheus myth.[95] But in early modern versions of that narrative, anxieties about retributive women may in part stem from and screen anxieties about creative men. That is, whereas many students of the Orpheus legend have suggested that Eurydice may be a side of him, his uncontrolled desires, it is at least as likely, I maintain, that the maenads are a side of Orpheus—they represent the dangers of lyric, which the myth deflects and, predictably, genders female.

A number of early modern texts attempt to resolve the conflict between male and female gendering of lyric in essentially the way I just suggested the Orpheus myth does. Much as theories of music repeatedly attempt to separate its beneficent and evil versions, so texts insistently distinguish various types of lyric, often through contrasts borrowed from classical literature. According to these reassuring versions of discrimination and distinction, the ode, the world of Pindar, is male, and it may be associated as well with stringed as opposed to wind instruments; love poetry, wind instruments, and so on are Othered as female. (Stubbes addresses the recurrent problem of negotiating ambivalences and contradictions not by separating wind and stringed instruments but rather by declaring that the private enjoyment of religious music is laudable while public performances or private performances connected with dancing are reprehensible.) These binaries often prove as volatile as the other binaries associated with gender. While the lute is represented as male in certain texts, notably Wyatt's "My lute awake" and "Blame not my lute," elsewhere it represents the female body. That pun on "minikin" may on one level reassuringly define the lute itself as female and the lyric poet as the male who controls its strings. Yet this bifurcation is compromised by the concurrent associations, noted above, of the lute with the male body, activating the homoerotic versions of Orpheus's legend.

In short, the gendering of lyric is overdetermined in its functions: it is a source of anxieties in its own right; it figures both positive and negative associations with lyric, ranging from spiritual and military achievement to sexual temptation; and it also reactively strives to counter such concerns. This reactive anxiety is not, of course, unique to the early modern period—discussing the annual Romantic volumes for women known as *Keepsakes*, Peter Manning writes of men "recuperatively self-constituting themselves against the women with whom they were too closely linked"[96]—but resolution of the anxiety through a heroic ideal was more accessible to, though again not unique to, the English Renaissance.

Extraordinary—and extraordinarily neglected—Herrick's "Vision" offers the best instance of all these responses to gender, as well as many other early modern approaches to lyric traced in this chapter. In particular, it recalls the implications of the tropes and myths whose centrality I have emphasized, for here lyric is associated with turning and transformation, with danger and opportunity, and with both power and impotence, including not least the physiological sense of the latter word. Herrick's lyric reminds us, too, of the continuing significance of classical conceptions of the mode and, in particular, of the predilection for discussing it through a prototypical example from Greek or Latin poetry.

Me thoght I saw (as I did dreame in bed)
A crawling Vine about *Anacreon's* head:
Flusht was his face; his haires with oyle did shine;
And as he spake, his mouth ranne ore with wine.
Tipled he was; and tipling lispt withall;
And lisping reeld, and reeling like to fall.
A young *Enchantresse* close by him did stand

Tapping his plump thighes with a *myrtle* wand:
She smil'd; he kist; and kissing, cull'd her too;
And being cup-shot, more he co'd not doe.
For which (me thought) in prittie anger she
Snatcht off his Crown, and gave the wreath to me:
Since when (me thinks) my braines about doe swim,
And I am wilde and wanton like to him.

This lyric is modeled on the rueful first poem in a collection of lyrics, includ-ing texts by Anacreon, that was very popular in the early modern period; but Her-rick wears his rue with a difference. In particular, although "lispt" (5) was not associated with homoeroticism in that era, in many other respects he rewrites the original to associate instauration as a lyric poet—indeed, as a surrogate for one of the prototypical lyric poets—with genderings and re-genderings that involve rapid slides between success and loss.[97]

The stereotypically masculine and even masculinist behavior attributed to Anacreon in many of his lyrics—drinking and kissing in particular—in Her-rick's adaptation involves several interlocking forms of emasculation. Anacreon is rendered impotent; his lisping suggests childishness and thus sexual immatu-rity, while the enchantress's wand on the thighs clearly alludes to and on some level transfers, re-gendered, Anacreon's phallic power. By substituting this fe-male figure for the personage of Eros in the original, Herrick also characteristi-cally transfers blame for the emasculation to the frailty whose name is woman. Many of Herrick's other changes in his source intensify Anacreon's involuntary loss of his intertwined poetic and sexual prowess; in particular, in the source Anacreon embraces his successor and apparently hands over the crown, while here it is snatched from him, and his drunkenness is played up more in Her-rick's version.

In any event, poetic and sexual power are not simply transferred to Herrick's speaker; his possession of them, like so much else in the poem, is rendered un-stable, warning us yet again against a monolithic contrast between the putative impotence of female writers and the imputed agency of their male equivalents. In the source he takes up the crown; here it is placed on him by a woman, demonstrating the role of feminine power in masculine instauration and also an-ticipating the possibility of his later unwilling loss of this icon of achievement. As in many instances cited earlier, masculinity is associated with impotence, in this case in the literal physiological sense as well as others. And by imitating a text de-scribed as spurious in the edition he almost definitely used, Herrick tropes these uncertainties: he himself is taking up Anacreon's crown, becoming a masculine poet, by echoing a lyric that, like Anacreon's masculinity, is spurious, deceptive.[98]

In short, as Herrick's lyric reports "reeling" (6) slips in motor functions, it not coincidentally performs a series of slippages, displacements, and replacements itself. They occur metrically: the trochaic substitutions in the opening feet of lines 3 ("Flusht") and 5 ("Tipled") mime the physiological unsteadiness to which they allude. Slippages occur in the poem's allusion to and displacement of sonnet conventions and in its ontological reelings, with the dream blending into so-called reality at the end. The closural stability and objectivity often attributed to the sonnet's closural couplet (and as often destabilized by its sixteenth-century writers in ways that anticipate this poem) are here destabilized both by the implication that this speaker is likely to replicate Anacreon's loss of the crown and by the tension between apparently objective statement on the one hand and on the other its attribution to someone with swimming brains, and by the "me thinks" (13). Indeed, in the source, the element of fantasy is introduced at the beginning, then submerged in the vivid story; here the appearance of "Me thought" (1) and its cognates no fewer than three times calls both reality and dream into question.[99] Above all, of course, the stability of gender is questioned and queered.

Herrick's "Vision," then, supports methodological premises central to this chapter in particular and to the larger study in which it appears: close attention to language, whether of an individual text or of a recurrent trope for lyric, is one of the best methods of understanding the cultural history that informs that mode, and vice versa. Herrick's poem also encapsulates several issues explored throughout Chapter 1 about the workings and attributes of lyric poetry during the English Renaissance. Gender, "The Vision" reminds us, variously intensifies and suppresses the guilt and other tensions associated with that mode. More specifically, in turning back towards Anacreon's poem, this text overturns gender categories; and the coexistence of those categories figures the recurrent representations of lyric as the site of both extraordinary power and of impotence, as the property of both Orpheus and the sirens, as the realm of military and spiritual achievements and of erotic failures. Would you buy a used lyric from this man?

# CHAPTER 2

# The Domain of Echo

*Lyric Audiences*

Technological advances in the use of glass have facilitated compelling architectural experiments that transform the relationship between a building and its audiences, complicating the latter's perceptions of the edifice and representations of their own presence within it. In particular, in so-called curtain wall design, the exterior enclosure is attached like a curtain to the structural frame of concrete or steel; that enclosure's independence from its structure enables experiments with the properties of glass. Many contemporary architects, notably Cesar Pelli, have triumphantly pursued those potentialities, but no better examples of such achievements in design—and no examples more relevant to the audiences of early modern lyric poetry—can be found than recent edifices by Renzo Piano and Jean Nouvel. Although both were previously known largely for their buildings abroad, of late they have received important commissions in the United States. Piano's include additions to the Morgan Library in New York City, the High Museum in Atlanta, and the Isabella Stewart Gardner Museum in Boston, and he is the architect for the new headquarters for the New York Times. Nouvel's Guthrie Theater recently opened in Minneapolis.[1]

In his high-rise edifice on Macquarie Street in Sydney, Piano giftwraps in glass the bricklike terracotta he so often uses in his buildings, creating the transparency and immateriality he celebrates when writing about architecture. Similiarly, the Morgan Library juxtaposes glass with stone and steel. If transparency "is very important on the plane of poetic language"[2] in the senses of "poetic" Piano apparently intends (expressiveness, intensity, and so on), it also, with apt paradoxes, introduces ontological opacities very germane to poetry. Is the space between the terra cotta and the glass within or without the edifice? Is the viewer on Macquarie Street who is reflected in the glass, or the diner sitting in front of it at an outside table of the café, inside or outside the building? In like manner, as one faces the far wall in the court of the Morgan Library, one wonders whether the images one glimpses are representations of activity on the street behind it or reflections from another wall behind the viewer; louvers with panels of glass visible between them can further complicate this play of images. As these effects suggest, Piano's glass confounds the planes in many of his buildings; "we have often created spaces with multiple and successive vertical planes," he writes of his work, and the observer is likely to encounter multiple reflections of herself, occupying different planes.[3]

Even more tantalizing are the questions raised by similar techniques in Jean Nouvel's Cartier building in Paris. On one level, when he replaced the stone wall that had previously cut off the surrounding gardens with a glazed screen, he opened up the space to those outside it. At the same time, however, he also opened up intriguing issues: the building itself is surrounded by two glazed screens that are considerably larger than the structure itself, and reflections also play off some walls within the structure, so when trees or viewers or inhabitants appear in the glass, it is impossible to tell what is inside and what is not, which reflections come from denizens and which from observers, and indeed, where the building should be said to begin and end. Enigmas are the principal plants in these gardens. Glass, Piano, and Nouvel demonstrate, not only teases and troubles in the way mirrors can do but delights in adding the additional complication of a claim to transparency that is itself far from transparent: neither simply true nor simply mendacious.

A particularly intriguing expression—and expansion—of these techniques and the issues they raise is Nouvel's Guthrie Theater in Minneapolis. Numerous enlarged photographs of earlier stage productions are reproduced with ghostly faintness on a material like air-mail paper that adheres to the stone walls; a huge representation of the Weird Sisters who haunted Macbeth, for example, haunts those walls as well. Especially apropos of my purposes, however, is the variation on that technique in the café on Level 5: the images from the plays appear not on stone but on back- and front-lit mirrors, so that the viewer sees her own reflection among those of the characters in the represented scenes. Thus the past of the theater merges with its present, spectators interact with actors on these reflective walls as they do during the play itself, and again inside and outside, here and there, are confounded.

Both the aesthetic pleasure and the epistemological conundrums of such buildings are replicated and analyzed in the work of the sculptor and designer

Dan Graham. Varied though Graham's installations are, many of them share an agenda of using mirrors and glass to confound boundaries between parts of the construction and between its audience and what they are observing. Subject is always becoming object, object always becoming subject. As Graham writes of these constructions, "they are not for one person. They are always for people looking at other people looking at other people inside and outside."[4]

In his installation in the sculpture garden of the Walker Gallery in Minneapolis, for example, greenery is partly enclosed by a series of wall-like planes, forming cubicles that resemble rooms but lack a ceiling and one or more walls. Some of the planes are transparent glass, some reflect spectators, landscape, and other walls. Hence the effect that Graham attributes to another, similar construction recurs here as well: "Reflections of people within are superimposed for them to view. . . . They [spectators] can perceive themselves perceiving; or they may perceive themselves as the subject of the perception of other (interior or exterior) spectators" (247). The movement between the passive construction of Graham's first sentence ("are superimposed"), the qualified ascription of agency in "to view," and the amalgam of positions in the concept of perceiving oneself perceiving enact grammatically his point about spectators themselves being both subjects and objects.

Graham's glass and mirrors raise the same problems posed by Piano and Nouvel, and his glosses on those issues render more explicit their relevance to this chapter. In particular, he draws attention to its central question: what is the relationship between an object and its audiences? More specifically, to what extent are onlookers detached, outside observers and to what extent participants? And how does their self-consciousness—"they can perceive themselves perceiving" (247)—affect their responses, an issue that will prove particularly relevant to the guilt associated with lyric? Graham also directs our attention to a problem especially germane to the multiplicity of audiences in lyric poetry: what is the relationship among and between various spectators, or, as he puts it, "people looking at other people looking at other people inside and outside" (77)?

Questioning and qualifying seminal statements by Northrop Frye and John Stuart Mill among others, the central contentions of this chapter are first, the need to acknowledge the multiplicity of audiences and audience positions in early modern lyric, and second, the far-ranging significance of that diversity. In particular, recognizing that range of positions reveals the fluidity and variety of the relationship of listeners and readers to the text and its speaker. For these and other reasons, the presence of lyric auditors is often as unstable as the reflecting echoes in the glass of Nouvel, Piano, Graham, and so many other masters of mirroring; yet, this chapter argues, it is often precisely through that instability, and especially through shifts between internalized and social direction of address, that the core meanings of a poem are expressed and core agendas, especially aggressive ones, pursued.

As my emphasis on fluidity suggests, in the form that is associated with *versus* in so many senses, the mutability and variety that this chapter posits typically involves several turns. Focusing on conditions of production and reception, Wendy Wall wittily observes that "Coterie circles thus encouraged a 'con-verse-ation' . . . a turning back and forth of scripted messages between writers"; this chapter explores many additional forms of turning that mime the types of circulation she traces.[5] Some texts evoke or hint at a wide range of audiences present simultaneously, establishing differing relationships with them; others dismiss or turn away from certain audiences and face others; members of a given audience may shift positions in relation to direction of address, themselves turning away, as God is represented doing in certain religious lyrics; the relationship of the diegetic addressees to the poem and its author may change not only in the course of a given reading but from one reading to the next.

Though the criticism it has attracted is often fruitful and sometimes brilliant, the very concept of lyric address can tempt one to neglect some of these complexities. Not the question "To whom is this text addressed?" but rather "Who are or will be or might be its audiences, whether addressed or not, at several different junctures?" is more encompassing and hence more profitable.[6] Such perspectives will, for example, demonstrate that early modern lyrics finesse many of the problems identified in Chapter 1 through strategies of deflected speech, turning away, or apparently turning away, from one potential audience to another. This chapter's principal argument—the multiplicity of audiences and the lability of their connections to the poem and to its poet—thus redefines lyric address. In so doing, as I will demonstrate at the conclusion of the chapter, that thesis also asserts a revisionist challenge to the widespread concept that the audience of lyric normatively engages in an identificatory voicing of it—the concept that the author erects for us a single mirror rather than an installation like Graham's.

⸺☙ ☙⸺

Pursuing those central arguments about multiple and shifting listeners insistently poses a number of difficult methodological challenges, best introduced by another analogue that is both visual and verbal. In the April eclogue of Edmund Spenser's *Shepheardes Calender*, the shepherds Thenot and Hobbinoll lament the fate of their colleague, Colin. Enchanted with Rosalind, he has abandoned his enchanting poetry. Thenot invites Hobbinoll to repeat one of the songs in question, thus moving from the position of Colin's auditor to his ventriloquist. The center of the accompanying woodcut is occupied by ladies in courtly garb, gathered in a partial circle around one figure, apparently the queen, who stands slightly forward; several of the ladies are playing musical instruments. In a lower plane to the left, a considerably smaller figure in the clothing of a lower class is piping in apparent isolation—though his rustic instrument is directed to the turned backs of some of the ladies. Above him and not seeming to attend to him are two other rustic figures. Since Colin created that lyric "as by a spring he laye" (35), the standing piper, near water that appears to issue from a cistern, might suggest that the artist read the text hastily;[7] critics do, however, have reason to believe that Spenser himself took a real interest in the woodcuts, even if he did not closely supervise them, so it is unlikely that they include significant reinterpretations of which he would have disapproved.[8] In any event, the woodcut aptly draws our attention to issues central to these and many other lyrics, especially my contentions that auditory positions are labile and that their shifts often express meanings at the core of the text.

Perhaps the most suggestive gloss on this illustration is Thenot's inviting Hobbinoll to "recorde" (30) one of the songs in question—a verb emphasized by its presence in a similar context in the Argument and by a note to that usage linking it to the Latin verb for remembering. The Oxford English Dictionary enlarges that annotation by citing contemporaneous usages of "record," some now obsolete, involving meditating, making a record, remembering, relating, bearing witness, and recording in song.[9] Like the tropes examined in Chapter 1, this word compacts many implications about lyric, notably song's role as a medium for memorializing something, thus recalling the connections with the inscriptions in posies I have already discussed, as well as links with monuments. In relation to the woodcut, the word suggests the privacy of meditation—Colin presumably lay by that stream alone—while also emphasizing an interaction with auditors, sharers of the fruits of that meditation, who could comprise both people to whom the poem is currently related and future generations with whom what it preserves will be shared.[10] In other words, "record" suggests multiple audiences, some present in the situation being mimetically represented and some not, and it implies that meditation is not necessarily an alternative to but in some instances a step towards social interaction, anticipating my analyses of the relationship between lyric and narrative.

This tension between lyric as the product of solitary reflection and as a version of social interactions is enacted in many levels in the woodcut, which repeatedly complicates the representation of both private and social performance. Piping in apparent privacy, the singer in the lower left is indubitably separated from his fellow shepherds spatially. And he is distanced from the courtly ladies by distinctions in space and scale, distinctions that underscore the differences in garb and in so doing trope the uneasy social divides manifest in the promulgation of numerous sumptuary laws, those regulations that based permissible attire on social status, during Elizabeth's reign. The backs of the women immediately in front of the shepherd form a wall, anticipating the "long fruitlesse stay" (6) searching for patronage that Spenser was to write about in his "Prothalamion." To this extent the illustration accords to Roland Greene's argument about failures of the dialogic in the poem itself.[11]

Yet the fact remains that several figures in the illustration may be audiences to each other's music, or performers to an audience, or both at once. To begin with, more than one courtly lady is a musician, raising the question of what happens to the distinction between performer and hearer in the instance of choral music. Moreover, the direction of the shepherd's musical instrument, like the direction of address it literalizes and materializes, hints that in some sense he is singing not only about but also to the court. Certainly the content of the April eclogue encourages that interpretation. And the use of "record" reminds one of the possibility, indeed the probability, of auditors who are not present now but will respond to the song sometime in the future, a likely eventuality given the content of this song. More immediately, despite those turned backs, is not our piper on some level at least potentially an audience for the courtly music as well as producer of his own songs? In fact, citing an early modern instructional manual, Carla Zecher has demonstrated that, whereas lute players usually faced the audience, players of the virginal often did not—thus anticipating Miles Davis's famous decision to perform with his back to his listeners.[12] These and other possibilities are, however, confounded by the planes in the illustration, which, in the ways they partially separate the courtly from the pastoral characters, may well recall the playful complexities of a Piano or Nouvel building.

Although the two shepherds in the background show no sign of attending to their colleague in the foreground, they are linked to him visually by their garb, by the similarity between the posture of one of them and that of the rustic musician, and by the triangle the three figures form, which is further emphasized by their crooks and by the presence of the same geometrical figure in the garments of some of the courtly ladies. So the isolated shepherd potentially at least has a coterie of his male peers like those about which Arthur F. Marotti has written so influentially, in this instance a sheepcoterie.[13] Yet, despite the claims of Marotti and many other students of the conditions of production, here the coterie audience is not the only or the primary one, a pattern that I will suggest also characterizes a number of early modern lyrics. This multiplicity of audiences recurs throughout the illustrations and texts of Spenser's pastoral sequence; the December eclogue, whose diegetic addressees include Pan, shepherd boys, sheep, Hobbinol, and Rosalind, is a particularly striking instance.

At the same time, the woodcut lends itself to a different explanation. Many early modern visual representations include an intermediary or onlooker figure who, often literally, points out the scene to the audience.[14] "I like to see someone who admonishes and points out to us what is happening there; or beckons with his hand to see," Leon Battista Alberti, author of the highly influential fifteenth-century treatise *Della pittura*, observes.[15] Demonstrating connections among such figures, the *festaiuolo* or master of revels, and choric actors in drama, Michael Baxandall explains that such characters are often involved in establishing relationships among diegetic participants and with the audience.[16]

Reading the piper in Spenser's woodcut in such terms is complicated but not obviated by the fact that Alberti was not readily available in the English Renaissance; the author of *The Shepheardes Calender*, or the illustrator, or the audience, or all of them could have been aware of such figures through their presence in illustrations. It is also true that Colin does not directly interact with the nondiegetic audience, as such figures customarily do. He is, however, literally marginalized, as they often are, and he does share their deictic, pointing, function. Adducing this tradition helps us to see that if his musical instrument most obviously represents his playing for and to the unresponsive court, it may also serve to point out the court to the viewers. Although he is not a textbook instance of the figures in question, he is related to them in respects viewers familiar with artistic traditions are likely to have recognized.

Colin is apparently powerless in his relationship to the court ladies. Yet when interpreted as a *festaiuolo*-like character, he asserts and achieves a significant measure of power in relation to the readers of the book. And what if, like other figures in this tradition, he is calling up the courtly scene, piping it into being, thus truly becoming a master of revels? If one admits that admittedly debatable possibility, he becomes at once the creature and the creator of the disdainful courtly ladies. The October eclogue encourages its readers to ask whether these paradoxes are the very point: might not the presence of a *festaiuolo* figure who does not directly address onlookers and a shepherd who on another level is master of even the court represent the ambivalences about poetry manifest in that lyric and others in the collection so clearly involved with poetic instauration? More to my immediate purposes, when one does read Colin as some analogue to or even reference to the mediating characters Alberti advocates, he embodies the multiplicity and variety of audiences traced in this chapter by himself becoming more than one type of auditor. He demonstrates, too, some recurrent corollaries of that multiplicity: like the spectators on Level 5 of Nouvel's Guthrie Theater, he is both inside and outside the diegetic scene, and the swerve between interpreting Colin as an excluded outsider, reduced in scale in more senses than one, and reinterpreting him as the *sine qua non* of the scene recalls the potential instability of such roles.

In these and many other regards, then, the woodcut reminds us that to study the issues it raises, one must distinguish among various types of audience, schooling oneself to note the variety and changeability associated with the role of listener and the range of possible interactions between author and auditor. For example, the senses in which the courtly ladies are openly and overtly auditors to each other's music should be distinguished from those in which they may hear and be heard by Colin. And an analysis should consider audiences who are not present and accounted for within the illustration; developing the distinction between diegetic and nondiegetic readers is a first step in doing so.

In fact, however, many of the categories used to classify audiences prove problematical on examination. If analysis of this woodcut is a first step towards reconceptualizing the audiences of early modern lyric, it is also a step down a slippery slope. In which category, for instance, should one place the future auditors emphasized by "record" (an audience through which many ostensibly atemporal lyrics in fact locate themselves within time)? If distinguishing the diegetic and nondiegetic has proved as challenging in narrative as many students of that form have demonstrated, that act is no easier in lyric.[17] Answer poems, whose popularity in the coterie circles of manuscript circulation has been established by Marotti among other critics, repeatedly raise a similar problem with the binary separation of diegetic and nondiegetic.[18] So too do the many love poems that intertwine but do not necessarily unite the lover within the poem and the poet. A lady who speaks in a poem to which I will return at several points in this chapter, Jonson's "Celebration of Charis in Ten Lyrick Peeces," addresses "Ben" ("Her Man Described by Her Owne Dictamen," 1); thus she implicitly calls into question her own status as a fictional character, the mirror image, as it were, of how a visitor to Graham's construction can insert herself into the composition by standing where she will be reflected in it.[19] If critics are tempted to finesse potential slippages by declaring that Astrophil addresses Stella within the diegetic world of the sonnet cycle, whereas Philip Sidney directs the poems to Penelope Rich, the pun on "rich" that recurs in Sonnet 37 undermines that solution. (Sidney's niece Lady

Mary Wroth was to go one better in the blurring of the boundaries separating "real" people, fictional characters, and fictional characters who insistently gesture towards their living counterparts: she names a minor character in the first part of her *Urania* Philistella.) These issues are far from unique to the early modern period or to literary texts; medieval religious paintings, for example, often insert donors into scriptural scenes, with their spatial marginality aptly figuring that of their ontological status. This chapter will, however, demonstrate how issues ranging from the guilt associated with writing and reading lyric to its conditions of production reshape these questions in the era on which this study focuses.

Considering a future audience crystallizes another methodological problem, the divide between physical presence and absence, though because it is explored more thoroughly in Chapter 3, I will only briefly gesture towards a few of its implications here. The impact of that apparently binary distinction is often less crucial than one might expect. A soliloquy delivered when another character happens to be on stage resembles other soliloquies more than it resembles dialogic interchange among characters on stage together. Conversely, a lyric like *Astrophil and Stella* 64 ("No more, my deare, no more these counsels trie") that directly addresses the lady even though she may not be physically present (like many sonnets, this one may rehearse what the speaker would like to say) in some respects is very similar to other instances of direct address, such as the appeal to the Muses in Sidney's fifty-fifth sonnet ("Muses, I oft invoked your holy ayde"), even though the issue of physical presence differs significantly in each case.[20] Indeed, texts that focus on engendering a response and those that provide one, whether or not they both mime solitary speech, may have more in common with each other than do a text that represents solitude but reaches out to an addressee and one delivered in isolation but without an addressee. Moreover, as George T. Wright points out, the letter format (a number of early modern poems resemble letters and others allude to that genre without unmistakably participating in it) encourages speech delivered as though both parties are present even though they are not; hence, one should add, the letter, icon of absence though it may be, often resembles the process of addressing an auditor who is physically with the speaker more than it does that of addressing an absent one.[21] As I will demonstrate at several junctures in this chapter, devotional poetry further complicates the distinction between physical presence and absence: many models of the relationship between speaker and audience were developed by critics envisioning the urn, not the Eternal, as the prototypical addressee.[22]

Closely related to the problematical divide between presence and absence are the overlapping ones between monologue and dialogue and between the solitary and the social, also issues to which this chapter will repeatedly speak. Because of these imbrications and for other reasons, the distinctions among various types of "lyric of address" posited in Gémino H. Abad's Chicago School study of the form prove deceptive.[23] In some instances a diegetic listener is not currently present but may be present—and may respond—on a subsequent occasion, another reason to see lyric as part of a process. Thus meditation may involve an obsessive rehearsal of what one plans to say on some future occasion; as I have argued elsewhere, the centrality of that and other forms of obsession in Petrarchism makes this form of thought very common in early modern poetry.[24] More broadly, Pamela S. Hammons has persuasively demonstrated how many female-authored texts from the period of the Civil War are in fact social in important respects, even if their mode of address appears private.[25] And dialogic propensities may be deflected onto a characteristic of the verse other than its direction of address, such as the interplay between words in correlative poetry. All language is social in many important regards, David Schalkwyk provocatively maintains when rebutting Helen Vendler's support for the customary ascription of solitude to lyric: "'solitary speech' is as marked by social specification as any other."[26] Yet if contentions like Schalkwyk's are adduced to read private, internalized discourse as a mere screen for the invariable centrality of the social in early modern poetry, lyrics are likely to be misread: the interplay of types of address is more often what is central and significant.

Like Spenser's use of "record," an etymology that would have been familiar to many early modern writers and readers encapsulates these problems of classification. The Latin verb "meditor" packs among its meanings not only contemplation but also "design, purpose, intend . . . practise."[27] In his seventh letter to Charles Diodati, Milton describes himself as growing wings "& volare meditor," leading the Columbia editors to offer the translation "meditating flight" but their counterparts in the Yale University Press to substitute "practicing flight," with the latter version supported by the subsequent phrase, which refers to a fledgling Pegasus raising himself on tender wings.[28] Because the verb in question also appears in the opening of a text that enjoyed a virtually iconic status in the early modern period, Virgil's first eclogue, readers in that period were surely aware of such resonances. To what extent, then, are lyric's meditative monologues, such as the one by Colin on which the April eclogue focuses, an exercise or practice for dialogues and for other social action?

In short, a principal, if not indeed the principal, methodological problem associated with the audiences of lyric is precisely that the clear-cut categories that the subject invites prove as deceptive as the divides between inside and out, reflection and original in the works by Graham, Nouvel, and Piano on which I opened. What many students of "race" have observed about that category is no less true of classifying audiences: there are typically more differences among members of a class than between classes. Commentaries by Wordsworth, Mill, Frye, and other theorists of lyric demand attention from students of early modern lyric in part because, for all their insights, they provide additional illustrations of such problems and how the commentators' investments generate such errors. Yet, at the same time, each of these highly influential statements provides useful directives for studying the audiences of Renaissance lyric, in particular by suggesting approaches to the multiplicity whose presence and consequences are the central arguments of this chapter.

—◌ ◌—

The Preface to Wordsworth's *Lyrical Ballads,* a document that went through significant editorial changes, is further compromised for the purposes of this chapter by its focus on all poetry, not just lyric, and also by the blurring of generic categories suggested by the author's title; moreover, many of the issues it raises demand an extended analysis, not a brief overview. Nonetheless, one can note in passing that the conflicting models of the democratic poet who speaks to other men and the inspired *vates* have obvious implications for the possibility of identificatory voicing. Also significant for this chapter is Wordsworth's repeated hope that the members of his audience will respond in a consistent way. As many readers of his Preface have noted, principles from the Enlightenment (that movement whose own variety is often collapsed in unenlightening maneuvers by those eager to make it a straw man) lie behind the author's generalizations about "the primary laws of our nature"; and one is not surprised that he emphasizes communalities in his readers, a model that may lie behind Frye's comparison of the audience to a chorus.[29] The idea of an audience offering communal and consistent response, as we will see, is as pernicious as it is pervasive in discussions of lyric.

John Stuart Mill's principal statement about the audiences of that mode, his essay "Thoughts on Poetry and Its Varieties," turns on two contrasts, each as problematical as the divides examined above: the distinction between narrative and poetry and the one between poetry and eloquence, which he describes as no less fundamental.[30] As I have observed, in discussions of poetry as of so many other subjects, comparisons often encode hierarchies, and this essay is no exception. I demonstrated above that Mill is not alone when he tellingly associates narratives with the immature stages of human life and the "rude state" of cultures (345);

similarly, his preference for poetry over eloquence is implicitly glossed when he establishes the former as the higher form and associates it with the English, in contrast to inferior creatures across the Channel from them.

Central to this essay and most crucial to its impact on later discussions of lyric is one corollary of the contrasts Mill draws: "eloquence is *heard*, poetry is *over-heard*," he affirms (348; emphasis in original). This contrast was to be singled out and seconded by Frye and more implicitly celebrated by many other commentators on lyric, though it has recently been interrogated as well, notably by Virginia Jackson.[31] Mill goes on to refer to "the poet's utter unconsciousness of a listener" (348) and to describe poetry as "the natural fruit of solitude and meditation" and eloquence as the product of "intercourse with the world" (349). He thus instantiates two divides whose limitations I have already flagged, positing an explicit distinction between the solitary and the social and an implicit one between presence and absence.

Elsewhere in the essay, however, he suggests that the "natural" solitude that involves "utter unconsciousness" of a listener (349, 348) is in fact an act that he compares to the so-called "fourth wall" of theater: "no trace of consciousness that any eyes are upon us must be visible in the work itself. The actor knows that there is an audience present; but if he act as though he knew it, he acts ill" (349). Much of this apparent paradox can be readily resolved by distinguishing the moment of poetic utterance from later reproduction of it motivated in part by consciousness of the marketplace, as Mill in fact does, and by distinguishing the speaker who is totally unaware of an audience from the poet behind him who creates a mimesis of solitude. But these distinctions do not completely resolve the contradiction in question: indeed, as Jackson also notes, the theatrical metaphor confounds the argument.[32] The actor, a figure more analogous to the speaker than to the poet, only pretends not to notice the audience, and the language of excluding vestiges is quite different from "utter unconsciousness" (348). That "fourth wall" is apparently transparent, and the effects may recall those of the walls by Graham, Nouvel, and Piano. Hence if the poem is the natural fruit of meditation, this is produce and product that has been carefully prepared and sauced.

Later in this treatise Mill contrasts the world of poetry and that of "the man of science . . . or of business" (357), thus flagging the hidden investments and agendas that impel him and others to posit the isolated lyric speaker. Behind the split Mill establishes, as well as behind the ambivalence about representing solitude as a performance if not a pretense, I suggest, lies the desire to establish poetry as pure, as the angel in the house uncontaminated by the marketplace or even by that language of the marketplace, rhetoric. Poetry, Mill believes, should be free

of exchange of all sorts, whether it be the exchanges of dialogue or the more pecuniary tradings of the marketplace. Thus Mill anticipates Adorno's drive to distinguish poetry from the social world, though their motives for that divide of
course differ, Adorno attempting to position poetry in a space that allows experimentation without ruling out its interaction with social formations.[33]

Although T. S. Eliot explicitly acknowledges the influence of the German
critic Gottfried Benn on his work, the impact of Mill is manifest as well. Insisting
that his system does not simply correspond to literary modes, Eliot distinguishes
three voices in poetry, the first and second being suggestively similar to Mill's distinction between poetry and eloquence: the poet may talk to himself or to nobody, may address an audience, or may speak through a character. The system is
shaped, and arguably misshaped, first by Eliot's dismissal of a category in which
the poet addresses only one person (surely such religious lyrics as Traherne's
"Desire" would fall under that rubric, and despite Eliot's claims on the subject
of love poetry, it sometimes would too), and second by his focus on dramatic monologue, which he attempts to differentiate from drama through some debatable
claims, such as the assertion that the poet typically identifies with the speaker.[34] A
more fundamental problem is Eliot's absolute distinction between talking to
oneself and addressing an audience.

Despite limitations like these—indeed, W. R. Johnson terms the essay "one of
the last and most effective of [Eliot's] smokescreens"[35]—some of his observations
can gloss or resolve the very problems that complicate other discussions of the audiences of early modern lyric. Especially significant are Eliot's brief but suggestive
comments on how the voices overlap—"I doubt whether in any real poem only
one voice is audible"[36]—which, although focusing on the speaker, invite the sort
of analyses of shifting auditory positions that are the agenda of this chapter. More
specifically, when Eliot talks of the poet "allowing himself to be overheard," he directs attention to what one might term "staged overhearing," the invited presence
of a bystander that interests Frye also and to which I will return.[37]

Although commentaries on Frye's approach to lyric understandably direct
most of their attention to his *Anatomy of Criticism*, his observations about the
mode in the collection *Lyric Poetry: Beyond New Criticism* provide a useful introduction to the more extensive treatment in his magisterial tome.[38] Citing the
psalms and the odes of Pindar, Frye stresses here that lyric may well be communal, an alternative that recalls the trope of posies and Wordsworth's reference to
group singing, and in so doing again warns us against establishing the solitary poet
speaking only to himself as normative. Also suggestive is his observation in this essay that, because of its association with music, lyric turns away not only from ordi-

nary space and time but also from quotidian language, "so often retreat[ing] from sense into sound." (34). This emphasis on what is tellingly described as retreat is echoed in the discussions of lyric audience in Frye's *Anatomy of Criticism*.

Arguing that the "radical of presentation" is the fundamental distinction among genres, Frye asserts there:

> Words may be acted in front of a spectator; they may be spoken in front of a listener; they may be sung or chanted; or they may be written for a reader. . . . The basis of generic criticism in any case is rhetorical, in the sense that the genre is determined by the conditions established between the poet and his public.
>
> We have to speak of the *radical* of presentation if the distinctions of acted, spoken, and written word are to mean anything in the age of the printing press. One may print a lyric or read a novel aloud, but such incidental changes are not enough in themselves to alter the genre. (247)

Although, as Jonathan Hart has demonstrated, an interest in history of several types informs not only the *Anatomy of Criticism* but other texts of Frye, the ahistoricity on which the concept of the radicals depends reflects the troubling universalism for which Frye is often faulted.[39] If the difference between a genre that is sung and one that is acted is fundamental in the ways Frye claims, surely the difference between singing or chanting a lyric in the early stages of that mode and reading it silently in a post-Gutenburg era should not be dismissed as "incidental." Nor is the history of reciting epics like *Beowulf* "incidental" to the ontology of epos. Frye stresses that he is considering not actual conditions but some sort of ideal, but that ideal itself changes in different periods.

More troubling—and more revealing—is what Frye does not say. Notice that whereas three of the four categories specified in the first sentence are defined in terms of both method of presentation and audience, in the instance of the radical of presentation he associates with lyric, only half that formula appears: "they may be sung or chanted." What tension produces this imbalance in a critic who is more prone to celebrate and demonstrate fearful symmetry? Frye's subsequent observations direct one towards answers.

He proceeds to comment on the audiences of lyric. Although his observations are varied and complex, many of them usefully distinguish the diegetic and nondiegetic audiences by assuming that the mode is publicly performed in some sense but involves a mimesis of solitary speech predicated on a fiction that there is no audience: "There is, as usual, no word for the audience of the lyric: what is wanted is something analogous to 'chorus' which does not suggest simultaneous presence or dramatic context. The lyric is, to go back to Mill's aphorism referred to at the beginning of this book, preeminently the utterance that is overheard." Immediately afterwards, however, Frye observes, "The lyric poet normally pretends to be talking to himself or to someone else," and whereas the first part of that statement is not surprising, the others whom lyric "normally" addresses comprise a long list, including friends and lovers (249).

Frye's conception of lyric audiences is, then, pulled between a model stressing solitude and another stressing interaction. The former is apparent when he compares lyric and irony, at first glance strange bedfellows indeed, on the grounds that both involve turning away from the marketplace and, more obviously, when he emphasizes the process of communing with oneself (271). Yet the social dimensions of lyric, emphasized in "Approaching the Lyric," achieve prominence when Frye lists friends and lovers among the audiences "normally" addressed by the mode (249). And to describe the lyric audience as choruslike, even though, to return to our woodcut, they are not present on the same plane as the speaker, is to imply interaction and again to trouble the divide between presence and absence.

That possibility of interaction emerges also in a tension in Frye's argument that deserves far more attention than it has received. "The fourth possible arrangement, the concealment of the poet's audience from the poet, is presented in the lyric" (249), he writes, and Frye's commitment to this formulation is evident in the decision to offer a version of it in the glossary, where lyric is presented as "characterized by the assumed concealment of the audience from the poet." (366). Although this phraseology indicates neither who is doing the assuming nor who the concealing, like the similar statement within the text itself, it implies that the poet is not himself involved in the process, except perhaps to join in assuming its results. But compare, "The poet, so to speak, turns his back on his listeners, though he may speak for them, and though they may repeat some of his words after him" (250). Some readers, including one distinguished poet, have claimed that the image of the poet with a turned back merely abbreviates Mill's point about overhearing;[40] but in fact the two models are substantially different. For although "so to speak" reminds the reader to interpret this metaphorically, not as a mimesis of someone literally turning a back, the statement does attribute more agency to the poet than Mill's commentary and Frye's own alternative formulations do. Notice, too, that it suggests a continuing consciousness of the presence of that audience rather than their concealment and the poet's "utter" unawareness of them posited by Mill (348). The model of concealment from — but not by — the poet suggests artlessness, the alternative of his turning his back, art if not artifice. At stake in the difference are the poet's agency and attraction to performance in several of its senses. Or, to put it another way, a statement like "the concealment of the poet's audience" from the poet turns those auditors into eavesdroppers, while in the alternative version that refers to turning the back they become participants of whose presence the poet is still aware. That second position also allows for the possibility they will shortly be addressed directly, that the poet who has turned his back will, as it were, turn back, as in fact arguably happens at the end of Donne's "Funerall," among many other secular poems. Similarly, as we will see, many religious lyrics may be read in terms of a returning to and turning towards God.

So acute about other distinctions, Frye nonetheless allows these alternative models to coexist uneasily. The explanation is the same one that lies behind the asymmetry with which he enumerates his radicals of presentation, not specifying the audience of the model for lyric: Frye, reenacting a tension often found also in other critics, is divided between two models for lyric—that is, he is divided between the competing claims of that bible Aristotle's *Rhetoric* and the literal Bible. On the one hand, his expressed commitment to rhetoric as the guiding principle behind genres leads him to emphasize a model for lyric in which the poet is performing the poem for an audience even if it is not diegetically present in the situation mimed in the poem; on the other hand, as hinted by his curious statement that lyric shares with irony a rejection of the marketplace, he joins Mill, Sidney, and many others in the drive to locate that mode, disengaged and unmediated, in a world of transcendent truth. He does not assign an audience to the radical of singing and chanting because on some level the author of *The Secular Scripture* wants to see lyric as uncontaminated by the negotiations of rhetoric, a field about which he has clear reservations. Thus we again encounter the drive to establish lyric as a pure sphere, adumbrated in my introduction and explicated by some of the tropes analyzed in Chapter 1. Indeed, Frye's suggestion that the relationship between lyric and epos resembles that between prayer and sermon exemplifies the predilection, encountered at many points in his study, for representing lyric as not only pure but holy.

The writings of Wordsworth, Mill, Eliot, and Frye, divergent though they are in a number of ways, thus crystallize questions central to early modern lyric. To what extent and in what regards is it private, and to what extent and in what ways communal? Does the poet implicitly communicate with audiences not directly addressed? And why are these subjects so unsettling for the critics examining them? To address these and other problems raised but not fully resolved by that quartet of writers, one needs a critical vocabulary as supple as it is subtle. Although the study of lyric audiences is not their primary objective, three groups of theorists—the narratologists, M. M. Bakhtin and his heirs and assigns, and the practitioners of discourse analysis—offer promising though not unproblematical routes for resolving some of the dilemmas and pursuing further questions about lyric audience, especially the types of diversification and profusion on which this chapter focuses. Analogues to the "implied reader" and to various forms of resistant reader, as well as the significance of epistolary communications, all concepts common to many narratological systems, recur also in lyric. But some of the principal differences between narrative and lyric, notably the centrality of a consciousness often identified with the first person in so many instances of the latter and the absence or submersion of direct address in the former, complicate adducing narratology when studying the interaction of speaker and audience in lyric poetry.

That interaction can often aptly be described as dialogic, and, as we have already seen, the indisputably canonical work of M. M. Bakhtin, as well as a number of essays that he may or may not have written under a pseudonym, provides an alternative to narratology. The potential value of Bakhtinian interpretation is confirmed by the students of William Wordsworth, notably Don H. Bialostosky and Michael Macovski, who have fruitfully approached that oeuvre in terms of its dialogics.[41] Bakhtin emphasizes an anticipated response: "the word in living conversation is directly, blatantly, oriented toward a future answer-word: it provokes an answer, anticipates it and structures itself in the answer's direction."[42] This aspect is especially relevant to lyric, suggesting, for example, that our common habit of describing certain lyrics as "answer poems" is an important step and yet still focuses, potentially misleadingly, on one stage in a continuing process of communication (and often miscommunication).

Reading poetry in general and lyric in particular from a Bakhtinian paradigm is, however, problematical, not least because the master's own position is not self-evident. The author of *The Dialogic Imagination* does not escape his characteristic predilection for straw men when discussing the mode in question. "Poetic style is by convention suspended from any mutual interaction with alien discourse," he asserts, and proceeds to associate poetic language with "one unitary and indisputable discourse."[43] On the other hand, though this assertion is often cited, it is not clear that it is his firm position on the subject; an essay widely attributed to him insists that both inner and outer speech are always oriented towards a listener, who is an active participant.[44] Another essay that may or may not be by Bakhtin himself makes a similar point by asserting that listeners are in fact especially important in lyric, and when the sympathy that lyric normally expects from them does not materialize, a dialogic irony ensues.[45] Several critics have seconded these positions; Bialostosky manages to make dialogics safe for lyric by focusing largely on the category of the novelized poetry, and Marianne and Michael Shapiro find widespread dialogic elements in lyric.[46]

In any event, in the case of lyric, Bakhtinian dialogical models need to be inflected with repeated reminders of how often a listener responds by refusing to respond, notably in the instance of the Petrarchan mistress who remains stony, or that of the deity whom the worshiper fears does not answer, as in George Herbert's "Deniall." Likewise, many poems of mourning focus on unresponsiveness in several senses, and we recall its illustration in the woodcut examined above. Numerous deconstructive readings of Romantic texts remind us that this lack of response is hardly historically specific to the English Renaissance; for example, building on the work on apostrophe by Paul de Man, Barbara Johnson, and others, Sara Guyer suggests that Wordsworth represents insomnia as a state where both subjects and objects are absent.[47] Given that the Lauras who do not deign to react and the Lucys who, rolled in earth's diurnal course as they are, cannot respond, are paradigmatic subjects for lyric, not the least valuable application of dialogics is an emphasis on what blocks dialogue in lyric, the form that Frye famously associates with blockage.

Similar and often preferable to the narratologists' or the Bakhtinians' ways of discussing the audiences of lyric is the work of certain students of conversational interaction, participants in a larger enterprise known as discourse analysis, a subject that has received too little attention thus far from literary critics. Most practitioners of these trades are linguists by training, but thinkers like the sociologist Erving Goffman and the psychologist Richard Gerrig have also contributed influentially. Although such studies are sometimes limited by a positivistic and inappropriately benign model of the workings of conversation, they are germane to lyric in many ways. To begin with, although these discourse analysts generally study quotidian social exchanges, their emphasis on the interactions between speaker and audience alerts us to the dialogic interchanges concealed within or facilitated by even those lyrics that appear to be straightforward monologues, such as certain Petrarchan laments and devotional poems. Also useful for the purposes of this chapter are discourse analysts' demonstrations of how even a largely silent listener can evoke or challenge the speech of a storyteller. (Those arguments may recall anthropological studies of how audiences participate in rituals, such as Ellen B. Basso's intriguing analysis of the crucial role of the "what-sayer.")[48]

Particularly valuable to students of lyric are the subdivisions in the position of both author and listener mapped through varying terminology by discourse analysts. Borrowing one of several comparable systems, the terminology proposed by Erving Goffman, one could distinguish the *animator*, or the person who fulfills a kind of ambassador role by speaking someone else's ideas, from the original *author* of the sentiments.[49] These categories, I will demonstrate at several junctures, gloss and demonstrate similarities among the relationships of lyric poet and audience, of poet and printer, and of printer and publisher, not least because in all three cases the participants can switch roles. But further complications present themselves immediately. What if the text frames its internalized meditations with a commentary, as is so often the case in lyric (Marvell's metalyrical "Hark how the mower Damon sung" ["Damon the Mower", 1][50] or, indeed, Shakespeare's opening line, "When I do count the clock that tells the time" [Sonnet 12])?[51] What if the animator changes a meaning through intonation?

Similarly, students of discourse analysis have subdivided the position of listener. It is common to separate the person or persons directly addressed from other hearers, termed by Herbert H. Clark and Thomas B. Carlson "side participants," although that label reduces them to a secondary status when, as I will demonstrate, they are really central in many lyric poems.[52] Adding further subdivisions, Clark and Carlson also distinguish participants, addressees, and overhearers; Goffman's system separates the ratified listeners, who are directly and openly addressed, from bystanders whose presence is assumed even though not acknowledged through direct address, and from eavesdroppers.[53]

William Waters's recent book, *Poetry's Touch*, another of the relatively few critical studies to deploy distinctions among types of listening, adeptly traces movements among the positions in question, though he focuses largely on modern poetry.[54] An overview of Ben Jonson's "Celebration of Charis in Ten Lyrick Peeces," however, demonstrates that discourse analysis is no less relevant to early modern lyric: its categories help us to see how many different types of audience are involved in the sequence, how often the author assumes the role of hearer, and how unstable the assignment of the label "auditor" to any personage may be. Picking up Jonson's "peeces," as it were, also summarizes other observations about the auditors of lyric and gestures towards some questions for future study, especially on issues related to tensions concealed in or broken apart by the poem.

"Celebration" is a series of loosely linked poems about love deploying a range of speakers and metrical patterns. The sequence opens on one of several lyrics in which the speaker addresses the lady directly, utilizing both first and second person pronouns. This reminds us, for the first of many times in this chapter, that in Renaissance lyric a typical dynamic is not solitary speech but rather a man speaking to a woman. But the lady is not the only audience: as Anne Ferry has pointed out, titles may at once assert ownership and put distance between the poet and his creation. In this instance, the title, "His Excuse for Loving," creates a vantage point from which the reader—and the poet framing the lyric in those four words—can evaluate the poem from a remove that permits the judgment involved in "excuse." In effect, the author and reader, like the lady, become auditors and judges; or, to return to discourse analysis, the lady becomes a ratified listener and the author and reader eavesdroppers.

In the next three poems the speaker uses the first person while referring to the lady in the third much or all of the time, depending on the particular lyric. But the reader is surely meant to speculate that she is a side participant, hence overhearing praise and complaint, an option confirmed by the subsequent lyric. In the fifth poem the speaker lauds his lady in a conversation with Cupid, but she is directly invited to attend to their conversation: "Heare, what late discourse of you / Love, and I have had" ("His Discourse with Cupid," 5–6). This invitation demonstrates the potential mistake in the term "side participant"; this invited overhearing is the very point of the poem at hand, and I will cite many other examples of it in other lyrics of the early modern period.

Whereas the sixth and seventh texts address the lady directly, the eighth includes both a narrative in which she is represented in the third person and direct address. In the ninth poem the lady responds, speaking to "Ben"; her list of the qualities she would ideally prefer in a man includes several that he obviously does not have, such as noble birth; her admission that she could be content with something less than her ideal may remind us of Jonson's "Inviting a Friend to Supper." In the tenth, "Another Ladyes Exception Present at the Hearing," someone who may have been either an eavesdropper or bystander responds with a bawdy joke about what part of a man she prefers. If one conceives of Jonson as audience, the comments are at once reassuring and flirtatious, recalling the artist Dan Graham's comment about "people looking at other people looking at other people inside and outside" (77). In short, this sequence resembles many other lyrics of its period in demonstrating the wide range of ways lyrics were conceived as interacting with their audiences and the resulting variety between and within specific poems; it differs from many of them in that it renders as realized dramatic characters the listeners whose implicit presence in the world of early modern lyric has been traced by Ilona Bell, among other scholars.[55]

What functions are served by this sort of game of musical chairs? On many levels, responsibility for lyric, the domain of the civilizing Orpheus and the seducing sirens, is variously acknowledged and deflected. A master of equivocation, Jonson delights in making and then breaking promises, avowing and then denying, as the menu attached to his famous dinner invitation indicates. That characteristic habit of saying and unsaying becomes literal here when the third person title implies that it was not the historical character Ben Jonson who spoke these words. Jonson was to repeat and intensify that gesture by assigning a song from his sequence "A Celebration of Charis" to one of the least savory characters in *The Devil is an Ass.* Often represented as prototype and even progenitor of modern conceptions of authorship, Jonson is here primarily concerned to deflect, to distance himself from that role—one of many early modern examples of such a response to the ambivalences about lyric anatomized throughout this book.[56] The other lady, who as eavesdropper or bystander ends the sequence on a risqué joke about the male body, serves the function of allowing Jonson to deflect the somatic anxieties that emerge elsewhere in his poetry; and for the purposes of this chapter she serves the function of alerting us to the implicit presence of figures like her even in poems where they are not so overtly realized.

In exemplifying the multiple and fluid positions taken by the audiences in early modern lyric, Jonson's poem demonstrates the central arguments traced in this section: the challenges of labeling and analyzing those stances and, in particular, the value of deploying discourse analysis in doing so. It also exemplifies many approaches to lyric audiences that recur throughout the poetry of the English Renaissance, notably Jonson's strategies of deflection and denial, and thus introduces the problem explored in the next two sections: how and why the early modern era represents lyric audiences in the ways it does.

Although illustrated by Jonson's Charis sequence and many other poems of the English Renaissance, the characteristics I am associating with lyric audiences are by no means unique to that period: to cite just a few examples from outside it, "The Dream of the Rood," Wordsworth's "Lines Composed a Few Miles above Tintern Abbey," and a little-known contemporary poem that creates a dialogue with that very author, Julia Randall's "To William Wordsworth from Virginia," all provide intriguing examples of shifting directions of address. Nonetheless, the lability in question sometimes takes distinct forms and is deployed to distinct ends in the early modern period; for example, as I have just indicated, the guilt about lyric in general and some of its subjects in particular traced in Chapter 1 impels poets to address multiple audiences as a strategy for deflecting anxieties about the mode itself. This is not to say that such guilt about poetry is confined to the Renaissance; but poets of the twentieth and twenty-first centuries, for example, are much more likely to worry about the irrelevance and impotence of lyric than about its immorality.

Why, then, are these proclivities for protean audiences so recurrent in early modern lyric in particular, and why do they assume the forms they do? One answer deserves particular attention initially because it is as significant as it is neglected in this context: devotional practices of the period, and particularly the congregational singing of psalms, profoundly influenced even secular lyric poetry.[57] The impact of the psalms on religious verse has hardly been ignored by students of early modern literature, yet that of communal singing on secular literature, especially its formative impact on lyric audiences and other underlying paradigms for the lyric, has received far too little attention.[58]

Resisting another binary, one should acknowledge the psalms' significance in Catholic religious practices (for example, the Sarum Pontifical orders the recitation of Psalm 116 after a death); but the fact remains that their presence and prominence in early modern Reformed spiritual practices is extraordinary, as signaled by the fact that over 700 editions of or including the Sternhold-Hopkins psalter appeared between 1562 and 1696.[59] Considered a crucial part of the Bible, the psalms of course assumed a range of roles in both ecclesiastical and private worship: devotional manuals included excerpts from them, numerous sermons elucidated them, many poets produced metrical versions of them or included allusions to them in their verse. Polyphonic arrangements like those of Gibbons were often viewed as seductively Roman, while the Sternhold-Hopkins version was widely, though by no means universally, seen as more appropriate for Reformed congregations.[60] But it is the Reformed practice of the entire congregation singing the psalms, a cultural watershed arguably as important in its way as the administrative reforms of the 1530s, that aptly signals their intensified significance in Protestant England—and their impact on conceptions of poetic audience central to the early modern lyric.

Many controversies attended the fraught question of who should sing the psalms. The congregation rather than the priest or choir as in Roman Catholicism? Was it actually perilous to sing them at all? Congregational singing was advocated by Luther and Calvin. The latter characteristically claimed, in a treatise reprinted in a 1571 edition of the psalms, that even this activity is directed by God, who "provoketh us too sing his prayses." Luther, who delivered lengthy and detailed commentaries on the psalms, agreed, asserting that everyone should own a psalter.[61] Practicing what they literally preached on the subject, Luther composed hymns and Calvin delegated first Marot and then Beze to create a series of them. Yet Zwingli at one point sedulously opposed hymnody, and even, or especially Calvin, in his lengthy discussions of the psalms, expresses some ambivalence towards it. In short, the contrast between the universality attributed to the content of the psalms and the divisiveness associated with their performance anticipates and tropes the practice of creating both a unified choral group and a series of shifting and conflicting positions for those performers, including the change from singer to audience.

As all of these debates suggest, on one level the psalms functioned as the prototypical version of the sanative lyrics that were so often contrasted with their opposite in the pairing traced throughout this study. In his *Goostly Psalmes*, Miles Coverdale reports that he prepared the book to supply the youth of England appropriate songs to sing, proceeding to contrast them to the "wicked frutes" of "unchristen songes."[62] Yet at the same time, doubts about the pleasure produced by singing the psalms and about the sexual proclivities of their putative author complicated the status of these texts, blurring the distinction between Good and Bad Lyric and incorporating a struggle between the two categories within the hymnal itself.[63] In other words, not the least way the psalms influenced even secular lyric was by participating in recurrent debates about its worth, variously providing an exemplar of and an antidote to moral concerns about it.

Initially the Reformed Church in England followed the Roman practice of assigning psalms to the priest and choir, but the continent was witnessing many instances of congregational singing (in Holland, for example, gatherings of Calvinists in fields included communal singing). Some Englishmen were attracted to the practice; himself the author of a collection of psalms, Miles Coverdale wrote a volume approvingly describing congregational singing in Denmark.[64] And when the English Marian exiles returned from Geneva, among the weightiest of their baggage was their commitment to that type of worship.

The uneasy and uneven development of the established church's position on how the psalms should be sung, who should sing them, and if indeed they should be sung at all is repeatedly manifest in the language and layout of the psalters, demonstrating the complex tensions that accompanied the shift of authority to the laity. Early psalters not only do not advocate congregational participation but also often reactively emphasize the authority of the church. An edition of 1566 announces that its poems are "Corrected and poynted as they shall be Song in Churches . . . Confirmed by act of Parliament"—notice the multiple linguistic markers of authority such as "shall" and "corrected."[65] In some passages, rhetoric that ostensibly resolves doubts about communal singing merely pours psalters on open wounds.

Other psalters, however, vigorously defend communal singing, the very intensity of their argument demonstrating the extent of the opposition and perhaps on occasion hinting that they are protesting too much. A frequently repeated Sternhold-Hopkins title page includes not one or two but three biblical citations defending the psalms and the singing of them. One of these passages declares that the ensuing texts are "Set forth and allowed to be song in all Churches, of all the people together and after Morning and Evening prayer: as also before and after Sermons, and moreover in private houses, for their godly solace and comfort, laying apart all ungodly songs and balades."[66] Notice how the practice of communal singing is mimetically advocated through a rhetoric of communality—that is, through conjunctive rather than disjunctive connectives and through adjectives that similarly stress coming together. Thus the word "and" appears five times in those forty-five words, while "all" is used three times. And these terms are surrounded by similar semantic, syntactical, and grammatical markers of unity: "together," "Morning and Evening prayer," "as also before and after Sermons," "and moreover." The warning of vice at the end of the passage—"laying apart all ungodly songs and balades"—suggests that all these references to unity are again reactive, the establishment of an us-them dichotomy: the common front displayed by the godly facilitates setting aside the ungodly alternative. In short, by promoting the use of the psalter for congregational singing in the Elizabethan period, the Church of England was uneasily working out yet another via media, this one involving a spectrum running between the assertion that the laity should not sing psalms and the claim that anyone could sing any psalm, including one of his own invention.

Despite the concern for community and harmony that choral music can trope, thematized in this and other passages, the performance of the psalms in fact involved precisely the unstable fluidity of audiences that is so central to early modern lyric. To begin with, the audience of a psalm sung by a congregation includes God, the members of that congregation, in many cases a group of believers elsewhere who are not yet singing but are being exhorted to do so, and in a sense the internalized individual singer (indeed, the first psalm celebrates meditation, including versions connected with this group of poems).[67] Many psalms address God directly; the performers of all of them surely believed that God was observing their worship. And inasmuch as the psalms were often represented as words the Lord had taught to David, this case is the first of many that merge the positions of author and auditor in the complex chain of this discourse. Similarly, early modern Protestants are represented as singing psalms David has taught to them, a shifting of the position of auditor to that of ambassador. (Hammons's study of Anna Trapnel demonstrates how her claim to take up David's harp figures and fortifies the agency of a female writer.[68]) Moreover, inculcating the Reformed focus on the laity's role in spiritual growth, the literature attached to the psalms repeatedly positions members of the congregation as each other's teachers as they sing—in other words, as both singer and audience at once. The excerpt from Colossians prominent on so many title pages refers to the congregation "teachyng and exhortyng one an other in Psalmes, Hymnes, and spirituall songes."[69] Given that a singer is being exhorted by another singer, she or he may be both performer and listener at once; thus the psalms also provide a pattern for divided and split subjectivity.

These patterns are further complicated by the Elizabethan figure sometimes known as the "singing man" or "singing boy," who would perform a line that the congregation then repeated. Resembling the Strasbourg custom of a congregation echoing a line the cantor had first intoned, this practice again shifts members of the community back and forth among the roles of speaker, auditor, and animator. This type of ventriloquization may even be suggested by the language of Psalm 136.[70] Furthermore, in another sense, too, the congregation is animator in that they are reading the putative words of David as they sing. The singing man becomes David's animator and the members of the congregation both David's animator and the animator of the singing man, who in turn becomes the audience of the singers who succeed him.

But at the same time, they are subjects assuming David's own position in that they command others to praise. Indeed, the literature that glosses the psalms and the process of performing them repeatedly insists on that identification with the extraordinary figure whose curriculum vitae includes stints as poet, prophet, soldier, and adulterer. So, to return to the role of the singing man, he is David's audience while also assuming the role of animator in performing David's words for the members of the congregation, who in turn are audience to the singing man and then themselves animators of the words of David and the singing man. The relationship between psalm singer and psalmist could be further complicated by titles like "A prayer of David," which at once encourage identification by stressing that the current singer is taking David's place, while at the same time inviting the early modern audience to observe David singing.[71] Both the role of the singing man and the coalescence of the congregation with David, then, model one of the most common theories about lyric, the argument that its reader identifies with the poet and in effect voices his words. Yet the shifting roles associated with the singing man and the invitation to watch rather than simply be David also involve multiple audiences, and in so doing they alert one to the problems in the conception of identificatory voicing that I will posit at the end of this chapter.

My argument so far assumes unified purposes and responses uniting the individual members of a given congregation, much as Wordsworth suggests that all readers of lyric will respond and participate alike. In fact, certain members may have reactions that further correspond to the shifting audiences and resulting divided subjectivities manifest in both secular and religious lyric. In the instance of the psalms, as in that of reactions to the words "under God" in the United States Pledge of Allegiance, surely in many instances a potential dissenter is temporarily carried away, or lulled into participation, only to recoil. Demonstrating that participants in a ceremony may read a text's formulaic insults in relation to their personal histories, the anthropologist Kenneth Kensinger trenchantly warns us against assuming that all observers react in similar ways to a ritual.[72] He invites us to rethink Ramie Targoff's assumptions about the coerciveness of public devotion, as well as Roland Greene's association of the psalms with what he terms "fictive" practices, which supply distance, and with ritualistic practices, which he maintains function coercively to produce unity: ritual, Kensinger's analysis encourages us to realize, may under certain circumstances foment dissent precisely because it provides an authoritative Other against which to define the self.[73]

Psalm singing in early modern England surely provided precisely the circumstances that would encourage some form of dissent; in particular, whether defiant, ambivalent, or simply confused, those who retained sympathies for the Catholic Church would be likely to have a complex relationship to the psalms they were singing. If a member of these groups did not share the sentiments of the psalm but was mouthing them to be polite or politic, then this dissenter was, in a sense, the judge of the lyric and the one judged by its strictures, perhaps even was the enemy to whom the poem refers. Other divisions are noted in Richard Rogers's 1603 treatise on the Scriptures, where he advises that those who cannot read and hence cannot sing the psalms should listen attentively to those who do so and attempt to participate rather than letting their minds wander.[74] In short, much as critics need to supplement the conception of dialogics with reminders of how often one member in the conversation is silent yet active in it, so too the history of psalm singing reminds us to include among the discourse analysts' classifications of audience members those who in some way resist that role.

Although the congregational performance of these songs attributed to David is the most complex and intriguing instance of these shifting roles in early modern religion, comparable transitions characterize many other devotional practices as well, thus preparing and alerting the devout, or the apparently devout, to the shifts involved in singing the psalms, and conversely such performances drew attention to similar reversals elsewhere. In private spiritual practices one might switch between internalized meditation with God conceived as bystander to direct address to the deity; John Donne divides the meditations in his *Devotions upon Emergent Occasions* into three stages, "meditation," "expostulation," and "prayer." Not coincidentally, devotion and lyric are thus both seen as processes, in part because in both instances the speaker's relationship to hearers may shift.

Moreover, manuals on meditation often emphasize interchange with God; Louis Martz reminds us that the stages of meditation include "colloquy" and "petition," both of which are by definition dialogic.[75] If that dialogue involves listening to and speaking with God, it also involves speaking for him, assuming an animator role. Indeed, much as David was sometimes represented as singing God's words (an analogue to the description of the Anglo-Saxon poet Caedmon which Susan Stewart analyzes trenchantly), so too prayers were often described as not only addressed to but also authored by God.[76] The doctrinal complexities of voicing the deity's words have been analyzed with particular acuity by A. D. Nuttall.[77] Despite the problems Nuttall documents, a number of poets celebrate that potentiality. John Donne, fascinated by communication and miscommunication in their many forms throughout his career, writes in one of his letters to Henry Goodyer, "And that advantage of nearer familiarity with God, which the act of incarnation gave us, is grounded upon Gods assuming us, not our going to him. And, our accesses to his presence are but his descents into us; and when we get any thing by prayer, he gave us before hand the thing and the petition."[78] Similarly, Milton implies that the suppliant is at once God's animator and his interlocutor when he writes in *Eikonoklastes* that God "every morning raines down new expressions into our hearts."[79] In short, like the psalms, meditation and prayer might well involve the suppliant shifting among the positions of principal speaker, animator, and audience.

In addition, the how-to devotional manuals of the period buttress my points about the problematical divide between the solitary and social by suggesting another presence besides that of God in a room where someone is apparently praying in private: another side of the believer, or even under some circumstances other believers, may in some sense be there as well. "As every good Master . . . is a good Preacher to his own Family; so every good Christian, is a good Preacher to his own soul," the minister Richard Baxter writes. His immediately subsequent observation that "soliloquy is a Preaching to one self" hints at the interaction between spiritual and theatrical models of audience to which I will later turn.[80] The obverse of Baxter's suggestion that meditation is a kind of preaching is the postulation of preaching as a kind of meditation: whereas Scripture per se was often the primary source for sermons, ministers also drew heavily on meditative traditions, as many students of early modern religion have demonstrated, and the subtitles of Thomas Gataker's published sermons include the phrases "Succinct Meditations" and "A Meditation on Genesis 25.8."[81]

This chapter will demonstrate the interacting influences of devotional and many other cultural practices on early modern lyrics in some detail, and one preliminary example can aptly introduce that interplay. Devoting its first seven stanzas to addresses to God that include pleas, queries, and praise, George Herbert's "Obedience" at first appears to have one clearly defined addressee. But as the poem progresses, Michael C. Schoenfeldt observes, its focus moves from God's power to the potential power of its own lines over its mortal listeners.[82] More to my purposes here, in so doing it radically shifts its audiences. The eighth strophe, which serves as a bridge between various types of address, generalizes about man's promises to God and the responses of moral readers to this poem, though without explicitly addressing the deity or those readers. The final stanza then declares:

> How happie were my part,
>   If some kinde man would thrust his heart
> Into these lines; till in heav'ns Court of Rolls
>       They were by winged souls
> Entered for both, farre above their desert!
>
> $(41-45)^{83}$

In these concluding strophes, direction of address in the narrow sense is far less significant than the potential presence of a number of hearers. In hoping that another human being would thrust his heart, and arguably his voice, into the lines, Herbert implies the range of audiences associated with the singing of hymns and with meditation: he appears to be meditating on this hope, while at the same time indirectly addressing God as a bystander as well as potential candidates for the role of "kinde man" (42). Thus the speaker is assuming a position quite like that of the singing man in hymns, and as is so often the case in that sort of discourse, one of the primary if indirect speech acts is invitation.

Although devotional practices, especially the singing of the psalms, were a particularly potent determinant of lyric audiences, they of course interacted with many other influences, notably the conditions of production, the practices of builders, the imperatives of rhetoricians and musicians, and the potentialities of popular genres. Most obviously, scribal and print cultures were as effective as the glass of Nouvel and Piano in changing the subject positions of reader and author (observe in particular the conjunction of images of actors reproduced on the glass with the reflections there of the current spectators in Nouvel's Guthrie Theater).

To that shift in positions I will return in detail in Chapter 4. Moreover, quotidian experiences repeatedly called into question, for both author and reader, the likelihood of meditation's remaining wholly private: the physical solitude often represented in lyrics of the Romantic period was hard to achieve in early modern culture. This is not to say that the relationship between speaker and listener in lyric necessarily represents daily life in any simple or direct way, but the assumption that privacy was at best temporary and partial surely influenced the changing subject positions in early modern lyric. Even when the central hall, so prominent in medieval and earlier sixteenth-century domestic architecture, was modified by building plans that included more private spaces, houses were not in fact private to the extent many twentieth- and twenty-first-century readers associate with that concept.[84] Witness the beds, outside whose curtains others might sleep in the room, fitting poster boys, as it were, for the limitations of solitude within houses. The emphasis on court spies in Donne's satires reminds one that true solitude was no easier to achieve in the more exalted world of the court. And while Arthur Dimmesdale and Hester Prynne found their privacy in the woods, in the early modern period that milieu was associated with threatening presences, notably robbers, as Falstaff's labeling thieves "Diana's foresters" suggests (1 *Henry IV*, I.ii.25–26). George T. Wright's persuasive assertion that Shakespeare's sonnets are a "silent speech" located on a border between the absence and presence of sound gestures towards a larger awareness in the culture that the silence of interiority might be compromised.[85]

Many literary texts enact the interruption of solitary speech that must have been common for these reasons—notice that Hamlet's soliloquies are sometimes cut short by others or by the speaker himself because of someone's approach, and observe how many of Shakespeare's other plot devices turn on someone's overhearing what is said. In prose romances, even the poems written in solitude are, like their poets, often found by other characters. All this suggests yet another reason one cannot neatly divide private meditation and social interaction: in the nondiegetic world, the former was liable to be either overheard or interrupted, a potentiality often staged within texts, famously in Sidney's "Soft, but here she comes" (Sonnet 47.12). Once again, lyric impels its readers to think in terms of process, not stasis.

Yet the contemporary reactions against the hypostasized image of the solitary poet communing only with herself, like many critical reactions, are exaggerated. If, as I have agreed, the diegetic social interactions of lyric mime conditions of transmission, the meditative solitude that is also a significant element in early modern lyrics mimes the conditions of production in that poets often spend time alone when writing, especially if they are working with the sort of vexing metrical and stanzaic forms in which Renaissance writers delighted. And even if dialogues within poems reflect the interchanges through which coterie literature is created, that is not to say, as one otherwise valuable study suggests, that the concern for love apparent in these poems primarily serves to encode responses to coterie exchanges.[86]

Numerous intellectual influences also shape the multiplicity and volatility of audiences in early modern lyric. Emphasized by Orpheus's association with both literature and eloquence—his gig in the underworld succeeds, at least temporarily, because of his powers of persuasion, musical and verbal—the connection between poesy and rhetoric was a commonplace. Training in rhetoric, a discipline as familiar and formative for Renaissance schoolchildren as video games are today, introduced those pupils at an early age to the significance of direction of address in particular. The rhetorical focus on debate, as Cristina Malcolmson points out, encouraged answer poems.[87] And the emphasis on persuading a listener, reinforced by the comparable mission of love poetry, alerted readers during their formative years to the suasive agenda that can underlie even texts that seem totally devoted to internalized cogitation, such as the farewell poems discussed below. Repeatedly stressed in rhetorical treatises is the need to address different audiences in different ways—for example, in III.210–212 of Cicero's *De Oratore*, a popular text in the early modern period, Crassus differentiates appropriate approaches to various listeners—and this principle also encouraged the multiple directions of address in lyric.

Especially relevant here are the rhetoricians' statements about the issue traced above in relation to Jonson, deflecting address. Apostrophe, so central to contemporary theories of lyric, is described in many manuals as a route towards, indeed a feint for, turnings and diversions. Quintilian observes, "*Apostrophe* also, which consists in the diversion of our address from the judge, is wonderfully stirring. . . . But the term *apostrophe* is also applied to utterances that divert the attention of the hearer from the question before them. . . . We may, for instance, pretend that we expected something different."[88] Although Quintilian's hearers are judges in the legal sense, the passage is also germane to the judges encountered throughout this chapter, those who may disapprove of the lyric poem and its author. In turning to love poetry, I will suggest that the Renaissance lyric effects through other means, including other versions of apostrophe, some of the forms of deflection achieved through prosopopoeia in eras when that trope flourishes.

Equally significant for lyric audiences were the ambivalences surrounding the practice of rhetoric in early modern England. Rhetoric's celebration as the art distinguishing man from the beasts and its status as the indispensable tool of preachers and statesmen contributed to the respect for one of its manifestations, poesy, that no doubt fueled many readers' drive to identify with the poet and, so to speak, voice her words. At the same time, the opening of *King Lear* famously reminds us of the distrust of "that glib and oily art" (I.i.224) that is apparent in so many other texts of the era. As a result of the Fall, according to widespread theories, the pure *lingua Adamica* was lost and man condemned to babble in his Babels. If language was corrupt and corrupting, silence was under many circumstances seen as a preferable "moving Rhetoricike," Christina Luckyj has demonstrated in a valuable revisionist study.[89] Such doubts surely encouraged the audiences of lyric poems—which often displayed their delight in rhetoric through prominent wordplay—to observe those texts with caution and even suspicion rather than simply identify with their speakers, a point to which I will return.

If rhetorical practices influenced direction of address, musical practices besides the performance of psalms surely did so as well. Music provided many analogues to and models for answer poems; as Carla Zecher points out, lute poems were often written in pairs, and in polyphonic settings, singers in effect change from auditor to animator of what has previously been sung.[90] In particular, some contemporary accounts suggest that, as James Anderson Winn puts it, "madrigals seem to have been primarily intended for an audience of performers."[91] In short, many types of early modern music encouraged listeners to become performers and vice versa in ways that mime the rapid changes in positionality involved in lyric itself. In addition, the declamatory songs that flourished in England during the seventeenth century, paralleling the development of operatic recitatives on the continent, provide some intriguing analogues to lyric's change in direction of address. For example, in Henry Lawes's *Ariadne*, set to a poem by William Cartwright, the eponymous heroine starts by calling to Theseus but proceeds to incorporate appeals to gods, nymphs, death, and heaven, as well as internalized meditation, into her lament.

Probably the most important of the many literary influences on lyric direction of address is drama, again an influence that is certainly not unidirectional. The impact of theater on the changing positions of lyric audiences was arguably especially intense during the early seventeenth century because the masque—a form acted by members of the court that incorporated further members when the audience joined in the final dance—flourished then. But throughout the early modern era theater evidently provided many models for an interactive relationship between author and auditor and, in particular, for the changing and often indeterminate positions of audience that this chapter traces throughout. Famously but by no means uniquely, *Hamlet, A Midsummer Night's Dream,* and *The Taming of the Shrew* all cast their actors as audiences for part of the action.

Students of drama continue to debate a number of questions about soliloquies. Does Shakespeare's practice differ from that of earlier playwrights? Should we envision the speeches as spoken? To what extent if at all is the audience involved? And so on. Whether or not one agrees with the workings of all of his categories, Raymond Williams's taxonomy of the different forms a soliloquy can assume in these respects offers particularly useful solutions.[92] In any event, it is clear that when and if one defines the role of theatrical audience as that of a side partici-pant or bystander, let alone if one assumes that it may be addressed as a ratified listener, patterns very like those in lyric address can ensue in the course of solilo-quies. Those auditors may, for example, become complicitous in dubious plans, as they were when Bolingbroke compellingly addressed his theatrical listeners in Steven Pimlott's RSC production of *Richard II* in 2000 or when Edmund asked his theatrical auditors which of the sisters he should marry in the same com-pany's version of *King Lear* that Bill Alexander directed in 2004. Similarly, when Hal famously announces that he "will . . . imitate the sun" (1 *Henry IV*, I.ii. 197), if one envisions the theatrical audience as side participants of whom he is aware, let alone as addressees, the soliloquy changes dramatically: he is trying out on us—and, significantly, with us—the ruses he will later try on a broader public, much as some love poems implicate male hearers, realized or putative, in the strategies of seduction. In other instances, the audience assumes the role of con-fessor; in the production of *Richard III* that Libby Appel directed in the Oregon Shakespeare Festival in 2004, Tyrrell sat on the edge of the stage and directly ad-dressed the audience when describing his "tyrannous and bloody act" (IV.iii.1). Once again, the binary divide between the solitary and the social is troubled. One particular version of the soliloquy further troubles such distinctions: Seneca went to school at Bakhtin in that Senecan monologues often represent a divided subjectivity through the speaker's address to a part of her body, so in this instance, too, the apparently solitary is in fact often dialogic.

Yet again demonstrating one of the methodological arguments of this book— the value of studying the interaction between formal issues demonized in many circles and more recent cultural questions—these and other influences on lyric audiences typically interact with generic ones. Four literary types that flourished in the early modern period—love poetry, devotional verse, pastoral, and the liter-ature of patronage—encouraged addressing multiple audiences and facilitated shifts in positionality. Of course, this, like so many other questions about lyric, re-sists a simple cause-and-effect explanation, since a predisposition towards the types of multiplicity this chapter explores may well have heightened interest in the literary forms in question.

First, then, whereas the Renaissance is hardly the only age when love lyrics flourished in England, it is surely the preeminent arena for that type of verse; and the ways Jonson's "Celebration of Charis in Ten Lyrick Peeces" deflects direction of address to negotiate gendered tensions—and to gender tensions—recur in many other poems. In particular, Petrarchism encouraged, even in lyrics that would not be classified as members of that movement, a stance towards the lady in which respect and resentment vie with each other in a constantly moving Möbius strip. By addressing a range of audiences at once, or by shifting from one listener to another, poets often finesse the resulting tension. They may praise the lady without, as it were, in the process miming the sycophancy intensified by addressing such compliments to her. More often, through a strategy that we might term "staged overhearing," they introduce the possibility and even likelihood that the woman is a bystander and then proceed to criticize her by mimetically evoking a situation in which she is apparently not supposed to hear the criticism. That type of antagonism may also be suggested and intensified by implicitly inviting other men to overhear. Relevant in more senses than one, the adjective "staged" again alerts us to the similarity between these feints and Mill's comparison of the poet to an actor who pretends not to see his audience.

Thus *Amoretti* 1, which imagines the lady as reading a book of these lyrics, ostensibly delimits the speaker's power by rendering his property, the poems, alienable from their author, and positioning them in a subaltern status ("lyke captives trembling at the victors sight" [4]). The diminution of the power of both poet and his poems is signaled as well by denying his instruments, those lyrics, the instrumentality of verbs throughout the first eight lines: presented in such phrases as "Happy ye leaves" (1) and "happy lines" (5), they are enfolded into syntax that generally focuses instead on actions the lady performs ("those lilly hands . . . shall handle you" [1, 3]). Later, when the poems are granted verbs, the action in question involves worshipfully beholding the lady and trying to please her.

Yet, as is so often the case in Renaissance love poetry and in families with teenagers, respectful subservience generates a reactive surliness, and vice versa. Not the least effect of opening on this note is establishing the fiction (and quite possibly acknowledging the nondiegetic reality) that the lady is audience to all the other poems, including ones ostensibly addressed to another reader. In so doing, the opening also increases the likelihood that the nondiegetic reader, who is literally holding a book at this point, will identify with the sonnet mistress, the subject position that Wendy Wall acutely argues is characteristic of this genre.[93]

More to my purposes now, on the one hand the deflection of address from the lady to another addressee delimits the imputation of sycophancy. "The glorious pourtraict of that Angels face" [Sonnet 17.1] sounds less cloying than "portrait of your Angels face" or even "this Angels face" would have done. Yet on the other hand that same deflection also interpellates the Petrarchan mistress into the position of bystander when she is criticized in poems as bitter as the forty-seventh sonnet, the lyric that begins, "Trust not the treason of those smyling lookes"—and, to the extent that one imagines a male coterie audience reading such poems, the lyric also interpellates her as witness to her own humiliation.

The type of passive-aggressive staged overhearing that Spenser exemplifies recurs frequently in the love poetry of the English Renaissance and takes a range of forms. In the subgenre of meditative farewell poems, complaints and regrets are transformed into threats and attacks if one assumes the lady is overhearing. Discussed elsewhere in this study, Wyatt's "My lute, awake!" is a particularly interesting version of the pattern in which the indirect assaults implied by the possibility that the lady overhears as a bystander culminate in a more direct second person onslaught in the image of her as alone and unattractive. In a mirror version of this pattern, "Blame not my lute" addresses the lady directly but becomes a far nastier poem if one allows for the possibility of overhearers, notably the courtiers who might be side participants. Like the rhetorical orations that so deeply influence early modern poetry, such poems also implicitly placate judges, in this instance establishing their writer as immune from and critical of some of the worst follies of love poetry.

In other words, aggression may also be slyly released by allowing the possibility of a side participant other than the lady. The description of his lady's aging in the eighth sonnet of Michael Drayton's 1619 *Idea* ("There's nothing grieves me, but that Age should haste") is unpleasant enough to suggest that the verb "grieves" in that first line is disingenuous.[94] The second person pronouns evidently establish the lady as the ratified listener, and, because she reads or hears those descriptions, this lyric seems more antagonistic than many comparable *carpe diem* poems. But if one supplements that model of audience with the recognition that a coterie of gallants or other women or both might overhear within the diegetic world of the poem—a possibility readers might consider because of the nondiegetic lack of privacy to which I referred—the poem, like "Blame not my lute" and many sonnets in the *Amoretti*, becomes even nastier. Once again, anxieties about judges shape the direction of address. (Occasionally, though rarely, the aggression in question is re-gendered; Andrew Marvell's "Nymph Complaining of the Death of her Faun," another arena for multiple audiences, changes if the reader acknowledges the possibility that Sylvio is meant to overhear.)

Multiple directions of address may serve the multiple agendas of love poems in other, less aggressive ways as well (in so doing reminding us that persuasion poems may be hidden in lyrics ostensibly serving other purposes, while overt persuasion poems may in fact pursue quite different aims too). The audiences of Herrick's writings are often unspecified, allowing us to imagine a range of listeners, diegetic and otherwise. If his erotic lyrics on the lady's body, such as "Fresh Cheese and Cream," assume a particular, desirable lady as their primary audience, they are probably attempts at seduction; if, recalling the final poem in Jonson's "Celebration of Charis in Ten Lyrick Peeces," readers posit that woman as an overhearer, he is ostensibly filling the informative function that the discourse analysts associate with speech, but in the interests of seduction; if one imagines another woman, not a target of seduction, as overhearing, he is trying to shock; and if one thinks about a male coterie readership, the poems have the odor not of fresh dairy products but of locker-room socks.

No less than love poetry, devotional poetry typically encompasses multiple addressees, especially when, as in the Reformed verse of the early modern period, interiorized meditation is prototypical.[95] In these poems, as in the work of Graham, Nouvel, and Piano on which I opened, one sometimes perceives the audiences only through a glass darkly: in a phrase like, "May Christ's sacrifice always be remembered," how does the reader distinguish, for example, an injunction directed to the self, a prayer directed to God, and an injunction directed by a priestly figure to a congregation? Critics variously read Donne's La Corona as the voice of a priestly celebrant participating in communal devotion or as that of an individuated private believer.[96] Moreover, positions often switch in the course of a lyric, so that God may be represented as a bystander at some points and an addressee at others. Nonetheless, in many instances it is possible—and fruitful—to analyze seriatim how a given devotional poem addresses its many audiences.

As we have seen, in many religious poems the speaker addresses another side of the self; and meditation based on a conversation with God, as so many poems of the era are, may be at once monologue and dialogue. Michael C. Schoenfeldt has incisively anatomized that pattern in George Herbert's "The Collar," and such a conflation appears in many other poems by that author as well.[97] In another such lyric by Herbert, entitled "Dialogue," the interaction between the two voices is emphasized when it culminates in an interruption by the grieving but grateful sinner: "Ah! no more: thou break'st my heart" (32). If the number of Herbert's poems that open on a direct address (often to God though also to his own heart, a book, the church, and so on) is striking, no less telling is the habit, manifest in such poems as "Sinne (I)" and "Sion," of apparently turning inward and addressing the self in addition to or instead of the external audience addressed later in the same text. In some such lyrics, God's voice is represented directly and in others just implied in the speaker's reactions, a situation comparable to the one Ilona Bell has posited for the interaction of lover and lady in many secular poems.[98] Indeed, in a study that resists seeing the solitary speaker as normative, Gémino H. Abad describes the "lyric of interaction," a category that includes both explicit and implicit responses from a listener, as a significant subdivision of the mode.[99]

Many authors of religious poetry were, of course, ministers, and their verse is often implicitly and sometimes explicitly addressed to a congregation, a third audience that is typically present as some form of side participant. The interest in exemplarity that characterizes both medieval and early modern culture encourages the representation of the struggles of a single soul as a case study for other believers. The presence of side participants is, of course, often hard to demonstrate conclusively, but discussions of the *ars praedicandi*, as well as gestures towards such listeners in a number of poems, do encourage this type of reading. In the seventh chapter of his *Priest to the Temple*, Herbert encourages exemplarity: "Sometimes he tells them stories, and sayings of others . . . for them also men heed, and remember better then exhortations" (233). In Herbert's own canon, a number of lyrics, such as his allegorical "Pilgrimage," appear in narrative form; in other instances, the juxtaposition of an earlier and later version of the self, so characteristic of this poet, thus incorporates an implicit story of change. Practicing what he preached, as it were, Herbert opens one poem, "Mark you the floore?" ("The Church-floore" [1]), thus drawing attention to the speaker's position as a minister addressing a congregation.

Joyously celebrated as a glorious vocation, guiltily distanced because of the speaker's unworthiness, and finally gratefully accepted with the help of Christ, a calling to the ministry is the subject of Herbert's "Aaron." The movement from internalized meditation on whether the sinful speaker is capable of assuming the role of priest to its assumption is signaled and staged by a change of address: the poem concludes "Come people; Aaron's drest" (25). That conclusion is complicated, as critics have acknowledged, by reminders of remaining vestiges of sin and of Christ's status as the only true preacher.[100] But the fact remains that here, as in so many other texts analyzed in this chapter, a shift in direction of address enacts and emphasizes the central issues of the poem: in this instance the speaker's achievement of his calling is staged when he calls out to his congregation.

When poets represent the role of preacher, they sometimes do so to negotiate a source of dissension that was far from covert in early modern England: a number of doctrinal divisions were often expressed in the widespread and recurrent debates about whether private worship facilitated or compromised communal devotion and vice versa. The case that the culture, favoring "common prayer," discouraged its more individualistic alternative has been powerfully made by Ramie Targoff; but in alluding to devotional manuals only briefly, she neglects the ways they not only permit but encourage devotional idiolects.[101] Not the least agenda of many religious poems of the period, I maintain, is establishing a type of via media where the conflation of the voice of the individual sinner addressing himself and God with that of a priestly figure calling up a communal activity produces a both/and model that exemplifies and implicitly advocates an interaction between private devotion and communal worship and thus among various audiences.

This and many of the other patterns I have been tracing throughout this discussion of religious poetry appear in textbook form in Herbert's "Collar," which can be adduced relatively briefly here, since it is discussed from cognate perspectives in Chapter 5. Because a penitent Christian is telling the story of an earlier rebellion, we need to distinguish the original conceptions about audience from those of the later version of the speaker.[102] Providing a new perspective on comments by Frye and Mill about the overheard lyric, the rebellious would-be traveler may be turning his back on God as a potential listener, a formal action that is a dry run for the abandonment of faith he intends; or he may be initiating that rebellion by defying God through direct address in lines like "Shall I be still in suit?" (6). Or, in a subtle possibility that also recalls Frye, he may be pretending to turn his back while glancing over his shoulder at the omnipresent deity, a formal position whose imagistic analogue is the inclusion of references to wine and thorns in lines that ostensibly attempt to deny spirituality. In contrast, the reformed speaker may be seen either as addressing God directly in a global speech act of confession or at least assuming God's presence as side participant. The Lord has, as it were, collared this particular miscreant—and that process provides an exemplum for wannabe runaways among Herbert's readers.

No less illuminating in its approach to lyric audiences but far more controversial in its doctrine and quality is Donne's "Litanie." Whereas John Carey, not unpredictably given his emphasis on apostasy, argues that its stanza on the Virgin would have troubled many Protestants, Helen Gardner firmly, even defiantly, labels it "in many ways . . . the most Anglican of the *Divine Poems*."[103] Analyzing direction of address in the poem, and hence recognizing Donne's agenda of rec-

onciling private and public worship, offers a different perspective on the disagreement of these critics.

Incorporating but not referring directly to the four standard parts of a litany, the
poem moves from direct appeals to the members of the Trinity, to a discussion of
beings such as apostles and martyrs, some of whom served intercessory functions
in the Catholic tradition, to a series of prayers. In certain of these stanzas, Donne
clearly refers to his personal experience, thus suggesting meditation—in particular,
the eighth strophe expresses fears about "Poëtiquenesse" (72)—while others enun-
ciate general problems and fears, such as "being anxious, or secure" (127). This
movement between the personal and more general operates in linear form via the
pronouns of the poem, with the first person singular predominating early on and
the first person plural later.[104] But the movement is not clear-cut; some stanzas, for
example, use both pronouns, and the image of physician and patient in the final
stanza at once evokes the universal application of such images for sinning Christians and refers very specifically and personally to Donne's own illness.[105]

In a letter about the poem to his friend Henry Goodyer, Donne observes,

> Since my imprisonment in my bed, I have made a meditation in verse, which I call
> a Litany; . . . [other verse litanies] give me a defence, if any man; to a Lay man, and
> a private, impute it as a fault, to take such divine and publique names, to his own
> little thoughts. . . . [Pope Nicholas V] canonized both their Poems, and com-
> manded them for publicke service in their Churches: mine is for lesser Chappels,
> which are my friends.[106]

The suppliant protesteth too much, but Helen Gardner takes him at his word,
declaring that this is "an elaborate private prayer, rather incongruously cast into
a liturgical form."[107] But that incongruity is part of Donne's strategy: as a catalogue of its audiences suggests, he is creating a poem that is private meditation
intending towards, verging on public worship. Even my brief description demonstrates that, despite all the orderly repetition intrinsic in the litany form, direction
of address careens throughout the poem. It shifts in almost the same way it does
when a congregation sings psalms. Clearly the members of the Trinity are the ratified listeners in the beginning stanzas and at the end, and the repeated versions
of the pleas "deliver us" and "hear us" establish God as the predominant listener
throughout. Although this poem is Reformed enough not to appeal directly for
help to martyrs, prophets, and so on, arguably the stanzas referring to them in the
third person hint that they are listeners, side participants, thus relying on the
porous categories of address at once to incorporate and to distance the Catholic
emphasis on intercession and its forfended status in Protestantism: these figures

are located on the margins of the poem spatially, much as they dwell on the margins of Reformed belief and of Donne's own spirituality.

I do not suggest that Donne literally expected his readers to recite this litany, but both he and they were surely aware that he had adapted a form associated with communal worship, and that type of litany shapes responses to this one. The move to the first person plural in the recurrent phrase "deliver us" and elsewhere encourages us to see other Christians as listeners and quite possibly fellow participants singing its words. In other words, Donne takes a role something like that of the singing man or boy, recalling Herbert's "Obedience." A cognate imbrication of the personal and communal also occurs in Milton's Nativity Ode, discussed in Chapter 3.

Citing "A Litanie" and Herbert's "Prayer" among many other instances, A. B. Chambers rightly demonstrates how religious poets of the seventeenth century often incorporate and adapt liturgical forms.[108] Their motives in so doing, I am suggesting, are more polemical than Chambers acknowledges. In "A Litanie," Donne implicitly but powerfully supports the attempt, common in many devotional texts and, as it were, among their political pit crew, to finesse debates about the relative worth of private devotion and public worship, arguments in which participants often not only diminish but discredit one or the other. Less polemically but no less powerfully, this poem itself bridges the two types of devotion in several respects: by adapting for partly private contemplation a genre of public worship, by turning the fruits of that contemplation into a text analogous to those used publicly, and, again, by implicitly suggesting that the individual speaker could provide an exemplum.

Having multiple addresses is no less significant in pastoral than in love and devotional poetry, but since my opening discussion of the woodcut for Spenser's April eclogue focused on that issue, a brief discussion can suffice here. Address is central to the workings of pastoral, as Paul Alpers has demonstrated in his magisterial book on that mode.[109] In particular, like the soliloquies of drama and the poetry embedded in romances, pastoral poems are often overheard by eavesdroppers or bystanders. The world of nature, it transpires, is no more given to privacy than the world of the Elizabethan or Jacobean house. Songs delivered in the absence of the beloved may still envision her as a side participant; as in the instance of the April eclogue, a shepherd who was originally an auditor may become an animator by repeating the poem to a different audience. Overt in the structure of many pastorals, the dialogic propensities of the genre are manifest as well in the way a poem recited by a single shepherd may be the product or subject of a conversation among shepherds, as is again the case in the April eclogue. The multiplicity of diegetic audiences in many pastorals is mimed by a similar nondiegetic pattern: Alpers's important article "Pastoral and the Domain of Lyric in Spenser's *Shepheardes Calender*" argues persuasively that whereas on the one hand pastoral allowed a degree of autonomy because Spenser's primary audience was not the monarch or the court, on the other he was not unaware of the traditional poetic role of counselor to a prince.[110]

As Alpers's essay reminds us, if writing of love and religion complicate the evocation of audiences in intriguing ways, so too does another distinctive practice of early modern England, seeking patronage. In particular, the poetry of patronage, like love poetry, often hides its sycophancy by turning its principal audience into side participants. "To Penshurst" (a poem whose classification as lyric is not unproblematical) praises the house, not its owners, thus complimenting the Sidneys lavishly while pretending, in that and other ways, to exemplify the moderation it advocates. Similarly, whether or not, as some critics have claimed, Aemelia Lanyer's "Description of Cooke-ham" deflects to a tree a kiss ideally meant for the "Mistris of that Place" (11), the poem indubitably deflects address; whereas some passages speak directly to the Countess of Cumberland and her daughter, in many others the second person pronoun refers to the house, but with the clear implication that its noble inhabitants are bystanders. If Lanyer turns away from them and towards the edifice, she too, like other poets I have examined, clearly is looking over her shoulder. This is a soliloquy meant to be overheard. Indeed, the fact that the referents of the second and third person pronoun in the concluding section are, at least initially, confusing enacts the way the text earlier conflated and confounded its audiences:

> This last farewell to *Cooke-ham* here I give,
> When I am dead *thy* name in this may live,
> Wherein I have perform'd *her* noble hest,
> Whose virtues lodge in my unworthy breast
>     (205–208; emphasis added to pronouns)[111]

Similarly, as its title suggests, in "To his Verses" Herrick addresses his poetry itself directly. Yet, as any sociologist of dinner table dynamics will attest, parents all too often speak to side participants, especially their spouses, in the guise of talking to children; and in this case Herrick clearly envisions his desired patrons, the potential "fost'ring fathers" (13) to his verse, as bystanders.

Different though the genres and texts examined above may be, certain patterns and strategies recur. As the rhetorical treatises recommend, shifting from one audience to another is often associated with deflection and concealment, particularly the attempt to avert guilt. And audiences are not only invoked and incorporated but also thematized; thus many poems, notably Herbert's "Collar" and Wyatt's "My lute, awake!", analyze the dynamic between speaker and listener, or its absence.[112] Indeed, absence is often relevant, and if lyric is typically preoccupied with loss, in many instances, such as Herrick's "To his Verses," the presence of audiences is an antidote, whether wholly curative or not, to emptiness. In other words, the recuperative motives that Jonathan Culler and others have associated with prosopopoeia in particular also impel other types of lyric address.[113]

—ৎ ৎ—

We have just seen how the genres and other potentialities of early modern English poetry create a range of positions and functions for the audience. How are those conditions relevant to the function most often—and most uncritically—attributed to these and other lyrics, voiceability, the most straightforward version of the mirrors on which this chapter opened? In discussing this subject, critics of both early modern versions of the genre and its realizations in other cultures too often subscribe exclusively to one of a small group of paradigms. Most prevalent, of course, is the concept of an identificatory voiceability, which provides a version of the role of animator as described by the discourse analysts. Characteristically, Steven Winspur asserts that "it is the very function of lyric to create and sustain this blending of audience and utterer in the formal patterns of a text"; and theories of dramatic monologue, notably the powerful work of Ralph W. Rader, sometimes contrast it with lyric on precisely the issue of voiceability.[114] One of the most distinguished and determined proponents of this theory, Helen Vendler, encapsulates it in the affirmation that "because lyric is intended to be voiceable by anyone reading it, in its normative form it deliberately strips away most social specification. . . . One is to utter [secular lyrics and other 'private' poems] as one's own words, not the words of another."[115] Despite the verb "utter," this theory does not, of course, assume literal reading aloud but rather a merging of subjectivities that can aptly be troped as ventriloquism or, to return to my original architectural and sculptural examples, as a glass wall that confounds inside and outside or a mirror that merges author and viewer. (Might recent scientific discoveries about mirror neurons, which function as though a spectator is actually performing the actions she is merely watching [someone observing another person eating will have the physiological responses of eating] support the argument that Vendler's process does occur on occasion?[116]) But I maintain that on the whole heteroglossia is a more apt model than ventriloquism for the relationship of audience to text: identificatory voicing is only one of several alternative positions readers may assume, and it is often an avenue towards, not simply an alternative to, those different roles.

The recent interest in the social and cultural determinants of lyric utterances has in fact drawn attention to a range of alternative models that rely on diverse theoretical paradigms and ideological investments. Arthur F. Marotti's pioneering work on coterie readers, developed by many subsequent scholars, posits not a generalized audience who would inevitably identify and, in effect, recite back a poem but rather a group of listeners with more specific agendas and interests, who on occasion expressed them by writing answer poems or changing a text they had copied into a commonplace book.[117] Neither precludes the possibility that such readers would also voice the poem when reading it, but both practices render absolute, uncritical identification with the speaker less likely. Moreover, copying yet altering a text at once literalizes and materializes voiceability while at the same time radically redefining it from, as it were, homophony to polyphony. Happily, the second-generation feminism that replaces laments for the silencing of women with discovery of an often limited but nonetheless present agency has also encouraged gendered descriptions of lyric audiences that emphasize active participation; for instance, locating love poetry within the dynamic practices of courtship, Ilona Bell argues that the responses of nondiegetic audiences to such lyrics are often mirrored by hints of responsive addressees within the poems themselves.[118]

Drawing on the work of linguists, including, on occasion, the discourse analysts, other critics have pioneered different but compatible descriptions of the responsiveness that they too consider characteristic of lyric. David Schalkwyk, who emphasizes communalities rather than contrasts between dramatic and lyric registers, advocates studying what he terms the "embeddedness" of lyric; he shows, for example, how the use of speech act performatives implies social interaction even when the addressee is not clearly specified, as in Shakespeare's sonnets.[119] Although she focuses primarily on drama and on letters, Lynne Magnusson's insistence on a type of social interaction that anticipates a reply is germane to lyric as well.[120]

To what extent, then, do the audiences of early modern lyric engage in identificatory voicing? Many transhistorical and transcultural characteristics associated with lyric support that paradigm; but I argue that such voicing is often limited and sometimes undermined. To begin with, the seductiveness of many lyric poems, like so many other forms of seduction, invites unthinking involvement: one hardly imagines the victims of the sirens arriving on their island with a checklist of criticisms of the song. Remembering Northrop Frye's emphasis on the sound effects of the genre that he associates with "babble" (275–278) and Andrew Welsh's cogent analysis of its connections to chant invites us to adduce anthropological studies of the sound effects of ritual; in particular, Richard Schechner's suggestion that repetitive rhythms create arousal and even ecstasy neurologically implies that comparable responses to poetry are more likely to involve enthusiastic identification with its speaking voice than critique.[121] Mark W. Booth's contention that the audience of song in effect merges with the singer, an assertion often though not invariably true, demonstrates ways identification may occur in lyrics that are literally sung or resemble song especially closely.[122]

The generic palette, conditions of production, and ecclesiastical practices all further encouraged identificatory voicing in the early modern period in particular. In three forms of poetry especially prevalent in the Renaissance, the poet models animating for the reader: pastoral involves sophisticated writers taking the voice of a shepherd, who then may well repeat the words of another shepherd; sonneteers, even more than most other poets, are conscious of their progenitors in their form; and devotional poetry is sometimes seen as voicing the words of God. Furthermore, as Harold Love reminds us, many texts were read aloud, literally voiced, in colleges and universities.[123] Devotional practices are yet again germane, since choral singing, like ritualistic recitals of a previously established text, encourage merging one's own voice with those of others.

Yet identificatory voicing needs, as it were, to be queered in ways that acknowledge the other positionalities it competes with and generates; this reinterpretation creates a revisionist model for early modern lyric that has implications for the poetry of other eras as well. To begin with, as my analysis of congregational singing suggests, identificatory voicing may be temporary. A reader may identify with the speaker completely for part but not all of a specific reading, though a rupture in that identification is less likely when a poem is close to those analogues to lyric—chant and magical incantation. Alternatively and more frequently, she may identify throughout an initial reading but, troubled by the poem on reflection, may assume a more distinct and critical stance on subsequent readings. The very brevity of lyric renders the process of reviewing the poem, studied by narratologists in relation to much longer texts, highly likely. That process may sometimes intensify identification—Stephen Owen compares returning to a poem with repeating the steps of a dance in a way that binds one to it—but I will demonstrate that this version of iterative performance can and often does instead facilitate distancing.[124] Shifts during the process of reading may be effected grammatically as well, especially since the second person pronoun, a powerful recruiter in the ways William Waters has traced so cogently in *Poetry's Touch*, often does not appear until relatively late in a lyric; and when it does it may not only interpellate but re-interpellate.

Thus in lyrics like Vaughan's "World" (I) or "Waterfall," the reader well may start by merging his subjectivity with that of the speaker and voicing his words; but in "World," unlike "Waterfall," as the poem progresses, the evocation and monition of wandering sinners provides a subsequent positionality that may well encourage a shift in identification. Responding sympathetically to an elegiac opening, a reader might well participate in identificatory voicing when beginning to read "The Nymph Complaining for the Death of her Fawn," only to distance her- or himself—as it were, inserting quotation marks in more senses than one—when voicing subsequent passages that hint that the speaker might be not only vulnerable but also culpable.

Similarly, an audience may initially identify with the speaker in Wyatt's "Whoso list to hunt," especially since the opening word defines the addressee in the vaguest terms, but as the poem progresses may become increasingly identified with that addressee. Moreover, whereas Vendler claims that identificatory voicing trumps specific social and cultural positionalities, surely a female reader may well identify more with the deer than the frustrated hunter. Ilona Bell comments acutely on the distanced irony with which a female reader might voice a male-authored love poem, thus introducing yet another version of dialogue.[125] Yet the extent to which a given reader will identify with one component of her status and rank, or identify with it more than with another component, is by no means obvious; and in cataloguing interacting coordinates of subjectivity, literary and cultural critics need to encompass not only the three commonly cited traits—race, class, and gender—but also such issues as age and geographical region.

One should recall as well that in Wyatt's lyric the speaker is animator of the deer's words, which the deer may in turn be displaying for Caesar, thus in turn assuming the role of animator or that of ambassador, the distinction between those possibilities depending in part on whether the reader envisions the final line of the sonnet, "And wylde for to hold though I seme tame," as that hind's addition to Caesar's message. In this and other instances, the heteroglossia so common in early modern and other lyrics clearly complicates straightforward identificatory voicing.

As identificatory voicing may be temporary, it may also be delimited, even ironized. The performance of the psalms signals yet another qualification to the voiceability of lyric, the need to separate repetition from endorsement of sentiments and identification with their speaker, an issue we will also encounter in

Shakespeare's Sonnet 35. The categories of the discourse analysts are again useful here, reminding us that someone who takes on an ambassadorial role, for example, may supplement a message with his own comments or, more subtly, deliver it in a way that implicitly comments on it. Pace Roland Greene's contrast between fictional and ritualistic modes, iterability does not necessarily assume a unified and constant relationship to what is being repeated.[126] Consider the range of identificatory possibilities for a male reciting one of Sappho's lyrics at a Greek symposium.[127]

Moreover, many of the texts discussed in this chapter would encourage readers who did voice them to do so with some measure of ironizing distance, either throughout or at some junctures. Frye's initially unsettling connection between lyric and irony usefully glosses this process, though he deploys it quite differently.[128] The voicing of the April eclogue might well be complicated, but not precluded, by political reservations about the queen or the frustrations of a disappointed courtier. As that text also demonstrates, if pastoral's Chinese box effect of people voicing words voiced by others can encourage identificatory voicing, the self-conscious performativity of the mode also suggested by those boxes within boxes can in turn encourage distance. Voiceability is further complicated in the many poems, notably religious and love lyrics, whose speaker, troubled by a divided subjectivity, in effect becomes an audience to a side of himself, often a side he condemns. Whereas a reader could identify with and in effect voice all parts in a psychodrama, it would also be possible, especially on later readings, to identify more with one voice than another. In short, whereas Marshall Brown's revisionist claim that skeptical distancing is not only a potentiality but the norm of lyric is a somewhat hyperbolic corrective, these examples remind us how a range of conditions, varying from one culture to another, can on occasion produce exactly the response Brown traces.[129]

If the material conditions of production encouraged identificatory voicing in the ways noted above, from another perspective they also further abetted and modeled this type of delimited voiceability. As noted, many texts were read aloud, literally voiced, in colleges and universities. But much as a reader copying a text into a commonplace book might change it, given the association of the Inns of Court with satire, can we assume that voicing by readers there was always straightforward, as opposed to ironic or otherwise transgressive? In other words, voiceability, like that cognate mode of lyric iterability the refrain, is often in fact repetition-with-a-difference. One might usefully compare the psychological version of repetition-with-a-difference, the game Freud labels *fort-da*, which not coincidentally aims to achieve mastery and revenge.[130] Or, to put it another way, voiceability is often rhyme, or even slant rhyme.

I am arguing, then, first, that the degree of voicing may vary from one reading to the next or within the same reading; second, that it may not involve total, uncritical identification with the speaker; and finally, that it coexists with and helps to create alternative positions for the audience, positions whose shifts often themselves produce important meanings. One of the most significant of these alternatives to voicing, the adoption of the position of addressee, I have already traced in detail in several texts above, in so doing noting William Waters's cogent arguments in *Poetry's Touch* about the forcefulness the second person pronoun may carry with it. Early modern literature offers a host of other instances of this type of compelling second person pronoun. For example, when Shakespeare's Sonnet 73 ("That time of year thou mayst in me behold") repeatedly uses the second person in connection with verbs of looking or observing, it connects the external reader beholding the text and the diegetic lover beholding its speaker. Similarly, to return to the opening of Spenser's *Amoretti*, when a woman—or, indeed, a man—reading a copy of the volume in which the work appears encounters the introductory poem in which the lady is represented as holding the book, that nondiegetic audience is clearly encouraged to identify with the diegetic one. Opening a poem on a reference to reading, a pattern Wendy Wall traces from the different but cognate perspective of the consciousness of production and circulation thus reflected, fosters that type of identification, and many poets deployed the device.[131] Compare, too, Donne's "Funerall," in which the diegetic audience coming to observe and shroud the dead body is in a position analogous to that of the reader coming to observe the text; this need not prevent identificatory voicing, but it does complicate it by offering an alternative subject position. And it is no accident that the instance from "The Funerall" involves the opening of Donne's lyric: much as the first day of a class profoundly shapes the relationship of teacher and student, so the beginning of a poem is especially potent in defining the position of an audience (though often it is easier to revise an audience's position during the first or subsequent reading than to rewrite the implicit contracts established at the beginning of a course). Hence opening a poem on one of the speech acts involving instruction or command—the line quoted above, "Mark you the floore?" from Herbert's "The Church-floore" (1), for example, or Donne's "Marke but this flea" ("The Flea," 1)—can readily interpellate the nondiegetic reader into the position of observer, at least temporarily, in lieu of encouraging identificatory voicing.[132]

This is not to say, of course, that readers always identify with the figure evoked through a second person pronoun: if any proof beyond that supplied by common sense is needed, it is readily provided by the many poems of the period addressed to God. But on this issue, too, a spectrum is a more useful heuristic instrument than a polar division between identification and its absence, and in some instances the movement between identification and separation is itself intriguing. Witness Herrick's "To Robin Red-brest," which is more complex in this and other regards than a cursory reading might suggest.[133] Anticipating his own death, Herrick asks the bird to cover him with leaves and sing his dirge: "For Epitaph, in Foliage, next write this, / *Here, here the Tomb of Robin Herrick is*" (5–6).[134] The proximal deictics in the lines quoted above establish the spatial contiguity of the bird and the poet and also achieve a cognate temporal contiguity, making the grave and the moment of the poet's death present. Intending in many of his other poems to blur the boundary between the natural and the human world (perhaps because of his anxieties about the political and sexual tensions in the latter), Herrick here proceeds to turn contiguity into virtual identity through many techniques; for example, the bird is the ratified listener who is directly addressed in the final lines, but that couplet enjoins that creature to switch positions with its creator and write the words itself.

Given the fact that few of Herrick's audience will consider themselves and the addressee birds of a feather, surely most readers are likely to voice the poem instead; alternatively, or in addition, the concluding inscription interpellates us into the position of its reader, the perusal of the inscription synecdochically representing a detached, observatory stance towards the whole lyric. On yet another level, however, the poet is implicitly asking his human audience to respond much as he wishes the bird to do—to be kind, to memorialize him. Arguably the act of voicing the poem is an analogue to what the bird does; and hence when the reader accepts the invitation "Sing thou my Dirge" (4), the lyric not only invites but becomes the dirge in question. Thus, in a limited but not insignificant way, we can identify with the position evoked by the second person pronoun; yet again the reader is offered multiple and overlapping roles.

As this poem and many of my previous analyses illustrate, in addition to and often in lieu of the positions of speaker and addressee, nondiegetic readers may adopt the role of an observer, distanced from rather than identifying with the first and second person pronouns within the lyric. Third person titles like those in Jonson's Charis sequence enable and even encourage this stance, in so doing activating the doubts about even "good" lyric that some readers surely shared with the authors of those poems.[135] Herrick's "To Robin Red-brest" demonstrates one of several ways this observer function may work: given the elegiac impetus that so often drives lyric, it is not surprising that a number of poems end on an inscription, an example of the performed "product" studied in my chapter on immediacy and distance, hence interpellating the reader of the poem as the reader of its epigraph as well. And even a lyric that does not end by representing an inscription may well achieve closure through a comparably detached and aphoristic saying, such as the concluding line of Wyatt's "Ffarewell, Love, and all thy lawes for ever": "Me lusteth no lenger rotten boughes to clyme" (14).[136]

More often, however, the position of observer involves making ethical judgments on the lyric, its speaker, and its poet. Because of the guilt widely associated with lyric, only partly obviated by that Good Girl–Bad Girl divide between versions of the mode, early modern texts encourage these judgments. (This is not to say that this effect is unique to early modern poetry, of course; many confessional poems of the twentieth century, for example, encourage an amalgamation of empathy and evaluation, while a Romantic lyric like the one examined above, Wordsworth's "Lines Written a Few Miles Above Tintern Abbey," scripts the grounds for judgment, inviting the reader to assume the position of judge.) Jonson's Charis sequence, as well as this example from Wordsworth, recall the frequency with which the position of observer is, or in the course of the poem becomes, contiguous to, or even identical to, that of the poet, who may criticize his own discourse in ways that invite the reader to do the same. Alternatively, the speaker may assume the role of observer even more directly, as a previously uncouth and now much more knowing swain does at the end of "Lycidas." In instances like these, identificatory voicing can overlap with judgment.

A sibling to the role of moral or ethical critic, the stance of aesthetic critic, is a no less significant option for early modern readers. The fact that a reader who might voice a poem may also, or instead, study its formal and other literary strategies—its meter, how it changes its source, its responses to generic conventions, and so on—may seem too obvious to require attention; but the ways such examinations interact with or substitute for voiceability have not been adequately analyzed, perhaps because many critics, impelled by a drive to locate prelapsarian purity in this mode, still attempt to focus on naïve, not sentimental, responses to it. In point of fact, the audience of a lyric frequently examines it as an artifact, a mode of reading that is more likely to occur after the first contact with the text but by no means impossible on that initial encounter, and certain textual strategies common in early modern poetry encourage the reader to adopt this role. Indeed, by thematizing the position of observer and deploying obtrusive formal devices such as the numbers that are sometimes printed on correlative verse, many texts compromise any attempt to separate an initial, "pure" reading from the later sentimental ones. Perhaps the most extreme version occurs in the *Vita nuova*, where sonnets are analyzed formally in some detail, and the English tradition itself offers many analogues, especially in the paratextual materials so often associated with lyrics. The extensive notes in Spenser's *Shepheardes Calender* urge us to study the poems. (Because this paratextual exposition may be written by Spenser himself, however, once again a position that seems antithetical to identificatory voicing may in fact incorporate it.) Similarly, the text may incorporate aesthetic judgments directly, as George Gascoigne does when he comments on the lyrics incorporated within his *Hundreth Sundrie Flowres,* or encourage them by discussing the sources and structure of the poem in the third person, as Thomas Watson does in his headnotes. When the use of superscript numbers draws attention to the workings of correlative verse, the reader is encouraged to approach the text as a student of poetry.

While the literature of other periods certainly sometimes generates this aesthetic or academic observation, several circumstances made this especially the case in early modern England. Many readers were themselves amateur poets and hence as likely to identify with the formal challenges of crafting a poem as with the sentiments within it. Contemporary debates about quantitative meter alerted many sixteenth-century readers to the prosodic choices of the poet at hand. Scribal practices allowed readers to see and compare several versions of a text, demonstrating that, besides considering how reactions would vary between successive encounters with the same poem, we should acknowledge that they might shift in response to a new version of a text one had previously read.

In short, the original audiences of early modern lyric, like their counterparts today, no doubt participated unreservedly in identificatory voicing on occasion; but in other instances they did so temporarily or ironically or not at all. The subject matter of these poems and their conditions of production both complicated and in some circumstances obviated voicing. And early modern culture encouraged alternative positionalities, especially those involving ethical and aesthetic judgment. These patterns, then, again demonstrate my contentions about the lability of early modern audiences. And the issue of identificatory voicing also substantiates and develops issues analyzed earlier in this book. Most obviously, the types of voicing posited here involve further versions of turning. They also involve an intensification of the anxieties associated with reading and writing lyric: the reader may move from complicity in, say, the aggression of a farewell poem to a critique of it, and the author may be uneasily aware that her audience is likely to shift from identification to criticism.

⸺ ᥐ ᥐ ⸺

A textbook example of the interrelated questions I have been tracing—the variety and motility of the positions the audience of lyric may assume, the imbrication of the roles of audience and speaker, the variations on and alternatives to voiceability, and the relationship of all these patterns to the central issues in the text—Shakespeare's thirty-fifth sonnet thus encapsulates the problems and theses pursued throughout this chapter. Above all, it again demonstrates that changes in direction of address often enact and thematize issues at the core of an early modern lyric.

This sonnet enacts a process in which the speaker starts by excusing the addressee ("No more be griev'd at that which thou hast done" [1]), then moves to the realization that the act of excusing is itself culpable, that he has caught the addressee's case of a sensual fault. If among the poem's purposes is establishing a clear divide between the guilty party who speaks and the magisterial magistrate who observes and judges, its praxis is the dissolution of that divide: "Such civil war is in my love and hate, / That I an accessary needs must be" (12–13). Once again, a poem that directly addresses the question of blurred subject positions itself effects their dissolution in the relationship of author and nondiegetic audience.

Notice, first, how the opening line—"No more be griev'd at that which thou hast done"—urges readers into not one but several different roles. The very vagueness of the line may permit and even encourage us to voice the poem, yet readers are held back from that option, instead encouraged to see ourselves as eavesdroppers, by a sense of entering *in medias res* ("*No* more be grieved"; italics inserted) a situation we but imperfectly understand. And both reactions are intensified, not resolved, by the comparably vague reference to the "sensual fault" (9) later on. These types of concealment resonate with the gloss that Colin Burrow assigns to "stain" (3) in his splendid edition, "obscure."[137] But if readers are both drawn into and distanced from the role of animator, the second person address, as immediate and intense as some of Celan's openings, may lead us to see ourselves as the accused party, the ratified listener. Yet, as Paul Alpers points out in one of the few acute readings this curiously neglected sonnet has received, the images in the first quatrain sometimes lose touch with the auditor; to the extent that he is right (I would argue that the intensification of the criticism gestures towards some continuing awareness of the principal addressee), the nondiegetic reader's identification with the accused is likely to weaken.[138]

As the poem progresses, its role as metalyric intensifies. In particular, as a lyric about the dangers of speaking lyric excuses, it both seduces us into and warns us against identificatory voicing. The speaker watches himself making excuses: "All men make faults and even I in this" (5). Such confessions, as noted earlier, invite us to assume the more distanced role of judge—a position that both discourages voicing and encourages it inasmuch as the speaker himself is adopting the role of judge as well as that of plaintiff and defendant.[139] And this distancing may intensify on subsequent readings as one meditates on the price the speaker pays for his excuses and the possibility that his confessions are in fact lies to himself or his reader or both. Yet the poem is generalized enough to encourage identification even or especially with the corrupt and corrupting process of making excuses; indeed, as its tropes of disease suggest, other people's cases of confessing may prove contagious. At the same time, much as the poem enacts the speaker's impulse to identify with the accused (notice how the auditory homology in "sensual fault" and "sense" [9] suggests a homology between accuser and accused), so too the reader may continue to see himself as addressee. Thus yet again shifts in position, especially those associated with direction of address, enact and express meanings at the core of the lyric.

As striking an instance of anticlosural closure as the conclusion of *Henry V*, the final four lines intensify the predilections I have been tracing: "And 'gainst myself a lawful plea commence. / Such civil war is in my love and hate, / That I an accessory needs must be / To that sweet thief which sourly robs from me." Notice that formally this ending both stages the epigrammatic certainties associated with closural couplets and breaks down that sense of control. On the one hand, the epigrammatic antitheses of the final line gesture towards decisiveness and closure; on the other hand, at the same time, the dissolution of the usual binary couplet into a curious three-line statement enacts the dissolution of such certainties. This resolution is about the inability to achieve resolution and especially the inability to distinguish oneself from the sweet thief through clear-cut binary moral judgments. If this pull between moral resolution and amoral or even immoral confusion is enacted formally, it is also staged in two ways of reading the lines. One could see them as a summary of the eleven preceding lines, in effect placing a period after "commence" (11). Or if, as other editors do, one posits a colon at this point, the lines become not a detached summary but yet another version of the illicitly lawful pleas that constitute—and corrupt—the rest of the poem. From this perspective, "commence" emphasizes not closure but the anticlosural continuation of a series of such pleas, a continuation flagged by the workings of enjambment, and lines 12–14 create an ending as abrupt and indeterminate as the final shot in "The Four Hundred Blows" and many other New Wave films. All this is relevant to voiceability in that the multiple interpretive possibilities represent positions the reader may assume, becoming an accessory to the speaker by voicing the excuses, or a judge of that excusing who distances herself from its practitioner, or a version of the sweet thief. Thus we, like the speaker, change roles rapidly, suborned and seduced into the reflections and refractions that constitute this poem no less than the sculptural and architectural creations on which this chapter opened.

# CHAPTER 3

# The Craft of Pygmalion

## *Immediacy and Distancing*

Poetry, Paul Celan declares, is a handshake.[1] Or, following William Waters's acute and suggestively revisionist translation of this poet who so often resists translation, the phrase becomes a "pressing of hands," an expression that, Waters demonstrates, deploys the double meanings of the German *"Handwerk"* to suggest both craft and the actions of literal human hands.[2] "Handshake" gestures towards the honesty and immediacy so commonly attributed to lyric. Waters's translation implies several sources and symptoms of that immediacy: a lack of intermediaries (no third hand intervenes in the pressing), an expression of what is directly apprehended (in this case tactilely experienced), an emphasis on the present and on presence (what better instance of the sense of touch so often associated with lyric than the meeting of hands).[3]

Yet in turning to a lyric that might at first appear to be a textbook example of everything Celan's observation evokes, whichever way it is translated, one encounters a sleight—and a slighting—of hand. Indebted to the so-called ugly beauty tradition, the libertine defiance of the opening stanza is immediate in many respects:

> I can love both faire and browne,
> Her whom abundance melts, and her whom want betraies,
> Her who loves lonenesse best, and her who maskes and plaies,
> Her whom the country form'd, and whom the town,
> Her who believes, and her who tries,
> Her who still weepes with spungie eyes,

And her who is dry corke, and never cries;
I can love her, and her, and you and you,
I can love any, so she be not true.

("The Indifferent," 1–9)[4]

Donne's characteristic creation of a distinctive voice calls up a sense of the speaker's presence, and that figure eschews temporal shifts by addressing the reader in the present about attitudes that appear unchanging. The presence of an audience is established as clearly as that of the speaker: the deixis that, as many students of lyric have acknowledged, so often encourages immediacy is here literalized, inasmuch as "her, and her, and you and you" (8) achieves signification through an act of gesturing or pointing. A poem that glorifies in emotional distance insists in another sense on an immediate relationship with its readers, both the internal audience and other women and men as well.

The second stanza continues these types of immediacy. But Donne is the master of endings that turn the poem and in so doing often turn on and against the addressee.[5] In the third strophe he engineers a different but related type of reversal:

Venus heard me sigh this song,
And by Love's sweetest Part, Variety, she swore,
She heard not this till now; and't should be so no more.
She went, examin'd, and return'd ere long,
And said, alas, Some two or three
Poore Heretiques in love there bee,
Which thinke to stablish dangerous constancie.
But I have told them, since you will be true,
You shall be true to them, who'are false to you.

(19–27)

Pace Carew, the stanza reminds us that Donne does not always exile the gods and goddesses of earlier poetry; here, however, the introduction of Venus is characteristic, both in the fact that it startles the reader and in its insistence that Venus, rather than occupying a more elevated realm, shares the world and the values of the speaker. Indeed, whereas he seems to cede authority to her, she in fact serves his purposes.

But if it sustains the amoral values introduced earlier, the conclusion, eschewing any aesthetic temptation of its own towards "dangerous constancie" (25), involves a number of abrupt shifts in the immediacy the text had so firmly established. The reader is pulled from the present tense commonly associated with lyric to not one but two alternative time sequences. The poem removes the observations in the first two stanzas from the lyric present, establishing them instead as a song performed on a particular occasion; moreover, the third stanza contrasts the sequential events about Venus being narrated, what narratologists call story time, and the discourse time in which they are being told. Venus's own words, though enlivened by direct discourse, also lack the immediacy we encountered, or thought we were encountering, in the first eighteen lines of the poem: they are reported as occurring on a specific occasion in the past, and they themselves incorporate the reportage of indirect discourse, thus mirroring the changed status of the opening two stanzas. John Carey acutely asserts that Donne typically writes of "unique instances," and one might add that this poem supports his point precisely by rejecting the alternative temporality on which it opens.[6] To be sure, the deictic in "sigh this song" (19) re-creates some of the immediacy at the beginning of the poem—Donne is not constant even in his literary inconstancy—and arguably the intensity associated with singing contributes to that recovery as well. Yet the primary effect of those three words is to distance the opening stanzas by removing them from their apparent status of speech to that of an aesthetic performance in several senses of that noun.[7] Conversely, Venus's location in the world of myth emphasizes fictiveness at the same time that her presence is associated with the apparent move from the fictiveness of the previous song to a more quotidian world.

In these and so many other respects, then, Donne's poem demonstrates the central arguments that will be pursued in this chapter. What is most characteristic of lyric in the early modern period, I maintain, is not the sense of immediacy that its proximal deictics, like a number of other devices, evoke but rather the coexistence of those techniques suggesting immediacy and those creating forms of distance. And it is precisely the presence, and on occasion the interaction, of those two types of technique that impels important attributes of this mode, such as how it is an event and why lyric, that domain of the intangible and ephemeral, is represented as a product in the sense of something produced, or in the sense of a literal, tangible object, or both. That interaction is often relevant as well to the agendas of a given poem, which may thematize and problematize it.

Numerous critics, however, continue to posit immediacy as normative, the default position for early modern lyric and its counterparts in other eras, and distancing devices as secondary or even aberrant; others, especially poststructuralists, assume that presence is the illusion that the text tries to maintain, while representation is the dirty secret that it tries to conceal, the aesthetic principle that dare not speak its name. However powerful demonstrations of lyric immediacy have been, they have typically unbalanced interpretations of the mode by neglecting the interaction in question; however persuasive theorized denials of presence in certain senses have been, they have too often dismissed as a mere ploy its survival as a poetic effect. This chapter attempts to calibrate the balances by instead looking more closely at the too often neglected ways the lyric poetry of the English Renaissance creates the impression of various forms of distance, and by tracing their relationship to the creation of forms of immediacy or apparent immediacy. Thus it directs its attention primarily to strategies for creating those impressions rather than to the extensive philosophical debates about presence, though the latter inevitably figure in my analyses at certain points.

My argument is, in short, revisionist in its rejection of several alternative approaches to the effects of immediacy in early modern lyric poetry (and thus, too, it adumbrates—though it does not address—similar challenges to the ways lyric texts of other periods have been read). Critics should not regard those effects as the norm for lyric during the English Renaissance and their reverse as what linguists call the marked case. Nor should we simply dismiss all such impressions of presence as mere ruses; my aim is not to substitute a privileging of distancing devices for the widespread privileging of those that suggest the opposite.[8] Despite the contemporary fascination with hybridity, neither do I posit a hybrid relationship between immediacy and its opposite as normative. The dynamics in question are too various to support any of those agendas. Instead this chapter develops a series of templates for the ways lyric avoids or modulates the very impression of immediacy that it also is concerned to establish, typically tempering or contrasting effects of presence with impressions of distance, and then traces the consequences of those practices.

⸺ ◦, ◦ ⸺

Studying immediacy and distance in early modern lyric poses a number of methodological problems, addressed in this section. The first step in both analyzing and avoiding common misreadings of all these issues is clarifying the terms in question, in the process explaining how the rest of the chapter will deploy them. Immediacy and distance assume a wide range of forms, including some that blur the line between them, while in other instances a single technique, such as a refrain, may generate both members of the pair. These varied forms can fruitfully be scrutinized as effects without definitively resolving the theoretical issues they raise, which is necessarily the task of a different book; but a resolution of the methodological challenges of discussing immediacy and distance does demand analyzing the investments both early modern writers and critics in our own day have brought to those challenges.

My use of "forms" in the preceding paragraph indicates a distinction between my own and some other approaches to these issues: not only may a given version of immediacy engage in an irenic dialogue or a heated argument or both with a type of distancing, so too multiple versions of each apparent pole typically interact with each other. The apparent denial of presence in one form, such as a reminder of fictiveness, does not only preclude but may even encourage its assertion in another form. Jonathan Bate's insistence that the early modern recognition of the problematical relationship between *res* and *verba* did not entail the poststructuralist radical distrust of *res* is very much to the point (indeed, I emphasize below that poems that acknowledge their own status as representations nonetheless may culminate on a proffered material product).[9]

Not the least slippery of the many fraught concepts associated with lyric, immediacy may be suggested in lyric through several effects, in particular, the sort of tactility suggested by Celan's statement, types of vividness that may or may not involve the other four senses, voice in the senses emphasized by critics of twentieth-century poetry, and the type of rhetorical positioning accomplished by linguistic devices, notably deictics. This chapter approaches the concept of immediacy in terms of those devices and traces versions of all of them.[10] (As this brief summary suggests, I do not propose an equation between presence and realism, a term no less slippery and in most of its senses far less relevant to the early modern lyric; nor do I assume that the impression of immediacy resolves poststructuralist doubts about the linguistic and ontological impediments to presence.)

John Keats's poem, or possibly fragment, beginning "This living hand, now warm and capable" exemplifies the impressions of presence summarized immediately above and demonstrates how they often unite in creating the sense that the poem is speaking directly to the reader. It cries out to be included even in a study of early modern lyric, not only because it is arguably the best single example and examination of those patterns in the language, and thus a useful gloss on their manifestations in the English Renaissance, but also because it will provide a textbook comparison with early modern poems to which I will turn shortly:

This living hand, now warm and capable
Of earnest grasping, would, if it were cold
And in the icy silence of the tomb,
So haunt thy days and chill thy dreaming nights
That thou would wish thy own heart dry of blood,

So in my veins red life might stream again,
And thou be conscience-calm'd. See, here it is—
I hold it towards you.[11]

A poem that thematizes touching, this extraordinary lyric enacts—or attempts to
enact—analogues to tactility in many other ways as well, thus creating a sense of
presence. It invokes other senses besides touch through the synesthesia so characteristic of its author. The physical cold and warmth to which it refers mirror the
subtle shifts between their emotional analogues. The poem moves between implicit threats and reassurances, and this intensity helps to create voice in the
sense of realized subjectivity and hence one version of presence. And the deictics
"This" (1) and "here" (6) build yet another version of it. These effects may be further intensified, for, as Lawrence Lipking points out, if readers identify as addressees and imagine the poet's living hand reaching towards them, "most . . .
will strain toward Keats in sympathetic grasping."[12]

At the same time, all these assertions of the immediate are complicated by the
unresolved paradoxes and ambiguities of the conclusion. A number of distinguished critics have commented acutely but not decisively on whether the living
hand is extended as a peace offering or the dead one as a threat; the question of
in what senses, if at all, the hand is present is further troubled by the issue of
whether the addressee is in fact the reader, or a character in a play, or, as critics
formerly assumed, Fanny Brawne.[13] These questions anticipate cognate ones, addressed below, about the shepherdess's speech in Lady Mary Wroth's Song 1.
However one resolves these dilemmas and disagreements in the instance of
Keats's text, a corpse's hand is certainly vividly invoked in the course of the
lyric—and gestures, as it were, towards further complications in discussing and
defining presence. A vividly realized image may be a sign of absence and loss: the
corpse's hand can be present precisely when and because the living hand cannot,
much as the poststructuralists have repeatedly emphasized that words, like other
surrogates, testify to the lack of what they introduce. Moreover, the uncanniness
that Brooke Hopkins incisively traces in the poem can make readers recoil from
the very poem that so intensely invites and enacts touch.[14]

As these lyrics by Donne and Keats demonstrate, putative presence may assume a range of forms, many of them unstable enough to recall the poststructuralist position that apparent presence is a response to and even symptom of loss.
So too does mediation of presence take many shapes. I am defining mediatory elements for the purposes of this chapter as textual strategies that delimit or distance the immediacy of a lyric, typically through a type of intervention or

standing-between—encasing that pressing hand in a glove, as it were. But versions of mediation vary in their structure from a headnote to the introduction of another voice, and in their effects from evading anticipated judgments of the text to showcasing such evaluations. In response to such variety, I focus below primarily on types of distancing that are in some sense part of the text—as it were, immediate to it—such as titles; the many other types involved in the category Gérard Genette analyzes as paratexts, such as title pages and dedicatory epistles, are treated only in passing here, though some of them are discussed elsewhere in this study.[15] Often the strategies I chronicle achieve their ends by introducing an alternative spatial or temporal dimension; they may also remind readers that they are encountering a literary representation of an event rather than participating in it as it unfolds.

Yet certain methods of mediation, however effectively they distance the text in some instances, can heighten an impression of immediacy under other circumstances, or even increase and diminish it simultaneously within the same passage of a poem—thus further complicating the agenda of this section, defining the concepts in question and addressing cognate methodological challenges. Metapoetic allusions to holding the poem as a physical object, for instance, can both intensify and qualify the presentness of lyric. Refrains sometimes strengthen and sometimes lessen the presence of what the stanza evokes. Above all, reminders of representation often qualify immediacy in certain respects while intensifying it in others. Mediating, one may recall, implies bringing about or conveying, and sometimes part of what it effects is a different version of immediacy.

Many methodological challenges in analyzing immediacy and distance are explicated by earlier critical commentaries on these subjects; some of these passages also gesture towards the investments readers in both early modern England and our own era bring to those concepts. To begin with, Renaissance discussions often emphasize the rhetorical roots of immediacy, which for that and other reasons are an important perspective throughout this chapter. Those roots are, however, somewhat tangled by the verbal and conceptual similarities between the concepts of *enargia*, which can roughly be translated as a vividness that makes it possible to see in the mind's eye, and *energia*, which suggests activity or energy.

Describing the workings of *enargia*, Quintilian declares that "vivid illustration, or, as some prefer to call it, representation, is something more than mere clearness, since the latter merely lets itself be seen, whereas the former thrusts itself upon our notice."[16] In the same book, he goes on at some length to discuss how these intense portrayals, created by specified rhetorical figures, move the listener and "[place] a thing vividly before the eye" (VIII.iii.81), and he subse-

quently discusses how "vivid illustration" may appeal to the senses (IX.ii.40). Notice in particular the aggressive agency implied, which recalls my previous analyses of connections between lyric and blocked or imperiled agency in early
modern texts. In Book 3, Chapter 3, Puttenham seconds Quintilian's emphasis
on vigor when he tries to designate *enargia* as appealing only to the ear and *energia* as involving meaning: to the latter he attributes "strong and vertuous opera-
tion . . . efficacie by sence."[17]

Both the focus on an energetic depiction and the concern with its rhetorical
effect on the reader recur when Sidney famously observes, "But truly many of
such writings as come under the banner of unresistible love, if I were a mistress,
would never persuade me they were in love; so coldly they apply fiery speeches,
as men that had rather read lovers' writings . . . than that in truth they feel those
passions, which easily (as I think) may be betrayed by that same forcibleness or
*energia* (as the Greeks call it) of the writer."[18] Whereas "betrayed" could simply
signify "to reveal" in early modern English, it is tempting to wonder whether Sidney's preoccupation with the treacheries of love, of rhetoric, and of their interre-
lationship unwittingly impelled his choice of the term (and no less tempting to
observe that when its more common sense is adduced here, Sidney anticipates
the poststructuralist emphasis on how apparently effective language in fact compromises itself).[19]

In any event, all of these early modern passages explicate how their authors
conceive immediacy: it is produced by vivid descriptions, presented in language
that evokes stereotypically male characteristics, and analyzed in terms of its
rhetorical agenda, that is, in terms of how it is meant to shapes the reader's responses. Most relevant to my purposes, these discussions indicate some reasons
for the seesaw between immediacy and distance posited by this chapter. The efficacy of contrast, a commonplace of rhetorical theory, argues for playing vivid
passages against less intense ones; the hints of aggressive control, or even manip-
ulation, of the reader activate anxieties indisputably common in early modern
England, about the dangerously suasive power of rhetoric, and hence could impel the writer to disown or at least distance its effects (as Sidney arguably does
through the double meaning of "betrayed").

Whereas rhetorical sources and effects remain crucial in modern discussions of
presence, many other perspectives have been explored as well; a few examples chosen from a multitude will demonstrate the range of assumptions many critics bring
to early modern texts, at times importing them from commentaries written about
and more suited to other poetry. Discussions of *Erlebnis*, still powerful despite the
many attacks on them, stress the speaker's consciousness and voice more than the

poem's rhetorical impact on the reader; and in the sense of a realized subjectivity, voice remains a crucial concept, especially in analyses of modern poetry.[20] Committed to emphasizing the figural elements in lyric, especially prosopopoeia and related figures, many other critics attribute presence—or apparent presence—to their handwork. In an influential analysis of apostrophe, Jonathan Culler focuses on its role in producing "a detemporalized space with forms and forces which have pasts and futures but which are addressed as potential presences"—in other words, many of the characteristics of lyric immediacy.[21] Yet observe how "potential" hedges the bets and allies Culler's argument more closely with how Paul de Man and others approach the limitations and even bad faith of such figures. At the same time, the concern for tactile and other forms of vividness expressed by early modern commentators has not been neglected by their counterparts today. In particular, in organizing her brilliant analysis of poetry around the five senses, Susan Stewart draws attention to how presence may be realized on sensory and sensual levels; she also shows how deixis can contribute to such effects.[22]

Other commentators, adopting a range of perspectives, have emphasized that lyric is distant from actual, lived experience (and in so doing, of course, often challenged that category itself). To begin with, treatises by poets may complicate assertions or implications of immediacy presented elsewhere in the same document. While he praises the immediacy created by *energia*, in developing the Greek concept of the poet as maker Sir Philip Sidney also turns to Platonic models; he draws attention to the element of artifice in art, an element redefined, defended, and celebrated when he famously compares the golden world of the poet to that of the First Maker: "Only the poet, disdaining to be tied to any such subjection, lifted up with the vigour of his own invention, doth grow in effect into another nature, in making things either better than nature bringeth forth, or, quite anew, forms such as never were in nature. . . . Her world is brazen, the poets only deliver a golden" (100).[23] Later in the treatise, when defending poesy from the charge of falsehood on the grounds that it does not claim to tell the truth, he rebuts the equation of representation with misrepresentation in the sense of deceit, a point that I have already emphasized and to which I will return. On very different grounds, Wordsworth distances poetry from the here and now, famously defining it in terms of recollected emotion, while Shelley, for all his emphasis on the incarnational force of poetry, also stresses its role in representing something prior and separate from it: "Poetry . . . reproduces all that it represents. . . . Poetry is the record of the best and happiest moments of the happiest and best minds" ("A Defence of Poetry").[24]

The past century has witnessed numerous critical denials and rejections of the several types of immediacy traditionally associated with lyric. Most obviously and most influentially, the deconstructionist attack on the concept of presence, famously spearheaded by the work of Paul de Man, has often included labeling its apparent exemplification by the lyric illusory.[25] Statements like these, however, were preceded by many challenges on other grounds. W. R. Johnson, for example, argued that the "I-You" structures that he finds in the mode establish it as discourse in the sense of "description and deliberation" rather than "unpremeditated warblings."[26] In both theory and practice the Language Poets have condemned the concept of voice in the sense of the realized subjectivity of the speaker; an analogue, often impelled by the putative association between the concept of the individual and capitalism that typically informs Language Poetry as well, may be found in recent studies of the sonnet tradition that eschew the earlier focus on the character of its speakers. The more sophisticated studies of lyric time often at the very least complicate a bald association of that form with the present tense.[27] Supplementing these theorized overviews, a number of powerful recent studies of specific poetic elements, such as titles and other paratexts, have also qualified or queried the immediacy of lyric.[28]

As the relative brevity with which I summarize these and related debates suggests, my primary goal is neither to produce an alternative theoretical position nor to engage at length with previous ones. The focus of this chapter is more rhetorical than ontological in that it focuses on how and why effects of immediacy—and, even more important for my purposes, distance—are produced in a given historical period rather than on the transhistorical potentialities and betrayals of language; and my focus is more on process than teleology in that I show throughout that discouraging or blocking certain versions of immediacy does not preclude and may even encourage its assertion in other senses. The same is true of distancing devices. Above all, I aim to dislodge immediacy as the putative norm for lyric and instead look at its coexistence with, and occasional interaction with, its opposite number.

Nonetheless, poststructuralist and related debates do undergird some of my discussions and the methodological assumptions propelling them. I assume throughout, for example, that texts are representations, and I demonstrate that early modern texts in particular often devote considerable energy to establishing their status as such. But, as I will argue, that does not preclude significant effects of presence nor establish those effects as ploys. As Sidney encourages us to recognize, the poems in question often signal their mediation of what they represent rhetorically, and even address it semantically, potentially obviating the charge of "bad faith."[29] In lieu of concentrating on broader generalizations about all language, I emphasize the varied forms that strategies for establishing presence and distance may assume, and I demonstrate how and why the balances and imbalances of those effects vary significantly and intriguingly from text to text.

Given the impact of poststructuralism on linguistic theory and the impact of the mediating devices I analyze on poetic practice, why are references to presence and the qualities associated with it so frequently—and often so uncritically—adduced in critical discourse? Certain explanations lie in the cultural and psychic work lyric performs. Poets and their readers often turn to poetry, whether in a spirit of nostalgia or of grief, for recuperation, restoration, and reassurance. "In contrasting the rhetoric of warmongering . . . with the exact and creative powers of poetry, the poet assumes that the immediacy of lyric will counter the abstraction of rhetoric and propaganda," Susan Stewart observes.[30] An analogue to the drive she identifies may occur on the level of more personal experience as well: the preface to the collaborative dialogue between two poets, Allen Grossman and Mark Halliday, insists, "Poetry is a principle of power invoked by all of us against our vanishing."[31] Although the authors are talking about poetry in general, given the preoccupation of lyric with loss these observations are especially germane to that mode. Or, to put it another way, since lyric so often confronts death in its many forms, its readers often want it to call back the dead, to make the past an unchanging present. (In this and a number of other respects, pastoral is metalyric.) And given that, as so many of its students and practitioners have claimed, poetry begins and ends in silence, in those frozen deserts of the blank page, one wants it to give voice as clearly and fully as possible.

From another perspective, explored in more detail in Chapter 4, lyric is involved in both scattering and reclaiming, as the founding myth of Orpheus indicates; an emphasis on presence reassuringly emphasizes the latter. Even if Eurydice must return to the dead, even if Orpheus's body is dismembered, the poem itself remains, at least putatively, alive and well and whole. Hence the interlocking drives to associate lyric with the magical, the pure, and the sacred further help to explain critics' resistance to seeing it as mediated: fears that the magical is inherently unsubstantial increase anxieties about presence, while at the same time the drive to recuperate and celebrate the special, even holy, world that lyric can represent intensifies the desire for that presence in its several senses, a desire experienced by an individual writer or critic and realized in the cultural work Theodor Adorno attributes to lyric.[32]

Discussing the concept of performance in relation to cognitive theory, Mary Thomas Crane has powerfully argued that representation and experience are "mutually constitutive"; many texts analyzed in this chapter will support her claim, thus demonstrating why an acknowledgment of representation does not necessarily preclude immediacy.[33] These poems will demonstrate, too, how frequently representation interacts with presence. Another anthropological study offers a useful parallel. In describing a form of ritualistic speaking event practiced by the Weyewa tribe, the anthropologist Joel Kuipers demonstrates that the term they use for it, li'i, suggests, on the one hand, "a message, a mandate, a promise, and a duty" and, on the other, aspects of the immediate performance, such as rhythm.[34] Within many early modern lyrics, as within this Weyewa term, is a juxtaposition of the mandates and promises often established by distancing elements and equally potent forms of immediacy.

The juxtaposition of effects of presence and distance is obviously not unique to the early modern period, but that era's lyrics are shaped by some distinctive reasons for pursuing immediacy, as well as distinctive types of and motivations for qualifying it, a few of which I have already indicated. Those reasons involve the interaction of etiologies and hence again demonstrate the virtues of dovetailing numerous critical approaches; genre, the conditions of production of both literary texts and art, the availability of relevant models, and theology all contribute to the combinations of immediacy and distance in lyrics of the English Renaissance.

Certain genres popular in the period intensified this predilection of lyric: much English Renaissance religious poetry invokes or attempts to embody a scriptural event, while the agenda of songs in masques is often to call forth a presence, the aesthetic analogue to the machinery that literally brought forth nymphs and goddesses. Thus, famously demonstrating the affective intensity of so much devotional poetry, Robert Southwell's "Burning Babe" gives presence to the vision through repeated tactile references to heat; demonstrating both the instrumentality and immediacy masques associate with lyric, at one moment in Thomas Campion's *Lord Hay's Masque* the text explicitly states that trees move in response to a song. As I have already pointed out, rhetorical treatises widely circulated in the Renaissance preached what Southwell and Campion practiced by drawing attention to techniques for making what is evoked immediate. *Demonstratio*, the *Rhetorica ad Herennium* informs us, ensures "that the business seems to be enacted and the subject to pass vividly before our eyes" (IV.lv.68), and in the *Apology for Poetry*, Sidney's advocacy of *energia* promises similar results.[35]

Less familiar but no less important are the period's distinctive approaches to mediating immediacy and to combining an impression and a denial of presence. Most obviously, poets did not regularly attach titles to their work. The dissociation of titling and authoring is neatly reflected in how George Gascoigne talks about poems he pretends were written by someone else: "adding nothing of myne owne, but onely a tytle to every Poeme, wherby the cause of writinge the same maye the more evidently appeare."[36] Moreover, a poet who attempted to affix a title risked the changes to it that scribal practice facilitated. Despite—and precisely because of—many authors' inability to attach a title, the period saw certain cognate practices that filled some of the same functions, such as the lengthy headnotes most memorably used by Thomas Watson.

The increased use of titles during the seventeenth century again demonstrates the importance of registering changes within an era; all-encompassing generalizations about early modern England are among the the unfortunate legacies of second-rate new historicist work, though the first-rate versions cannot be faulted for this. Ben Jonson was one of the earliest poets regularly to assign his own titles; in many poems by Herbert, such as "The Collar" and "The Pearl," the title's contribution is no less central than subtle. If, as many have rightly demonstrated, the growing ability and desire of poets to attach their own titles reflected and contributed to early modern changes in the status of the author, it also contributed to changes in the status of the text by rendering it more distant and more clearly framed as a work of art. But practices of titling have further implications for our own critical practices, warning us against positing a neatly linear historical movement that corresponds to what we want or expect to find—in this instance evidence of shifting conceptions of the author—rather than fully acknowledging the survival and coexistence of competing systems: despite changes in authorship that would apparently encourage authorial assignment of titles, that practice was followed sporadically in the seventeenth century and by no means became universal.[37]

Also located in the early modern period, crucial changes in both the conception and execution of the literal framing of pictures certainly paralleled and arguably influenced the framing of lyrics. During the sixteenth century, as Rayna Kalas demonstrates in her acute study of those artistic practices, the word "frame" shifted from suggesting making something to denoting enclosing it, though both meanings coexisted for some time. Inasmuch as that process of construction could literally suggest hands-on work, the word itself contains the paradoxical juxtaposition of a pressing of hands and distance that I have been tracing.[38] In England, Kalas goes on to show, the sixteenth century witnessed as well a movement from the so-called engaged frame, which is part of the picture, to the type of frame that is separate from it. This change, I suggest, alerted writers and readers to the potentialities of verbal framing, and especially to the types of distancing they could produce. If alienable frames emphasize the distinction between subject and object, as Kalas persuasively maintains, they would have been a particularly attractive analogue for writers ambivalent about the poetry they were producing.

Certain texts and traditions that were exceptionally popular in the period both encouraged and modeled mediatory strategies: Psalms 1 and 2 can be seen as a type of headnote or frame for the ensuing poems; Dante's *Vita nuova* provided an influential precedent for an authorial decision to situate a lyric in relation to some sort of explanatory prose; many sixteenth-century editions of Petrarch's *Rime sparse* demonstrated editorial glosses; and the emblem tradition exemplified the interaction among different types of representation that gloss and extend each other.[39] Especially significant was the widespread familiarity with the Geneva Bible, which went through nearly one hundred fifty editions between 1560 and 1644; the commentaries with which it framed the psalms anticipated paratextual headnotes, while in this, like other editions of the Bible, the metapoetic references to singing and to the status of the psalms as poems also anticipated widespread practices in both spiritual and secular lyric.[40]

Theological traditions more indirectly influenced the early modern dialogue between techniques evoking immediacy and those suggesting distance. Often debated not only in this but earlier eras was a broad and multifaceted problem: the extent and ways scriptural episodes could be immanent in the mind of the believer, alive in her or his culture, or both. Liturgical events were seen as happening in the present even though they were associated with a distant historical moment and with recurrent previous celebrations of it.[41] The artistic practice, common in both the Middle Ages and Renaissance, of portraying historically specific biblical stories in a contemporary setting implies the presentness of the Christian past; in a painting by Duccio in the Frick Museum, for example, the devil tempts Christ in a locale with recognizable Sienese buildings, while in Rogier Van der Weyden's famous canvas of St. Luke sketching the virgin, that disciple has the artist's features, and the people outside the window look like his, not Mary's or Luke's, contemporaries. Even devotional works that do not themselves explicitly evoke their own culture in many cases do so implicitly; for instance, frames used in altarpieces typically incorporate architectural elements, implying that the figure within it is, as it were, alive and well in that very church at that very moment.[42]

Augustine, for Protestants the most influential patristic writer, explicates these issues in his commentary on the psalms. Challenging the assertion that Christ dies anew every Easter, he insists that it "happened but once," yet "the yearly remembrance brings before our eyes, in a way, what once happened long ago."[43] The emphasis on sight, as well as the qualifying "in a way," recalls to us, as it must have to many of his Renaissance and earlier readers, Paul's observation that fallen man sees through a glass darkly. In "Goodfriday, 1613. Riding Westward," Donne's question "Could I behold" (21, 23), repeated and stressed through anaphora, also emphasizes the limitations on human vision, and later in his discourse on the psalms Augustine stresses our inability adequately to mourn Christ's death.

While acknowledging those restrictions, however, Augustine is concerned to emphasize the affective power of representation: that yearly remembrance, he explains, "stirs in us the same emotions as if we beheld our Lord hanging upon the cross" (207). Earlier in the same discourse he draws attention to the motive impelling the re-creation of the event: "for fear we should forget what occurred but once, it is re-enacted every year for us to remember" (207). Augustine in effect warns us against oversimplifying the putative contrast between the immediacy of presence and the detachment of representation.

Indeed, a number of theological treatises and traditions devote themselves to techniques through which our ability to re-create and represent scriptural events can be heightened within the parameters of its inevitable limitations. In particular, both Catholic and Reformed meditative traditions emphasize strategies for creating a mental image of a scriptural episode or character. One stage in the Ignatian meditation is the *compositio loci*, in which one pictures the place being contemplated, attempting to create physical immediacy.[44] Also highly influential in early modern England, as Barbara K. Lewalski insists in her corrective to an exclusive focus on Catholic writings, were the extensive Protestant writings on meditation.[45] Here too, despite the predictable recommendations to meditate on sermons and other linguistic texts, making scriptural events and characters present visually is promoted; Joseph Hall, for example, assures his readers that if one masters the art of meditation, "wee see our Saviour with *Steven*, we talke with God as *Moses*."[46]

The significance of these issues in early modern England was intensified by their connection to two distinct but related theological cruxes especially germane to the relationship between immediacy and distance: the eucharistic debates about Real Presence and the millennial controversies. Whereas the Reformers distinguished their interpretations from Catholic doctrine on eucharistic presence, they are divided among themselves on the issue, and their positions are complex enough that a brief summary risks oversimplification. Zwingli's "memorialism," the most radical of those position, defines the sacrament as a so-called "ordinary" sign representing what is absent—in other words, a sign with no natural link to what is being signified. Luther's "ubiquitarianism" or "consubstantiation," in contrast, maintains that Christ, present in all things, is hence present as well in the Eucharist. Calvin effects a kind of compromise through his "virtualism," the assertion that Christians do not receive Christ's body and blood carnally but are invested with the virtue of it.[47]

Apocalyptic and millenarian assertions, which intensified in their frequency and their political ramifications during the seventeenth century, in a sense involve the obverse temporality, that is, the possibility that events prophesied in the Bible will be realized immediately or shortly. In commenting on the proximity of the apocalyse, early modern writers were, of course, drawing on a long exegetical tradition, but the Reformation encouraged its application to contemporary events. That practice was modeled and stimulated in particular by John Bale's presentation of the pope as the Antichrist and by his friend John Foxe's application and extension of this and other connections between Revelations and the Reformation. Many other Protestant thinkers followed suit, for example, by emphasizing that the number of letters in Archbishop Laud's name adds up to eighteen and that the devil is associated with the sequence 666.

All these theological debates about presence and presentness are germane in that two texts I will examine closely, Marvell's "Bermudas" and Milton's Nativity Ode, deploy literary strategies for suggesting both immediacy and distance in the course of exploring to what extent fallen man can experience Eden and the birth of Christ respectively with the immediacy of the original time and place. Arguably the rise of religious poetry in the seventeenth century, like the increasing urgency of apocalyptic and millenarian debates, intensified the culture's interest in the relationship between immediacy and distance, a relationship explored through lyric as well as in many other venues. Once again one is reminded that English Renaissance lyric needs to be discussed in terms of many historical subdivisions. Yet one must posit those subdivisions with care; although it is likely that the seventeenth-century vogue for religious lyrics heightened interest in the dialogue between presence and distance, these issues were actively debated in prose texts of the sixteenth century. As Debora Kuller Shuger has cogently shown, the concerns about absence and loss that surface in the religious lyrics of the seventeeth century appear also in prose by Lancelot Andrewes, Richard Hooker, and other sixteenth-century theologians.[48]

In any event, much as the psalms profoundly influenced even secular lyrics, so too the doctrinal disputes in question offered models and analogues for many texts that have nothing to do with religion; these debates may be heard as a significant though subterranean subtext when early modern lyrics attempt to negotiate the relationship among presentness, representation, and distance. As the

Donne poem on which this chapter opened reminds us, many early modern lyrics resist being classified in terms of either the immediacy conventionally associated with lyric or the distance and deceit commonly linked to representation; like the theological discussions, they move among various versions of apparent poles, and often that movement is itself part of their meanings. Moreover, as we have seen, meditative practices stress that the immediacy of spiritual vision sometimes is achieved only gradually and laboriously; and, similarly, many poems examined below, present both immediacy and distancing as processes.

⟋ ⟍

At poetry readings in the twentieth and twenty-first centuries, the author often intersperses patter with the presentation of the poems. Although the styles of delivering these conversational remarks are as varied as the styles of the texts they accompany, certain functions do recur—demonstrating that the term "patter," though regularly used by writers themselves for this practice, inappropriately attributes to it a kind of casualness and even pointlessness that is far from the case. Usually the patter is more conversational and quotidian than the poems; thus it creates a contrast with their linguistic registers, in its close juxtaposition with the lyric representing the default position from which, Jonathan Culler rightly claims, lyrics typically deviate.[49] (Typically, not universally, one might add. One measure of Billy Collins's refusal of the intense registers associated with lyricism is that at his readings it is not always clear when the patter ends and the poem itself starts. Indeed, his work could usefully clarify the distinctions between lyric and lyricism.) The function of creating a contrast with the text itself is, of course, particularly marked when what Frye famously called the "radical of presentation" is song. But the poet's interspersed comments can serve to provide not simply a contrast but also a bridge, allowing the reading to encompass poems of very different types and moods. I myself have sometimes switched from a couple of lyrics about my mother's death to poems on, say, dill or irises, wanting to provide some relief from the wrenching subject matter of the first texts; to move from one to the other without the sort of preparation for the audience that patter can provide would itself be wrenching.

Patter may simply serve to explain otherwise obscure references; poets sometimes use it for a different type of explanation, filling in autobiographical details of events behind the poem. In this second function, the comments are frequently attempts to gain the audience's attention and sympathy (much as opening a lecture on a personal anecdote can counter the anonymity of a large classroom and engage students who may be thinking about the previous lecture or about the previous night's party). In the instance of the poetry reading, to reduce that aim to commercialism would be to oversimplify, but to deny that poets at these readings, which so often literally end in attempts to sell the poet's books, implicitly incorporate that agenda into the patter would be an equal misrepresentation. One technique through which the poet may seek sympathy is to anticipate, incorporate, and defuse the audience's possible negative responses—"this is an early poem," "this is work in progress which I'm including because it relates to the previous poem," and so on.

Although one has no way of being sure, it is likely that some version of this sort of patter accompanied the voicing or singing of early modern lyrics as well. A bridge, for example, would have been necessary when reading aloud sonnets like those composed in the sixteenth and early seventeenth centuries, in which tones can change abruptly; the contrast between Spenser's laudatory and accusatory sonnets is so intense that readers have even improbably speculated that the latter were written earlier, perhaps for an entirely different relationship, and were simply slotted into the sequence. Sonnets might also encourage disclaimers about or confessions of their autobiographical resonances.

In any event, the versions of patter practiced in our own and probably the early modern era suggest both some functions and some likely origins of the mediatory devices explored in this chapter. Like patter, many of these techniques are attempts to win over readers or to distance the author from guilt that could be engendered by writing the text, a response not unique to early modern England but very characteristic of it for the reasons traced in Chapter 1 and elsewhere. In fact, when written transmission became increasingly common, mediating devices developed in part as surrogates for patter, responding to the diminution of opportunities for this and other types of oral paratext. (Diminution, not destruction, however: a copy of a book could still be handed to someone with comments, whether oral or written.)

A preliminary catalogue of mediating devices prepares us to analyze their shared functions in more detail. Some of these instruments are paratexts that precede the text in close conjunction with it; they generally provide information about the lyric, variously focusing on its literary sources, its meanings, or its biographical significance. The right to name, as narratives of the Garden of Eden tell us, is the right to reign. Most obviously, titles and subtitles may assume these and many other functions, as Anne Ferry has acutely shown in *The Title to the Poem*. The poem generally known to us as "Break of day," appears in one manuscript identified as "D$^r$ Donne. / To his Love, who was too hasty to / rise from him.in y$^e$ Morning."[50] If this title, unlike the more familiar one, identifies the author and the obvious meaning of the lyric, in so doing it also demonstrates the ability of whoever assigned it to assume significant power over the text and its readers. Witness the consequences of referring to the poet, who attributed such secular works to "Jack Donne," as "Dr. Donne" and of gendering as male a speaker who many later critics have thought might have been a woman.

An intriguing analogue to how literary titles, as well as the authorial identification often associated with them, may both activate and complicate meanings latent in the text is the decision of the Palestinian artist Mona Hatoum to label her outsized kitchen grater "Grater Divide"; the effects of that title are telling enough to inspire juxtaposing it with the early modern ones I am examining, despite the evident difference in their eras and their media. Had Claes Oldenburg been the artist, the assumption one might well make before reading the placard, one would have interpreted the object as another instance of his practice of defamiliarization, on one level a playful and unthreatening act but on the other a demonstration of how a change in size can make a well-known object from our homes *unheimlich*. These interpretations are localized and reconfigured by Hatoum's title, which interacts with her Lebanese nationality and her involvement in politics to suggest Middle Eastern divisions. From this perspective the potential playfulness of the object itself is lessened and in a sense transferred to the pun in the title—and the violence in the serrations, which now come to resemble weapons, is emphasized. Like much of Hatoum's other work, the object juxtaposes the comfortably familiar and the dangerous, and her title indubitably establishes political interpretations of those dangers.

But recall, too, Hatoum's own complaint that "most people look for a very specific meaning, mostly wanting to explain [a work of art] specifically in relation to my background. I find it more exciting when a work reverberates with several meanings and paradoxes and contradictions."[51] Alerted by this comment, one may respond more fully to the puckishness one would have seen had Oldenburg created the grater, as well as noting more formal achievements, such as the interplay of shapes on the object. Sometimes a grater is partly, if not only, a grater. This one divides and cuts but is also itself divided into many units and patterns. In short, titles, like other mediating devices, often participate in a kind of teamwork with other signals; and they, like other mediating devices, often themselves give mixed signals, sometimes by highlighting certain possibilities without discounting others.

Headnotes provide another type of mediation that precedes the text proper and in this way can substitute for what might have been covered during an interval of patter. Defining space as amorphous and place as defined and bounded, not least by the boundaries that are social rules, many students of space theory have variously offered paradigms for how space is turned into place.[52] As Thomas Watson's identification of his sources demonstrates, headnotes, like other forms of mediation, often transform space into place in that they give both the material white space and the ensuing text a local habitation and a name. And, much as the transformation of space into place is often an assertion of power, so too headnotes substitute several interrelated forms of power for many authors' inability to attach titles: like patter, they may establish authority, even while they sometimes acknowledge its limits.

In their studies of marginalia, William W. E. Slights and Evelyn B. Tribble demonstrate how those devices can control and educate the audience.[53] Similarly, the long paratextual commentaries that accompany Watson's sonnets, possibly the most extensive and intriguing instances of headnotes in the early modern lyric, typically instruct the reader on how to approach a given text, encompassing background information (in his ninety-seventh poem, for instance, the fable behind the poem is identified), advice about the attitude to adopt towards the text ("the contrarietie ought not to offend," we are told in the paratext for the first sonnet), and information that encourages the "academic" readings for which I argue in Chapter 2.[54]

Headnotes can also negotiate a relationship with an author whose work is being borrowed. When such a prefatory passage attributes the succeeding poem to the writer who is being translated or otherwise incorporated, it defines the text as what Dickens's Wemmick so intensely advocates, portable property. In one sense it belongs to, say, Ronsard, and Watson is merely borrowing, or appropriating, it, a process that, as many critics have demonstrated, often delimited authorship in the early modern period. Yet in another and not coincidental sense, through the act of writing the headnote, Watson is asserting a kind of authority and ownership. Particularly interesting in that and other respects are the many headnotes that not only identify a source but quote part of it; when, as is often the case, the lines in question are translated at the beginning of the text proper, the boundary between text and paratext blurs. The book thus enacts visually another type of power play—the appropriation of someone else's words—while at the same time acknowledging the status of the original author. In other words, such headnotes establish not absolute ownership or freehold but rather a kind of leasehold; they effect the types of partial and limited ownership discussed in more detail in my chapters on audiences and on the size and shape of lyric.

If they thus gloss contemporary critical debates about authorship and authority, headnotes have wider implications for many debates surrounding lyric. Pursuing his valuable revisionist agenda of relocating lyric poetry from ahistorical literary contexts to social ones, Arthur F. Marotti demonstrates that by evoking a social world, headnotes and titles create a situation like that of manuscript circulation. Sometimes, notably in George Gascoigne's *Hundreth Sundrie Flowres*, they function in just the way he describes.[55] But Marotti's reading is limited by his long-standing rejection of aesthetic analysis as a distortion of and distraction from the cultural and material. In fact, in this case as in many others, all those realms can profitably be studied together. Watson's headnotes, like the paratextual materials in Spenser's *Faerie Queene*, more often instead evoke a literary context, even on occasion implying that the poem is an exercise, and thus yet again encourage us to revise the revisionists by linking the current focus on the social to a historicized formalism. Dead writers, especially those who experimented with the same form, are members of the poet's social circle and no less important than the coteries about whom Marotti and others write. Indeed, one might profitably think more about the interaction between these groups.[56]

Sometimes an introductory poem assumes certain though not all functions of a headnote: it situates the reader and the other texts, in so doing qualifying or in some instances complicating their immediacy. The opening lyric in Petrarch's *Rime sparse*, discussed at the beginning of Chapter 1, is a textbook example of this, as it is of so many other lyric predilections. Numerous English sonneteers follow suit in introducing their own cycles. Giles Fletcher the Elder begins *Licia* with a text that is entitled "To Licia the Wise, Kinde, Vertuous, and Fayre" and not numbered in the way the ensuing sonnets are: it establishes and announces a respectful relationship to the eponymous character who may or may not also be his patroness. When one contrasts Fletcher's "I send these Poems to your gracefull eye:" (3–4) with, say, the opening of the Keats poem quoted above ("This living hand, now warm and capable / Of earnest grasping"), the primary impression is that the early modern poet holds readers at bay while his Romantic counterpart insistently, even alarmingly, reaches towards them. Fletcher's lines separate the text from its audience through the reminder that it is precisely that, a literary representation, and through the suggestion that the principal addressee is not present but rather engaged in an act of reading at some remove from the lyrics ("send" [3]).[57] A related difference, whose relevance to this chapter is pursued below, is that Fletcher's version stresses the materiality of the book, not of a part of his own body. At the same time, when one compares the succeeding line in Fletcher, "Doe you but take them" (4) with Keats's "I hold it towards you" (8) affinities are as apparent as contrasts; indeed, Fletcher's direct appeal for participation may make the poem even more immediate in some senses. Thus his lyric recalls the pressing of hands so relevant to the immediacy of lyric, demonstrating again the interaction between distance and contiguity and among various versions of each that is so common in that mode.

Similarly, the first sonnet in Daniel's *Delia* performs a range of mediatory functions. Explicitly inviting the lady to peruse the text ("Reade it sweet maide" [13]), it offers a similar invitation to the reader as well.[58] Like the instance from Fletcher, it at once distances us from this and the ensuing lyrics by emphasizing their status as representations, while at the same time insisting on the material presence of the poem as a physical object, an assertion buttressed by the insistent repetitions, often in the form of anaphora, of "heere": "which heeere my love" (4), "Heere I unclaspe the booke" (5), "Heere have I summ'd my sighes, heere I enroule / How they were spent" (7–8). That type of opening poem is analogous in some respects to a strategy to which I will turn later: the introduction of a voice apparently, though in fact not invariably, separate from that of the speaker that comments directly on the text.

The introductory poem that, like patter, provides additional information, and the introduction of a second voice are both related in some important ways to the strikingly common practice of embedding a lyric within another text, frequently of a different genre, that frames and comments on it. Dante's *Vita nuova* and Machaut's *Remedy of Fortune* exemplified and encouraged this predilection. Although prose romances and drama offer a wealth of examples, discussed from different perspectives elsewhere in this study, among the most intriguing instances is George Gascoigne's *Hundreth Sundrie Flowres*. The lengthy prose narrative in this extraordinary bouquet, "The Adventures of Master F.J.," interjects a number of lyrics relevant to F.J.'s courtship. They are often preceded by a commentary positioning them in relation to a particular time, place, and mood through a phrase that complicates the subsequent immediacy of the text, such as "walkinge abrode devised immediatly these fewe verses followinge" (146). Notice as well how "devised" also draws attention to the craft and planning involved in the poem, as does the use of the word "devises" for the title of the collection of poems that follows this work. At the end of Gascoigne's poems commonly appear informative comments like the headnotes and footnotes examined above ("This is the translation of *Ariosto* his .xxxi. song" [189]). Also common in these conclusions are evaluative comments—"This Sonet was highly commended, and in my judgment it deserveth no lesse" (156)—that prompt readers to assess the texts aesthetically, thus distancing themselves. Sometimes, too, such observations have, again like patter, a type of apotropaic magic in their agenda, the warding off of criticism: "This is but a rough meter, and reason, for it was devised in great disquiet of mynd, and written in rage, yet I have seene much worse passé the musters . . . the truth is that

F.J. himselfe had so slender liking thereof" (162). Also similar are the paratexts in Gascoigne's "Devises of Sundrie Gentlemen," the group of poems that follows "The Adventures of Master F.J." and is presented in A Hundreth Sundrie Flowres as primarily the work of other poets but acknowledged as Gascoigne's own in the subsequent edition. Many of these commentaries within "The Devises of Sundrie Gentlemen" emphasize that Gascoigne is putatively the compiler but not the author of the poem. Others serve the deictic function so common in mediatory paratexts or their analogues within a poem: "Now I must desire you with patience to hearken unto the works of another writer" (245).

Among the numerous examples of a lyric embedded within another poem are the songs sung by the nymphs in Spenser's "Prothalamion" and by Alcyon in his "Daphnaïda." Less familiar but equally intriguing as an instance of the relationship between distance and immediacy is the eclogue that provides a setting for the epithalamium proper in the poem Donne wrote for the notorious Somerset-Howard nuptials. In it, a figure called Idios, clearly identified with the author, claims that he wrote a poem but does not wish to send it to court; if, as is likely, the figure Allophanes represents not only or primarily a friend but rather another side of Idios and of Donne, his insistence that the poem be delivered to court enacts the poet's internal conflict about participating in the games of patronage. Idios's reference to the poem as a "sacrifice" (104) for the event at once extends the religious language that attempts to lend dignity to this singularly sordid match while on the other hand hinting at the sacrifice of principle in the service of patronage that is an undertow to the disagreement between Idios and Allophanes.[59] Recalling the reference to Venus in Donne's "Indifferent," the outer, enveloping poem qualifies the presentness of the framed one by positioning it within an event and hence at a particular time and place. Such framings, an analogue to a play-within-a-play, distance the poem-within-a-poem; Donne's desire to separate himself from the sycophancy of patronage is thus enacted formally.

Like such poems-within-a-poem, metapoetic devices, notably an allusion to a musical instrument or to the acts of writing, singing, or reading, draw attention to the ontological status of the text as a whole. This practice, like others catalogued in this chapter, is not unique to Renaissance poetry; witness, among so many other examples, the pastoral poems "Virgil: Eclogue IX," "Glanmore Eclogue" in Seamus Heaney's collection Electric Light, and William Carlos Williams's "To a Young Housewife." But this version of metapoetry frequently assumes certain distinctive (though again not unique) forms in the period, such as the address to the lute and the reflexive introductory poem in a sonnet cycle. Often, as in the introductory poems by Daniel and by Giles Fletcher the Elder examined above and the twentieth poem in the anonymous collection *Zepheria*, these allusions occur at the beginning of a poem or a cycle; but in certain instances, such as Wyatt's two famous addresses to his lute and the fourth sonnet in Daniel's *Delia*, they are interspersed throughout.

Such references may serve a range of divergent functions, some of which I will explore in more detail later in this chapter. Though they share the agenda of abruptly distancing the reader from what has come before and what ensues by the reminder that the text was a performance, the conclusions of "Lycidas" and the Eighth Song in *Astrophil and Stella* ("that therwith my song is broken" [104]) intriguingly differ in that the first poem distances the speaker and his actions, while the second insists on the presentness of an event and the presence of the poet who had hidden behind a persona.[60] There is no better example in the language of how a metapoetic device may intensify certain types of immediacy and limit others than Philip Sidney's use of it in the latter work. In some cases, notably Gascoigne's "Lullabie" and Donne's "Hymne to God my God, in my Sicknessse," the text's status as a representation and literary creation is thematized. Similarly, in his twenty-second sonnet, Robert Sidney declares that he "read[s] the story" of his "wrack of rest" (4).[61] Although the line does not refer primarily to the poem, it does serve to unite its speaker's experience with that of his audience (and thus, incidentally, to connect the lyric's present and the present in which the reader peruses the text). In any event, he is creating distance by telling a story about himself telling a story. The poem thus offers a particularly clear and explicit example of an observation developed by John Shawcross, among other critics: lyric is often not about an experience but about the reporting of it, locating the poem at two removes from the experience.[62]

This chapter has already flagged the cognate type of ontological positioning in lyrics, such as the first poems in Spenser's *Amoretti* and Giles Fletcher the Elder's *Licia*, that establishes the text as a physical object that can be held. Recalling Susan Stewart's emphasis on touch, such references clearly make the poem more immediate in one sense, as do Wyatt's allusions to touching the strings of his instrument, while in another reminding us forcefully that it is indeed a representation. Again one sees that distancing generally but by no means always counters immediacy and that it moves in strange and often contradictory ways. If the poem is variously established as an aesthetic achievement and a material object through this form of distancing, its author is separated from its speaker to some extent and established as a poet—thus potentially classifying him both as an artist committed to craft and as a rhetorician committed to craftiness.

Refrains vary in any number of respects, not least in the fact that they sometimes assume and sometimes refuse the several mediatory functions my brief survey of types of framing has introduced. Recalling the new historicist insistence on the hyphenated version of "re-presentation," refrains enact and trope that process by quite literally presenting again what was said in a previous refrain, while at the same time their incantatory power may intensify the presence of what occurs earlier in the stanza. Indeed, it is no accident that refrains are often deployed towards a purpose so many critics consider central to lyric, calling up what is absent: their own returning tropes that mission, and their repetitiveness awakens lyric's root in magical charms, discussed so acutely by Andrew Welsh.[63]

Yet refrains may also form a kind of metaframe by fulfilling many mediatory agendas, in so doing drawing attention to their own status as frames. They may, for example, turn space into place by providing the familiarity of a predictable element; moreover, if one seconds Yi-Fu Tuan's observation that space involves movement and place pause, refrains create a momentary stopping place.[64] Sometimes they refer directly to the text's status as poem or song, as Spenser famously does in all three of the refrains cited above; in an intensified version of that process, the one in "Daphnaïda" itself alludes to refrains ("Weepe Shepheard weepe to make my undersong" [245]). That device may also draw attention to the text's artistry and hence its identity as an art object through its very existence as a formal feature of poetry. Similarly, returning to "Daphnaïda," the structure of the lament within it, a series of seven groups of seven-line stanzas, is emphasized by the fact that the final strophe in each group terminates on a refrain, encouraging us to notice Spenser's architectonics. And if other types of mediatory elements contest the presentness of lyric by introducing different time sequences, refrains trope temporality, representing as they do a form of repetition that looks backward to previous occurrences and forward to future ones; the refrains of Spenser's wedding poems reinforce this emphasis on time semantically through a number of techniques, notably the change in the final line of the stanzas of the "Epithalamion" and, in the "Prothalamion," the usage of the word "long," and the references to ending the song. In their Janus-like stance towards the poem, refrains substantiate John Hollander's analysis of how they are connected to the act of remembering—an act that is the antithesis of the immediacy associated with lyric and the invocatory potential of the refrain itself.[65]

⁓

This brief, individuated catalogue of some principal mediating elements in lyric and of functions distinct to them allows me to generalize further about common features of the poetic processes they effect. Like Orpheus walling the citizenry within towns, these devices may establish boundaries; they may position the text spatially and ontologically, notably by signaling that it is an event or an object; and they may define the status of the poem's author and reader. In so doing, these elements intensify effects and processes that I have scrutinized in earlier chapters; for example, they negotiate the guilt so often associated with lyric and expressed in the trope of turning, they establish multiple positionalities for both audience and reader, and, as those instances suggest, they contribute to the many types of process and change lyric typically enacts.

The establishment of these boundaries assumes a range of forms. For all that Watson's headnotes sometimes blur distinctions, headnotes and other mediatory devices more often establish them. Thus they can negotiate the transgressive elements within the text, distancing them from author and reader in ways that enable their continuing presence. Because guilt about writing secular lyrics was so intense in the early modern period, we encounter many versions of this mediatory pattern. Gascoigne both writes salacious love poems and claims they are composed by someone else. He thus invites us to think that although he is virtuous, there will indeed be cake and ale; or to put it another way, he has his cake and pretends not to eat it. In distancing the reader from the lyric by stressing its literary antecedents, Watson's headnotes also distance himself from it by referring to "the author" in the third person. (In his collection, like a number of others, the impression of boundaries that is achieved semantically is enforced visually: the headnotes at the top of Watson's poems interact with the prominent borders at the bottom to create a frame.) Whereas recent scholarship has focused on Ben Jonson's pioneering assertions of authorship, the instances in which he qualifies or conceals it are no less intriguing. Like Watson, Jonson on occasion protects his authority precisely by hedging his authorship: the third person pronouns in the subtitles of "A Celebration of Charis in Ten Lyrick Peeces" ("His Excuse for Loving" and so on) must have been attractive to a poet who elsewhere claims he does not write of love, while "Excuse" distances him not only from love per se but also from the process of defending it. Similarly, the type of frame that locates a poem of courtly praise within another narrative and in so doing assigns it to a speaker ostensibly separate from the author offers some shelter from accusations of sycophancy; Donne's Somerset-Howard epithalamium is the most obvious example, but Spenser's *Shepheardes Calender* offers many more.

Several types of mediation listed above involve erecting a different form of barrier: as we have seen, they create distance from the lyric through mechanisms that in effect allow the author to reject it. Or, from another perspective, they build in judgments on the poem and thus deflect judgment on its author: he may become not the cryer of dubious wares but rather the voice that cries foul by rejecting some of the values and assumptions of the text. Helen Vendler has noted how many of Shakespeare's sonnets are what she terms "morning-after" reflections, and she proceeds to demonstrate how retrospection enables the incorporation of judgment.[66] In many instances, of course, the judgments on the text in question are more subterranean and ambivalent. By turning the April eclogue in praise of Elizabeth into a poem-within-a-poem and assigning it to the intermediary Hobbinol, who repeats the song of the absent Colin, Spenser at once participates fully in courtly rituals and builds into his text some distance from the poem; as we saw, Donne erects similar barriers when praising a distasteful courtly wedding, thus anticipating negative judgments.

Mediating devices, especially when they function as frames, establish boundaries in another sense as well. Renzo Piano, like his fellow architect Jean Nouvel, is committed to transparent walls that do not wall in. Piano writes dismissively of the attempt to construct by constricting: "We instinctively seek enclosure, a fixing of limits, in what is built. Space does not exist except insofar as it is precisely — and solidly — circumscribed. This is a concept of space that disturbs me."[67] Desirous of, rather than disturbed by, circumscription, lyric poets often use mediating devices as barriers against transgressive meanings. Most obviously, a title like "The Lover Complains to his Mistress" excludes homoerotic meanings, and, as we have seen, the title some manuscripts assign to Donne's "Breake of Day" excludes the possibility of a female speaker. Reflecting the commitment to positivistic interpretation often characteristic of structuralist narratology, Genette's claim that paratexts ensure that the ensuing text is read correctly does not adequately gloss some texts I have examined, but it encapsulates this type of intermediary.[68]

If many mediating devices, as observed above, locate the text ethically by passing judgment on it, another function they often share is locating it spatially and ontologically, in a sense an additional version of establishing boundaries. We may learn who is speaking, where, when, and to whom, all of which can at least complicate the universality and timelessness sometimes attributed to lyric. To return to questions about voicing discussed in Chapter 2, surely the ways Marvell's "Bermudas," analyzed in more detail below, positions the singers in terms of a particular place, historical moment, and nationality precludes simple identification with them. But if giving lyric a local habitation and name delimits it in those ways, it also delimits an anxiety associated with it in Chapters 1 and 4, the scattering of the voice (and implicitly the body) of the latter-day Orpheus who writes it. Marvell's Juliana may refuse the poem like its speaker's other gifts, but the narrator and the audience invited or commanded to "Hark" (1) do hear Damon's song in "Damon the Mower."[69]

Especially intriguing is how such frames may establish a lyric as an event in the sense not only of something localized temporally and spatially but also flagged as significant, worthy of or even demanding our attention—not coincidentally, the very function Rayna Kalas attributes to alienable picture frames.[70] Many other devices may emphasize this status; as George T. Wright points out in his compelling essay on the lyric present, for example, tense may do so,[71] and a headnote may do so by connecting the text to a well-respected source. The intensity of a refrain, I observed, may contribute to the ritualistic numen of a text, thus making it an event in the sense that ceremonies are. Again demonstrating the connections between that ritualistic mode lyric and anthropological practices, Herbert Blau adduces Henry James's usage of the term "ado" to argue that rituals involve *ado*, rather than just *do*.[72] The implications of the term—something that is astir, something forced on one, something involving trouble—gloss the consequences of establishing lyric as an event. Herrick suggests *ado* in some of these senses when he entitles two poems, one of which I examined earlier, "A Vision." (As we will see shortly, Marvell's "Bermudas" plays on such commands and the expectations of significance they often entail, by reversing them.)

Establishing a lyric as an event also distinguishes it from what has come before, thus enabling the kinds of changes in linguistic registers and communicative rules that the mode often entails. Anthropology, as well as cognate disciplines, can yet again help us to understand these processes. Many recent studies in that field advocate focusing attention not merely on the ritual per se but also on the "warmup" practices that prepare for it and the "cool-down" after it.[73] Similarly, studies of games, which are often compared to rituals, emphasize the need for procedures that distinguish the time and space of games as marked cases, suspending certain rules and instituting others. Erving Goffman's theory of keying, where something is assigned a significance different from its ordinary one, such as the reinterpretation of fighting gestures as playful ones, is a case in point.[74] Barnabe Barnes attempts to excuse the transgressive sexual fantasies and their realization in a violent rape in the fifth sestina of *Parthenophil and Parthenophe* by emphasizing the fictive, which is keyed by the mythological references; "it's only a poem" functions like "it's only a game." To return to Marvell's "Damon the Mower," the insistence on a conventional pastoral name in effect identifies the rules of the game generically; and given the generic conventions in question, the reader is also aware that Damon's performance is likely to involve *ado* in several senses—something troublesome, something over which he does not have control.

If they transform a poem into an event, several of the mediating devices enumerated above also turn a poem into an object, drawing attention to it aesthetically, materially, or both, as Spenser does when he envisions his lady holding the book and, again, as picture frames do. The contrast identified above between Fletcher's poem and Keats's seemingly similar one highlights the impact of stressing the materiality of the text. Emphasizing its artifactuality in this way speaks to—though without resolving—the concerns about the insubstantiality of lyric that we have encountered at many junctures. A second effect of treating the poem as an object relates variously to gender, as do so many other issues about lyric. In a sense the text is stationed in the female subject position as an object that can be held by someone else, thus giving the lady the impression—or illusion—that she herself is subject, not object. At the same time, the poet bifurcates himself: he becomes both the text, an instrument that is thus effeminized, and the writer who creates it and at least partly controls it, reminding us that the extent to which the lady herself is subject, not object, is real but limited.

As this bifurcation suggests, while the kinds of distancing listed above may define the status of the text, they also reshape that of author and reader, as well as, on occasion, the relationship between writer and reader. Generally, though not universally, they do so by participating in the interlocking assertions of authorship and authority whose development in the period, traced by so many contemporary critics, is discussed in more detail in my chapter on size and structure. Given the uncertainty in the early modern period about the concept of speaker and the ambiguity in many instances about whether someone is in fact editor or author, these assertions about who is speaking can be reassuring. Moreover, many forms of mediation establish the author's authority, thus contributing to the era's construction of conceptions of authorship. As we have already seen, in the seventeenth century writers did begin to assign their own titles; whoever does so, as Anne Ferry and John Hollander both rightly observe, asserts authority and ownership.[75] Again, the turnings of poetry turn space into place. Similarly, one consequence of, so to speak, establishing title is establishing the right to sell; as I have already observed in another context, titles, headnotes, and related devices in effect may announce that their creator is hawking the wares that will follow, crying his lament in the sense of that verb established earlier, and that she or he has the right to do so. For all the respectful devotion announced in the initial poem addressed to Licia, Fletcher still represents himself as the architect of a temple. At the same time, however, the devices also qualify or screen the author in order to negotiate anxieties about writing whose recurrence in the early modern period we have repeatedly encountered. We have seen how assuming the subject position of intermediary can be a ploy to shield the author from the dangers of erotic and epideictic verse — reminding one again that the early modern period witnessed many attempts to conceal authorship as well as the efforts to assert it that have been more widely studied.[76]

The lack of title to the title experienced by many early modern poets made them all the more concerned to establish their power in other ways, thus establishing surrogates for their ability to assign and change their titles: headnotes like Watson's, a narrative frame like Gascoigne's, footnotes like those apparently written by Spenser, all allow the writer to lay claim to the text intellectually through the acts of elucidating its literary history or establishing its interpretation. Similarly, to the extent that lyric originates in a summoning of the lyric voice, as Allen Grossman, Susan Stewart, and others have suggested, these frames may also be seen as a reactive redefinition of roles: originally the summoned, the author may demonstrate power by summoning other speaking voices, other landscapes, and audiences through the mediating language of the poem.[77] Yet again Marvell's "Damon the Mower" is telling, for its opening line, "Hark how the mower Damon sung," accomplishes all those ends. Here, as so often, the same line may create immediacy in some respects and compromise it in others.

In some instances, of course, mediating elements do not merely summon but also dismiss through the act of introducing a new speaker or distinguishing one side of the speaker from another, a characterological equivalent to the way they may demarcate an *inside* where transgressive language and behavior may thrive and an *outside* where they are not permitted. Arguably the ending of "Lycidas" involves not a commentary by a completely distinct voice but a separation between the speaker as pastoral shepherd and the side of him that wishes to move to new pastures, new genres. The newer self appropriates the poem (an act recalling Thestylis's defiance in "Upon Appleton House") with the anticipated move to a different territory enacted through the take-over bid on that territory the page. Ernst Häublein rightly notes that a change in speakers serves closural functions very like that of a quotation and that the two are in fact sometimes identical; another function they may share, one might add, is closing off in the sense of pushing away an alternative.[78]

No less important than their effects on the author's subject position are the ways mediating techniques shape the reader's. Again, though, these processes are complex and contradictory. If one form of mediation, the refrain, is a bridle for the text, other forms serve as it were to bridle the reader's autonomy, assigning us a role, a vantage point, even an attitude. There is an imperiousness behind the command to harken, as well as an emphasis on the significance of what is going to be heard; orders to hearken or see, so often included in mediating devices, not only remind us that the ensuing lyric will appeal to the senses but suggest that it is, as it were, imperative that we respond to that appeal. If the film camera directs the eye of the viewer while stage productions allow individual members of the audience to decide what they are going to look at and for how long (though those decisions may be guided in part by blocking and lighting), mediating techniques attempt to make the process of reading lyric more cinematic. (Indeed, the pressing of hands about which Celan writes can on occasion precede the twisting of arms.)

In other circumstances, however, mediating devices may serve not as counterpart but rather as counterbalance to the types of coercion Roland Greene perceptively identifies with lyric.[79] As Milton demonstrates in a passage from *Comus* discussed in my last chapter, the immediacy of the mode contributes to its seductiveness: its touch may be not a pressing of hands but the embrace of a siren or even of Circe, often associated with that dangerous glee club. Mediating devices often provide a safely distanced vantage point from which not only the author but also the reader can listen to the siren song. If two poems paired above, Fletcher's opening sonnet and Keats's "This living hand, now warm and capable," are published with titles, those devices can provide a barrier when the poems reach out, reminding the readers that, as parents assure anxious children, it's only a story.

As Chapter 2 demonstrated from another perspective, the reader may also be distanced by being invited into the "academic" role; a headnote like those in which Watson discusses his sources in detail or a paratextual comment like those in which Gascoigne evaluates the meter of the immediately preceding poem encourages the audience to study the text at a remove from it.[80] Again, an audience containing many writers, as early modern audiences did, would respond with particular alacrity and intensity to such invitations. In so doing, they would assume a stance that again recalls anthropological studies of ritual, in this instance observations about the separation between the person performing the ritual and observers.[81]

Varied in other respects, many techniques catalogued above also unite in affecting, and even on occasion effecting, the temporality of lyric, creating the multiple time sequences that the more acute studies of the mode substitute for an unremitting emphasis on its presentness. Refrains can both figure and trouble temporality. The devices that comment on what happens in the lyric establish a second time frame corresponding to the discourse time that narratologists contrast with the story time of the narrative itself. These temporal movements may be troped and complicated by shifts in speakers. When Robert Sidney writes in his third song, "Thus sayd a shepheard, *once*" (63), the abrupt and unexpected introduction of another speaker, which distances us from the original voice, not only effects but also mirrors the results of the intrusion of different time sequences. As in Donne's "Indifferent," the shepherd's present-tense lament is now narrowed to a specific moment in the past, and the presence of the commentator adds yet another temporality, the discourse time in which he speaks.

The most intriguing and subtle function that connects otherwise distinct mediating devices is creating a kind of wind-up that, like the cognate anthropological processes to which I refer above, enables or at least encourages the performance that follows. Although in some instances headnotes and other framing devices may lessen the intensity of the ensuing lyric by inviting, for example, a detached and scholarly study of its meter, in other instances they form a crescendo of intensity. "Performances seem to gather their energies," observe Richard Schechner and Willa Appel, who proceed to discuss "this gathering of intensity" as characteristic of not only tribal rites but also the games, sports events, and theatrical productions to which they compare ritual.[82] Alerting and activating the senses can prepare readers for the experience of lyric, which is, as Susan Stewart and so many students of Romantic poetry have shown, often an appeal to all five. Notice how often mediating passages refer in particular to sight and hearing, though other senses may be evoked as well—thus the use of "See" (22) in the stanzas that precede the hymn within Milton's Nativity Ode prepares us for the sensuality of many images in that hymn and in particular for its culmination on "But see!" (237), the vision of the Christ child.[83]

Frequently metapoetic through their references to the act of writing or singing, frames in effect may summon up their own song, another type of warm-up and another analogue to prosopopoeia. Crashaw's hymn on the nativity celebrates the arrival of the Son by effecting the arrival of the sun and of a song:

> Come we shepheards whose blest Sight
> Hath mett Love's Noon in Nature's night;
>     Come lift we up our loftyer Song
> And wake the Sun that lyes too long.
>                    (1–4)[84]

The Chorus's injunction "Come lift we up our loftyer Song" (3) is both a performative, in the most precise sense of a statement that effects the action to which it refers, and a warm-up for the subsequent songs by Thyrsis and the Chorus. In short, early modern refrains, like many of their classical precedents, not only may invoke a god or other luminary but also often encourage the creation, delivery, or dispersal of the text, their incantatory repetitions adding emotional power to that invitation and implicitly aligning it with ritual invocations: "The woods shall to me answer and my Eccho ring" (18) Spenser famously announces in his "Epithalamion," the echo of the refrain troping and proleptically enacting the dispersal of the poem.[85]

The same writer's "Daphnaïda," discussed from other perspectives above, provides an intriguing mirror image of and commentary on all these forms of warm-up: the narrator attempts to rein in Alcyon's tension in the frame to his lament, and it is precisely that restraint that generates the intensity of the lyric:

> Then gan I him to comfort all my best,
> And with milde counsaile strove to mitigate
> The stormie passion of his troubled brest,
> But he thereby was more empassionate:
> As stubborne steed, that is with curb restrained,
> Becomes more fierce and fervent in his gate;
> And breaking foorth at last, thus dearnely plained.
>
> (190–196)

In another, related sense, encountered above, mediating devices involve coiling the spring that will uncoil dramatically in the lyric itself: they may perform an action analogous to establishing the rules of the game or turning a quotidian locale into a sacred area where a ritual may be enacted. Citing Eliade, Mary Oates O'Reilly has traced the association of odes with such spaces;[86] the same linkage occurs in many other lyric genres as well. The type of keying Goffman describes in a sense prepares a sacred space by changing the meanings of what would otherwise be ordinary words and objects. More literally, as we will see shortly, the opening stanzas of Milton's Nativity Ode both establish and problematize the idea that the poem not only describes but also takes place within the sacred space where Christ was born (4–5).

So far I have focused largely on the successful deployment of various procedures for qualifying immediacy. But in a painting by Grant Wood in the Minneapolis Institute of Art, a very small figure, clearly a version of the *festiauolo* analyzed in Chapter 2, points towards the landscape that virtually engulfs him. Unsettling in the way its artist's work so often is, the canvas implies that the figure is attempting vainly to assert authority through his deictic gesture: this master of ceremonies lacks mastery. Whether or not one interprets this figure as a type of artist and hence the painting as an ironized undercutting of the act of painting, the implications for the deictic and other mediatory gestures examined here are extensive. Is the self-confident framing that motivates a statement like "Hark how the mower Damon sung" ("Damon the Mower," 1) no less narcissistic and futile than the posturing by Damon from which the narrator is apparently distinguishing himself? Are the frame and framer, so to speak, really part of what they attempt to frame? Mediating devices are often in turn mediated, moderated, and even mocked by their own limitations—as well as by the types of immediacy with which they interact. Hands may be pressed, pushed away, then pressed again.

A close and detailed analysis of texts, the agenda of the next section of this chapter, is the best approach to such issues. These poems demand and repay scrutiny primarily because they so aptly demonstrate how the interplay between immediacy and distance that is the central contention of this chapter plays out in the course of particular texts; but in so doing they also exemplify why interplay is so significant not only for individual lyrics but also for their culture. They remind us that, as the briefer instances adduced above suggest, the dialogue between immediacy and distancing in their varied forms is often semantic as well as structural. Many of the principal concerns in both early modern lyrics and their counterparts in other eras—notably the authority of speaker and author, the reliability of representation, and the relationship of speech and writing—are analyzed and negotiated precisely through that dialogue. In addition, it can be employed to explore questions about the accessibility of biblical events in contemporary culture that, as indicated above, acquired culturally specific valences and intense force through seventeenth-century millenarian movements.

⁓

In the first song in Lady Mary Wroth's *Pamphilia to Amphilanthus*, a shepherdess laments the betrayal and inconstancy of her lover; anticipating her own death, she concludes on the lines that she hopes will appear on her tombstone:

And thes lines I will leave
    If some such lover come
Who may them right conseave,
    And place them on my tombe:
She who still constant lov'd
    Now dead with cruell care
    Kil'd with unkind dispaire,
And change, her end heere prov'd.
            (41–48)[87]

The poem again demonstrates that it is through the interaction of immediacy and distancing that certain issues central to lyric are expressed. In this instance, the text deploys that interplay to stage a problem of interest to many critics today, the relationship between the immediacy of voice, emphasized by the recurrence in close conjunction of the word "sayd" (17, 21), and the permanence, or apparent permanence, of writing.[88] The issue of stability in love mirrors that of the stability of texts recording love; the poet who ended the 1621 version of this sequence with a tribute to constancy here evokes a speaker who wants to create a tribute to her own constancy in a medium that will itself have the immutability, or apparent immutability, of inscription. But the feasibility of that project is no more certain than the survival of true love: even if a lover does come, she or he may not "conseave" (43) the lines rightly, and that in turn raises the question of how readers will "conseave" the lines. Moreover, the verb suggests not only comprehension but impregnation; the lover would be a kind of second maker, thus beginning the process of distancing the lines from the shepherdess that will culminate in the inscription.

These concerns are part of a larger semiotic preoccupation throughout the poem, the issue of what type of signs offer representation that is reliable in its message and lasting in its effects. We start with a reversal of the pathetic fallacy, so nature clearly does not always read the emotions of those within it accurately, nor can it necessarily be read as a register of those emotions; and the shepherdess proceeds to look for other signs she can deploy, announcing, for example, that the willow branches she will wear "shall my wittnes bee / My hopes in love ar dead" (27–28).

Juxtaposing this poem with others involving epitaphs reveals just how distinctive Wroth's approach to both the putative immortality of her poem and the related issues of representation are. As William Waters has shown in his acute analysis of such lyrics, the inscription must depend on "a voice that it also, ceaselessly, hopes to ambush."[89] In many instances, ranging from Horace's ode 3.30 to its heir in Shakespeare's Sonnet 55 to some of the Rilke sonnets Waters analyzes, the dead person is closely associated with, if not necessarily completely identified with, the stone. But in weakening that linkage by having the shepherdess express the hope that someone may someday carve her words on her tombstone, Wroth replicates and complicates the process of waylaying, establishing the need of two ambushes, which trope each other. She must waylay both the person who will find and inscribe the poem and that of the subsequent reader—or, to put it another way, the process of representation becomes a virtual *mise en abîme*, since the shepherdess's words, already a representation, will be represented on the tomb, which will then represent them to onlookers in the hope that one of them will perform a version of the same process in voicing them. This process anticipates the layering of Desdemona's willow song, analyzed in Chapter 5. In the case at hand, observe too that this sequence is further undermined by the two conditionals in, "*If* some such lover come / Who *may* them right conseave" (42–43; italics added), the first arguably emphasized through a spondaic or trochaic foot. In addition to the more general issues about language and immortality raised by Wroth's interpretation of the conventions surrounding epitaphs, might not these hesitations also encode Wroth's anxieties about whether her own work will be interpreted "right" (43) and about whether—for all the hermetic privacy Jeffrey Masten has found in her work—it will be widely read?[90] The related issue of exactly who is currently being addressed recalls Keats's "This living hand."

These and many other questions are enacted formally through mediating devices; thus the semantic core of the poem is embodied in the techniques that variously create immediacy and distance within it. Most obviously, the poem is full of references to representation in its many guises, reminding us that what we are reading is a text and encouraging us to think how our reactions to it are a sample of the problematical relationship between speech and writing. On one level we are perusing speech that is available to us precisely because it has been inscribed, and yet on another a recurrent concern of that inscription is its own potential unreliability. The relationship between the immediacy of voice and writing—between air and stone, two potentialities for lyric that are, as we saw in Chapter 1, suggested by early modern troping—is further complicated by our inability at several points to determine which we are encountering. Are we reading what is written on the bark or hearing her talk about the fact that she will write on it? And in the final stanza, are we on some level reading the inscription, which is immediate in the sense of addressing us even though it is in the most literal sense inscribed, or are we hearing her recite what it will say, or hearing her read from a paper on which it is written?

These alternatives evidently raise theoretical questions that recall the deconstructionist debates of the twentieth century, but they also gesture towards questions about the relationships among oral delivery, scribal, and print culture that must have been of interest to Wroth and her readers, poised as they were at a moment when texts were transmitted in all these ways. In particular, the appeal to the person who may find the poem and reproduce it on a tombstone registers authors' dependence on those who circulated manuscripts and those who published them. One may recall in this context the conditionals cited in the previous paragraph.

Furthermore, the whole issue of immediacy is itself made immediate and pressing by the way this lyric—much like Robert Sidney's third song and ninth pastoral—on first reading tricks the reader. We are plunged into the poem by hearing a voice that delivers a transhistorical and transcultural lament; for all the limitations on voiceability, the opening two stanzas certainly invite it. Then suddenly we read, "A sheapherdess thus sayd" (17) and another function of the repetition of that verb is to intensify the abrupt distancing. A specific speaker, defined by a profession shared by few if any of the readers, is named; the poem is further distanced by being located in a pastoral landscape, adumbrated but not clearly established by the opening lines. In short, then, the poem creates an intense impression of the presence of the shepherdess, only to distance her and her speech through doubts about exactly what one is hearing or reading. Thus it stages its semantic core in its workings—issues about loss, betrayal, and representation that call into question not only the promises of lovers but also the authority of the shepherdess and the reliability and permanence of her words.

Marvell's "Bermudas" was perhaps written in response to the experiences of John Oxenbridge, a persecuted Protestant minister who had twice gone to the islands in question. It records the hymnlike song of a group of rowers, apparently Puritans themselves, judging from the reference to prelates. The poem demonstrates how the interplay between effects of immediacy and of distance can, as I am arguing, negotiate theological and spiritual issues as well as broader poetic issues, such as the trustworthiness of representation. Most analyses of this charming lyric have focused on the song at the expense of the lines that precede and follow it. Such studies have typically concentrated on the spiritual and historical sources for that hymn, tracing its skilled paraphrases of Scripture, its quotation of lines from the psalms deftly woven into the song, its debts to other descriptions of Paradise, and its responses to Edmund Waller's mock epic, *Battle of the Summer Islands*. Especially acute is Annabel Patterson's positioning of the poem in relation to contemporary attempts to work out aesthetically and spiritually satisfactory means of praising God.[91]

In addition, the hymn within the poem exemplifies the immediacy that often characterizes the spiritual poetry from that and other traditions.[92] The song relies on the lyric present. Proximal deictics—"this eternal spring" (13), "here" (14), "these rocks" (31)—give the landscape presence, making it accessible to the sense of touch associated with lyric, while the frequent appeals to the senses and, in particular, the reference to figs that meet the mouth literalizes that emphasis on touch. (Similarly, at the beginning of the poem, the proximal usage in "this song" [4] locates the hymn as immediate to the text if not to the experience itself.) In lieu of the pressing of hands involving touch, this lyric offers us a spiritual pressing involving taste.

These types of immediacy are, however, framed in ways that demand our attention; having examined how the hymn is positioned in relation to literary and religious traditions, one needs now to look more closely at how it is positioned in relation to the rest of the poem. Not only is it an instance of the poem-within-a-poem pattern discussed above; the effects of that status are intensified because, like many other hymns, it begins with a reference to singing a hymn, another version of warm-up procedures ("'What should we do but sing his praise?'" [5]). The impact of this frame on the sense of immediacy is, however, limited: although it certainly reminds us that we are witnessing a representation (which, we soon discover, is itself a representation of the psalms), it is also part of the performance, a way of singing rather than just of singing about singing. Later these hints are sustained by the description of the island as "a grassy stage" (11).

Far more extensive, however, are the consequences of the other passages that frame the poem, in more senses than one. It opens:

Where the remote Bermudas ride
In th'ocean's bosom unespied,
From a small boat, that rowed along,
The list'ning winds received this song.

These seemingly straightforward lines in some respects provide textbook examples of how mediating devices can work in lyrics, while in other respects they simultaneously demonstrate and reject such mediation. To begin with, like many of the passages I have explored, they qualify the putative immediacy of lyric by identifying what ensues as a representation. The emphasis on the unusual setting prepares the reader for something special, for an event in the senses identified above; at the same time, however, the low-key language and the size of the boat arguably delimit the grandeur of what is about to ensue in a way that privileges the restraint Patterson and others associate with the Protestant—or, more specifically, Puritan—aesthetics of the poem over the process that anthropologists term warm-up.

Mediating devices, we have seen, frequently locate the lyric in a particular time and place; in so doing, they may distance it from the reader and author, though they may also intensify its vision in a way that makes the poem and its subject more present, more immediate. Gesturing towards those more common types of mediation, this stanza at first seems to position the ensuing hymn geographically, turning space into place, as lyric frames so often do: "Where" (1) holds out the promise of such transformation, and the proper noun that shortly ensues, referring as it does to an area about which many members of Marvell's original audience had been reading pamphlets, appears to deliver on the promise.

But of course the singers themselves are not on the island but rather at sea, a locale that prototypically represents space not place, especially when one recalls Yi-Fu Tuan's association of the former with movement and the latter with stasis. And the language of this stanza transforms the apparent positivism of the reference to the Bermudas, intensified by many readers' prior knowledge of those islands, into a description that is itself, as it were, all at sea. Initially, "remote" (1) hints that those expectations might not be met, and in fact the four lines proceed to overturn it. If the islands, like the boat, "ride" (1), one implication is that their location is unstable, hard to determine; similarly, "unespied" (2) could suggest that the reader is privileged to see what others cannot, but it also arguably hints that if the islands are hard for anyone to spy, a "small boat" (3) will be impossible to find. Subterranean and debatable though it may be, that hint is reinforced in the fourth line of the stanza, which draws attention to the absence of other observers. As Rosalie L. Colie briefly but suggestively notes, the poet and persona do not seem present and the readers "seem to happen in"; one might extend that statement by suggesting that even we have trouble happening in on this landscape.[93]

In other words, this opening at once undertakes the task of locating the poem spatially and evades it, hence refusing one of the principal functions of mediating passages; as in many Winslow Homer paintings, the viewer is denied a shore of dry land from which to view the action at sea. If mediating devices summon up and position a vision, the detachment that Colie acutely stresses complicates but does not obviate those processes.[94] Thus the interplay of immediacy and distance is rendered semantic and thematized, as is so often the case, and the viewer's relationship to the poem crystallizes questions about representation.

The conclusion reads,

> Thus sung they, in the English boat,
> An holy and a cheerful note,
> And all the way, to guide their chime,
> With falling oars they kept the time.

(37–40)

Like other frames, this modulates the suggestions of presence and presentness by defining the song as part of a particular moment: "Thus sung" (37) is tellingly different from the alternative Marvell could readily have chosen, "Thus sing." In the same line, however, "English" relates the experience in the remote Bermudas island back to that of readers on Marvell's island, many of whom had also been victimized by prelates.

Framing is a thematic and imagistic focus of the poem: the pomegranates are jewel cases, the oranges "golden lamps in a green night" (18), the worshipers' temple "frame[d]" in the rocks (31). And framing and its discontents enact the ethical stance of the poem. This apparently straightforward lyric was composed by the poet whose "Garden" represents Eden as not only the locale of temptation but also itself an epistemological temptation for readers who might unwarily assume that fallen man can return to a prelapsarian paradise. It was written by the man who warned us that his mourning nymph's attraction to an innocent joy is itself a temptation. A similar agenda, I suggest, compels the frames that both exemplify and eschew mediation here. Marvell is trying to suggest that the paradisiacal world the poem evokes is not available to his readers, who live in a fallen world of prelates and other sea monsters; but, as devout Puritans themselves, they may approach that ideal in limited ways.[95] Hence the poem on the one hand establishes the boat as "English" (37) while on the other distancing it. In this as in so many other respects, the dialogue of immediacy and mediation speaks the principal concerns of the poem.

Allied to Marvell in multiple ways, Milton also enacts a drama of limitation and caution through that dialogue. In his Nativity Ode, both immediacy and distancing are repeatedly invoked, thematized, and questioned (as of course is mediation in both the narrow sense this chapter deploys and its theological ramifications). Thus the text explores the transhistorical questions about authorship and representation, as well as more local theological problems that, I am arguing here, are often negotiated through the dual effects on which this chapter concentrates.

Seldom known for achieving irenic consensus, Miltonists have parted company, especially in recent years, on fundamental interpretive problems about this text. That this poem celebrates not only the birth of Christ but also Milton's triumphant instauration as poet-prophet remains a popular and predominant position in many quarters.[96] Among the dissonant voices, however, are the critics who draw attention to the suppression of the speaker's presence at a number of junctures; J. Martin Evans maintains that that erasure contributes to a dehumanized scene that ends on a negative note, while Hugh MacCallum sees it as contributing to the poise and balance he finds in the poem.[97] Other readings emphasize not the celebration but the limitation of poetic achievement; David Quint finds the putative personal and spiritual triumphs of the poem significantly undercut by its emphasis on the impossibility of achieving a pure world and the purified poetry the speaker seeks.[98]

Inconsistencies and unresolved conflicts in the text lie behind these opposing readings. The poem—not coincidentally the celebration of a divine mediator—stages the tension between the assertion that scriptural events may be immediately present at the date flagged in Milton's title, 1629, and the countervailing claim that they can be approached only through types of mediation that may create an impression of presence but also carry with them aesthetic limitations and spiritual dangers. In so doing, Milton does not eschew the celebration of poetry and his own position as poet that most critics still find in the text—the answer to the rhetorical question in stanza three about whether the Muse has a song is clearly a resounding yes[99]—but he does demonstrate the limitations of that version of mediation, together with those of other versions. In other words, whereas the shifts in the poem between the speaker's presence and its disappearance or redefinition through first person plural pronouns has previously and persuasively been traced to Milton's exploration of his personal role in interpreting scriptural events, those changes also help to construct an unresolved debate about the potentialities and limitations of both immediacy and mediation in lyric poetry.

In exploring all these issues, Milton of course focuses mainly on Christ's nativity; but in so doing he responds to millenarianism through a comparison of the immediacy of the nativity and that of the Second Coming. His interest in Protestant apocalyptic visions at this point in his career is not surprising for many reasons. Whereas Bale and Foxe were among the many prominent sixteenth-century figures in this tradition, prophecies about that event were becoming increasingly prominent in Milton's culture, possibly reaching their peak in the 1640s. More specifically, in 1627, two years after Milton was admitted to Christ's College and two years before he wrote the Nativity Ode, Joseph Mede, a Fellow of that college, published his influential *Clavis Apocalyptica*, which included the prediction that the Antichrist would fall within twenty-five years. Once again, historical developments in a smaller temporal unit within the early modern period encourage potentialities of lyric.

Witness above all the paratextual material that precedes the text proper in this poem. Although students of Milton have interpreted his decision to add the subtitle "Composed in 1629" in the 1645 edition as an announcement of his poetic instauration, in fact those three words also establish a dialogue with what precedes them, "On the Morning of Christ's Nativity," providing an example of the concerns of this chapter. Is the subtitle in apposition to—or in opposition to—the title? In other words, is 1629 indeed a version of the morning of Christ's nativity, or does the poem draw attention to a major temporal gap that marks other types of distance as well? From a different perspective, the title poses another unresolved question: to what extent is its author using "on" in the common sense of the Latin *de*, translated as "about," "on the subject of," a usage that Milton deploys in much of his early poetry? That is, is the poem "on" that morning in that it is a meditation on a prior event, a meditation occurring in 1629 rather than the year of the nativity? Or is Christmas Day 1629 itself the morning of the nativity in the sense that the event *is* happening on that day? Or is it through the very act of meditating on and writing about the event that it recurs? Conceivably, too, the classicist who wrote this poem was aware as he did so that *de* could be used spatially, signifying "down from, from an origin," thus casting in spatial terms the distance that is implied temporally by "Composed in 1629." If so, this is the first of many instances in this text where spatial positioning interacts with the temporal questions more overtly established through shifting verb tenses.

As the lyric progresses, through the temporal shifts noted by many readers and other strategies, Milton pulls us back and forth between those possibilities.[100] "This is the Month, and this the happy morn," the ode opens; emphasized by the anaphora and the meter of the opening foot, which may be either spondaic or trochaic, the deictic "this" stresses immediacy, hinting that the event is occurring even as we watch. "Did bring" (4), however, locates that momentous occasion in the past, one of many instances where deictics and verbs conflict rather than cooperate. From one perspective, the distancing effect of the verb tense is intensified by the line that follows it, "For so the holy sages once did sing," whether that statement is read as separating the poet's song from that of the sages or as suggesting that the first four lines quote them rather than merely repeating the gist of their song. The former reading anticipates and mirrors the rivalry with other singers established by reading "prevent" (24, quoted below) in terms of poetic competition.

Yet this is the first of many points in this lyric where one needs to qualify the widespread contemporary assumption that to establish a text as a representation is to establish it as well as a mere ruse, for, from another perspective, the line merges the poem we are reading and the sages' song, thus anticipating the presentation of this very text to the Christ child and also hinting that it is a material product, a tangible gift (a point to which I will return shortly). Moreover, it is conceivable, though by no means indisputable, that the repeated "this," in addition to all its other meanings, gestures towards the text itself, implying that the morn can be re-created in—and as—a lyric. In short, the opening stanzas, like the title and subtitle, raise unanswered questions about in what ways and to what extent the spiritual act of meditation and the poetic act of representation can draw us closer to their object.

Such questions are further complicated in the next few lines. Line 5 works like the metapoetic references I have explored to distance us from what the words make present with the reminder that we are reading a representation. And after another stanza, whose three past tense verbs emphasize the historical gap between 1629 and the birth of Christ, the ensuing reference to the poem itself suggests an extraordinary immediacy of time and place: "O run, prevent them with thy humble ode, / And lay it lowly at his blessed feet" (24–25).

In short, the opening stanzas that frame the hymn themselves repeatedly run quickly to the original scene of the nativity, only to block that movement through various strategies for distancing the birth of Christ and the act of writing about it. This tension between immediacy and distance is also established metrically: the hexameters that end the stanzas slow them down, creating a pause (which in the third stanza mimes aesthetically the decision to abide which the line expresses: "And chose with us a darksome House of mortal Clay" [14]).[101] As the poem progresses, changes in verb tenses continue the veering between presentness and distance. For example, whereas the first stanza in the hymn proper commences, "It *was* the Winter wild" (29; italics inserted), the strophe immediately following it begins, "Only with speeches fair / She woos the gentle Air" (37–38).

Such shifts are all the more striking when one compares other poems on the same subject. Crashaw's nativity ode, examined earlier from a different perspective, shifts between immediacy and distancing as well. For example, Thyrsis first refers to the baby in the third person, then moves to the second; later the Christ child is addressed by the poet immediately after he lifts his head, and it is as though that motion, with its sense of physical presence, enables the address. Moreover, the later version of the poem intensifies the immediacy by changing the tenses of lines 65–69: the infelicitous earlier version, "streight his eyes advis'd his Cheeke, / 'Twixt Mothers Brests to goe to bed" (49–50), becomes "See, see, how soone his new-bloomed cheek / Twixt's mother's brests is gone to bed" (67–68). Yet the movements in Milton's poem are more startling. In Crashaw's version temporalities and positionalities generally remain stable: with the exception of the rewritten lines 65–69, the poem records impressions from the past reported in the present; the persistent anaphora on "We saw" and "I saw" (33, 35, 36, 51, 58, 72, 74, 76, 77) emphasizes this structure. In Milton's lyric, in contrast, the reader repeatedly shifts abruptly from a sense of being present at the scene to watching the speaker watching the scene or hearing him report on doing so. Herrick's "Ode of the Birth of our Saviour" achieves some immediacy through the direct address to the child and the use of epiphora to emphasize that the baby was born "here" (3, 4, 5, 8, 27, 28, 31), but most of the time it regards that birth from a time period clearly distant from it; the one apparent exception, the promise to dress the baby in silks and jewels and make for it a room of ivory and amber, in fact reminds us that this adornment is metaphorical, involving adornment with praise and celebration rather than with literal clothes, and thus could be read not only as the product of a time period considerably after the birth but also as a reference to acts of representation like writing this poem. Thus Herrick, like Crashaw and Milton, moves from more immediate to more distanced responses; but like Crashaw and unlike Milton, he significantly limits the effects of doing so in that he does not repeatedly shift temporalities.

Those shifts carry with them many implications for authorship in general and Milton's putative instauration as poet-prophet in particular. Whether or not Milton is identifying with Christ in all the respects that Richard Halpern sometimes compellingly but sometimes unpersuasively enumerates,[102] he is surely allied through the role of intercessor. "But see!" (237), the final stanza opens, in the most overt of many reminders that poetry's gifts include intermediation, that is, it makes the scenes from the past present. But yet again that gift functions paradoxically, delimiting the very presence it apparently creates with reminders of the act of representation: much as the opening of the poem did through its references to those "holy sages" (5), the newly minted sage composing this lyric almost immediately qualifies the effects of "But see!" (237) with "Time is our tedious Song should here have ending" (237). This line shifts us from story time to discourse time and draws attention to the question of where the lyric is located, temporally and spatially, without conclusively resolving it. Indeed, that question is further complicated by the plural pronoun. To be sure, the text and its reader are "here" at the manger—there is apparently no room in the inn for poesy, its creators, and its readers—and yet, by reminding us that we are reading a poem, the line distances us from the scriptural events while simultaneously locating itself within them. "Here" could, after all, refer to a point in the text as well as a place in the stable.

Earlier, the implicit contrast between "humble ode" (24) and "lowly" (25) on the one hand and "Have thou the honor first, thy Lord to greet" (26) on the other is another technique through which the poet's achievements are both celebrated and interrogated. The Wife of Bath, one might remember, was eager to give her offerings first, and it is tempting to speculate how the Lady of Christ College would have responded to his proximity to this strange but enthusiastically inviting bedfellow. These reservations are intensified in the millenarian passages acutely analyzed by Quint. Song can apparently hasten events—

> For if such holy Song
> Enwrap our fancy long,
>     Time will run back, and fetch the age of gold.
>         (133–135)

—but "wisest Fate" (149) warns the makers of even holy songs against attempting to do so. Five years after writing this masque-like poem, I have argued elsewhere, Milton tries in his Ludlow masque to call up another type of Second Coming, the birth of a reformed masque—but finds that he cannot in fact completely do so.[103] Moreover, the debates here about the extent to which a poet can make Scripture immediate and the dangers of hubris and haste he faces in doing so anticipate the concerns that were to become more prominent in *Paradise Lost:* the author of an "advent'rous song" (I.13) is at once celebrated and cast into dubious company by that adjective. In that instance, the adventure and the dangers revolve precisely around questions of presence and mediation, issues whose resonances for Milton and many of his readers, as suggested above, were no doubt intensified by Reformed debates about the Eucharist and about the apocalypse. To put it another way, if an ode is, as Paul H. Fry incisively maintains, "a vehicle of ontological and vocational doubt," with the possibility of presence in many forms central to that doubt, in these Miltonic examples it is more specifically located in current theological issues.[104] Once again, generic potentialities acquire a local habitation and a name.

As we have seen, whether one reads the poem as celebrating or interrogating poetic instauration, or both, it is clear that Milton is performing it in several senses of the word. And it is no less clear that the result of that performance is an entity that, like the gifts of the Magi, can be laid at the "blessed feet" (25) of the child. Thus the ode invites us to look more closely at the senses in which early modern lyric is an object resulting from a performance, an examination that will develop some issues about the physicality of lyric introduced in Chapter 1 and also encapsulate and extend this analysis of how distancing devices work in that tradition.

—⁂—

As I was drafting this chapter, a morning news program announced that Martha Stewart's personal assistant had given "a teary performance on the stand," thus demonstrating the multiple denotations and connotations of the term that has recently generated a whole new field of performance studies. In social and aesthetic situations, to what extent if at all does "performance" necessarily suggest deceit? In textual analyses, does it refer to theater in the more literal sense, the meaning often dubiously ascribed to Judith Butler's influential work on performance, or should it be used primarily for the type of repetitive gestures on which her most influential work on the subject in fact concentrates? Different though they are, the several meanings of "performance" raise a number of broad issues relevant to lyric though not immediately relevant here, such as whether, and if so how, the presence of an audience is essential. It is more to my purposes, however, that performance in its several guises, particularly the specifically early modern one on which this section concentrates, involves a dialogue—often, indeed, stichomythy—between immediacy and mediation. I concentrate here on a meaning particularly relevant to questions of immediacy, mediation, and framing, that is, the creation of a material product or something analogous to it.

Other meanings of "performance" do need to be adduced in passing, if only to remind oneself that in the final decades of the sixteenth century and in the seventeenth, when increasingly theatrical companies focused on London playhouses rather than traveling extensively, people living outside London were at least as likely to associate performance with the recitation or singing of lyrics as with the presentation of plays. When early modern lyrics were read aloud by their own author, the situation of performance would in some important ways effect both immediacy in general and presence in particular. Indeed, as David Schalkwyk has pointed out in an important study, in many circumstances the speakers of lyric were literally embodied; lyric, he acutely insists, is performed socially through linguistic performatives.[105] And if the author sang them, as not only Wyatt but many of his counterparts clearly did, the special power of such music could achieve the aural equivalent of a tactile pressing of hands: the intensity associated with song and its ability to fill a room and command the attention of the inhabitants all create the kind of heightening that contributes to an impression of presence.

Importantly, it is an impression of presence, for in other respects performance in these senses could build distance. The circulation of poems in scribal culture facilitated their recitation by animators who had not written the texts (as students of discourse analysis would put it), much as Hobbinol repeats Colin's song in the April eclogue, thus emphasizing the distance from both the original performer and the earlier performances. "When I have done so, / Some man, his art and voice to show, / Doth set and sing my paine" (12–14) Donne complains in "The Triple Foole," reminding us that song, or verse that could readily be turned into it, was as alienable as other forms of portable property.

Many attributes of lyric's interplay between immediacy and mediation can also be read in terms of other theories of performance. Students of Romantic and other poetry that frequently uses prosopopoeia might gloss its workings with Butler's conception of performance as the repetition of an action that creates something that did not before have a stable existence. Reiteration is also central to the anthropological theories of performance adduced above; Herbert Blau's assertion that rituals have no originary moment, just reproductions, is suggestively similar to Butler's paradigm.[106] Such studies, influenced by Turner's emphasis on parallels between ritual and the stage, typically adduce drama and dance rather than lyric. In fact, as the instance of Barnes may indicate, their work, like Butler's, is at least as useful for lyric—perhaps more so, given all the formal versions of repetition characteristic of that mode. The mode that, as Frye points out, stems from the repetitions of babble is a virtual echo chamber, and its formal repetitions, like those of refrains in particular, can function ritualistically to call up a spirit of some type. Witness the insistent rhythms through which Barnes evokes Hecate in his fifth sestina, as well as the repetition of that creature's name and the use of anaphoric structures. Examined above, Crashaw's "Hymn in the Holy Nativity" effects a similar process, though with antithetical moral dimensions, by repeating "Tell him, Tityrus, where th'hast been" (15, 16) in successive lines.

Although these and other theories of performance could usefully be deployed further to study lyric in both the early modern and other eras, a different sense of the term is especially germane to the subject of this chapter. In her important essay cited from a different perspective earlier in this chapter, Mary Thomas Crane teases out the shifting and varied usages of "performance" in early modern England, emphasizing in particular that the word was frequently applied to carrying through a task or exercise, especially for processes that could result in turning something immaterial into the material.[107] She proceeds to demonstrate that this terminology establishes theater as being like a trade that can generate a material effect, especially something that can be "used" or "kept," and adduces plays like Jonson's *Alchemist* to trace the processes she posits. Yet again, a model previously deployed for the stage proves at least as useful in analyzing lyric.

The multiple senses in which lyric is an artifact have hardly been ignored by students of the mode. Roland Greene, for example, redefines the term in order to posit the "nominative" option, in which the speaker is a single self, against what he terms the "artifactual" alternative of several voices.[108] Moreover, as I have already observed, many early modern texts invite us to see them as physical objects in someone's hands, "lyke captives trembling at the victors sight" (Spenser, *Amoretti*, 1.4), yet another sense in which lyric invokes touch. But Crane's article urges us to consider other respects in which lyric can usefully be seen as performed in the sense of not merely representing a product but also resulting in a product that is often in some sense material. First, early modern linguistic usages demonstrate the connections between the mode and the material work of artisans: I have already explored the term "turn," and Chapter 4 will demonstrate that by referring to stanzas as "staffs" and "staves," as well as by deploying architectural vocabulary, early modern writers represent lyric as a physical object, thus containing in its well wrought urn anxieties about its propensity towards diffusion.

Second, and more to my purposes now, if the entire lyric may in some regards be artifactual, lyric is also performed in the sense that it may culminate on a product like a motto or couplet that, to borrow Crane's useful categories, may be "used" or "kept." John Shawcross hyperbolically asserts that the creation of an artifact, not the expression of emotion, is typically the principal aim of lyric (the claim is itself a problematical artifact of his otherwise fruitful emphasis on craft), but his statement prepares us to observe that often an artifact in these senses is indeed the product and goal of the emotion.[109] The very process of representing an experience in ways that intensify its immediacy may result in a physical object or an analogue to one. That product may be characterized by its distance from, and often distancing of, the original experience. At the same time, the object may introduce other versions of immediacy; the inscription on a tombstone, for example, may command attention as forcefully as a singing voice, and in some senses, as many have observed, it at once makes the absent person present and reminds us of the absence. Once again, in other words, the relationship between presentness and representation can involve not conflict but cooperation.

Frequently, though not invariably, the product in question is a representation of a material object, most obviously the inscription on which a text may end. Hence we return yet again to the tensions between the ephemeral and insubstantial and apparent material solidity present in the tropes analyzed in Chapter 1. If the first song in Wroth's *Pamphilia to Amphilanthus* omits the introductory warm-up so common in lyric, the whole poem may be seen as building up to the inscription. Pattern poems and anagrams, both exemplified by the pillar that is the eighty-first text in Watson's *Hecatompathia*, are cognate; it is no accident that Herbert, engrossed in examining the fraught relationships between devotion and the often sensual physical fabric of worship, creates pattern poems that are themselves physical objects. Analogous to that inscription, though usually not explicitly seen as physical, are mottoes and couplets, notably the "posies" at the end of the lyrics in Gascoigne's *Devises of Sundrie Gentlemen*. And the very word "posy" can refer to bouquets of flowers and writings within rings as well as to a short section of verse; thus it too flags connections with materiality.

Categorizing these types of conclusion also crystallizes some of their near kin. Sometimes the second voice on which the poem concludes functions similarly, to the extent that the poem builds up to it; like the presence that may result from an operatic serenade, it can seem to be a product of the song that preceded it even while delivering its own song. The serenade in opera is often a lyric that is designed literally to call forth a presence. Witness, too, its literary analogue and precedent, the literary tradition termed *paraklausithyron* or "by the open door."

In texts using it, which range from ones by Propertius to the folk song "Silver Dagger," the speaker, barred from the home of his beloved, attempts to gain entry, thus reversing the agenda of the serenade.

How and why do so many early modern poems "perform" a product in this sense? The briefer warm-up that may precede the body of a poem hints that, in these alternative instances, the bulk of the lyric may be seen as a warm-up for the final product. Yet again their authors are reacting to fears of the evanescence of their mode: these fragments they have shored against its ruins. Marvell's grieving nymph cannot protect her faun from the troopers or her own innocence and trust from Sylvio, but she can create a memorial. Or, to put it another way, although they cannot be classified as prosopopoeia in that, with the exception of the second voice, they generally do not speak, these concluding products perform what one might think of as a type of prosopopoeia function in testifying to the generative power of the text and its speaker or author. Bereft in other ways, Wroth's shepherdess may nonetheless inscribe. She moves from a semiotic system of branches, which will hardly be widely read (even by those who believe in supporting their local branch library) to a translucent inscription. Although they characteristically appear at the end of a lyric, these objectified sayings operate like titles in that they may announce a kind of ownership and entitlement; and they literally have the last word. In particular, if the refrain has, as it were, a roving eye, looking backwards and forwards and at itself, such artifactual assertions insistently stare straight ahead at the audience they are controlling.

The frequent result, however, is not a straightforward tribute to the agency of verse and its creator but rather a reexamination of that issue. Stone, though more stable than air, nonetheless wears away, as I suggested in Chapter 1 and as other students of lyric have noted as well.[110] At the same time, representing the poem or some section of it as a material object leaves open both the potentialities and the dangers of a kind of surrogate parenthood: if the fruits of one's conception will be, in Wroth's own term "conseave[d]" (43) and then inscribed by others, on the one hand the shepherdess has insured that someone will care for her story but on the other she has surrendered it for adoption. The text risks becoming a trinket others can hold in their palm rather than a tornado that may envelop them. And when these codas are the detached sayings whose gathering the humanist tradition advocated, they substitute a collective wisdom for the insight of the individual author.[111] Some of the closural strategies adduced in this section, like the mottos at the end of the eclogues in Spenser's *Shepheardes Calender,* resemble the "cool-down" phrase studied by anthropologists because of their detachment from and sometimes passing relevance to the intense emotion and events that precede them.

Nor are such conclusions a straightforward demonstration of the move from immediacy to distance. Clearly many of them are textbook examples of shifting from voice to inscription; clearly, too, the sort of generalizations expressed through posies and mottos can distance the reader from the experience rendered in the text, a movement often mimed by the shift from English to Latin. Yet the deictic "here" and the direct address to the reader that so often characterize inscriptions remind us yet again that the hand that presses another one and the hand that pushes another away frequently belong to the same body.

# CHAPTER 4

# The Predilections of Proteus

## *Size and Structure*

Lyric poems, unlike lyric poets, seldom wander lonely as a cloud. Typically neither solitary not unitary, they variously and sometimes simultaneously establish and resist links with other texts around them, while similarly binding and loosening subdivided units within themselves. To define lyric poetry in the early modern or any other period as short is risky, in part because that descriptor is vague and relative. For example, Edmund Spenser's "Epithalamion," though technically distinguished from the so-called "epic" version of its genre through its classification as a "lyric" epithalamium, is substantial enough to make that designation problematical; although William Wordsworth's "Intimations of Immortality" is a typical, indeed prototypical, example of lyric in many respects, it is 203 lines long. And even if one attempts a broad description, rather than a precise definition, of lyric in terms of brevity, trouble arises precisely because of the genre's predilection for forging and loosening links among constituent units. On occasion it is even difficult to say where a given poem begins and ends. For example, is Spenser's *Shepheardes Calender* a single poem or a collection of them, and how about George Meredith's *Modern Love?* Moreover, in the more common instances where lyrics seem to be separable but related, the shortness of individual poems may be far less important to their workings than the connections among the parts; the answer poems that are so common in the early modern period obviously interact with each other, as do analogous pairings in William Blake's *Songs of Innocence and Experience*. In other words, the brevity of lyric is not infrequently a problematical criterion, and it needs to be recast in terms of a larger perspective—the potentialities for fluidity and malleability that in effect shape and reshape the dimensions of a single lyric by breaking it into parts or inserting it into larger entities.

For many reasons, especially the influence of the conditions of production, those potentialities have been variously realized in different historical periods and subdivisions within them. Establishing the anthology as the characteristic format for medieval lyrics, Seth Lerer observes that readers typically purchased unbound sheets that they then bound themselves.[1] Romantic lyrics were often packaged in volumes known as "Keepsakes," annuals that were designed, one critic asserts, "as a status gift rather than a book to read."[2] In the early twenty-first century, numerous publishers have expressed a preference for collections of lyrics linked by a narrative structure, and, given the difficulty of getting poetry published, that preference has had a considerable impact on writers.

This chapter explores the forms these issues about the dimensions of lyric assume in regard to early modern poetry in particular. It approaches the putatively characteristic brevity of the mode in terms neither of the cohesiveness of a well-wrought urn nor of the shards into which a generation of iconoclastic critics have transformed that urn but rather of the potentialities of a series of units, notably the stanza. The precept that the size of an early modern lyric should be interpreted in relation to its malleability is my underlying presupposition but not my principal thesis: the changeable and permeable dimensions of lyric in the English Renaissance have been so thoroughly demonstrated that they require only a brief overview, not lengthy documentation, here. Nor is intervening in contemporary debates about such issues as the impact of print on changing conceptions of authorship the primary agenda of this chapter—though I do engage briefly with those questions—if only because an adequate discussion of them would have required extensive commentary on more than one genre and more than one historical period. Rather, I explore two consequences of malleable size, one related to the units that comprise a given lyric and the other to its role within larger units: I argue that stanzas, as well as other devices, provide more fixity than studies of lyric often have claimed and that groupings of poems, as well as other techniques, allow a more powerful assertion of authorship than students of early modern lyric have recognized. Clearly, these two issues are potentially connected: the fixity of stanzas may on occasion contribute to authorial agency and the combining of poems may build fixity, though, as studying the interventions of printers and examining Lady Mary Wroth's poems will demonstrate, these connections are by no means inevitable.

Because of the contemporary interest in conditions of production and their impact on authorship, questions about the size and structure of lyric have hardly been neglected, and much of the resulting criticism is at least sound and at its best powerful. Many recent critical statements about the English Renaissance have rightly emphasized certain consequences of the malleable dimensions and structure of its lyric poems and their relationship to adjoining texts. That scribal and printing practices can shape interpretation has been demonstrated with particular acuity by one of the most influential students of the scribal and print cultures, Harold Love: "Clearly a Pindaric ode on the bible means one thing read as part of a collection of godly verse and quite another wedged between two segments of 'Seigneur Dildoe': equally clearly it would not be within all communities of readers that such a juxtaposition would have been possible."[3] Tracing the malleability of specifically scribal production, Arthur F. Marotti coined the apt term "social textuality."[4] Numerous examples support his influential analyses.

Yet two common presuppositions, widespread though not universal, about the fluid size and form of early modern lyric are more dubious. First, many critics are prone to stress the instability resulting from its changeable size and structure. Fair enough. But, much as Chapter 3 maintains that, while seconding the conventional wisdom about the impression of immediacy created by lyric, one should look as well at its techniques for suggesting distance, so here I emphasize that the fluidity of lyric variously coexists and interacts with important techniques for creating stability in size and structure. As with the relationship between lyric and narrative elements, this interaction sometimes takes the form of a victory for one side or the other, sometimes of a continuing struggle, and sometimes of co-existence. My aim is not to replace an exaggerated emphasis on the protean and malleable with an equally hyperbolic model of solidity, but rather again to right some balances. Analysts of early modern texts need to devote more attention to strategies for countering instability other than that widely discussed event, the advent of print; in particular we need to look more closely at one such strategy that has been largely overlooked, the unit of the stanza itself.

One reason the potentialities of the stanza have not received the attention they deserve is the continuing impact of Elizabeth L. Eisenstein's *The Printing Press as an Agent of Change*, which traces the development of fixity, as well as a wide range of other changes, to print.[5] Subsequent scholars have, however, challenged her on both the sources and the workings of fixity, a concept that itself paradoxically risks slipperiness when deployed in so many different ways; asserting that "fixity is in the eye of the beholder," Adrian Johns, for example, argues that it, like other characteristics Eisenstein and her heirs and assigns attribute to print, in fact has other sources, such as perceptions of reliability.[6] This chapter suggests that stanzas themselves can provide (and on occasion, though less frequently, undercut) an important and often overlooked version of fixity, one that stems from a visual impact that is in the eye of the beholder in a sense more literal than Johns's, as well as from other sources. My first main argument, then, involves a reconsideration of how the indubitably protean size and structure of early modern lyrics relates to their putative fragmentation.

Second, students of early modern literature and culture also need to rethink the relationship of the size of a lyric to authorial agency. Positing the stability of print as a precondition for authorship, certain discussions associate malleability with a widespread lack of any significant agency and control or transfer the possibility of agency from author to reader, printer, and publisher. This book is hardly the first study to challenge such readings; to choose one example among many, Roger Chartier famously traces many conditions contributing to authorship, including some present in the Middle Ages, even while also acknowledging the impact of print.[7] Nonetheless, the linkage between the malleability of lyric and the absence of authorship is still repeated in discussions of the mode, and it remains alive and well for a number of reasons. The dubious assumption that a lack of fixity in the sense of a stable, incorruptible text necessarily issues in a lack of authorship, in several significant senses of that concept, has been buttressed by a number of other critical predilections. Although rebutted in some influential recent collections, the widespread demonizing of the aesthetic has recently discouraged analysis of how aesthetic challenges and triumphs can create an important sense of ownership.[8] Also contributing to contemporary statements about authorial agency in lyrics is a model relevant to my discussion of lyric and narrative as well: that is, a winner-take-all, either/or system which assumes that the readers and the producers of the material text co-opt the role of author rather than coexisting as rivals or coauthors or even cooperating with the poet. "In a system of manuscript circulation of literature, those into whose hands texts came could, in a real sense, 'own' them," one study observes; another adds that "the dedicatee (as well as the subject) can own or seem to originate the work."[9] Yet another reason many early modern poets are not seen as authors is that some recent studies have redefined the concept in question to focus on the text as commodity and authorship as proprietorship, a model that does not appear readily to fit the alienable texts of the period. In doing this, Joseph Loewenstein relates conceptions of authorship to how books were sold, especially the development of monopolies, and Mark Rose emphasizes the significance of copyright.[10]

For these and other reasons, then, scribal culture still is often discussed in terms of the severe curtailment or virtual absence of authorial agency. ("The manuscript system was far less author-centered than print culture and not at all interested in correcting, perfecting, or fixing texts in authorially sanctioned forms," as Marotti puts it in another study, tellingly ascribing agency himself to the "system" rather than any of its participants.)[11] Print, in contrast, is seen in many quarters to enable and encourage authorship; but critics often interpret conceptions of the author in the sixteenth and early seventeenth century as at best rudimentary anticipations of our own category, whether because they see the impact of print as gradual or because they believe that factors that developed later contribute significantly as well.

Although these assumptions are in certain respects justified, a blanket application of them has too often led studies of early modern lyric astray. Admittedly, my discussion of that apparent breeding ground of subjectivity the sonnet will demonstrate that its authors' agency in relation to the poems was as various and indeed in many instances delimited as the lovers' control over their ladies. In the sonnet and many other genres, one reason writers so often glorified their role as second makers, as Sidney so memorably does in his *Apology for Poetry*, is their uneasy awareness that third and fourth makers were just around the corner. Numerous studies have shown that both humanist doctrine and the material conditions of production enabled, even encouraged, readers to excerpt and redeploy a section of a lyric. The circulation of manuscripts and the popularity of commonplace books further encouraged those processes. And because so many readers in the period were also occasional poets, their own breaking apart and recombining of sections of poems surely alerted them to the structural fluidity of the texts they read.

Yet at the same time reading early modern lyrics drives one to reconsider a number of widespread presuppositions about the relationship of the malleability of their size and structure to authorship, and on this issue, too, my agenda is largely revisionist. Authors, I will demonstrate, reassert agency, even, or in some instances especially, in scribal dissemination, notably through the process of grouping their texts. That such agency is sometimes circumscribed from the perspectives traced here is not to say that it is insignificant: many instances that contemporary paradigms might tempt us to dismiss as further cases of an author virtually absent or silenced by the power of readers and publishers can better be seen in terms of an interaction among these agents. The second- and third-generation feminist work that, while still acknowledging cultural constraints on the female voice, questions earlier paradigms about the putative silencing of women would be a useful model for revisionist work on the putative silencing of the author for much of the early modern period. The malleability of texts is counterbalanced in certain important respects; so too is the curtailment of authorial control over the size and shape of lyric.

Authorial agency, however limited, on occasion has important consequences for the aesthetic workings of the text and the development of authorial subjectivity. The malleable may become modular, the protean plastic: the very alterability of early modern poetry carries with it opportunities for semantic exploration and artistic impact that transform chaotic malleability into controlled modularity—that is, into a skillful deployment of subdivisions and other units. In particular, as I will demonstrate, in both theory and practice poets often deploy stanzas to create an impression of a stable structure. Moreover, the plasticity of texts allows not only the intervention of readers, printers, and publishers but also the continuing engagement of writers with their work, a process that contributes to a sense of power and ownership.

In short, this chapter supports and extends a widespread consensus about the fluid size and architectonics of early modern lyric; but in focusing on stanzas and on groupings of texts it challenges two associated corollaries of fluidity: the downplaying of important structural devices and the denial or downplaying of authorial agency when it interacts with or supersedes other possible masters of the text. This is a fruitful moment to examine such questions because of their implications, though often tangential, for a field currently very much in flux, the study of the conditions of production. Earlier contrasts between scribal and print culture have been challenged by many recent studies stressing their coexistence.[12] Earlier assertions about the fixity of print in contrast to the fluidity of manuscripts have been questioned through a more sophisticated interpretation of those media and, in the instance of David Kastan's work in particular, of their relationship to electronic heirs and assigns.[13] As noted above, earlier histories of the chronology of authorship have been challenged, with certain medievalists ascribing that concept to their own era.[14] Despite the powerful achievements of such projects, however, the malleability of the text is still stressed far more than the potentialities for containing that flux, and in many circles the widespread commitment to linking authorship to the advancing impact of capitalism has preserved some longstanding and dubious assumptions, especially about the virtual erasure of the author for much of the sixteenth and even the early seventeenth century.

⁓⁓

In exploring its dual interlocking challenges to how the size and structure of the early modern lyric are often read, this chapter focuses in particular on two arenas, stanzas and groupings of poems. But because the patterns found in these two elements of structure recur in so many other venues in early modern lyric poetry, a short overview of malleable size and its implications will provide the best introduction to stanzas and clusters of texts. Admittedly, in many cases the text has no close affiliations; in many others the reader is aware of it as a separate entity engaged in a dance with another clearly separate text, distinct though intimate partners who sometimes press against each other but may at other points whirl apart: if we cannot tell the dancer from the dance, we can still tell one dancer from another. Thus, for all the connections between Samuel Daniel's sonnets to Delia and his "Complaint of Rosamond," most other critics would challenge reading them as a single text.[15] Influenced by Pietro Aretino, Sir Thomas Wyatt forges links among the psalms he translates, yet the poems are still distinct. But, as I suggested above, even in these instances of separable but closely related poems, the interplay of texts within larger units may be no less important to their workings than the brevity that is stereotypically associated with the genre. In any event, these examples of poems that are closely related yet readily separable occupy a point on a spectrum that includes instances where the distinction between texts may blur until seeing them as fully individuated separate poems becomes trickier. This slipperiness is very common in the early modern period, in part because of a delight in rhetorical figures and other poetic practices that build links, a vogue for genres that encourage them, and a reliance on conditions of production that facilitate them. To return to Daniel, when he connects individual sonnets with *concatenatio*, in what senses if any is their status as single poems compromised?

Because manuscript circulation made it especially easy to combine and recombine texts, such questions recur repeatedly concerning scribal versions. Appearing in the collection *Liber Lilliati* and a number of other manuscripts are a riddle attributed to Sir Walter Ralegh and its answer, attributed to Henry Noel; are these one poem or two or a hybrid that calls into question those very categories? The riddles play on the names of these two authors, thus semantically introducing the concern with identity that is involved in their pairing.[16] Other types of answer poems raise similar problems. Ashmole 1486, as Marcy North points out, in effect establishes Marlowe's "Passionate Shepherd to his Love" and Ralegh's reply as a single poem: Simon Forman places the word "finis" only at the end of the second poem, not the first as he does with other lyrics.[17] Similarly, whereas one manuscript omits the "finis" between Marlowe's lyric and Ralegh's rejoinder, that fascinating collection the *Liber Lilliati* does not.[18] In another manuscript, apparently compiled by Henry Stanford, a series of sonnets its editor attributes to Stanford himself is linked through the repetition of the same opening words; given the many other similarities among these texts, they appear to be a cycle of sonnets more closely connected than such poems usually were, and in fact they read almost like stanzas of the same poem.[19]

Whereas many of the examples I have just cited involve a stable if complicated relationship, one of the multiple ways lyric is associated with process is the lability of its units, which, as numerous recent critics have demonstrated, was encouraged by both scribal and print practices. The same lyric may enlarge or contract under different circumstances; among its characteristic turns are moving towards and away from other poems. Sir Philip Sidney's "Fourth Song" is an intrinsic part of *Astrophil and Stella* in important respects, yet it appears as a separate poem at the beginning of *England's Helicon*, whose compilers were evidently attempting to take advantage of the cultural capital associated with its author; on another level, however, the title "The Sheepheard to his Chosen Nimph" encourages the reader to relate the lyric to other pastoral poems in the same volume. Also witness Sidney's "Eighth Song" ("In a grove most rich of shade"), which is printed with a musical setting—and without the seven stanzas in which Stella responds to her lover's entreaties—in Robert Dowland's *Musicall Banquet*. Again, the conditions of production often render structure even more fluid, with manuscripts (and on occasions printed books, a point to which I will recur) combining what had previously been separate texts or truncating what had been an apparent whole. To return to the manuscript of *Liber Lilliati*, it also includes, as its eighty-fifth entry, three stanzas of a poem that first appeared in John Dowland's *Second Booke of Songs or Ayres*, conjoined to a fourth sixain initially published in George Peele's *Polyhymnia*; in it may also be found a poem by Robert Devereux, Earl of Essex, that is present in no fewer than thirty-one copies made during the English Renaissance, some boasting fourteen stanzas and some fifteen.[20]

If size and structure are amorphous, the agents controlling them are multifarious and often ambiguous as well. A given eclogue might be circulated with a few related instances of that genre by its author, then juxtaposed with a different group of sonnets in a collection he published, then excerpted by someone else for an anthology, then copied in conjunction with a different sonnet in someone's manuscript or commonplace book, then perhaps harvested for a nugget of epigrammatic wisdom that would be written down with one or more similar observations, and so on. The interaction—and often the tension—between linkages flagged by the author and those created or undercut by other agents is not the least source of the fluid structures we are tracing and of reactions against them as well.

Petrarch's *Rime sparse* is prototypical even of English Renaissance poetry in more senses than one, as I suggested in Chapter 1, and many literary techniques popular during the period may be interpreted as defensive responses to the perceived scattering of manuscripts. Early modern poets and their readers surely saw lyric in terms of a dynamic interplay between scattering and gathering in their many forms, an interplay expressed on a range of levels, from the workings of particular prosodic forms and other poetic practices to the mythological narratives studied in Chapter 1 to the structure of particular texts and collections. Acutely traced to gendered antagonisms by many critics, the scattering of the female body in many love poems may also be glossed as a response to the poet's fears of being scattered: they do unto others what they fear will be done to their texts.[21] Exhaustive and incisive, Mary Thomas Crane's *Framing Authority: Sayings, Self, and Society in Sixteenth-Century England* cogently traces an apparently opposite activity, the humanist practice of gathering fragments of text, which she relates to one strain in the lyric poetry of that period.[22] Studying the size and structure of lyric, however, fruitfully extends Crane's argument by positioning the scattering and gathering that she primarily attributes to humanism in multiple other contexts.

In the English Renaissance, both mythology and diction, identified above as arenas for implicit discussions of lyric, offer decisive evidence of those preoccupations with the interaction between gathering and scattering in their many forms. In her acute study of Victorian lyric, Yopie Prins maintains that, in part because of her association with fragmentariness, Sappho in her many avatars was one of its principal exemplars.[23] In early modern England, as Chapter 1 demonstrated, Orpheus served cognate functions. The dismemberment of his body is not *sui generis* but rather the climax to the many types of dispersal associated with his death; in Ovid's version, the departure of Hymen foreshadows the tragic murder initiated by a woman whose hair is flying in the breeze, a crime that involves the fleeing of peasants and the scattering of their agricultural implements, often symbols of civilization ("vacuosque iacent dispersa per agros / sarculaque" ["Scattered through the deserted fields lay hoes"] XI.35–36), a crime that is mourned by trees shedding their leaves.[24] Yet Orpheus is also associated with types of gathering; as Chapter 1 indicates, he draws together listeners, even beasts, and political readings of the myth emphasize his drawing together and confining people in towns.

Individual lyrics often thematize the interplay between scattering and gathering enacted in their genre, with the latter typically serving as a preemptive strike against the possibility that the text will be scattered. "Lycidas" literally embodies scattering through the fate of Orpheus and King and enacts it formally through the irregular rhyme scheme of the canzone form and thematically through the *ubi sunt* tradition; but the end of the poem involves many forms of binding and reintegration, especially when Lycidas is gathered in by dolphins and the song that advertises itself as a monody concludes on the communal singing of choirs of angels. A lyric whose images focus on types of dispersal, George Herbert's "Collar," ends when its speaker is not poured out like water but rather gathered in, or at least apparently gathered in, by God. George Gascoigne's *Hundreth Sundrie Flowres* purports to gather the work of other authors, but it actually scatters Gascoigne's work among multiple fictive poets; not the least of the many valences of the title of the second edition, *The Posies of George Gascoigne*, is a reactive tying together.

A Claes Oldenburg sculpture on the campus of the University of Nebraska at Lincoln represents notebooks whose pages are blowing apart. Separated completely from the original binding, some of these leaves suggest uncontrolled dispersal; others, half torn, form graceful, avian patterns with other leaves in the same book. These images aptly represent the energetic and often unpredictable spread of knowledge that is the mission of the sculpture's setting—and they resemble as well the structural propensities that, I argue, characterize the early modern lyric. The best approach to those propensities is to turn now to two arenas where the principal foci of this chapter, attempts at stabilizing the text and asserting authorial agency, are played out in particularly intriguing forms: the micro-level of stanzas and the macro-level of collections of lyrics.

—⚬ ⚬—

Often though not unproblematically considered characteristic of lyric, stanzas are common in early modern English poetry, with many writers clearly delighting in crafting a range of them; and a fascination with especially challenging strophic patterns marks the period. Nonetheless, systematic discussions of stanzas, as of so many other issues about lyric, are rare, the principal ones occurring in brief passages within treatises by Gascoigne and George Puttenham, while suggestive though even shorter remarks appear in the note to the reader that precedes Michael Drayton's *Barrons Wars*. But these limited treatments fruitfully gloss the workings of early modern stanzas, and their multiple implications for the size and structure of the lyric enlarge when such passages are read in light of the reliance on metaphor noted in Chapter 1 and in collaboration with the literary texts that practice what the treatises preach. In particular, stanzas typically provide the solidity associated with "posy" in the sense of an inscription in metal or stone, assert the masculinity variously celebrated and threatened in other representations of lyric, and imply the holy harmony of certain types of music. At the same time, the movements from success to loss in Orpheus's story may alert us to how the potency of strophes may on occasion be undermined.

Yet another reason for looking closely at stanzas is that they demonstrate the interaction among textual practices too often treated separately by critics. As we will see, the effect of the stability and stasis that stanzas generally give is the product of a dynamic involving theoretical conceptions of stanzas, the aesthetic impact of components like couplets, and the visual presence of strophes on the page, which is often related to material practices such as the use of catch-words. Chartier's insistence on studying authorship in terms of the interaction among quite varied mechanisms, including but not unduly privileging print, is thus also a useful approach to many issues connected with stanzas.[25]

Particularly striking for my purposes is how intensely Drayton, Gascoigne, and Puttenham respond to that interaction by associating the stanza form with a cohesiveness and restraint that are antidote and antithesis to scattering. Or, to return to the framework introduced above, these three early modern writers insistently redefine malleability as modularity, thus rendering it a source of, not a threat to, the unity of the text. That insistence is probably a response to not only the general dangers of fragmentation but also a more local and reflexive peril: lyrics in general were prone to be reconstructed, even cannibalized, and rearranging stanzas was, as Marotti has shown, one particularly common type of scribal change.[26] Arguably these reactive efforts to assert the unity of a stanza also emphasize, even figure, that of its maker: authority over the text, potentially scattered among readers, printers, and copyists, is thus located in its builder. As Ernst Häublein suggests in his study of the stanza, the very term gestures towards unification—"The Italian etymology (a room of a house) implies that stanzas are subordinate units within the more comprehensive unity of the whole poem"—and in the rhetorical treatises in question and the poems themselves, this implication is crystallized and substantiated, often through architectural tropes that recall that etymology.[27] This is not to say that the fluidity of early modern lyric is absent from its stanzaic structure; rather, this prosodic unit often encompasses both protean shape-shifting and its reactive restraint, but with the latter typically dominating in both theory and practice.

"There is a band to be given every verse in a staffe," Puttenham writes, and by choosing "band" for rhyme in this context emphasizes not *rime sparse* but rather *rime raccolte*.[28] The anxieties behind this emphasis on collection and tying together, yet another instance of the dynamic of gathering versus scattering catalogued above, emerge explicity in the succeeding part of the sentence: "so as none fall out alone or vncoupled, and this band maketh that the staffe is sayd [stayed?] fast and not loose" (102). Later in the same section he further emphasizes the danger countered by these banding and binding rhymes: "Sometime also ye are driven of necessitie to close and make band more then ye would, lest otherwise the staffe should fall asunder and seeme two staves" (102). Keenly conscious of courtly hierarchy, Puttenham reveals his cognate consciousness of class when he suggests in passing that poetry written for the "rude and popular" ear needs more obvious rhyme (100), not a system where the rhyming words are distant from each other. Behind this comment may lie not only the assumption that the vulgar are not attune to subtlety but also a transfer of the fear of unruly mobs onto the fear that the poetry they favor will also be unruly if not carefully contained. Puttenham focuses here on audiences, but the association of the makers of lyric with artisans, traced in my first chapter and developed below in this one, may well have intensified such anxieties. A similar concern for unifying what might otherwise be scattered emerges in Gascoigne's *Certayne Notes of Instruction* when he describes the scheme of rhyme royal in terms of dialogue, a telling instance of the dialogic propensities discussed from another perspective in my examination of lyric audiences: "the first and thirde lines do aunswer (acrosse) in like terminations and rime, the second, fourth, and fifth, do likewise answere eche other in terminations, and the two last do combine and shut up the Sentence."[29] Later he again deploys that revealing verb "aunswere" (461), thus again drawing attention to the dialogic propensities of lyric. He also uses "crosse meetre" (460) for the *abab* stanza, while other early modern writers label that form "cross couplet"; these usages render the couplet form, that exemplar of unity, normative and pervasive. In short, the emphasis on restraint that glosses the versions of the Orpheus myth that stress his role as civilizer is apparent in these discussions of stanzas crafted by his heirs and assigns in the English Renaissance.

Also recurrent in the treatises in question is vocabulary that stresses the solidity of stanzas, thus again shoring them against the ruins of fragmentation: lyric is represented in terms of orderly and firm units, not ones that can fracture and splinter. Moreover, that solidity is seen as an implicit antidote to the anxieties about the evanescence of voice apparent in the usages of "air" discussed above: lyric is represented as not a breeze but a brick. The implications of these usages are literalized in the type of text known as a pillar poem. Drayton compares the eight-line stanza he uses in *The Barrons Wars* to a column—"this sort of stanza hath in it maiestie, perfection, and solidite, resembling the piller which in Architecture is called the Tuscan"—and he describes the couplet as its base. Puttenham establishes a similar point by presenting a poem in the shape of a pillar, which he terms the "most beawtifull" geometrical form (100), and a few pages later referring to the construction of a stanza in terms of masonry.[30] (The indentation of the couplets in several editions of Drayton's work published during his lifetime makes them appear an unreliable base at best, probably because the printer determined the layout of the poems. To this, too, this chapter will return.)

If such metaphors establish the strength of stanzas directly by connecting them to an icon of solidity, they accomplish the same end through implicit gendering, thus continuing the reactive interplay between masculine and feminine that, as we saw earlier, characterizes representations of early modern lyric. Masonry is evidently man's work, not the preserve of the women and children with whom lyric is sometimes associated. This vocabulary also protects and distinguishes the stanzas to which it is applied not only from the female and feminine but also from the accusation of effeminizing: columns suggest not the physical swaying and immoral suasion often attributed to lyric but rather rootedness, not the ravishment or seduction that, as we saw earlier, was associated with turning men into women but rather a type of solidity generally gendered male. Much as the massiveness associated with stanzas counters the evanescence of air, so the masculinity of their mason contravenes the femininity and emasculation that, as Chapter 1 demonstrated, were often though not always linked to lyric in general and the expression of voice in song, so often seen as female, in particular.

Although he does not refer explicitly to stanzas as columns, Gascoigne, in repeatedly deploying the cognate terms "staff" and "stave," raises many similar issues. Whereas "stave" referred to an individual piece of wood, the word was also frequently used in the period for the components of a barrel and the rungs of a ladder, as well as other kinds of sticks; thus some of its meanings draw attention again to construction based on the processes of gathering and binding together potentially disparate parts.[31] Literally denoting a stick, "staff" was also used in the early modern period to mean a support, the very role I am arguing stanzas served. More specifically, the term was applied in that era to certain kinds of material supports in particular—the bar between the handles of a plough, a part of a chair, something used in making a grid or case, a rung of a ladder, or, as in the case of "stave," part of a barrel—in other words, material objects that tie together otherwise separate parts. Since the association with a musical staff was already present in the early modern period, the term also adduces that symbol of unity in music, thus itself tying together artisanal production and aesthetic endeavors.[32] The references to pillars and barrels carry with them implications about not only the poem but also the poet. He is an artisanal maker, and, like the references to columns and the obvious phallic resonances of "staff," these allusions to the labor of artisans serve further to counter the conception of poesy as effeminate, effeminizing, and childish. Real men may not make sestinas, but they do make ploughs.

The resonances of this artisanal vocabulary are further emphasized by Gascoigne's orthography in the phrase "at the end of every staffe when you *wright* staves" (461; italics added). "Wright" was, to be sure, a variant spelling for "write" that did not necessarily carry associations of creating an artifact, as numerous instances of its usage insist, but the combination of the word with "staves" activates those punning associations. Their presence is also supported by the linkage of making stanzas to making artisanal products in the passages examined above, as well as in Puttenham's comparison between crafting a stanza and crafting a building: "even as ye see in buildings of stone or bricke the mason giveth a band" (102). (It may be argued that the connections between writing and manual construction also occurred in the next century; an English translation of the French author Paul Scarron includes the phrase "no higher a Rank than that of a Verse-Wright," where the reference to rank emphasizes the association with lowly manual work.)[33] Behind allusions like these lie a widespread association between manual crafts and literary endeavors of many types, not just the writing of lyric, brilliantly traced by Henry Turner.[34] More to my immediate purposes, the connection between the poet and the artisanal maker may reflect anxieties related to those that motivate the act of countering the scattering of verse with forms of gathering: in many arenas in addition to genre, definitions often function via making distinctions, and in this instance the definition of the poet as maker implies a rejection of the alternative Platonic model and hence of a kind of uncontrolled frenzy not unlike that of the Maenads and the many types of scattering that may be laid at their door. *Techne* replaces *furor*. Above all, this parallel between constructing stanzas and constructing useful and durable objects suggests that the poet orders and ties together.

The etymology of "stanza" evokes different but related resonances of the language of tying. Rooms can contain, confine, control. In describing the achievements of Orpheus, the verse attached to Emblem 81, "The force of eloquence," in Thomas Palmer's *Two Hundred Poosees* declares that the singer "Broughte those dispersed soules in one, / and walde them in a towne" (11–12).[35] That sorcerer Orpheus performs his apotropaic magic against the bestial by gathering in, tying together, much as stanzas might be said to do; the walling at once hints at protection and government. In other words, the act of making stanzas asserts dominion and mastery.

Stanzas can imply the author's power in other ways as well. If on one level the association of stanzas with binding and connecting linked the poet to lower social strata, these implications were effectively countered by contemporary theories of harmony as the fundamental principle of the universe, theories that are triggered by explicit references to harmony and music in the passage from Drayton we are examining, as well as in many other venues. The model of the world in Plato's *Timaeus* repeatedly stresses binding and coherence. Similarly, the emphasis on pairings and opposites in Boethius's *Consolation of Philosophy* conveniently encapsulates widespread assumptions that the universe joins together disparates, so that unity and goodness are one and the same. If the disparates fail to be one, he writes, things will perish and dissolve. Thus the vocabulary of constructing binding units aggrandizes the writer even as it associates him with manual labor; some mundane forms of earthly making are linked to the First Maker. And thus, too, the couplet and its *abab* cousin, tellingly described as "cross coupling," represent heavenly harmony. Moreover, while elevating the poet, these associations do the same for lyric, implicitly offering yet another rejoinder to the notion of that mode as childish toy or lubricious pandar. The frequency with which poems were set to music in the period fostered the linkage between stanzaic form and harmony in more ways than one. As Häublein points out, because such stanzas had to have the same melody, writers were encouraged to use similar syntactical units in them.[36] And, lacking the visual evidence of stanzaic form, the audience would have been alerted to it by those aural repetitions.

The association of celestial harmony with stanzas should prompt us to consider aspects of their more earthly potentialities. In practice, lyric poets frequently achieve what the theorists of the stanza preach. The often lengthy process of crafting a complex stanza form in particular counterbalances threats to authorial identity in two respects. Pragmatically, while printers, readers, and copyists may indeed, as students of early modern literature have emphasized of late, appropriate and modify texts, complicated prosodic structures do resist certain types of tampering. Although it remains possible to insert or delete words, it is much harder to switch or add lines to a sestina or sonnet. As noted above, Marotti has demonstrated how often scribes move stanzas;[37] but rhyme schemes like that of the sestina discourage deleting or appending stanzas, and in general the most complex stanzaic arrangements could prove daunting to those amateur poets among the readers wanting to dabble as Third Makers. And, whereas the widespread claim that authors took little pride in and felt little ownership over their work in the sixteenth century and even the early seventeenth may be easier to justify in relation to texts that were rapidly and easily produced, the labor of creating one of these complicated strophes is likely to produce a sense of pride and possession. *Techne* and title are related by more than alliteration: compare the masons' marks in cathedrals and in particularly impressive houses, such as that of the ill-fated Thomas Arden. To these points too I will return later in this chapter.

Solidity and its concomitant implications of harmony are the primary valence of the vocabulary of columns and masons. Yet an era that saw the literal breakup of monasteries, whose fabric was on occasion put to other uses, and that witnessed frequent large fires—Stratford-upon-Avon, for example, suffered three major blazes during the 1590s alone—would not necessarily associate buildings with permanence.[38] The emphasis on pillars, the most solid element in a building, may be a response to this, but the threat remained. Literal columns, like the stanzas they troped, were liable to be scattered. Thus latent in the vocabulary of materiality that provides an antidote to fluidity is a reminder of its ever present threat.

That peril not only remains but surfaces in stanzas that refuse or redefine their role as exemplar of binding and controlling. Ben Jonson's "To the Immortall Memorie, and Friendship of that Noble Paire, Sir Lucius Cary, and Sir H. Morison" explores versions of separation and reunification (the "infant phenomenon" who is born only to think better of it, the death of one of the eponymous heroes and their continued twinning, the hyphenation of "twi-Lights" [93–94], and so on) and also embodies those patterns in its stanza forms.[39] Jonson's anglicization of the three parts of the Pindaric ode into "turn," "counter-turn," and "stand" emphasizes a movement from debate to achieved stasis and harmony, in other words, to the functioning of stanzas as a bulwark against fluidity. Much as the relationship between turn and counter-turn is mimed within strophes through syntax like "Alas, But Morison fell young: / Hee never fell, thou fall'st, my tongue" (43–44), so too the linear structure of individual stanzas progresses from change and potential scattering to gathering. Consisting until the end of lines of varied length yet concluding on an iambic pentameter couplet that indeed binds, visually and aurally, they enact a movement towards containment and stability. And this realization of the potentialities described by Drayton, Gascoigne, and Puttenham remains a significant component in the workings of the poem.

Yet at the same time, the prevalence of such patterns makes their violation when Jonson famously scatters words and the structure of the stanza as a whole through an extraordinary enjambment, emphasized by the metrical variation created by the poet's last name—

And there he lives with memorie; and *Ben*
The Stand
*Jonson*, who sung this of him, e're he went
(84–85)

—all the more startling. One critic rightly observes that this passage is multivalent, suggesting at once overflowing and separation, disunity and unity;[40] but surely the scattering predominates. This transgression mimes the semantic content of the first of the two stanzas in which it appears, which involves "holy rage" (80) and "leap[ing]" (79), but it also serves to question the stability celebrated by the poem as a whole and symbolized by its stanzas.[41] Often himself associated with the assertion of authorship, Jonson thus complicates it here.

That master of the interrogative John Donne repeatedly asks similar questions about and through his stanza forms. To be sure, by concluding the first and last lines of all the stanzas in "The Canonization" on "love," he not only comments on the ubiquity and significance of that state but also suggests that the stanzas celebrating it are themselves cohesive and contained, again exemplifying the principles theorized about stanzas. Elsewhere, however, he more characteristically undercuts the predominant conceptions of the stanza form that I have been identifying. Donne often plays the putative solidity of a stanza against challenges to that stable unit, and the challenges often, but by no means always, triumph. On the one hand, "The Sunne Rising" concludes each stanza on couplets which semantically and aurally express the assured victories of the speaker; on the other, the varied line lengths and enjambments earlier in the stanzas suggest scattering more than gathering. Similarly, in Donne's couplets, themselves a kind of little stanza, we encounter in miniature this variation from exemplifying to defying the common potentialities of the stanza. These couplets sometimes deploy the closural propensities of their form by expressing epigrammatic sentiments in a balanced iambic pentameter unit, but elsewhere they juxtapose balance and imbalance through the contrast between semantic cohesion and a striking variation in line length. Enacting an aural inconstancy appropriate to its subject matter, "Womans Constancy" concludes on this type of heterometrical couplet: "Which I abstaine to doe, / For by to morrow, I may thinke so too" (16–17).[42]

Printing and scribal practices typically reinforce the role of stanzas in restraining potential fluidity or even chaos, but sometimes, as in certain of these instances from Donne and Jonson, they destabilize or at least complicate that function. If Drayton's commentary on his *Barrons Wars* compares the stanza he uses to a pillar, the frequency of stanzas that are comprised entirely of iambic pentameter or that use another line consistently often creates a similar effect in the work of other writers as well. The visual impression of a column may be intensified when the printer puts only one stanza on each page and frames it with a border, as is the case with Spenser's "Epithalamion" in his 1595 volume, which mimes the effect of capital, shaft, and base.

That well-wrought urn the sonnet is sometimes presented and represented as though it consists of separate stanzas. Echoing the usage analyzed above, Gascoigne's *Certayne Notes of Instruction* refers to the units within the form as "staves" (460), and some manuscripts and printed books adhere to this assumption by leaving noticeable blank space between the sections of these poems; Mary Wroth, for example, generally does so in the manuscript of her poetry, Folger V.a.104. Similarly, when the term "quatrozain" or "quaterzain" is used for a sonnet, as the titles of the paratextual poems in Thomas Watson's *Hecatompathia* and the subtitle of the 1594 edition of Michael Drayton's *Ideas Mirrour* do, might not these texts draw attention to the fact that those lyrics are primarily comprised of four-line subunits even though the term in question explicitly refers to the fourteen-line structure of their poems?

Such practices deserve more attention than they have as yet received because their effects are multiple and varied. On the one hand, as we have seen, "stave" can connote the units of a barrel, hence emphasizing cohesion, and a succession of visually similar units can appealingly create that very effect. On the other hand, however, under some circumstances such divisions can look unbalanced and unstable, notably when the couplet is indented. Such hints of dispersal do not completely disappear, but they are typically contained and restrained with considerable, though by no means unimpeachable, success. The syntactical and semantic links between the units and the repetition of rhymes in the Petrarchan and Spenserian versions of the sonnet evidently draw together its parts. Many poets craft additional ways of doing so, as when Thomas Lodge begins every quatrain in the thirteenth sonnet of *Phillis* on the word "love."

Above all, often the couplet both visually and semantically functions as a base to the column and a basis for drawing together the potentially scattering units, again allowing poets to practice what the treatises on stanzas preach. As we have observed, in discussing his eight-line stanza, Drayton explicitly refers to it as such, and arguably this potentiality is not the least reason for Elizabethan poets' attraction to the so-called Shakespearean sonnet. This integrative function may be emphasized when the couplet is written or printed flush left, thus creating the visual impression of a base on which the column of print above it securely rests. In Richard Lynche's *Diella*, the capitalization of both lines of the couplet and their positioning at the left of the page emphasizes their function in providing stability and unity, with these material effects being emphasized by semantic markers of that role, such as opening on "Then" in the sense of "therefore," as the eighth, ninth, and fourteenth poem do.[43] In Wroth's manuscript Folger V.a.104, the couplets are generally positioned flush left (sometimes, though by no means always, she intensifies the impression of a firm base by capitalizing both lines). In short, the poststructuralist attraction to the unsettled certainly should not blind one to the frequency with which other poets also create that representation of solidity: the primary effect of stanzas and their subunits in early modern English verse is indeed to reassert firmness and order.

Yet once again we are encountering a potentiality for stability, not its inevitable realization. Practices in printing sonnets, like their scribal counterparts, vary considerably; and in instances where one or both lines of the couplet are indented, especially if the second line is not capitalized, the base may seem far less reliable, and the visual effect can be that of a column whose base is apparent but insecure. The column may even appear to be threatening to topple over, its *rime* potentially *sparse*, its customary function as an icon for restraint hence toppled as well. Arguably such couplets iconographically represent, or at least gesture towards, the instability of ethical principles and emotional resolutions in the world of the sonnet, form thus adeptly mirroring content; if so, in this as so many other instances, studying the materiality of a text is not an alternative but a route to studying its aesthetic and ethical agendas, and vice versa. Lodge's edition, for example, indents the first line of his quatrains and of his couplet, thus creating a pictorial impression of imbalance.[44] Whereas the Petrarchan rhyme scheme does not as obviously lend itself to either the impression or the refusal of a base, the visual arrangement of its sestet may comparably suggest stability or its opposite. One of the most extreme instances of the latter effect is a sonnet near the opening of Young's translation of *Diana*, where Selvagia's distress is mimed by repeated trochaic inversions, by feminine rhymes, by the syneciosis-like phrase "doe undoe" (14), as well as by the appearance of the final lines:

> Then will I trust in hopes that not forsake me,
>> When I have staide her wheeles that overtread me,
>>> And beaten down the fates that doe undoe me.
>>> (12–14)[45]

The 1595 edition of Daniel's *Delia* prints the first line of each quatrain and both lines of the couplet flush left, with other lines presented as hanging indents, so each section as well as the poem as a whole seems to rest on a base. In the 1592 editions of this text, however, the first line of each quatrain and both lines of the couplet are indented, and the border appears only at the bottom; although one needs to resist the temptation to exaggerate the difference, it is clear that in the later version the sonnets appear more securely poised, an effect intensified by the use of a thick border at the top and bottom, the latter replicating and echoing the effect of the flush left couplet. And for all his expressed commitment to the couplet as the base to a column, those written by Drayton are typically indented in editions of his work that appeared during his lifetime. Did he acquiesce to the impact of printers' practices on authorial agency? Did he simply accept them, manifesting his position as a transitional figure in changing conceptions of authorial authority? Or, pulled between the desire for the solidity of a base and the attraction to unsettling ideas and language that becomes increasingly prominent in his work, did he accept and even delight in the tension between the couplet's ostensible stability and the countervailing visual effect in these editions? Couplets almost always trope but by no means always perform the desire for closural unity, and printing and scribal practices offer a visual analogue.

The potential instability of such couplets is simultaneously intensified and delimited when they fill their customary role as aphoristic summaries. On the one hand, as Mary Thomas Crane has shown, humanistic practices focused on the detachment of such nuggets from their original context, on a gathering of them that necessitated a scattering of the text in which they had originally appeared;[46] and a couplet that does not seem securely attached to the preceding lines might well appear especially ripe for the picking. Yet by providing a reassuring summary, such epigrammatic units could stress their connection to the preceding lines. Hence if stanzas in early modern lyric poetry typically involve countering the uncontrolled dispersal of texts through the agency and skill of the author, these prosodic units may also enact the tension between scattering and unification.

As Chapter 3 indicated, with characteristic incisiveness John Hollander has outlined the workings of the poetic refrain; the striking similarities between several of his points and the issues I have been exploring here demonstrate that in many regards refrains synecdochically figure the stanzas they terminate.[47] Tracing the term in question to the French for bridling, Hollander examines how this prosodic element restrains or ties; in so doing, I suggest, it bears to its stanza a relationship not unlike the one the stanza typically assumes towards the lyric as a whole, thus again demonstrating how gathering can attempt to counter scattering. For stanzas generally bridle discordant elements that threaten to gallop away out of control and in so doing bridle anxieties about the workings of their mode. If, as Hollander claims, the refrain at once breaks off and reclaims part of a line, the stanza does so as well, restraining and tying together elements whose epigrammatic neatness or metrical irregularity threatens to detach from the whole poem. And if, as Hollander demonstrates, refrains are allusive, drawing attention to previous refrains, one might add that stanzas are also typically metastanzaic, directing the reader's attention to how both the poet at hand and others have used the form. To Hollander's analysis one can append the gloss that the processes of breaking off and reclaiming that he traces, whether in the refrains he is analyzing or the stanzas we are scrutinizing, is a form of *fort-da* that, like other versions of the game, attempts to achieve and assert mastery. And, as in *fort-da*, success is by no means guaranteed. In short, in writing stanzas lyric poets of the English Renaissance both acknowledge and attempt to rein in the potential dispersal of lyric, with varying degrees of success re-forming and re-formulating its potentially threatening fluidity as controlled pattern and redefining their own role as masculine master rather than effeminized and effeminizing siren.

⁓ ☙ ❧ ⁓

Moving from stanzaic practices, notably divisions and recombinations within a given lyric, to the macro-level of pairings and larger groups of texts reveals that authors use the potentiality of combining and separating units of writings to assert more agency than many critics attribute to them, whether in cooperation or conflict with other would-be masters of the text. But somewhat less of that agency is apparent in certain venues where we might expect it, notably the putative narrativity of sonnet cycles, while more is visible in manuscripts.

Generalizations about all these patterns are, of course, inflected by the range of strategies through which texts are grouped, as even a brief survey reminds us: the breadth of possibilities extends from a group of unconnected poems by other hands that someone may copy into a commonplace book to a crown of sonnets by a single writer. Medieval readers typically purchased unbound sheets that they then bound themselves, as I noted in passing above, and anthologies of lyrics were common in the early modern period as well as the medieval; they range from well-known ones like *Englands Helicon* to groupings of poems by divers hands brought out in response to events like the death of Prince Henry. But Lerer's reminder of the differences between miscellanies and anthologies is very much to the point here: whereas a collection like *Englands Helicon* is obviously unified by its commitment to pastoral, and the most popular of Elizabethan miscellanies, *The Paradise of Dainty Devices*, is tied together by a predominant piety, it is harder to discern a common thread in many other volumes. This is not to deny, however, that some readers, accustomed to linking texts in commonplace books, may have attempted to find links among the poems, yet again demonstrating their contributions to the process of making meaning.

Lyrics may, of course, be grouped by many other criteria as well, as we have already seen. In some instances, titles stress the connections among poems, a predilection Susan Stewart traces with her usual incisiveness in analyzing Thomas Watson's *Passionate Centurie of Love*.[48] The early modern period also witnessed the popularity of certain generic and prosodic forms that encourage or mandate the binding of texts into collections. Most obviously, the model provided by Petrarch invited later poets to realize that sonnets could mate much more readily and successfully than most sonneteering speakers, although that example also demonstrates how tenuous and ambiguous the links among sonnets can be (a pattern we will shortly encounter in Petrarch's English heirs). Similarly, as *The Shepheardes Calender* and some of its classical ancestors demonstrate, eclogues can be related to each other by the recurrence of names and situations, as well as by their genre, and the same is true of versions of the psalms. Cognate subject matter can link other types of religious poetry too; Richard Crashaw's three hymns about the Christmas season, celebrating respectively the nativity, the circumcision, and the epiphany, are further connected by parallels in their images and structures. Encouraged by scribal culture, the practice of writing answer poems produced further pairings; some of Donne's verse letters appear to be replies of this sort, and Helen Vendler has categorized some Shakespearean sonnets this way.[49] George Gascoigne's "Devises of Sundrie Gentlemen" links its thirty-fourth and thirty-fifth entries through the title, "Another shorter discourse to the same effecte" and their common motto (247). Also popular in the period was the crown, a form with which Samuel Daniel, John Donne, Robert Sidney, and Lady Mary Wroth, among others, experimented.

In the case of printed collections, one encounters, as many previous critics have observed, significant but limited authorial control over connections between lyrics, with multiple implications for size and structure; since that argument has been persuasively established in numerous venues, this chapter can develop it relatively briefly. Often it is precisely by positioning a single poem within a larger unit that authors assert some of their principal preoccupations, and that drive to arrange their lyrics in a significant order has been traced in detail.[50] Even lyrics whose form did not necessarily mandate or invite grouping were frequently tied together by their authors—and, indeed, at times tied in ways that intriguingly complicate one's notion of what the unit is. As the instance of Gascoigne, discussed at length elsewhere in this study, demonstrates, authors experimented with these potentialities in the middle of the sixteenth century, earlier than some would expect a significant assertion of authorial agency. And seventeenth-century examples are, of course, legion. In rearranging the texts in *Hesperides*, in whose production he apparently closely participated, Herrick often creates ironic pairings, like the juxtaposition of "Delight in Disorder" and the poem that succeeds it immediately, the tribute to his muse that celebrates her bashful, virginal tastes. Here the ordering playfully connects the two poems in the service of showing how separate and separable they are.[51] Jonson, having rejected other literary forms, concludes the tenth poem in *Forest* on a promise to deliver an epode, which is in fact the genre of the succeeding work in the volume. These two texts, then, are also separate but related. Although critics dispute the significance of how Milton ordered the lyrics in his 1645 *Poems*, that he did so with care is beyond dispute; most obviously, the final lines of *Lycidas* are appropriate to the poem's position as the concluding text in its section.[52]

It is tempting to cite sonnet cycles as further evidence of authorial control, and in fact Wendy Wall has developed a powerful argument on a related subject, asserting that the very concept of an author encouraged readers to see cycles of sonnets as unified and to read them as a consecutive narrative.[53] But did authors foster that response by structuring their collections as narratives? If so, we may have a textbook example of the principle, a commonplace among narratologists, that telling stories is an assertion of agency, as well as another instance of collaboration among producers of meaning. But once again the evidence is mixed; often it is through tropes and images rather than a story that the units in a sonnet collection are united. To be sure, individual sonnets frequently include narratives, as when *Astrophil and Stella* 41 recounts the events of a tournament and Stella's reactions to it or *Amoretti* 67 famously represents a successful hunt. Etiological myths are common in the genre; the ninth sonnet in Robert Barnfield's *Cynthia* attributes Ganymede's beauty to Diana's having created him from blood and snow (a sonnet, incidentally, that through its echoes of the creation of the snowy Florimell may implicitly tell another story, that of the author attempting to rechannel antagonisms and guilt). The frequency and the specificity of the stories within particular sonnets, however, varies considerably and tellingly from one cycle to the next. Narrative elements recur with some frequency in Sidney's work, for example, while they are virtually absent from Lodge's.

To what extent, then, does narrativity structure an entire group of sonnets and thus provide an arena in which its author can assert control over the story line even while cataloguing evidence of his lack of control over the lady, much as stanzas reactively announce restraint in certain arenas in response to its absence elsewhere? At one end of the spectrum, the calendrical allusions in the *Amoretti* certainly insist on some linearity, and the religious events behind it are often clearly and specifically portrayed; the reference to Easter, for example, is tellingly signaled with the deictic "this" in "this day" (68.1). Yet even within this instance, the arrangement of certain poems seems arbitrary: whereas Sonnets 30–32 exemplify the presence of certain types of narrative link, there is no apparent reason why, say, Sonnet 56, one of the many additional laments about the lady's cruelty, appears where it does rather than with Sonnets 30–32. As Neil L. Rudenstine has demonstrated, Astrophil does indeed change in the course of Sidney's sequence,[54] while in certain other respects as well a linear order is apparent: the collection opens on the problems of falling in love and writing about it, the concluding poems are related, and so on. Yet even some claims like those are debatable: for example, given the other signs of disdain throughout the sequence, the linkage between 85 and 86 is at best a sensible hypothesis. David Kalstone's warning that "we must look for shifts of viewpoint rather than for narrative progression" is characteristically shrewd.[55] While some of the links within these sonnet collections seem more problematical than others, at the other end of the spectrum we encounter cycles like Robert Sidney's, whose poems are no more connected by a linear story than those in the miscellany by the Scottish Petrarchist Alexander Craig, *The Amorose Songes, Sonets, and Elegies*. And, as I have argued at length elsewhere, Shakespeare's collection has far less of a plot than many critics have assumed.[56] In short, the presence of narrativity varies so much from one collection to another and often within a given collection that we should discard the term "sonnet sequence" in favor of "sonnet cycle" when generalizing about the English tradition.[57]

Why, then, do authors only intermittently and imperfectly use the potentialities of narrative to assert control, in effect avoiding opportunities to bind their sonnets in the way they bind lines in stanzas? The Petrarchan tradition gestures towards yet resists two qualities often associated with narrative, the expression of certainty and the exposition of events. Gérard Genette observes that narrative's "one mood, or at least its characteristic mood, strictly speaking can be only the indicative," while Gerald Prince insists, "Narrative, which is etymologically linked to knowledge, lives in certainty." Although these formulations have hardly gone unchallenged, they remain widespread, as my discussion of the relationship of lyric and narrative will demonstrate.[58] The Petrarchan world does rest on a few versions of certainty, such as the surpassing—though temporary—beauty of the lady and the overwhelming power of love. But the signature figure of that literary tradition is the oxymoron, that embodiment of obsessive doubting. Indeed, Helen Vendler rightly maintains that indeterminacy is "intrinsic to the sonnet sequence as a genre."[59] All this may explain why if telling a story is a method of asserting sovereignty, as so many narratologists have suggested, it is a method many early modern sonneteers eschew.

In any event, many sonnet cycles demonstrate how conditions of production could produce further limitations on that sovereignty. The printer might cooperate by publishing the poems in the order the author intended, but he also might arrange them randomly or change their order or deploy, whether wittingly or not, devices that undermine the structure the author established. Elsewhere I have argued against Katharine Duncan-Jones's defense of Thorpe's Shakespeare edition as a faithful rendition of the author's intended order.[60] Whereas Colin Burrow's magisterial edition of the sonnets and other poems largely supports Duncan-Jones's assertions about order, his commentary on the 1609 edition aptly draws attention to the types of fluidity scrutinized throughout this chapter. Hence it is worth quoting at some length:

> While there are good grounds to believe that the order of poems in Q is authorial . . . , there are grounds for being less certain than Duncan-Jones that Q represents that ideally convenient thing for an editor, an "authorized" final version which accurately reflects its author's intentions. "Authorized" can mean many things. At its most minimal it would mean that Shakespeare assented to publication of the volume. At its maximal it would mean that Shakespeare assented to publication of the volume and that he gave Thorpe a manuscript which accurately reflected his final intentions, and that those final intentions were completely realized in the book which resulted. . . . If one accepted the maximal it would still be the case that the volume which resulted would be subject to the thousand material uncertainties which preyed on early modern printed texts: foul case (type which had got into the wrong box), foul papers (rough working manuscript copy), shortages of type, and tired compositors.[61]

Witness too Spenser's volume *Amoretti and Epithalamion*, published in London in 1595. No gardener has planted borders more insistently than the printer of this edition: each page is adorned with a smaller one on top and a more substantial one at the bottom, thus separating each sonnet in the sequence, each stanza of the epithalamion, and even subdividing the Anacreontic poems between them. Catchwords bridge the pages, sometimes complicating the signals of the borders. Those paratextual decorations add to the closural firmness of the final line of the first sonnet in the *Amoretti*—"whom if ye please, I care for other none"—visually holding the poem together and holding at bay other voices and other Elizabeths for whom the poet may care.[62] Thus in some important ways the printer supports the author's endeavors, whether or not he consciously intended to. On the other hand, the catchword "Unquiet" mimes its own semantic content, rendering unstable that closural final line. In short, if on the one hand Spenser's allusions to the Christian calendar structure at least in part establish a linear progression—witness, for example, Anne Lake Prescott's argument that scriptural and liturgical references link *Amoretti* 67–70—on the other the physical appearance of the book presents sonnets and stanzas as distinct units.[63]

Indeed, as I have already noted, in the case of not only sonnets but other types of collections, certain kinds of groupings were outside the agency of the author, indeed an affront to it. A printer could purloin a text for inclusion in an anthology, perhaps in so doing changing its valences, as the compilers of *Englands Helicon* did when they turned a song from *Astrophil and Stella* into a pastoral. Furthermore, the appearance of a text in print did not prevent readers from copying it and inserting it into a very different context, thus establishing connections the author might not have intended. To return to a telling instance discussed earlier in this chapter, when Marlowe's "Passionate Shepherd to His Love" is copied together with Ralegh's reply in a format that omits the word "finis" between them, the copyist is undercutting alternative forms in which the poems had been printed, thus denying the author the power of closure and the ability to stabilize meaning that it can on occasion entail. Similarly, adhering to the medieval practices Lerer charts, someone bound together a printed copy of Watson's *Hecatompathia* and a number of poems by John Lilliat and other obscure authors of the period, forming a manuscript that now resides at the Bodleian, classified as Rawlinson poetry 148.

Yet one should not assume that the relationship among would-be authors and those rival poets the reader, the publisher, and the printer was inevitably or even normatively conflictual. Although Arthur F. Marotti's influential model of coterie circulation has been qualified trenchantly by Wendy Wall and others, it still serves to remind us that the act of pairing an answer poem with the original was often performed cooperatively, not antagonistically in both scribal and print transmission.[64] To emphasize the interaction among one or more playwrights, members of a company, printers, the theatrical audience, and so on, many recent students of drama have been discussing theater in terms of collaboration, a concept that, though variously interpreted, does not necessarily presume—and can even offer an alternative to—a combative relationship necessarily suppressing the agency of a particular author.[65] Stephen B. Dobranski's important study of Milton demonstrates the collaborative genealogies of his poems and prose.[66] Too often critics of lyric presuppose a battle for control which the author loses; adapting studies of collaboration from other modes would be more useful in a number of these instances.

One case study provides a particularly telling example of both the presence and limitations of authorial agency in shaping lyrics into larger units—and of the resulting implications for collaboration and conflict. Whether or not one subscribes to the theory that Samuel Daniel's juxtaposition of his sonnets, an Anacreontic ode, and "The Complaint of Rosamond" initiated a widely imitated pattern, the "Delian tradition," the fact that he wanted to link those texts is indisputable.[67] Daniel himself stresses the links at several points: Rosamond directly invokes Delia, and numerous thematic parallels further unite the volume. Yet the connections are by no means consistent: markers of the relationships among the texts, notably the use of "finis" and of half titles, differ from edition to edition, including variants published in the same year.[68] In the first 1592 edition (STC 6243.2) "finis" appears between the sonnets and the ode and between the ode and the complaint; the latter texts are not, however, introduced with a half-title, and this omission encourages readers to link them to the previous poems. In the same year, though, the same printer and publisher brought out a version (STC 6243.3) that incorporates some corrections within the sonnets that had been noted on a prefatory corrigenda sheet in the previous volume. More to the purposes of this chapter, the relationship between the sonnets and "The Complaint of Rosamond" changes significantly in the later edition: although the placement of "finis" remains the same, the two texts are distinguished by the use of the half title page. Moreover, because that sheet, which displays a version of the architectural drawing on the principal title page, locates the title of the complaint in small letters within an archway, visually it enacts its effect on the relationship among the texts: that is, Rosamond's story is distanced and enclosed, cut off. All these patterns are further complicated by the inclusion of *Cleopatra* in some subsequent editions; for example, in an edition from 1598, *Cleopatra*, unlike the complaint, acquires its own half title, and the connections among the lyric members of the volume are implicitly emphasized through the contrast.

In short, although we cannot be certain how closely aligned Daniel considered the two texts in question to be, he must have been aware of the thematic and imagistic links between them, and by referring to Delia within the complaint, he impels the reader to note connections. Hence, rather than assuming that he requested changes in this revised version that would increase the separation between the texts, it is likely that the publisher added them, quite possibly hoping that the separate half title would make readers think they were getting more for their money. (This is not to deny, of course, that in other instances, aesthetic, not pecuniary, considerations might shape the decisions of a publisher or printer; for example, italicizing a lyric within a prose text implies its special status.) In any event, these editions remind us that the semantic and the visual content of a book can give a reader mixed messages about how unified the volume is, leading her to debate that issue and uncover or suppress signs of unity or disunity. Thus author, printer, and reader all interact, sometimes cooperatively and sometimes not, in determining structure.

Although many critics would take issue with my position on the linearity of sonnet collections, in other respects I have been buttressing commonly accepted assumptions about the interaction of agents in collections of lyric—and in so doing demonstrating again how and why the presence of other agents complicates but does not preclude the workings of authorship. Can one, however, second another widespread assumption by asserting that whereas authorial agency was apparent though limited in early modern print practices, an examination of groupings of poems reveals its virtual absence, traceable in large measure to the lack of fixity, in scribal practices? Admittedly, in some respects scribal practices evidently curtail authorial control over poetic units, as many scholars have demonstrated. Harold Love has pointed out that manuscripts virtually invite interpolations by other hands, and, similarly, Marcy North has analyzed how the white space left in many manuscripts seems to facilitate the addition of further texts and hence the possibility of further combinations.[69] Thus a reader could readily combine texts that had not originally been conceived as a unit or even written by the same author, or excerpt lyrics from the larger context in which the author had positioned them. For example, poems that also are printed within Sidney's *Old Arcadia, Certaine Sonnets,* and *Astrophil and Stella* make cameo appearances in the scribal collection apparently compiled by Henry Stanford.[70]

More important and more surprising, however, are the ways scribal practice contributed to authorial agency, thus challenging widespread assumptions. Scribal culture is an obsessive-compulsive's paradise, the world of second thoughts and second chances, and writers could and did take advantage of this opportunity to arrange and rearrange their unpublished poems, often significantly changing their impact. Not the least effect of scribal transmission, though one of the most neglected, is the author's ability to rewrite—and, more to my purposes right now, reorder—not only individual poems but also a collection in response to changes in his or her conception of them.[71] Marotti has noted the extent of Robert Sidney's continuing revisions.[72] I have emphasized how scribal transmission allows readers and publishers to rewrite at the expense of closely considering the effects of that same possibility on the author. For lyric poets the fluidity that is the central focus of this chapter can entail freedom and creative challenges rather than their destruction.

Moreover, while acknowledging how scribal culture permitted readers to reshape texts through groupings, critics need to observe as well how fruitful those same potentialities could be for authors. It is easy to speculate that Donne, fascinated as he was with pairings and matings of all types, might have copied and circulated to friends lyrics that either supported or resonated ironically with each other, such as "Womans Constancy" and "The Good Morrow." And he might well have shifted those groupings to fill different ends; for example, by substituting for "The Good Morrow" the epithalamium he composed for the ethically dubious wedding of Frances Howard and the Earl of Somerset, he could have introduced a similar implication but with a pointed topical reference that it would have been dangerous to express more directly. Such speculations are, admittedly, just that, but one can observe with more certainty that the poet who wishes to reorder printed texts could do so informally through correspondence with friends but that, for a larger impact, he has to hope for a selected or collected edition of his work or, even less probably, a second edition of the book. In contrast, the recent variorum edition of Donne's *Holy Sonnets* persuasively documents his control over how scribal versions of these poems were grouped.[73]

Although it is usually not read from this perspective, the manuscript of Lady Mary Wroth's poetry in the Folger Library, V.a.104, further demonstrates how an author could arrange and rearrange units of her writings, hence asserting authority not despite but because of the workings of scribal culture.[74] Thus this text supports my contention that, if from one perspective lack of fixity diminishes the author's ability to, as it were, have the last word—the power to effect closure—from another perspective it offers continuing opportunities to assert authority over the text. Cognizant of Josephine A. Roberts's deservedly high reputation as a textual editor and grateful for her many contributions to subsequent work on Lady Mary Wroth, most critics have accepted Roberts's description of the putative manuscript of *Pamphilia to Amphilanthus* in the Folger Library, Folger V.a.104.[75] That text, according to the standard edition meticulously edited by Roberts and to an earlier article by her, comprises neither the copy-text for the 1621 edition nor a collection of discrete groups of lyrics; rather, it represents an early version of Wroth's sonnet sequence, though some poems were excerpted from it for the *Urania* when it was subsequently revised.[76] Recognizing that two lyrics are signed "Pamphilia" ("How like a fire doth love increase in mee" [P55] and the text she assumes terminates the sequence, "My muse now hapy, lay thy self to rest" [P103]) and that the manuscript includes blank pages, Roberts also posits subdivisions within Wroth's sequence; P55, she asserts, concludes one of those sections, while the signature on P103 flags its status as the final poem in the sequence.

Yet if, as I have demonstrated elsewhere, we attend to Wroth's use of catchwords and of her distinctive closural symbol, a slashed S, as well as to how she numbers the poems, the structure of the manuscript appears quite different in several ways, and more wholly distinct groupings emerge. In particular, it is more than likely that V.a.104 comprises not simply a collection of poems originally conceived as a sonnet cycle but rather a preliminary version of that cycle, ending at P55, plus a number of other poems, some of which Wroth envisioned as separate groups. For example, P63, P17, P30, P66–67, P18, P69, P19, P71, and P25 appear consecutively in the manuscript. Each has one slashed-S closural mark and a catchword, with the exception of the final poem in the group, P25, which has two marks and no catchwords. In addition to the catchwords, these poems are linked by numbers 1–10, suggesting that they were at some point conceived as a series. Subsequently, of course, Wroth folded into the sonnet cycle that originally ended at P55 many of the poems after P55; she extracted others and positioned them in the *Urania*; and she changed some of her original groupings. Pamphilia could not control Amphilanthus, but she could attempt to reshape her own responses, and her alter ego, Wroth, could reshape the collection, or collections, that record them. Harold Love has demonstrated with his usual acuity how the possibilities for rewriting offer agency to scribes; for authors as well, Wroth's collection thus suggests, agency may be expressed and realized not through fixity but rather through opportunities for revision.[77] Moreover, if, as many critics have claimed, the manuscript was shared with a small circle, the renumberings were a way of directing readers' attention to the new form it had assumed; if scribal culture under some circumstances allowed readers to become coauthors, in instances like this it allowed the author in the customary sense to guide them.[78]

Whether one accepts Roberts's analysis of the manuscript or my revisionist interpretation, the crown of poems within it unmistakably demonstrates other, often neglected, potentialities of scribal culture. Wroth deploys a range of techniques to bind together the sonnets within her crown. The lack of even a single slashed-S at the end of all but the final sonnet suggests they are virtually a single poem, an impression intensified by another scribal practice: whereas she generally starts a new page at the opening of a new text elsewhere in the sequence, she begins succeeding sonnets in the crown on the same page as the previous one if there is room for an additional text. Leaving about the same space between poems that she elsewhere leaves between sections of a single poem, she marks the end of one sonnet and the beginning of the next only with an Arabic number. (Similarly, Robert Sidney does not separate the lyrics within his crown with his customary closural marker.) Already chained by the repetition that defines a crown of sonnet, Mary Wroth's lyrics are, then, further chained visually. Her scribal practices thus draw attention to how Wroth, and arguably her father and other poets as well, conceived a crown of sonnets: the texts within it are more tightly linked than the common habit of printing each poem on a separate page would suggest, and in the instance of Wroth's poems, as with several other crowns, their connections trope the entrapments of and in desire. In short, in its crown as elsewhere, V.a.104 emphatically demonstrates the ways scribal culture often did not impede the poet's agency but rather facilitated authorial workings and reworkings of the text, including, in some instances, regroupings—and facilitated as well the pleasing aesthetic effect of a union of form and content.

If Wroth's manuscript encourages one to question the association of scribal culture with the erasure of the author, the 1621 printed edition of *Pamphilia to Amphilanthus,* like certain editions of Daniel's poetry, from one perspective complicates the linkage of print with increased authorial agency, recalling my earlier observations about how the fixity of print could instantiate not the author's intentions but some rival to them. Whereas the manuscript visually emphasizes the connections among the poems in the crown, in this edition they are printed exactly like other texts in the collection: in both instances, more than one poem appears on the same page, and they are all spaced the same way. It is surely more likely that Wroth would have preferred to retain the connections among the poems in the crown that she visually flagged in her manuscript. Thus her work is a microcosm both of the often acknowledged interaction between the author and other agents in shaping a printed text and of the often neglected potentialities open to the author in scribal transmission.

I have argued, then, that if texts disintegrate, they are also stabilized, and students of early modern literature should not privilege one part of that process at the expense of others. If the conditions of production can interfere with aesthetic effects, as in the instance of Daniel's title pages, they can also contribute to them. If authors lack agency under some circumstances, they reassert it at other junctures, whether in collaboration or conflict with other agents. But, as my concluding chapter will demonstrate at greater length, intellectually fuzzy consensus is neither the goal nor the necessary outcome of these and other "both/and" arguments. Rather, they may produce focused and fruitful insights in themselves; thus studying those title pages in Daniel's texts extends our knowledge of the interaction among the agents contributing to them. Moreover, in literary criticism identifying both/and structures is often not the culmination of an argument but a route towards other insights. For example, recognizing the interaction of scattering and gathering expands our interpretation of the consequences of the malleability of texts, notably the implications for authorial agency.

Although I have developed such points in relationship to early modern lyric poetry, they do offer opportunities for future inquiry in other areas, especially the broader questions about authorship and materiality that are currently being debated. Recent studies, as I have indicated, have redefined authorship in terms of proprietorship and commodity, but further redefinitions are called for: despite or because of all the recent interest in collaborative theatrical practices, twentieth- and twenty-first-century critics of lyric have tended to impose their own concept of possession onto a period where it operated quite differently.[79] "Literary property is not fixed and certain like a piece of land," Mark Rose observes, and Chartier warns us against equating the ownership of real property and that of a text.[80] But land ownership is in fact relevant in one significant respect: it can be argued that the types of partial and limited rights land ownership involved provided an applicable model of which early modern writers and readers were very aware. Hence future studies could profitably emphasize and further explore how versions of shared and partial ownership worked, concentrating particularly on how poets, like playwrights, participated in the interaction among various owners and types and degrees of ownership even very early in the period. Both the medieval and early modern period offered alternative models of property rights that could be far from binary. Inheritance practices involved limited but still significant forms of ownership, notably the medieval option of holding in fief and the leasehold practices that still survive in English law today. An early modern lyric poet, I maintain, could see himself as, so to speak, holding in leasehold a text over which he did not have total sovereignty.

Similarly, recognizing that Shakespeare repeatedly uses "author" for "parent" reminds us that the author of a text could also have the major yet limited rights accorded fathers in early modern patriarchies. Imposing in more senses than one, the scope of those rights is expressed in Theseus's disturbing celebration of fatherhood ("To whom you are but as a form in wax, / By him imprinted, and within his power, / To leave the figure, or disfigure it" (I.i.49–51).[81] Yet the same scene recalls as well the limitations on those rights—many early modern conceptions of marriage stressed the importance of children's assent in marriage—and in this instance happily it is Egeus's wish, not his daughter, that is disfigured and melts away. But the point remains that parenthood, like land ownership, offered early modern poets and their readers potent models of limited but far from insignificant agency.

The analyses above also raise another important issue. The distrust of aesthetic analyses in many quarters is one of the most profound differences between contemporary criticism, especially as practiced in the United States, and its predecessors. In a series of important articles, Robert Kaufman has trenchantly maintained the need to distinguish the aesthetic and aestheticization, and I have argued in a number of other venues that we should not evaluate formal analysis through the categories of outdated versus cutting edge or formal versus material.[82] Similarly, this chapter has demonstrated that formal and other aesthetic considerations are neither ideologically nor practically inimical to the projects of many contemporary critics. Indeed, an analysis of the stability so often attributed to stanzas requires deploying intellectual history, aesthetic analysis, and materialist criticism. In this and other ways, few if any arenas better illustrate the compatibility—indeed, interdependence—of formal and material analysis than the size and structure of the early modern lyric.

# CHAPTER 5

# The Myth of Janus

## *Lyric and/or Narrative*

Even when representing other issues with the precise detail and complex coloration of Mughal painting at its best, many literary studies adopt the bold gestural strokes of Franz Kline to discuss the relationship between lyric and narrative: lyric is static and narrative committed to change, lyric is internalized whereas narrative evokes an externally realized situation, lyric attempts to impede the forward thrust of narrative, and so on. Offering a more theorized but still diametrical contrast, Jonathan Culler posits the narrative and the apostrophic as the two poles for poetry, with lyric typically "the triumph of the apostrophic."[1] But the chapters preceding this one have already called some of those assertions into question. And what happens if one plays these commonplaces about the two modes against the complexities of a few texts that not only participate in but also thematize them?

Much as the lyric by Donne examined at the beginning of Chapter 3 impelled a reexamination of the conventional wisdom about immediacy, so two very familiar poems, Sir Thomas Wyatt's "My lute, awake!" and George Herbert's "Collar," defamiliarize putative generic norms and thus invite a reconsideration of the relationship between lyric and narrative. In the sixth stanza of Wyatt's lyric, the speaker is continuing to assert—or is he continuing to threaten?—the ending of his relationship with his lady, a declaration that is at once intensified and undermined by the refrain's repetition of "I have done." Participating in, even exemplifying, the *carpe diem* tradition, the passage in question anticipates the lady's loss of beauty:

Perchaunce the lye wethered and old,
The wynter nyghtes that are so cold,

> Playning in vain unto the mone;
> Thy wisshes then dare not be told;
> Care then who lyst, for I have done.
>                         $(26-30)^2$

On one level this is a clear example of narrative, at once invoking and explicitly addressing the sequential temporality conventionally associated with that mode through its emphasis on the ravages of time. Repeated twice (29, 30), Wyatt's "then" apparently exemplifies the narrative use of deictics that Roland Greene has acutely traced when distinguishing that mode from lyric.[3] So one might entertain the hypothesis that here, as at a few other points in the text, a lyric encases a narrative, a reversal of but not a radical challenge to the more common models of narrative incorporating but ultimately rejecting lyric.

Yet, as we will see throughout this chapter, even, or especially, metalyric and metanarrative do not necessarily firmly establish, let alone triumphantly celebrate, the power or even the presence of the mode they concern. In fact, by this point the poem as a whole has complicated our attempts to ascribe narrativity to it, and lines 26–30 exemplify Gerald Prince's concept of the "disnarrated," events to which the text refers but that do not occur, a category to which I will return.[4] (Arguably, however, that categorization is further complicated. Whereas on one level the "Perchaunce" [26] certainly governs the whole stanza and the auxiliary "will" is understood, might the omission of that verb form and the *enargia* of the description tempt us to read "Thy wisshes then dare not be told" [29] as something more than mere possibility?)

In any event, the repetitions of "I have done" throughout the text paradoxically imply that the speaker may be protesting too much (an implication emphasized by the possibility of a spondaic stress on both the auxiliary and final verb in "have done"). The termination of the relationship is less a story he is recounting than one he is trying to effect, or, in other words, it is a story he is telling himself he is telling. It is a story whose repetitions are mimed by internal rhyme on "Playning" and "vain" (28), a story that is blocked, at least temporarily, by a poem whose agenda is revenge as much or more than leavetaking, as is so often the case in that intriguing subgenre of lyric the farewell poem.

Moreover, the reader is very aware of the mind that is imagining these events, a common characteristic of lyric. The refrain "I have done" slips and slides between an apparently factual narrative of an action ("I have given up the relationship") to its counterfactual double ("I am pretending I have given it up") to a version that involves not action but brooding and in that way veers towards lyric ("I am thoroughly tired of being in this relationship"). And the refrain is but one of several junctures at which the stanza emphasizes its speaker's internal dynamics. In the stanza I just examined, the word "Perchaunce" (26) signals the senses in which this is a vengeful fantasy from a mind whose own aggressive wishes dare not be told directly, again recalling the internalization that sometimes, though of course by no means always, characterizes lyric. One might speculate, too, that the stanza also deflects onto her his fears that rather than giving up the relationship decisively or reaching the lady with his threats, he is plaining in vain unto the moon. In short, this stanza, like the rest of the poem, includes both textbook examples of the distinctions between narrative and lyric, such as the emphasis on sequential temporality in the former and the meditative intensity of the latter, as well as usages that cannot readily be classified as one or the other. Jane Hedley has commented acutely on destabilized time sequences elsewhere in Wyatt's work, and throughout this particular song temporalities and modalities slip and slide.[5] Thus elements of narrative and of lyric participate in a relationship as entangled and unending as that of the speaker and his lady.

No less complex is the interplay between lyric meditation and narrative action in Herbert's "Collar." One reason the pattern is so complicated is that the valences of both modes shift in the course of the text. In brief, the early rejection of "sigh[ing] and pin[ing]" (3), activities frequently associated with lyric, is a symptom of the speaker's spiritual failings. The poem proceeds to display a different version of that mode: morally and logically tainted lyric reflections about the possibility of action and about the rejection of spirituality which that action represents in this instance. And its speaker's repentance is signaled by a lyric meditation on the episode he recounts. But these variously deployed versions of lyric are only part of, as it were, the story: "recounts" is indeed an operative word, for narrativity functions here both as figure for spiritual rebellion and as an alternative to that rebellion, much as lyric both expresses and critiques it. The restlessness of the verse, whose extraordinarily varied line lengths and frequent enjambment have been glossed acutely by Achsah Guibbory, Joseph Summers, and other critics, enacts the restlessness of thought; it might also be said to mirror the process of traveling, of going abroad, and the related journeys back and forth between lyric and narrative elements.[6]

More specifically, much as my instance from Wyatt not only locates itself in but also comments on temporality, so "The Collar" opens by both portraying and thematizing action: "I struck the board, and cry'd, No more. / I will abroad."[7]

Narrativity is figured in the opening lines through the physical gesture on which the poem begins and prefigured in the anticipated restless movement of the speaker's body ("I will abroad" [2]). Michael C. Schoenfeldt's acute reading of this poem draws attention to its implicit rejection of silence, a form of passivity; one can add that when these initial lines recount and also discuss the action conventionally associated with narrative, the author is also turning storytelling itself into an alternative to that silence and hence into a trope for its alternative, the assertive autonomy that Schoenfeldt scrutinizes here and elsewhere in his study.[8]

Yet notice that the central activity in question, leaving the spiritual world of travail for an earthly pleasure dome of travel, is located in the future, much as Wyatt's fantasy is. And, indeed, on one level almost all the succeeding lines, like their analogues in the selection from Wyatt, emphasize mental activity and anticipation, rather than events. As Richard Strier points out, our expectation that the opening will be followed by a story about what its speaker does abroad is frustrated.[9] For example, immediately after declaring he will go abroad, he strenuously affirms his right to do so, recalling Wyatt's insistence that he indeed is done and has done:

> What? shall I ever sigh and pine?
> My lines and life are free; free as the rode,
> Loose as the winde, as large as store.
> Shall I be still in suit?
>
> (3–6)

If the opening two lines thematize action, the third line does the same for lyric meditation, at once continuing to sigh about its limitations and apparently rejecting the world of complaint for the freedom of action.

The speaker's lines may or may not be free, but in the passages between the queries in lines 3 and 6 and the conclusion, the lines between lyric and narrative modes indubitably blur yet again. His spiritual state is on a cusp, with rebellion certainly represented and the redemptive power of grace arguably adumbrated through references, however distorted in their current form, to wine and thorns.[10] Similarly, the meditative mood of these lines is on a cusp for several reasons. If he is reflecting on the past, at the same time, as I suggested, the initial lines of the poem encourage us to read what ensues as a story about the consequences of the decision to travel, a story whose multiple audiences become more explicit in the final lines.

In some important senses the conclusion of the poem is the final incident in a narrative:

But as I rav'd and grew more fierce and wilde
>    At every word,
>  Me thoughts I heard one calling, *Child!*
>  And I reply'd, *My Lord.*

(33–36)

Indeed, the poem might be said to follow some of the formulas narratologists have established for that mode: the initial action is followed by the complications in the central part of the poem and by the resolution, a spiritual version of *nostos*, in the concluding four lines. Through the very act of telling this tale, the speaker assumes the role of dutiful child to God and perhaps preacher to other would-be sinners as well, the latter possibility recalling arguments also made about Herbert's "Aaron" and "Church-floore"; as Chapter 2 indicates, that poet, like many other ministers, emphasizes the role of storytelling in preaching. Yet not the least effect of the use of "Me thoughts" (35) is to direct our attention again to the speaker's mental processes. On one level this conclusion is a reflection on the perception expressed through "Me thoughts." Much as he moves from fantasies of an outer world of pleasure to the presence of grace, so the text moves here from the fruits of the secular world of pleasure outside the speaker to the fruits of spirituality and inner peace. Notice, too, that in that transformation it is narrativity in some of its senses, not lyricism, that is associated with the transgressive and childish. All this is further complicated, however, by the anticlosural force of "Me thoughts" (35), which, like a comparable usage in a poem examined earlier, Herrick's "Vision," introduces the possibility of the repetition and entrapment so often associated with lyric.[11] In short, modally as well as spiritually, the text abruptly moves between apparent opposites and thematizes other types of movement through that one.[12]

The two texts I have examined are not, of course, chosen at random: their methods of troping literary modes and their complex temporalities are not universally found in early modern lyric. But neither are they unique in these or many other respects, and the problems in the relationship between lyric and narrative that they crystallize recur repeatedly in early modern texts. Hence in demonstrating the complex relationships between narrative and lyric, my two opening poems mimetically invite the move from reflection to action enacted by the next section of this chapter, which aims to craft alternative methodological protocols for approaching the dilemmas those two lyrics reveal. In addition to resolving such methodological challenges, the critical community needs to design a series of new models for the relationship of the literary types in question. The texts by Wyatt and

Herbert introduce a number of patterns to incorporate in doing so, such as the use of the future tense and the troubling of the boundaries between the two modes.

My purpose in opening on those poems is certainly not to suggest that a monolithic paradigm of hybridity should replace the equally rigid contrasts between lyric and narrative that are currently in use: their relationship assumes so wide a range of forms that no single pattern should be privileged as normative. Even when the line between lyric and narrative blurs, as it not infrequently does, hybridity, a concept used too readily and loosely in contemporary parlance, is sometimes but certainly not always the most apt description. This chapter aims to explore the range of ways elements of narrative and lyric variously supersede one another, suppress one another, and coexist, emphasizing that very variety.

In so doing, however, it also aims to redirect attention to one issue in particular. In re-envisioning the varied interactions of lyric and narrative, literary critics—not coincidentally members of a professional community too often roiled and soiled by a competitiveness that can destabilize the very concept of community—should also be especially alert to a pattern that is frequently neglected. In many instances, rather than attempting to impede or suppress each other, lyric and narrative may further common agendas. In some of these cases their boundaries blur, as they do in the poems by Wyatt and Herbert, and in others they remain distinct; but in either instance cooperation replaces co-option, and interplay is a more apt description than interruption.

—☙ ☙—

As I just suggested, discussions of the connections between these two modes, like analyses of lyric audiences, insistently pose methodological challenges. Neither these problems nor their solutions are specific to the early modern period; but this chapter proceeds to demonstrate how they are related to that era's more distinctive characteristics. Three such problems in particular need to be acknowledged and addressed: dubious definitions and the rankings they often encode or justify; that expectation of a combative relationship issuing in a clear victor; and the absence of historical distinctions.

The first problem, definitions, is initially complicated inasmuch as the ontological status of the narrativity in question may vary considerably, ranging from storytelling clearly represented within the text to its analogues in paratextual materials to its versions in the nondiegetic world, such as the situation in which a lyric is passed on as an event in an ongoing courtship. Moreover, in considering the interaction of the modes, critics too often rely on definitions and evaluative descriptions that are partial in more than one sense. Whereas the poems that I just examined demonstrate the range of temporalities that can characterize passages that are indubitably lyric, let alone those in which elements of lyric and narrative merge, students of narrative often repeat the commonplace that lyric is rooted in, and rootbound by, a static temporality. Conversely, critics whose primary work is in lyric risk associating narrative only with clear-cut events and unambiguous closure, ignoring the poststructuralist—and earlier—emphasis on the edginess of what may or may not be happening. Splendidly subtle as a lyric poet, the contemporary writer Heather McHugh falls into this very trap as a critic: poetry, she maintains, excitingly offers "a constant unsettling [that] undermine[s] the constitutional groundwork of narration," neglecting the fact that narration itself often in fact posits seismically shifting ground.[13]

Such problems are endemic to the relational analysis of genres. To be sure, literary forms invite and often reward such comparisons; for example, the formal verse satire of the 1590s achieves some of its rhetorical energy from its determination not to be love poetry; science fiction both is and is not pastoral. At the same time, this type of relational definition is perilous, impelled as it often is by a covert agenda of privileging or defending one of the forms being compared, or, alternatively, denigrating the other. The Virgilian wheel tempts us to see pastoral, the form associated with the fledgling poet, as less sophisticated and less valuable than the epic putatively written during his mature years. Later critics have, as it were, reinvented the Virgilian wheel; thus Mikhail Bakhtin misreads romance in his eagerness to establish contrasts. Comparisons of genres are often driven less by an objective drive to explore than a covert need to celebrate one form as lacking the limitations and dangers of another, a variant of a schoolyard game: "My genre is bigger than your genre."

In this instance, many students and celebrants of narrative represent it as the norm and lyric as hence both deviant and less powerful. Such a hierarchization of lyric and narrative would lead us simply to read the ending of "The Collar" as a return to narrative, authorized by the most powerful of all storytellers, after the temporary divagations of lyric complaint. Similarly, an analysis of Sir Philip Sidney's *Old Arcadia* represents its distinction between lyric and narrative as a contrast between "a static, idolatrous verse of the past ('Petrarchan') and fluid, allusive, emerging prose ('Ovidian')" and goes on to assert that the eclogues "present the author's nostalgia for a lofty, rhetorically intricate, and conventional verse, even as they affirm, by contrast, the superiority of prose as a more supple means of literary expression."[14] Whereas this reading misrepresents Sidney's verse (not least because it downplays the poetic experimentation and variety), the passage does map the territory of the author's (and many other critics') presuppositions

and agendas; it reflects in particular how she historicizes her own rejection of a critical interest in aesthetic achievement, an approach putatively static in its relationship to newer critical methodologies and idolatrous in its enthusiasm for the text.
Readings like this are often impelled by the move, incisively challenged in Robert
Kaufman's revisionist interpretations of Theodor W. Adorno among other studies,
of associating lyric with an aestheticization that resists the engagement with historical change facilitated and troped by narrative.[15]

On the other hand, as the passage by Heather McHugh implies, those critics
who identify themselves with lyric, whether because of its putative gendering or
its centrality in their own work or both, are prone to establish narrative as a masculinist rival mode associated with an authoritarianism that should be and can be
combatted by the excitingly powerful semiotic force of lyric. Susan Stanford
Friedman effectively warns against such errors when emphasizing the polyvocal-
ity of narrative.[16] And my samples from Wyatt and Herbert caution one about
these oversimplified and self-serving rankings; for example, Wyatt's narrator
sometimes reaches out towards narrative for authority that he cannot in fact
achieve.

However dubious, that comparative privileging of lyric by twentieth- and
twenty-first-century critics has a distinguished lineage, though these predecessors
often contrast narrative with poetry in general, taking lyric's prototypical status as
implicit but not unambiguous. Examples from many eras abound. Shelley's
comparison privileges the poetic, contrasting its organic and divine power with
the limits of historical narrative in particular: "a story is a catalogue of detached
facts, which have no other bond of connexion than time, place, circumstance,
cause and effect; the other is the creation of actions according to the unchangeable forms of human nature, as existing in the mind of the creator, which is itself
the image of all other minds. The one is partial . . . the other is universal."[17] The
Platonic values shaping the passage are apparent in the way the phrase "no other
bond of connexion" trivializes precisely what narrative respects, that is, the workings of "time, place, circumstance, cause and effect." Later in the century, the hierarchies adumbrated in such documents were to prove grist to Mill, though the
author of the *Principles of Political Economy* is more explicit about his rankings
than Shelley: the love of narrative, John Stuart Mill declares, is associated with
the childhood of an individual and the "rude state" of a society.[18]

If the difficulty of defining lyric and narrative and the often related appetite
for ranking them constitute the first methodological challenge, those implicit
and sometimes explicit rankings generate a second problem: critics too often assume that encounters between lyric and narrative are a battleground on which

the most powerful army enjoys a clear-cut final victory, though perhaps not without skirmishes where the other side gets in and temporarily appears to triumph. These readings typically and not coincidentally replicate the assumption that when rival narratives struggle for power, one of them, often identified with the discourses of the dominant culture, eventually suppresses and replaces the others.

In the instance of narrative and lyric, the winner-take-all paradigm depends on the type of clear contrast between narrative and lyric that the examples from Wyatt and Herbert call into question, as well as on an essentially conflictual conception of their relationship undermined by, for example, the multiple readings of Wyatt's "I have done." Feminine and potentially effeminizing, lyric, according to one version of this winner-take-all story, plays Dido to the Aeneas of narrative. Witness the critic who, while on the one hand stressing the role of the eclogues in presenting and inculcating the moral values of the text, nonetheless on the other hand draws his diction from commonplaces that recall that ill-fated Carthagian queen: "Writing eclogues was Sidney's pastoral *retreat* from the responsibilities of narrative," "an *escape* from another kind of constraint," "as Sidney *retreats* from poetry into prose," "an *escape* from the *constraints* of his narrative" (italics added).[19] Or, to shift metaphors though not peninsulas, the ultimate powerlessness of lyric is reflected in the fact that it cannot and should not prevent the trains of narrative from running—and running away from Dido—on time. In the obverse, twinned version favored by many other feminist scholars and numerous poststructuralists, feminist and otherwise, lyric, enhanced with the power of the semiotic, is an excitingly transgressive force that overturns the power of narrative; here, too, as the connection with Kristeva's concepts of the semiotic and symbolic might imply, lyric is often gendered.

Encountered at many other junctures in this study, a third and closely related problem in studying the interplay of lyric and narrative involves incautiously importing generalizations from the period in which the critic specializes into the poetry of other time zones. Thus, for example, one scholar assumes the normativeness of a narrative that focuses on the quotidian.[20] But, as Mary Thomas Crane reminds us, in the early modern period narrativity was associated with romance in particular and errancy in general—thus, one might add, not with a genre that makes those trains run on time but rather with one that transforms the trains into cavorting magic carpets.[21]

Early and enthusiastic registrants at most academic conferences, straw men are also all too likely to populate scholarly books. So it is important to acknowledge that the idols of our tribe catalogued above, powerful and perilous though they are, have in fact variously been avoided and critiqued by studies before this one. Although some of the alternatives that have been offered are not without their own problems, my study gratefully builds on these important revisionist attempts. For example, highlighting the interplay of lyric and narrative, Timothy Bahti fruitfully avoids the oversimplified dichotomies that cannot speak to the complexities exemplified by the texts on which this chapter opened; but in so doing he attributes to lyrics a narrativelike movement from predication to conclusion, an argument that is at the very least compromised by, for example, the interpretation that suggests that Wyatt's speaker is unreliable throughout.[22] Having argued in an earlier essay for the gendered victory of a transgressive lyric, Susan Stanford Friedman subsequently stresses the interplay of the modes and then posits a continuing need for narrative by many women and people of color; Friedman does not, however, fully consider how lyric could and does serve some functions comparable to those she assigns to narrative.[23]

Particularly relevant to my study are the recent writings of a number of narratologists: although they focus mainly on nineteenth- and twentieth-century texts, as they rethink their mode in relation to lyric they suggest directions for the reverse undertaking. James Phelan has astutely complicated the relationship of the two types by denying the linkage of lyric to stasis, an important revisionist position supported at several junctures in *The Challenges of Orpheus*.[24] Phelan adds further subtlety to that relationship by positing a third term that shares certain qualities of each mode, "portraiture," and by tracing the interaction of the modes, and particularly their relationship to ethical criticism, in what he calls "lyric narrative."[25] Jay Clayton acutely explores what he terms "visionary moments" in narrative, moments that are clearly related to lyric, thus, like Phelan, modeling some ways of tracing the interaction of narrative and lyric.[26] And, as we will shortly see, the reinterpretations of narrative temporality by a number of narratologists are particularly useful in addressing the future tense narrations in some of the passages on which this chapter opened.

—◌ ◌—

To avoid the problems in even these revisionist studies, critics need to refine the models currently deployed for the interaction of narrative and lyric and develop new ones. Although the first group of models involve conflicts variously won by narrative and by lyric, the succeeding varieties of cooperation are, I argue, no less significant and no less intriguing. To begin with, however, much as clear-cut contrasts between the modes are by no means hard to find, so too do hostile takeover bids occur in early modern texts, as in the poetry of many other cultures.

The writing of lyric provides a moratorium from cultural struggles and yet at the same time enables a more effective participation in them, as Theodor W. Adorno so famously observes in "Lyric Poetry and Society"; so too does the participation in it sometimes provide a temporary break from the responsibilities and pressures of narrative, but in such instances not lyric but the rival genre may insist on the termination of that hiatus.[27] At once writ large and rewritten in Book VI of *The Faerie Queene*, with Pastorella representing not only the genre to which her name refers but also lyric in general, this pattern appears as well in many individual lyrics. The temporality that will turn Richard Lovelace's eponymous grasshopper from verdancy to green ice is represented through the shift from the exclamatory mode we often find in lyric ("Oh thou that swing'st upon the waving haire / Of some well-filled Oaten Beard" [1–2]) to the declarative past perfect statements often associated with narrative ("Golden Eares are Cropt; / *Ceres* and *Bacchus* bid good night" [13–14]).[28] Offering an intriguing parallel to this and other victories by narrative, in Giacomo Puccini's opera *Turandot*, our hero Calaf sings of his love for Turandot while a procession related to the impending execution of a previous suitor moves across the stage, a spatial analogue to the narrative about the victim; Calaf's song and its values only briefly interrupt the music and tale related to that slaughter, and, indeed, we are ironically aware that the sentiments he expresses potentially impel, not impede, the story of death inasmuch as he risks becoming Turandot's next victim.

But if narrative sometimes conquers lyric in these and related respects, in other poems it is lyric that emerges victorious, supporting again, though with the relative strength of the warring camps reversed, the model of hostile takeovers. Incisively glossing one of the most intriguing examples of the interruption of narrative and the permanent triumph of lyric and what it symbolizes, Susan Stewart points out that the praxis of Augustine's *Confessions* is a turn from his sinful life, a world of narrativity described in the past tense, to a spiritual world associated with the present tense and implicitly linked to lyric.[29] A similar spiritual dynamic impels the triumph of lyric in certain early modern poems. As we have already observed, whereas on one level the conclusion of Herbert's "Collar"—"Me thoughts I heard one calling, *Child!* / And I reply'd, *My Lord*" (35–36)—is the final incident in a narrative, on another the lines apparently effect the transformation from a world of action to one of meditation, though they do so through what could aptly be described as a version of narrative resolution. Northrop Frye suggests that what he terms the "private poem" is often the product of a blockage, such as frustrated love; as the instances of St. Augustine and Herbert again demonstrate, lyric may also itself effectively frustrate narrative.[30]

*Pace* St. Augustine and Herbert, however, the conquest of worldly narrativity by lyric spirituality may be qualified and partial. At first glance, Donne's "Goodfriday, 1613. Riding Westward" appears to offer a textbook example of that victory, contrasting as it does the material body's movement in the fallen world with the soul's meditations about Christ: "I am carried towards the West / This day, when my Soules forme bends toward the East" (9–10).[31] In other words, to borrow the term Stewart uses so skillfully at many points in *Poetry and the Fate of the Senses,* in a poem that is about leanings in many senses of the term, the soul arguably "intends" towards lyric, away from narrative; according to this reading, it is "fully persuasive," as one fine reader puts it, in its staging of the effects of grace.[32] But in fact that pattern is complicated and compromised: "bends" (10) obviously also suggests a version of movement, and, as some of the most acute readings it has received have argued, the turn towards Christ, like many of the other turns in verse, is partial and ambiguous.[33]

Of course, the victory or partial victory of lyric over narrative need not be imbued with spiritual resonances. In Donne's "Sunne Rising," the invasion of the sun represents the apparent victory of narrativity, subsequently contested by the battalions of lyric. Not only does the poem in effect tell a story about the sun, but the sun's entrance carries with it the preconditions for narrative, the assumption of a before and an after, in this case the unchanging world of consummated love and the subsequent time when it has been threatened. It is telling that both the challenges to the sun's power and the closural assertion that such challenges have triumphed banish the grammar of action verbs and substitute the stillness of predication, the grammatical formula "x is y": "She is all States, and all Princes, I" (21), Donne famously writes, and the poem concludes on another instance of predication, "This bed thy center is, these walls, thy spheare" (30).[34]

Although the examples of lyric impeding narrative that I have just been examining are intriguing, the generalization about the conflictual relationship between the two modes that they substantiate is no surprise. More surprising and no less important is how often, rather than blocking narrative, lyric enables it, matching not Dido but Lavinia with Aeneas and in so doing making sure the dynasties are founded in time.[35] In its revisionist emphasis on these instances, this chapter, like several other sections of the book, attempts to counter a tendency in literary studies to project its own competitive hierarchies onto a number of literary arenas.

One reason lyric enables narrative is that, unlike Lavinia, it often functions not as an icon of stability but rather as source and symbol of an intensification, a wind-up that must be released in action. In some of these instances, the result is

literally that end so often attributed to narrative, sexual consummation, so that
the lyric functions as a kind of heightening of emotion and sensation leading to
its release; we may recall the double meanings of "increase." Peter Brooks and
others have claimed that narrative itself effects a release; but in many such cases
it is precisely the interplay between that mode and lyric that is instrumental.[36] In
other instances, the intensification allows the speaker or the text to make war, not
love: what is released is aggression. As Robert Kaufman has incisively emphasized, Adorno makes lyric safe for progressive politics by arguing that it creates
the lyric moment, a ruptural space of experimentation that facilitates the recognition of the new; the lyric moment thus functions like the revolutionary moment often posited by some Marxist theorists, that is, the point when cultural
conflicts have intensified to the point of explosive change.[37]

Early modern texts provide many instances of how lyric meditation can pro-
pel narrative action. Arguably the song of the nymphs in the sixth stanza of
Spenser's "Prothalamion" creates a kind of energy that facilitates the swans'
progress to London; the breeding of the song in the "undersong" (110) of the
other nymphs anticipates the breeding of the brides, and the murmuring of the
water that enables their journey represents another echo of the song.[38] The direction of address in Donne's "Funerall" is not the least complexity in this splendid poem, but on some levels the author's reflections on the hair are internalized,
manifesting an increasing anger that culminates in the final stanza of the poem.
There his move from a partly playful religious reference and a command that
someone else bury the hair sometime in the future to the insistence that the
speaker is performing that action now—"since you would save none of mee,
I bury some of you" (24)—exemplifies the ways lyric reflection can lead to the activities of narrative. In other instances, the action in question includes the type
involved in speech acts. Not surprisingly, the meditations in Donne's other lyrics
also often culminate in commands: "Twicknam Garden" turns from laments to a
series of orders (and thence to reflections whose direction of address is ambiguous), while the grieving meditations that occupy most of the "Nocturnall upon
S. Lucies Day" lead to imperatives to other lovers and to the speaker's decision to
prepare for his own death.

Such poems thus encourage us to reevaluate yet another common assumption about lyric. Recognizing the types of heightening I am analyzing, many critics have observed that the mode often moves towards an epiphany, a pattern
of which this chapter has found numerous instances. But rather than achieving
insight—that is, rather than seeing into, seeing inwards—lyrics may enable, even
demand, the process of speaking out and in so doing reaching outwards to the

social circles that, as I have repeatedly observed, are so important a component of many types of lyric.

In addition to impelling action through this kind of heightening and tightening, lyric may more directly generate narrative action by releasing whatever is blocking it, which recalls Frye's brief but suggestive association of that mode with moments of blockage.[39] In a text to which I will turn in the concluding chapter, Milton's *Comus*, Sabrina's song literally releases the Lady, thus also allowing the praxis of moving towards the parents' house to continue. In another operatic analogue, it is Orpheus's song in Monteverdi's opera that releases a blockage and enables him to visit the underworld; in "La Traviata," Violetta's intriguingly echoed aria "Sempre libera" opens by reinforcing the barrier between the lovers but is echoed and reshaped in a way that advances the action and enables the love scene that directly follows, for that and other reasons assuming some of the functions usually attributed to recitativo. As I observed in my analysis of Spenser's *Shepheardes Calender* in Chapter 2, the Latin verb for meditation, *meditor*, can denote certain preparations for action, that is, exercise and practice, as well as designing and intending, while the Hebrew word for the same concept can suggest plotting.[40]

Also, of course, lyric may lead to action in another sense because of its rhetorical efficacy, though often this is action that presumably occurs after the poem has ended rather than within its diegetic confines. Early modern readers must have been aware how many sonnets and other love songs were persuasion poems, whether or not they advertised that aim. The titles in George Gascoigne's *Hundreth Sundrie Flowres*, a text that, as we have seen, repeatedly interweaves lyric and narrative, often stress the rhetorical agenda of the succeeding lines. The twenty-third poem in his *Devises of Sundrie Gentlemen* purports to be sent to accompany a ring, and Shakespeare's "Lover's Complaint" reminds us, if we needed reminding, that such gifts carry with them agendas. More subtly, the title "Corinna's Going A-Maying" assumes the rhetorical success of the persuasion poem it introduces, substituting its certainty for the invitation on which the poem concludes, "let's goe a Maying" (70).[41]

Lyric in the sense of a material text in that mode may also generate narrative in a different respect: many texts incorporate situations in which encountering a poem leads to an attempt to find an explanation for it. In the opening sequence of Lady Mary Wroth's *Urania*, attracted by a light and an apparently newly written sonnet, the title character soon also finds its author, Perissus. Indeed, texts are often discovered, deracinated from their author, in prose romances (thus miming conditions of production examined in the preceding chapter). In other circumstances too, lyric may create a puzzle that narrative attempts to solve, in so doing intensifying the effect of the lyric, as James Schiffer has shown.[42] The implicit "plot" of the procreation sonnets, he suggests, helps us to interpret Sonnet 20, and Sonnet 147 can be glossed through the triangle suggested in Sonnet 144 and elsewhere.

I have been focusing primarily on how lyric may lead to narrative and to action, but the opposite, narrative culminating on lyric, occurs in many different forms—and thus again encourages one to challenge the expectation that a conflictual relationship between them is normative, even virtually inevitable. This is not to deny that on occasion the lyric termination of narrative can be a rejection, even a rebuke: the stillness at the end of Milton's Nativity Ode suggests that not only the pagan gods but also narrative has been banished, at least temporarily.[43] Yet a poem examined earlier, Ben Jonson's "Celebration of Charis in Ten Lyrick Peeces," demonstrates how seamless the connection between storytelling and the lyric transcendence it introduces can on occasion be. Intriguing in this and so many other respects, this poem—or series of poems—introduces the narrative act in its first text ("if then you will read the storie" [13]) and devotes the second and third to recounting the events in this love.[44] "Her Triumph," a lyric celebration of the lady, seems to be the product of those narratives, as if the energies for this tribute had been released by them, the obverse of the lyrics whose energies release narrative. The twenty-third sonnet in Spenser's *Amoretti* ("*Penelope* for her *Ulisses* sake") exemplifies its genre's potentiality of starting on a story and culminating on a meditation on it, a predilection often facilitated by the movement from octet to sestet or from the body of the poem to its couplet. Generically complex in the ways I have already identified, dream visions may also move from a narrative about the dream to a meditation on it, and sometimes back again. In Chapter 1, I examined a fascinating instance in Robert Herrick, the poem "Vision" that begins "Me thought I saw (as I did dreame in bed)" (he writes two with that title).[45] Because of the relative paucity of dream visions in early modern texts, for another apt example we can usefully turn to Chaucer: in his "Book of the Duchess" the act of reading the story of Alcyone and Seyes leads to the dream of the birds, and the narrative about encountering the knight in black culminates on his lyric complaint.

The reader encounters similar shifts in item 109 in the manuscript of poems compiled by Henry Stanford, a poem about whether the speaker's eye and heart should be blamed for love. This lyric is structured around a series of episodes involving those organs, with the words "An other tyme" (7) and "At last" (14) emphasizing the temporal shifts associated with narrativity:

Calling to mynd myn eye went long about
to cause my hart for to forsake my brest
All in a rage I thought to pull yt out
by whose devise I lyved in such unrest
what could he saye then to regayn my grace?
forsothe that yt had sene his mistres face

An other tyme I cald unto my mynd
It was my hart that all my woe had wrought

. . . . . . . . . . . . . . .

I found my self the cause of all my smart
   and told my self my self now slaye I will
but when I saw my self to you was true
    I loved my self because my self loved you.
          (1–8, 15–18)[46]

But, as is often the case in love lyrics, the reader focuses not on those incidents but on the lover's responses and unchanging devotion, qualities that gesture towards lyric; moreover, the opening words, "Calling to mynd" (1) encourage us to read this as a reflection on previous reflections, like Shakespeare's twelfth sonnet.

My opening instances from Wyatt and Herbert draw attention to one of the most significant ways narrative and lyric may interact. It is no accident that both of those poems involve allusions to the future, for modal conflation often occurs in a form we might term the "anticipatory amalgam" inasmuch as in foreseeing events that may occur it blends modes and temporalities. Although Sharon Cameron does not comment specifically on this phenomenon, such conflations are related to patterns she traces throughout her study of lyric temporality, the overlapping of time frames and the attempt to convert fixed time.[47] Threats, prophecies, and promises—speech acts that are intriguingly similar in a number of ways—are all instances of anticipatory amalgams; and, returning to Wittgenstein's model of family resemblances, summarized in my introductory chapter as a model for studying genre, one might also link this kind of conflation to sexual fantasies and dreams.

These amalgams are types of text, often associated with future tense narration, that combine qualities of narrative and lyric by referring to events that generally are explicitly or implicitly flagged as not having occurred in what is diegetically identified as a "real" world—and that may and may or may not do so at some point. Hence on some level they occur within the speaker's mind. If these instances often involve events in the future, they may also blur and displace time sequences, creating the fuzzy temporality about which David Herman has recently written well, and, as I will suggest shortly, also in some respects imitating the lyric present.[48] For example, as we have seen, the sixth stanza of "My lute, awake!" opens on a line implicitly set in the future but without the auxiliary "will"; the central section of "The Collar" both enacts the freedom that will come from going abroad and anticipates it.

As this description and the Wyatt poem on which this chapter opened demonstrate, anticipatory amalgams recall Gerald Prince's category of "the disnarrated," which he defines as "all the events that *do not* happen but, nonetheless, are referred to (in a negative or hypothetical mode) by the narrative text" (italics in original).[49] Including as it does what could have happened but did not and many types of impossibility, Prince's concept is a broad one, and so his analysis of its functions includes many less germane to anticipatory amalgams in particular, such as making the logic of the narrative clear. One reason it is fruitful to distinguish the category of anticipatory amalgams is that they assume distinctive functions relevant to the workings of lyric; another is that they crystallize the relationship of that mode to narrative.

Uri Margolin's recent discussions of prospective narrative, one stage in his provocative and often convincing attempts to replace structuralist models of narrative with newer conceptions, could also usefully gloss anticipatory amalgams. My argument differs from his in enough respects, however, to justify, even mandate, a separate category. Above all, many texts about the future should not merely be classified as narrative but rather should be seen as modal hybrids.[50] For example, as the selections from Wyatt and Herbert discussed above suggest, this type of poem obviously involves a story of events, but much of the emphasis is on the mind experiencing them. Because of the emotions and the situations generating them, such poems are generally electrified by the emotive intensity often, though not unproblematically, associated with lyric. And they straddle temporalities.

How, then, do anticipatory amalgams function in practice? Whereas they can serve many purposes, as the instances from Wyatt and Herbert suggest, they often grant power and authority to those whose purchase on those attributes is limited or blocked. If, as Michael Riffaterre notes in passing about a related phenomenon, the use of conditionals directs one's attention to the speaker's voice, one might add that our anticipatory amalgams as it were magnify that voice.[51] The ability to foresee the future is indeed a power, though, as Cassandra learns to her cost, it can be intertwined with the tragic lack of the ability to forestall the events or even to be believed. In many instances, however, the direct speech act of threatening or promising or foreseeing embeds an indirect speech act of commanding; Wyatt's stanza, for example, has as its subtext, "Yield to me."

Through anticipatory amalgams, lyric poems can offer a type of power analogous to that of the signature verbal tense of lyric, the so-called lyric present. Associating the "sense of enchantment" of lyric with the lyric present, George T. Wright observes of its special type of present tense: "Deliberately bypassing all the modifiers that normal speech requires, the lyric present appears to offer as actual, conditions that we normally accept only as possible, special, figurative, provisional."[52] In other words, the approach to narrativity in many anticipatory amalgams tropes their approach to social interaction: they project an event from mental interiority onto an external space in the future, much as they aim to bring to pass certain types of desired behavior.

Donne's "Apparition," a poem similar in many respects to our stanza from Wyatt, opens on the speaker's apparent powerlessness: literalizing Petrarchan metaphor, as Donne so often does, his speaker assumes he has been killed by his unresponsive mistress.[53] In so doing, he establishes as a literal fact in the future an event metaphorically occurring in the present, her destruction of him, much as he projects onto the future a destructive fantasy of revenge currently in his own mind. Anticipatory amalgams, like lyric, are associated primarily with one temporality but often allude to others. As this narrative, a ghost of future events, progresses, the speaker's ghost attains power over the lady in the events that purportedly will occur in the future—an attempt to regain the power compromised if not lost by her scorn in the present.

The instance from Donne suggests that these amalgams are revealing in their effects not only on the speaker but also on the diegetic listener. Emphasizing the communicative processes of ethics, James Phelan's analyses of twentieth-century lyric narratives can gloss that impact on the audience.[54] Although, as Chapter 2 implies, his endorsement of the commonplace assumption of voiceability is problematical, his focus on interchange and communicative purposes draws attention to further functions of our anticipatory amalgams, and his systems of classification can be usefully deployed. For the story in question often has a rhetorical agenda more pronounced than that of the rest of the poem; in particular, borrowing Phelan's categories, we may observe that the purpose of these inserted narratives is frequently to deliver a threat in the hope that the listener will change, will, as it were, write or allow to be written an alternative story. In other words, when one again adduces Phelan's formulations, it is clear that these speech acts, unlike normative versions of narrativity, tell someone not that something has happened but that it will happen; similarly, in so doing, rather than demonstrating the change that he and many others associate with narrative, they attempt to make that shift occur. Or, to put it in a way that returns to the agency of the speaker, they project what purportedly will happen as a way of willing something else to happen.

In short, while remembering the dangers of painting with Kline's broad strokes, one can now locate the anticipatory amalgam in relation to other modes. If narrative generally, though of course not always, involves a story that is set in the past (which differs of course from the time of discourse) and located in a mimesis of physical space ("it happened in this place") and lyric is generally the mode that focuses on the lyric present or overlapping time schemes and a mimesis of mental space ("it is happening in my mind"), the hybrids in question are typically optatives located both in the mind in the present and in a physical space that may exist in the future. They are thus an extreme but revealing case of the admixtures of lyric and narrative exemplified by our two opening texts—and of an interaction between them very different from a winner-take-all contest.

⎯☙ ❧⎯

As noted above, the patterns traced thus far occur transhistorically: although my examples have been culled from early modern texts, analogues from other periods can readily be found. Variously characteristic of and specific to the early modern period, however, are the ways its literary heritage, its generic template, and its conditions of production shape the relationship between lyric and narrative, and on those effects the rest of this chapter concentrates. This section offers an overview of how all those factors inflect the modal interplay in question; each of the succeeding two sections focuses on an instance in which lyric interacts with another member of the generic template: the lyrics that appear within prose romances and the songs in Shakespeare's plays.

To begin with, the era had many influential models for locating a lyric poem within a narrative situation, notably the prose links in Dante's *Vita nuova*, the ones Thomas Wyatt borrows for his version of the penitential psalms, the headnotes and margin notes of a number of psalms, and Sidney's *Astrophil and Stella* and *Arcadia*. Theatrical practices also alerted early modern lyric poets and their readers to the potentialities for combining lyric and narrative, and especially to the cooperative interactions that this chapter reactively emphasizes. Devoted theater-goers, the Londoners in an early modern reading audience would have been especially conscious of the ways lyric heightening can lead to action. Songs in plays, such as the hunting song in Act IV of *As You Like It*, often work in that manner. And the praxis of the Senecan monologue is frequently reflection that culminates in a decision and its consequences. Indeed, not only the Senecan monologue but also the many other types of dramatic soliloquies, discussed in Chapter 2, offer enlightening counterparts and perhaps inspirations for the sort of lyric whose intensification generates a story or the action associated with narrativity or both. In Act II, scene ii of *Hamlet*, for example, the preceding meditations clearly lead to the action that is a plot for further action, and the speech culminates on "the play's the thing / Wherein I'll catch the conscience of the King" (II.ii.604–605).

The social and cultural circumstances under which lyrics were produced activated interest in such models and provided many opportunities to deploy them. Whereas critics studying periods other than the Renaissance often contrast the occasional genesis of Greek lyrics, which were typically written for particular situations like a military triumph, with the subsequent separation of the mode from particular events,[55] numerous early modern lyrics were in fact composed at least in part for and in relation to occasions and situations, which might appear within the resulting poem as a narrative episode. The imperatives of a patronage culture encouraged this type of writing: weddings, funerals, and visits to country houses all generated poems that can be classified as lyric according to many definitions but include stories about the events in question. In the decades towards the end of the period being studied, tumultuous political events similarly encouraged an amalgam of narratives about them and lyric reflections on them; Marvell's "Horatian Ode" and Milton's sonnets "To the Lord General Cromwell, May 1652" and "On the Late Massacre in Piedmont" are a few examples from among many. In addition, as observed in previous chapters, demonstrated by Catherine Bates, Ilona Bell, and others, and exemplified by Gascoigne's *Hundreth Sundrie Flowres* and *The Autobiography of Thomas Whythorne*, such texts could be deployed as one stage in the events of a courtship. Thus they offer another instance of a narrative that is very relevant to but not necessarily fully expressed within the diegetic world of the text.[56] Prudence warns that Gascoigne and Whythorne no doubt fictionalized events, a hypothesis supported in the former case by the differences between Gascoigne's versions of his text, but we can also safely assume that lovers and would-be lovers exchanged poems in the ways those two writers chronicle. Indeed, given how many readers apparently also turned out poems themselves, they may well have experienced at first hand the exchange of lyrics as an incident in an ongoing relationship.

The English Renaissance also favored a number of genres that encourage the interplay of lyric and narrative elements, with an interest in that interplay no doubt contributing to the popularity of the literary forms in question, and vice versa. These types often involve not a simple triumph of one mode over the other but rather a continuing dialogue between them or overlapping of them or both. On occasion, too, they cast that dialogue in a form that plays up lyric elements even within narrative passages, thus creating further overlapping.

First of all, sonnets and sonnet cycles, as we have seen, evidently permit the interplay of lyric and narrative: storytelling is not in fact very important in some cycles, as Chapter 4 indicated, but certain foundational stories (the first sight of the beloved, some incident showing her disdain, and so on) do recur, whether as the overt focus of a poem or as a subtext. Another popular genre, the psalm, often compromises the distinction between the two modes in question by emphasizing the events that lie behind and can be impelled by reflection: thus again the psalms provide a model for even secular lyric. Many of them, including ones that appear to meditate on a given event, were read as episodes in biblical stories, or even, as Mary Ann Radzinowicz has suggested, as points in a continuing journey, a metaphor that obviously draws on the linearity of narrative.[57] This interpretation is fostered by paratextual material; Henry Ainsworth's *Annotations Upon the Book of Psalmes*, published in 1617, precedes its version of the texts with a summary of David's life that implicitly provides stories for many of the ensuing poems, while many other editions include headnotes or annotations referring to specific events, such as a particular battle.[58] Commentaries like these establish the poem at hand as a product of and participant in narrative, not an interruption to or rival of it.

When early modern lyrics of these types do include narrative, however, they often favor a truncated version of it that veers back towards lyric, that is, a story that focuses on two points, *then* and *now*, and plays down or omits entirely the intermediary stage of further complications traced by many narratologists. Robert Scholes, for example, posits the triad of situation/transformation/situation.[59] The effect of a story or an adumbrated story that omits the middle is to pull us back and forth between the emphasis on change and the events that create it, often associated with narrative, and a focus on a moment and on reactions to the changed state it involves, often characteristics of lyric. That *then/now* structure is central to the Petrarchan tradition, as Roland Greene has incisively shown:[60] many poems contrast the period before the poet saw Laura and the interval after that cataclysmic event, or her life and her death, and so on. Refining and expanding Greene's analysis, one might add that if, as Claudine Raynaud has observed in her analyses of Donne, seduction clearly demarcates *before* and *after*, unfilled desire anticipates but does not achieve that demarcation, so the temporality of the static present is played against a kind of conditional or optative *then/now*.[61] And much as the structure of pastoral often turns on the contrast between the daytime of the poem and the night in which it ends, so too may its temporal underpinning also involve this sort of binary contrast—witness the garden of Eden versus the fallen garden, the experience or illusion of happy love versus its loss, the unviolated landscape versus its invasion.

The separation between lyric and narrative is further confounded in many texts of the period by poets' predilection for writing about love and loss, subject matter that encourages such erosions of modal classification, though that predilection obviously is not unique to this era. As the lyric by Wyatt on which this chapter opened and many other love poems demonstrate, when an event is repeated often enough in the mind, it becomes at once a narrative about past events and a moment in the lyric present. Notice that in another meditation on lost love, "They Flee From Me," he does not cast the first line as "The deer used to seek me and take bread from my hands; then they stopped doing so; now they are fleeing from me" but rather as "They fle from me that sometyme did me seke" (1). Witness a temporal inversion of the pattern in Donne's "Hymne to God my God, in my sicknesse," which is on the cusp (that edgy territory Donne's work so often occupies) between a present of preparing for death and that future event.

Although I have thus far been looking at literary forms that flourished for much or all of the period in question, historicizing lyric, as this study has repeatedly insisted, involves inflecting generalizations about the early modern period with attention to its subdivisions. The masques that flourished at the end of the sixteenth and first part of the seventeenth centuries offered, at least for their relatively small audience, additional instances of and inspirations for modal interplay. These texts encouraged a tendency to meld lyric and narrative modes, a process that, as we have seen, is one of the many ways they can interact. And masques provided prototypical instances of lyric and narrative as cooperating partners, not rivals; notably, they offered examples of lyric's encouraging, not impeding, linear events. The masque as a whole, of course, typically juxtaposes narrative, especially the expository passages on which these texts so frequently begin, and the lyric commentary on it; and often, as in the instances from prose romances to which I will turn shortly, a song leads to narrative action. For example, at the end of Jonson's *Irish Masque*, it is partly in response to a song that the masquers drop their mantles, a garment stereotypically associated with the Irish. Similarly, in George Chapman's *Memorable Masque* the earth obediently opens in response to a song that commands that action. Finally, the ability of lyric to engender action is nowhere better demonstrated than in the charms that are so prevalent in masques.

—୧ ୨—

If writers and readers in the early modern period were intrigued by the relationship between narrative and lyric, so too were the characters in romances. In *As You Like It*, only Orlando puts stiletto to bark; but in its source, Thomas Lodge's *Rosalynde*, Montanus also cannot resist carving poems on trees, a method of transmission favored by many characters in Lady Mary Wroth's *Urania* as well. In Sir Philip Sidney's *Arcadia*, even Basilius delivers poems and even Mopsa is the subject, or rather the target, of a parodic love lyric. Poems of many types, but especially lyrics, variously festoon, advance, and complicate many of the prose romances of the early modern period. Their versions of the relationship of narrative and lyric deserve attention in part because romances were so popular in the period and in part because examining them in detail substantiates and extends analyses elsewhere in this study while also opening some new avenues.

Thus the lyrics in these texts offer useful examples of the labile subject positions whose centrality to early modern lyric I emphasize elsewhere in this book. Characters are often represented as animators singing someone else's song, as when, near the opening of Book I of Bartholomew Young's translation of Montemayor's *Diana*, Syrenus performs for Sylvanus a song he had heard Sylvanus himself sing, thus exemplifying the shifts between the status of poet and audience that are so common to the period.[62] In Book II of Lady Mary Wroth's *Urania*, the title character renders a song that, as she explains to her brother and Pamphilia, she and the shepherdess Liana had overheard. Urania glosses it in terms that recall the complexities of address discussed in my chapter on lyric audiences: "the song was this, speaking as if shee had been by him, and the wordes directed to her, as his thoughts were."[63] Yet another way the prose romances substantiate my earlier analyses is by gesturing towards early modern conditions of production; although one may have some doubts about how often verse was written in sand or left on altarlike stones, such episodes draw attention to how varied the actual means of production and distribution were. Elsewhere these romances more precisely replicate activities in the more quotidian worlds of their readers; when Rosader and Rosalynd sing a madrigal together, they are miming actual courtly behavior, and in Book II of the *Urania*, when Pamphilia adds another stanza to a poem she has previously carved on an ash tree, she conveniently buttresses my point that scribal culture often permitted continuing control over one's text.

More to my purposes now, the lyrics in romances also offer intriguing examples of the relationship of lyric and narrative; in particular, they indicate how often and how variously the two modes cooperate to advance the story rather than competing. Although thus far I have primarily traced that pattern in terms of lyric elements within a particular text, its analogue, common in prose romances, is how the performance of a lyric—instrumental in more senses than one—influences the rest of the plot. Most obviously, in Book II of *Diana*, Syranus recognizes Selvagia by hearing her voice as she sings; symmetrically, he then performs a song that leads Selvagia to approach him. In the sixth book, Diana, Sylvanus, and Selvagia recognize Syrenus in the same way. In terms of the romance tradition, such incidents indicate that one way lyric can contribute to the plot is by effecting versions of anagnorisis. But such episodes also carry with them a larger implication for early modern culture: singing must be seen as a means of transmission connected to but distinct from print and scribal replication of a text.

Lyric serves many other roles as well. Demonstrating the wide range of functions assumed by the poems inserted within the text of the *Old Arcadia* (in contrast to the eclogues), Robert F. Stillman includes the roles of providing information about the plot and humorous exposition.[64] In an analogue to the suasive agendas I mentioned, Lodge's Salader hangs poems by his father's hearse to give the impression he is sorrowful, thus building the reputation that allows him to deceive others subsequently. Because the two episodes appear in close conjunction, the text contrasts this deceptive use of poetry with a more positive instance of its rhetorical instrumentality: the love poem Rosader sends Rosalynd early in their courtship intensifies her interest in him and thus advances the plot. I noted that lyric may advance narrative more directly by posing a problem that the story solves, and in Book II, Chapter 12 of Sidney's *New Arcadia*, reading a poem leads Zelmane to ask Philoclea for an explanation of it, thus inviting one of the many lengthy inset stories in this romance.

In prose romances, as in instances observed earlier in this chapter, the energy and intensification of lyric may also participate in the forward movement of the plot. The "Wooing Eclogue" (211) that Rosader and Rosalynd sing together is one incident in the courtship of our hero by a woman pretending to be a man, an episode prominent as well in Shakespeare's play; but in Lodge's version, a significant part of the wooing is actually conducted through a song, whereas in Shakespeare's, Orlando's atrocious poetry is more an impediment than an encouragement to the course of true love. (To be sure, if Rosader and Rosalynd literally sing the same song, thus symbolizing and abetting their desire to make many types of music together, this incident is implicitly contrasted with Phebe's poetic answer to Montanus's love poem, a response that blocks the love interest rather than advancing it.)

Story may also facilitate or advance lyric in episodes that suggest that lyric is in a sense the achievement and product of narrative, another pattern discussed above. The song Zelmane sings in Book II, Chapter 11 of the *New Arcadia* when he sees Philoclea bathing is described in terms of Platonic furor and the involuntary poetic outburst sometimes associated with it: this language encourages us to see the poem as an expression of sexual desire, in some senses even a consummation that temporarily replaces but also anticipates the more literal consummation of this love. An even more intriguing example occurs at the end of Book III of the first part of the *Urania*. Having previously refused Doralina's request to repeat her poetry, saying she is "weary of rime" (498), Pamphilia instead tells a story about Lindamira that she claims is lifted from "a French Story" (499); the tale, however, culminates in a set of seven sonnets. Although they are labeled, "Lindamira's Complaint," they obviously relate to Pamphilia's condition as well, and as we read we may suspect that the process of telling the story released the blockage that made her hesitate to recite verse earlier. Similarly, the pretense-within-a-pretense-within-a-truth that these poems concern a character in a French story both blocks and releases the fact that they are about Lindamira, and thus in addition really about Pamphilia, both of whom are, of course, characters in an English story.

All this is not to say that hostile takeovers, whether temporary or permanent, and other types of interruption are absent from the relationship of lyric and narrative in these prose romances. The songs at the end of Book I of the *Urania* temporarily delay boarding a ship and the literal and narratological advances that vessel represents. In the *Old Arcadia*, Sidney introduces his eclogues as easing the tediousness of his narrative (an apology for prose that he omits from his revised version): "whereof I will repeat you a few to ease you, fair ladies, of the tediousness of this long discourse."[65] Conversely, the idea that the eclogues—and the social class with which they are primarily associated—threaten the principal plot is both introduced and denied through Sidney's wording at the end of Book IV of his *New Arcadia*: "But yet to know what the poor shepherds did, who were the first discriers of these matters, will not to some ears perchance be a tedious digression."[66] Moreover, some of the lyrics within prose romances do not in any sense contribute to the movement of the plot or the development of its characters; when Basilius sings a song about sunset in Book III, Chapter 39 of the *New Arcadia*, even the most committed New Critic would have trouble finding evidence of organic unity.

On the other hand, in many other instances what would appear to be a lyric interlude that at worst impedes and at best temporarily suspends the plot in fact proves to be relevant to it in some respects, even if it doesn't directly advance the action. As David Kalstone has pointed out, when Strephon and Klaius famously address the "gotehead gods" in their extraordinary sestina, they are alluding to the situation of the princes and to lost harmony.[67] Similarly, some of the eclogues that conclude Book III gloss marriage in ways very relevant to the text. And the commentary on tyranny in Philisides's song in the Third Eclogues illuminates many episodes in the narrative, exemplifying Blair Worden's assertion that Sidney's political observations can be at their most piercing in those bucolic interludes.[68]

The neatest example of a delay that is something else as well occurs at the end of the first book of the New Arcadia. Hearing about Cecropia's "beasts ranging in that dangerous sort" (181), Basilius brushes aside the issue in favor of attending the performance of eclogues, much as he attempts to brush aside the ranging political discontents he should address and the familial responsibilities he subverts. This is a characterological parallel to the formal textual device of suspending the principal plot in the interest of eclogues, thus ignoring the parts of the story that are, so to speak, still roaming abroad, their teeth bared. This delay indubitably serves positive narratological ends of building suspense, but it also enacts one of the principal ethical concerns of the plot, the danger of suspending heroic action for the values troped through the related symbols of pastoral, poesy in general, and love lyrics in particular.

In addition, the lyrics in prose romances often serve functions specific to that genre. The suspension of action at the end of the first book of the New Arcadia demonstrates that these poems do not merely provide one version of the delays the genre requires but also enable a formal analogue, the interlacing of genres and registers, to the interlacing of plots that is also characteristic of romance. And they may also contribute to character development. As several students of Wroth have noted, in the Urania Antissia's uncontrolled effusions of verse participate in the exposure of her weaknesses, establishing her, too, as a kind of negative identity for both Pamphilia and their creator.[69] Most telling are the songs delivered by Pyrocles and, in a closely parallel episode that ensues shortly afterwards, by Musidorus: these lyrics demonstrate how the characters of these worthy princes are threatened by the demon desire.[70] Pyrocles's transformation via love and his disguise as a woman are closely associated with his delivering a love poem, that activity so often seen as effeminizing in Sidney's culture.

Songs and poems are, in short, typically integrated into the prose romances in a range of ways. Yet the extent to which this incorporation is signaled visually differs significantly from one romance to another. For those who read romances in manuscript, the songs would have necessarily lacked the distinction, in both senses, created by italicization, though they were set off by white space. In contrast, in printed texts such as the 1598 translation of George of Montemayor's *Diana* and the 1590 and 1593 editions of Sidney's *Arcadia*, poems, like many paratextual elements, are italicized; in those editions of Sidney's romance, generally though not with absolute consistency, a large capital further flags the shift into poetry. Once again the reader receives varied signals about the status of verse; once again the author does not have absolute control over those signals. This anticipates how song in Shakespearean drama is thoroughly woven into the texture of the drama in some respects, yet insistently distinguished from it in others.

—☙ ❧—

This chapter focuses on the mating rituals and rebuffs of lyric and narrative: emerging as they do when one examines speaker and audience, the dramatic qualities of lyric have necessarily been discussed at several other points in this work, notably in my chapter on lyric audiences. Nonetheless, at this juncture a coda on one particular instance of the relationship of lyric and drama, the songs in Shakespeare's plays, can usefully supplement those discussions because it supports and extends my arguments about the modal relationships traced in this chapter in one way while further complicating them in another. First, much as lyrics are often closely integrated into the romances and other narratives in which they appear, so too Shakespearean songs often advance the action of the drama rather than simply adorning or impeding it.[71] In particular, they typically do so through their many connections to issues about power and its limitations. And second, whereas many of the examples examined so far involve some blurring of modal categories, the Shakespearean analyses below demonstrate how and why in certain important respects songs in particular must be sedulously distinguished from other discursive registers.

Recognizing how song can impel action and why it differs from other forms of discourse provides a new perspective on, among other subjects, the relationship of song to marginalized characters. Many valuable studies of the Others who sing in these plays, such as the work of Leslie C. Dunn, attribute the newfound agency of these performers to characteristics of the social situation, notably the presence or creation of a community of women, or, alternatively, these studies concentrate on the content of what is performed.[72] Yet these analyses call for revisionist qualifications, for, although the thematic content and female circles associated with songs often contribute to their power, it is primarily through the distinctive qualities of song per se, notably its ability to substitute its own rules for others, that hierarchies of gender and social status are countered. Thus otherwise marginalized women and men can achieve a measure of agency.

A large subject in its own right, the issue of Shakespearean songs necessarily gestures towards the even vaster question of the role of such verses in early modern plays. The relationship of those two exemplars of performance, songs and plays, has received far more critical attention than the relationship of lyric and narrative in early modern literature. Especially useful is William Bowden's survey of the uses of song in seventeenth-century drama; in particular, in demonstrating that songs appear in some 70 percent of the 475 plays he examined, Bowden's study stresses the range of functions they serve, thus providing a useful warning against making the little world surveyed below an everywhere. No less valuable in its conclusions, though quite different in its focus, Diana E. Henderson's study of the role of song in Elizabethan drama achieves insights with broader implications through a more focused analysis of three test cases in particular, George Peele's *Arraignment of Paris*, Christopher Marlowe's *Dido, Queen of Carthage*, and Shakespeare's *Love's Labor's Lost*.[73]

Methodological and ontological problems confront any study of songs in early modern drama, even one with my more limited agenda. As my introduction noted, songs differ among each other in multiple ways; especially germane to debates about lyric is the extent to which a given song establishes itself as a performance, a self-conscious representation for an audience. Some Shakespearean songs are not lyrics in most of the senses in which I have defined the mode but rather ballads, while others are lyrics in some senses yet distinctly unlyrical in their mood, such as Silence's songs in Act V, scene iii of *2 Henry IV* or Autolycus's in *The Winter's Tale*. My analysis focuses largely on songs that are lyric, not narrative, in mode, but some of its observations apply to both types and to songs that, though primarily narrative, include lyric elements.

If we cannot always be sure which songs should be described as lyrics, neither can we invariably achieve certainty about which passages in plays were sung. To what extent and in what ways, if any, are the songs in drama ontologically different from types of discourse they resemble? Although Jonathan Culler has suggested a binary divide between lyric and the default position of ordinary speech,[74] in fact, as my analysis of the relationship between narrative and lyric demonstrates, many intermediary positions insistently present themselves. Similarly, it is not always possible to locate an inherent linguistic distinction between the songs in plays and other passages. In some respects the seductive language with which

Volpone attempts to court Celia immediately after singing "Come, my Celia, let us prove" is more lyrical than that classically restrained song itself. The sonnet delivered during Romeo and Juliet's courtship is evidently a passage of heightened lyricism but not literally a song. Despite and because of these category crises, Frye's radical of presentation—that the given words are sung—remains crucial. In particular, Shakespeare so often presents song as discursively ruptural, as a dramatic break from many other kinds of language, that this way of voicing words qualifies some of my earlier generalizations about the overlapping of discursive types.

This is not to deny the kinship of song with a few linguistic forms that are themselves ruptural. As Andrew Welsh has so cogently demonstrated, charm and chant are among the roots of lyric, and one is certainly aware of their connection in the songs of many Shakespearean plays.[75] "Charming your blood with pleasing heaviness" (III.i.215) is the effect predicted for the Welsh song in *1 Henry IV*.[76] In the opening of Act II, scene ii of *A Midsummer Night's Dream*, the fairies' apotropaic song at Titania's bedside is followed virtually immediately by Oberon's charm. Arguing as well that charms differ from songs in the former's characteristic emphasis on the private rather than the communal, irregular rhythm, and reliance on magic words rather than nonsense words, Welsh suggests that chants may combine elements of both charm and song;[77] spectators of the scene in *A Midsummer Night's Dream* are likely to be aware that while one of the two passages in question is a song aiming to protect Titania and the other a charm intended to harm her, their tones are similar, and both might be performed as chants. In short, the similarities between these types encourage the audience to compare and think further about each of these discursive registers, thus directing attention to their distinctive workings.

Song itself is not distinctive, however, in a way one might well predict, that is, miming of the properties of soliloquy. Shakespeare, as studies ranging from the classic work of Wolfgang Clemen to the recent revisionist analyses of James Hirsch have shown, was attracted to the soliloquy and redeveloped it from earlier models.[78] Given the association, however problematized and limited in the early modern period, between lyric and the meditative, we would expect to find a significant percentage of Shakespearean songs associated with or serving the functions of soliloquies. Quite the contrary. Shakespeare is interested in lyric as a form of speech that interacts with other forms, as we just saw; and in the characterological analogue to that concern, he is interested as well in how the singer interacts with those around him. Diana Henderson's acute observation about the work of Marlowe and Peele, as well as *Love's Labor's Lost*, applies to the rest of its author's canon as well: "Shakespeare's play is very much about lyricism as a social act."[79] Most of the time the use of songs in his plays, unlike those of some of his contemporaries, emphasizes interplay between people and registers of discourse, not isolation or removal. Exceptions of course present themselves; for example, although the song Julia hears in Act IV, scene ii of *Two Gentlemen of Verona* enables some puns on the behavior of the performer, its performance per se contributes comparatively little. On the whole, however, songs participate actively both in the dramatic action and in the forms of narrativity it involves.

In so doing, they serve a wide range of roles; for example, the Clown's love songs in Act II, scene iii of *Twelfth Night* and his duet with Sir Toby in the same scene establish the rowdiness against which Malvolio rails. One should, however, render Henderson's observation about lyricism as a social act more specific by acknowledging that Shakespearean songs are typically associated not only with social acts but with ones involving the assertion and achievement of power, whether it is the apotropaic magic of the fairies in the concluding scene and some earlier ones in *A Midsummer Night's Dream* or the different but not unrelated seductive strategies of Autolycus and Ariel when he is calling to Ferdinand. When Laertes alerts Ophelia to the danger Hamlet represents "If with too credent ear [she] list his songs" (I.iii.30), he is cautioning her about the potency of songs, literal and otherwise, implying that, like the vows against which her father shortly warns her, they may serve as "brokers" (127) in a campaign of "unmast'red importunity" (32).

Although Laertes also reminds Ophelia that Hamlet's agency is limited because of his social position, clearly his love lyrics can express and enhance his power as princely lover in predictable and conventional ways. In some particularly intriguing Shakespearean instances, however, the power of song is transgressive because of the type of sentiments being expressed or the type of person expressing them or both. Singing, so often a pastoral activity, may fill a liberatory discursive function similar to the role Paul Alpers attributes to pastoral itself.[80] Notice that the hunting song in Act IV, scene ii of *As You Like It* not only expresses the commonplace anxieties about adultery but links them to male prowess in that the hunter who killed the deer wears the horns. In other words, achievement in male pursuits like hunting is not adequate protection against failure in amorous ones; the song stages male competition, with jealousy of the hunter's achievements symbolically represented as the fulfilled desire to cuckold him.

The connection between singing and power in cases like that one is significant in part because it highlights the question at the core of this section: how and why do marginalized characters sing? In the instance from *As You Like It*, male courtiers perform the song, but it is striking how often in Shakespearean drama the singer is a woman, a Fool, or someone else whose power and status are delimited, as Leslie C. Dunn, among others, has observed.[81] Similarly, although she does not discuss *Hamlet* at length, Henderson's overall argument that song is often linked to both positive and negative responses to female power is as germane to that play as to the ones she does analyze. Ophelia's songs are transgressive: she is insisting, as Nona Paula Fienberg has pointed out, on becoming a subject not an object, and her subject matter is deviant and threatening in that she is talking about her father's death and about male betrayal of women.[82] The play is concerned throughout with how one can speak the truth in a world of spies, which is one of the many implications of the hall of mirrors, with people concealed, in the Branagh film version, and various solutions—Ophelia's turn to song, Hamlet's disguised and whirling words, the license of the gravediggers—are compared with each other.

The contrast between Hamlet's and Ophelia's songs alerts us to how often in Shakespeare's plays marginal characters sing to accomplish a very different function from Hamlet's: to find a means by which they can say what they otherwise dare not say, or, indeed, to have any voice at all.[83] It is no accident that, as William C. Carroll has demonstrated, Poor Tom sings frequently.[84] In the case at hand, song allows Ophelia two interrelated opportunities: she can introduce ideas that might not otherwise be voiced or voiceable, and she can express those ideas in a social situation, as a form of communication and even interaction.[85] One could readily envision a play in which madness is figured by the solitary singing of these words, but that is precisely the opposite of what Ophelia does; although her performance is a marker of madness, there is indeed method in it, and the method fills social functions. To the queen's "what imports this song?" (IV.v.27), she replies, "pray you mark" (28) and then delivers the verses that should be marked by the audience. And she repeats exactly the same three words six lines later. Insisting that her audience both interpret and participate in the songs, shortly afterwards she declares, "Pray, let's have no words of this, but when they ask you what it means, say you this" (46–47). What follows, the song she prefers to other types of words, concerns a man who seduces a virgin. Michael Boyd's 2004 Royal Shakespeare Company production emphasizes the social interactions performed by this and her other songs: she addresses them directly to specific characters (in this instance, Claudius, thus clearly linking his political transgressions with sexual ones and also, more debatably, perhaps hinting at her own Oedipal scenario). Shakespeare's Fools are, of course, another case in point of using songs not only to express the transgressive but to communicate it to others. Through ditties that, as the text tells us, are sung, Lear's Fool attempts to alert him to his mistake in surrendering power to his daughters.

How, then, does song grant a voice to otherwise marginalized Others? What gives song the power to empower? The answers, however complex and various, reside above all in three mechanisms of this medium. It rewrites ontological rules through its connection to ritual. It rescripts conversational rules by substituting an alternative discursive register. And it recasts closural rules through its ability to impose an alternative ending.

First, its connections with ritual, traced so acutely by Roland Greene and Andrew Welsh among others, imbue it with quasi-magical potency.[86] Chapter 2 demonstrated how the ritualistic characteristics of lyric can encourage the participation of the audience and even on occasion identification with the speaker; I argued that these processes are often seductive, though not necessarily as coercive as other critics, notably Greene in his very different approach to the ritualistic elements in lyric, have claimed.[87] When lyric takes the form of song, however, its coerciveness sometimes intensifies. For singing can do for discursive space what its analogue, ritual (like game), can do for space in the more literal, geographical sense: that is, song questions or unsettles other rules and imposes its own. Many early modern playwrights were surely aware of the common Neoplatonic links between song and magic. More specifically, those connections among song, charm, and chant contribute to its ritualistic practices. Especially relevant here is how charms substitute for the quotidian practices of the workaday world their alternative etiologies, which are often rule bound—anyone touched by this flower will necessarily fall in love and so on. Shakespeare's plays are full of examples of these patterns, even beyond the most obvious ones like the magical lyrics in *A Midsummer Night's Dream*. The utterances of Lear's Fool manifest a type of ritualistic power, and it is both invoked and ironized in Imogen's funeral dirge.

But the potency of song relates not only to the rules established by the world of the magical or quasi-magical but also those established in and about discourse, and this introduces the second source of the power of song. One of that medium's most intriguing aspects is its preemptive redefinition of the regulations of speech. If, as Mark W. Booth asserts, song builds a sense of communal identity, arguably the singer acquires authority from speaking for and with those around her.[88] But Booth's theory is limited by its assumption that listeners do not wish to take issue with the song; hence it needs to be supplemented by the work of the anthropologist Maurice Bloch. Bloch's observation that the special status of song precludes argument or interruption is very germane to how song entitles those who might otherwise be suppressed to speak despite potential opposition.[89] He also points out that such interruption would itself be transgressive. To put it another way, the turn-taking practices of conversation are suspended. In support of Bloch, observe that Lear does not interrupt his Fool's songs. And even if Ophelia sings an accusation directly at and about the king, as in the Michael Boyd production, he does not interrupt her musical mousetrap as he interrupts its spoken analogue.

Third, song plays and is played by its own rules when it concludes a play, thus again permitting an assertion of power. Characters often struggle for the right to bring about closure—which is, in effect, having the last word in a conversation or, in a heated one, hanging up the telephone before the other party can do so. Many of Shakespeare's dramas conclude on what might be termed "contestatory closure" in that several characters battle to create an ending and to achieve the other types of authority that act represents. Among the clearest examples is the conclusion of *King Lear* (however one resolves editorial debates about the assignment of certain speeches); similarly, at the termination of *Hamlet* Horatio and Fortinbras in effect compete for the right to end the play on their own terms, with Hamlet's team losing yet again. Especially interesting examples are the final scene of *As You Like It*, where in a sense Rosalind, Hymen, Jacques, and the Duke all try to bring about closure, and the ending of *A Midsummer Night's Dream*, where both the human characters and the fairies offer their versions of closure.

Song can be an appropriate ending to a play in such contested situations because it marks that conclusion with a change in registers, in fonts, as it were. Witness Feste's final song. Like an epilogue addressing the audience, a song that the hearers might recognize and hum under their breaths or even join breaks down the separation between players and spectators in a way appropriate to the liminal moment of closure. At the same time, as R. S. White points out in a thoughtful study of songs in Elizabethan romances and comedies, in Shakespeare's texts as elsewhere, a song may destabilize other forms of closure by calling into question comedic resolution. In these instances, too, singing enjoys agency and potency.[90]

I have been arguing, then, that the force of ritual, the workings of everyday speech, and the operations of closure in a range of circumstances all write special rules and thus give a song a force that allows previously powerless characters to acquire agency and instrumentality; in so doing, this medium often shifts the social dynamics and especially the hierarchies of power in a preexisting situation. The work of that controversial singer of songs Freud suggests additional ways song grants agency to Others. Whereas Freud persuasively associates dreamwork with the hidden agendas of jokes, one might usefully import his insights about both of those forms to create a category of "songwork."[91] Songs, like dreams and jokes, may condense a story, as in Ophelia's lament about her father or the Fool's commentaries on Lear's relationship to his daughters. They may deflect a story by associating it with people other than the original participants; arguably Ophelia's song about the betrayed woman is a version of her own experiences with Hamlet, while Feste's final song, apparently about his own sexuality, also refers to the shenanigans of the other characters.[92] And, again like dreams and jokes, songs may express something by seeming to say the opposite, as when Ophelia claims that young men are not to blame for seducing women and Desdemona similarly seemingly excuses male betrayal as she sings.

But if Shakespearean song bestows power on those who lack it by overturning ontological, discursive, and closural rules, as well as through its similarities to dreamwork and jokework, its own power to do so is sometimes constrained. The transgression it enables may be delimited, though not as consistently as a bald subversion/containment model would lead us to expect. A song functions the way speech acts in drama function according to J. L. Austin and other speech act theorists: it undermines its truth value, surrounds its statements with an "as if."[93] In other words, Ophelia is reading Derrida when Hamlet believes she is engrossed in a different type of prayer book. If on one level singers like her rightly imply that they are not only telling truths but telling ones of great import—"when they ask you what it means, say you this" (IV.v.36–37), she insists—on another level their medium produces a signature in quotation marks. In their potentially compromised but nonetheless significant relationship to empowerment, songs, whether they be lyric or narrative, playground jingles or ballads or performed sonnets, have more in common with each other than, say, the prose romance does with the novel.

Similarly, although songs give the singer the power and authority to express radically dissonant truths, they nonetheless do not guarantee an appropriate response on the listeners' parts, a fact learned and publicly lamented by many Shakespearean characters, as well as numerous sonneteers in the early modern period. (Thus too the work of jokes may be compromised by a listener who refuses to play straight man or replies with, "I don't get it.") A source of revelation, songs also are treated as a symptom of madness, as Dunn and Sophie Tomlinson have demonstrated, the latter having acutely adduced the Jailer's Daughter in *Two Noble Kinsmen* as well as Ophelia.[94] This linkage between bursting into song and mental instability obviously reflects the ambivalences about the power of lyric traced throughout this study, and in so doing it provides another way the agency of singers may be circumscribed.[95] The ability of song to achieve or chal-

lenge closure may be similarly curtailed. Ending on song, as Feste does, celebrates his power—but such lyrics were in many cases followed by the jig, a rival
form of music by which a rival author brings about closure. So, in this sense,
songs contributed to rather than terminating contestatory closure.

In another respect as well Shakespearean drama delimits the potency it assigns
to songs. If they are often associated with powerless but sympathetic characters
like Desdemona, songs are also treated ironically by being assigned to unappeal-
ing characters like Stephano or to those who at best evoke an ambivalent response, such as Caliban and Bottom—much as poems that are not necessarily
sung, such as the lyrics of Orlando and the courtiers in *Love's Labor's Lost*, are
mocked. Sometimes the content rather than the speaker will be ironized and even
discredited: the beautiful funeral dirge sung for Imogen in *Cymbeline* is as inap-
propriate as the intriguingly similar moment in the Coen brothers' film *Raising
Arizona* when the convicts wail for the baby they have left in the road.

This amalgam of power and powerlessness invites us to place the songs in
drama within the broader context of a linguistic form that I have elsewhere termed
"authorizers"—that is, types of speech such as riddles, stories, and prophecies that
negotiate power and authority, as well as their often contested relationship.[96] Authorizers function by impelling a process aimed at establishing the authority of the
speaker, even, or especially, if it did not exist previously, a process that often involves first establishing and then qualifying that authority. Thus, much as a song
grants power to the singer in the ways I have identified, so a riddle allows the person who poses it to determine what the appropriate answer is; but his or her status
changes dramatically if the conundrum is successfully solved. And in establishing
power and authority, these types of discourse, like song, typically abrogate the rules
for everyday conversation and substitute their own regulations.

Desdemona's willow song exemplifies the workings of authorizers and in so
doing provides intriguing encapsulations and extensions of issues discussed in
earlier chapters and previously in this one. In the course of talking with her own
maid, Emilia, and preparing for bed shortly before Othello kills her, Desdemona
delivers a lament she heard from her mother's maid, Barbary. It is a text about
someone who is singing a song by a stream and has been betrayed by a lover who,
like Othello, "prov'd mad" (IV.iii.27). Critics have noted that the geographical locale of the area termed "Barbary" shifts from one text to the next in the early
modern period.[97] No less significant are the shifts in its subject positions, modes,
and types of discourse.

To begin with, Desdemona's song, like those in prose romances sung by a
character who had previously been the listener, provides a useful analogue to the

shifting positions of lyric speaker and audience analyzed in Chapter 2. Barbary sings an "old thing" (29) sung by others; Desdemona then sings Barbary's song and sings about Barbary singing it; the song quotes the man involved; and Emilia subsequently refers to singing it before she dies. By adding Barbary, who has no counterpart in the original ballad, and by including Emilia's desire to repeat the song, the text enables and emphasizes these shifts in position. Thus it develops from a different perspective the cognate changes that occur elsewhere within the play, notably the ways Othello comes to mirror Iago; at the same time, the text draws attention to the changing subject positions characteristic of lyric itself, a potentiality and problem that, as my analysis of Sonnet 35 in Chapter 2 indicates, preoccupied its author.[98]

As that description suggests, the willow song also blends narrative and lyric in ways previously explored in this chapter. Although it is based on a very popular ballad and thus owes more to narrative than to lyric, it certainly includes lyric elements as well.[99] The narrative within the song ("The poor soul sat [sighing] by a sycamore tree" [40]) echoes the preceding narrative about it ("My mother had a maid call'd Barbary. . . . She had a song of 'Willow'" [26, 28]) until the two are hard to distinguish semantically, though they are distinguished by the move into the register of song; and the Russian-doll effect of stories within stories is extended by a tale within the song:

> "I call'd my love false love; but what said he then?
>     Sing willow, willow, willow;
> If I court moe women, you'll couch with moe men."
>
>                         (55–57)

At the same time, as is so often the case, those stories introduce the lyric complaint that is being sung: "'Sing all a green willow must be my garland'" (51) and the refrain emphasizes lyricality.

But if Desdemona's song exemplifies the larger contentions of this chapter about the relationship of lyric and narrative, it also enacts the arguments of this particular section about song. Until she sings, Desdemona has been attempting to excuse Othello. Here, albeit tentatively and obliquely, she acquires enough authority and autonomy to begin to blame him. From where does she draw and sustain the agency to challenge his plots in several senses of that noun?[100]

The answers are interlocking. First, the important issues about female community adumbrated earlier contribute to her power as a narrator. Second, she achieves that power in part through narrativity. Although commenting on the scene in question only in passing, Lloyd Davis's acute analysis of *Othello* traces the instrumentality of narrative, especially the ways in which telling stories about the past can be an important action in its own right and one that will influence the future.[101] Desdemona, unlike many other storytellers in the play, lays claim to an instrumentality that she did not previously have, or at best had in limited form, the power to attack Othello for his betrayal of her love and the grievously unfair accusations that result. As a result, two scripts, one authorizing Desdemona and one authorizing Othello, struggle for supremacy.

Above all, however, both Desdemona's agency as a singer and its limits relate to the ways songs reinterpret rules and other social practices. The procedures of ritual replace those of everyday interactions, and one of the many functions of the refrain here is to render the utterance more ritualistic.[102] In a sense this song is an apotropaic charm for women, a defense against the seductions of all too charming men. We could profitably extend the arguments of earlier critics about female community, summarized above, by recognizing that in such ways singing establishes and strengthens gendered bonds. And if, as I have suggested, songs resist interruption, this instance shows us that they may do so in part through what is the polar opposite of and a defensive strike against interruption: ensuring the repetition of their own words. Whereas Desdemona's complaint temporarily blocks the novella by Othello and his ghost writer Iago, reminding us that the power of song, like that of narrative, often derives from blocking another form of speech, it does so by means of patterns of repetition that both enact and figure the breeding of stories. In the refrain we find the most obvious instance, and that poetic device stages its own workings in the phrase "'Sing willow, willow, willow'" (56). Desdemona gives Barbary's song currency, makes it current, much as her own song will be repeated. The streams by which she sings echo the story, though if the mirroring effect of the water figures these types of recurrence, it also reminds us that iteration may involve distortion. In any event, all these echoes draw attention to the encouraging fact that Desdemona's story may be repeated just as Barbary's has been and just as Barbary herself has reproduced an old song. And, authorized in her transgressive defiance both by song itself and by Desdemona's previous deployment of it, Emilia does repeat a snatch of it. A stanza from one common version of the ballad omitted from the text requests the listener to note on the singer's tomb that he was true to his love: though on one level erased, on another level that stanza becomes dramatic action in that Emilia in effect inscribes in the play an epitaph about Desdemona's chastity.

In short, the very repetitions of the song both testify and contribute to its potency: each successive singer in effect authorizes the next one to sing it, demonstrating that one may control the future by ensuring that one's tale will be told again. If on the one hand the alienability of lyric demonstrates the destructive aspects of scattering, here one is reminded that both narrative and lyric may achieve power through dissemination in its most positive senses. Thus, in a play whose praxis is the contestation of rival stories and rival storytellers, Desdemona becomes not only a lyric poet but a narrative one, telling a tale that rivals those proffered by that master and slave of narrative Othello. She achieves this in no small measure through the iterability of song.

But singing often involves not only the assertion but also the delimitation of authority, and Desdemona's song is no exception. Reminding us of how the potency of that medium is impeded in instances like Ophelia's performance, Desdemona tellingly presents her performance in terms of lack of agency:

> That song to-night
> Will not go from my mind; I have much to do
> But to go hang my head all at one side
> And sing it like poor Barbary.
>
> (30–33)

Notice that she associates singing with the pitiful physical position and lower social position of Barbary; notice too that her phraseology here transfers agency to the lyric, literally the subject of the first sentence.

Although mitigated by the act of singing, Desdemona's culturally encouraged tendency to blame herself for being a victim does not disappear: "'Let nobody blame him, his scorn I approve'" (52). The limitations in her agency register in the limitations in the potentialities I have ascribed to song. If on one level Desdemona's song resists interruption from other storytellers, on another level she suspends it with her own interjections. Breaking into and hence breaking apart her own song, Desdemona complicates though does not obviate the anthropological work of Bloch on the ability of song to resist interruption inasmuch as these interruptions are partly subsumed into the tale. Nor is the ability of song to establish a rival version of closure fully achieved here; tellingly, Desdemona's song culminates on a series of questions. The only closure it achieves involves a tragic diminishment of power: as Emilia explicitly asserts, this is a swan song. Yet all these challenges to her authority do not erase the accusatory story she, like Ophelia, authorizes through song.

Thus, in a study that has repeatedly adduced paradoxes, a few more can now join the zoo of those cavorting creatures. Narrative and lyric, we have seen, assume a wide range of different relationships, and in many cases the distinctions between those modes can help us to understand each of them. Yet I have emphasized throughout that in early modern culture as well as other eras, in addition to exemplifying the conflict and conquest that critics generally anticipate, those two modes often interact cooperatively, at times even producing intriguing amalgams. In particular, whereas they may impede or interrupt narrative action, lyric passages often advance it.

The same is true of the songs in Shakespeare's plays, which, as Henderson observes in relation to *Love's Labor's Lost,* typically participate actively in the action and the relationships among characters rather than primarily expressing the emotions of a single personage.[103] In so doing, I have argued, those songs bestow agency and other types of power, even if they are circumscribed. The principal reason for that achievement lies in our final one, their peculiar ontological status. Although this chapter has drawn attention to blurred categories elsewhere in poetry, when songs are performed in Shakespeare's plays, as in many other venues, it is distinction, in its several senses, that matters most. In diction, mood, and rhythm such songs may resemble other passages in the plays, especially intense lyrical descriptions and chants. Under these circumstances, however, Frye's radical of presentation trumps other determinants. Even as song participates in the spectrum of various types of heightened or lyricized speech, it often insists on its difference from other registers and on its ability to authorize new types of insight and to write a new set of rules.

# CHAPTER 6

# The Rhetorics of Lyric

## Conclusions and New Perspectives

Beneficent spirit of the Severn's ominous borderlands, Milton's Sabrina harbors odd companions on her own borders.[1] So significant for the purposes of this conclusion is the song invoking her that its latter section merits a lengthy quotation:

> Sabrina fair                                859
>     Listen where thou art sitting
> Under the grassy, cool, translucent wave,
>
> . . . . . . . . . . . .
>
>         Listen and save.        866
> Listen and appear to us
> In the name of great *Oceanus*,
> By the earth-shaking *Neptune's* mace
> And *Tethys'* grave majestic pace.         870
> By hoary *Nereus'* wrinkled look,
> And the *Carpathian* wizard's hook,
> By scaly *Triton's* winding shell,
> And old soothsaying *Glaucus'* spell,
> By *Leucothea's* lovely hands              875
> And her son that rules the strands.
> By *Thetis'* tinsel-slipper'd feet,
> And the Songs of *Sirens* sweet,
> By dead *Parthenope's* dear tomb,
> And fair *Ligea's* golden comb,            880

Wherewith she sits on diamond rocks
Sleeking her soft alluring locks,
By all the *Nymphs* that nightly dance
Upon thy streams with wily glance,
Rise, rise.

    (A *Maske Presented at Ludlow Castle*,

      859–861, 866–885; emphasis in original)[2]

In line 878 references to the sirens begin to invade Milton's catalogue of more appropriate attendants for Sabrina, alluring the lyric away from the translucency, semantic and aquatic, on which it began. Five of the nineteen lines quoted above (878–882) directly invoke that treacherous glee club, while the "wily glance" (884) of the nymphs, not fortuitously an echo of Comus's earlier description of his own trains (151), at least mirrors the enticements of the sirens and, alternatively, may be read as an additional description of them.

Might one explain away the unsettling appearance of the sirens' narrative by claiming that these are not the seductive singers whom Comus links to Circe earlier in the poem ("I have oft heard / My mother *Circe* with the Sirens three" [252–253]) but rather merely the embodiments of Platonic celestial harmony invoked by Milton himself in "At a Solemn Music" and *Arcades?* Haemony, Louis Martz suggests, may represent sacred song.[3] Or one might join Stella P. Revard in glossing this passage as a description of "nurturing" water deities linked thematically to Sabrina?[4] Any attempt to finesse the sirens' presence in these ways is, however, countered by the reference to "soft alluring locks" (882); although the menacing implications of a woman plotting seduction coexist with the appeal of the phrase (as erotic menace so often does in Milton), its negative resonances are intensified by that use, only two lines later, of "wily," an adjective not only deployed earlier in this poem as noted above, but also applied twice to the snake in *Paradise Lost*. And the connection between the sirens' modus operandi and that of Circe and her son is surely more powerful and more immediate for most Renaissance and contemporary readers than the positive biographical entries Revard adduces for them. The point is not that those positive stories are completely erased; rather, if the presence of these dangerous singers casts a shadow over even Sabrina, the myth of the menacing sirens overshadows the alternative story of their unthreatening alter egos. A similar conflation occurs in the nineteenth-century English painter William Etty's illustration for the poem. Now in the Art Gallery of Western Australia, his "Scene from Milton's *Comus*" recalls the cast of characters in the woodcut by the seventeenth-century Italian Jiulio Bonasone, discussed in Chapter 1. Etty's canvas represents Circe, the Naiades, and the sirens; while the raised eyes of two of those singers suggest spirituality, their voluptuous bodies, so characteristic of Etty's nudes, as well as the company they keep, evoke the threatening seductiveness Milton associates with them.

The textual history of the poem registers its author's unease with the inclusion—and the exclusion—of the sirens. Their description was crossed out, then restored, a process that the most thorough student of Milton's editorial emendations, S. E. Sprott, believes occurred when its author was drafting the poem.[5] Moreover, the fact that the wily nymphs were inserted after the passage was initially composed is telling, as is the number of trochaic adjectives with very different valences that might have been substituted for "wily": "playful glance," "loving glance," and so on would have toned down the menace that is instead intensified by Milton's modifier. Not only the obvious semantic content of the passage but also the reference to Parthenope, associated in Virgil's *Georgics* IV.563–566 with the author's guilt about the genres of his earlier poetry, encourage us to read that menace in relation to the dangers of song.

For all the attention excited by other hints of inconsistency or anxiety in the poem, notably Milton's reference to "glutinous heat" (917), most critics have ignored Sabrina's unlikely attendants completely; a handful of acute readers, a select company ranging in critical approach from Douglas Bush to John Guillory, has noted their inappropriateness without offering any detailed etiology for the pathology of the passage.[6] In a brief but suggestive commentary on these lines, Nancy Lindheim acknowledges a "hint of danger" while maintaining that the masque as a whole successfully contains it, thus instancing the young Milton's attraction to sensuous beauty.[7] What, then, is a nice girl like Sabrina doing in a place like this?

Immediately before she rises up through the magic of the masque's engineering to exercise her sanative powers through the magic of lyric, a competing story about that mode rises up through dark regions in the poet and his culture. Yet the anticlosural relationship of those two tales can in fact effect closure to my own narrative about early modern lyric, for from the turbulent waters of this passage arise as well summaries of and supplements to many no less turbulent issues traced throughout *The Challenges of Orpheus*. Throughout early modern lyric we encounter, for example, the conflict between the positive valences of sirens and the negative ones. Manifest in the distinctions between various types of lyric instrument and various classical instruments, this ambivalence is often gendered, as it is here, with the result of intensifying anxieties about writing lyric. The resonances of the apparent binary in question, like those of many other gendered issues, frequently in fact involve the blurring of borders: much as the positive and negative associations of sirens cohere and even coalesce in this passage, so the attempt to associate Good Lyric with the psalms, in contrast to the ungodly songs they may drown out, is compromised by doubts about the moral value of singing even those heavenly songs. Milton's invocation is also about Milton's vocation, as is so much of his canon, and hence this passage reminds us, too, how often early modern poets discuss decisions in their careers as choices among genres or, as in the instance of the two versions of lyric, between positive and negative versions of the same genre. Above all, like many songs, this book has its refrains, and Milton's passage may recall my emphasis on the guilt engendered by lyric in the early modern period and on the many types of movement and process associated with that mode.

The excerpt from *Comus* also gestures towards key arguments pursued seriatim in the successive chapters of *The Challenges of Orpheus*, enabling recapitulation. Most obviously, it is appropriate to conclude this study on an excerpt about myth, since, as I have demonstrated in Chapter 1 and elsewhere, the early modern period often expresses the problems and potentialities of lyric through mythological narratives and tropes. The selection from *Comus* in turn draws attention to the complex issues about audience discussed in Chapter 2. Although it is indubitably a direct address to Sabrina, reminding us how frequently early modern lyric does speak to a *you*, in invoking other spirits, including some that literally dwell by the sides of the river, the poem demonstrates the significance of side participants in many lyrics. Moreover, Sabrina's reply recalls another predilection very germane to the audiences of lyric, the early modern attraction to answer poems, one of many dialogic propensities traced in this book. This extraordinary selection from Milton's masque also stages the interplay between immediacy and distance examined in my third chapter; not only are this song and Sabrina's reply to it framed in the sense that they appear in a larger text, but they are also called up in a way that draws attention to them, turning them into songs about singing and thus introducing some measure of distance. At the same time, the appearance of Sabrina can be said to figure the emphasis on the deictics *this* and *here* that we have so often encountered in lyric and the immediacy associated with them. The connections between this song and Sabrina's answer in turn recall the issues about modularity explored in Chapter 4. Chapter 5 demonstrated the limitations of applying a conflictual model to the relationship between lyric and narrative: in many instances, I argued, lyric encourages or even engenders narrative, thus representing not the stasis often identified with such poetry but rather a pathway to action, even a release of a blockage rather than the blocking effect associated with it in the myth of Orpheus and many other texts. And here it is through song that Sabrina appears in order to deliver her own song and then literally to release the Lady from the stasis imposed on her.

_____

Remembering that Orpheus, at once the bad boy and the patron saint of lyric, learned the hard way about the dangers of glancing backwards at crucial moments, this study concludes by looking ahead with some suggestions for future work on early modern and other literary texts, as well as for other shifts in our professional practices. First, then, *The Challenges of Orpheus* has indicated several subjects and problems that students of Renaissance English literature could profitably explore in the future. Since around 1980, the widespread materialist dismissal of lyric as hermetic, interacting with a reaction against the New Critical privileging of that mode, created not simply another pendulum swing but rather what might better be described as a virtual lurch towards drama among academics specializing in early modern literature in the academy in the United States. To avoid such overcorrections in the future, we need to be alert to how both an interest in and a recoil from a field of study can be as contagious as the air whose negative valences I explored in my opening chapter. A new faculty appointment can stimulate interest in what had been a dormant field, and seeing some students enter it will encourage their peers to do likewise; conversely, if the staffing in a given field is allowed to decline, enrollments may do so as well, thus seeming to justify the previous hiring decisions and guiding future ones. For this and many other reasons, basing these personnel decisions largely or entirely on current patterns of student enrollment, as too often happens in the United States, is dangerous. Moreover, those policies in hiring, faculty evaluation, and course assignment that encourage specialists in early modern literature and culture to define themselves as experts in either dramatic or nondramatic texts but not both contribute to the current imbalance between drama and lyric. A stockholder in both the companies in question, I am hardly denying the value of studying theater; but if lyric is associated with disease in more troubling respects, I hope that this book will help early modern scholars and students catch and transmit a serious case of lyric.

In particular, future students of early modern lyric might profitably reconsider its relationship to subjectivity, an issue treated pervasively but relatively briefly in this study because a full analysis of its complexities would demand a book in its own right. The connections between lyric and subjectivity have been incisively, but again only briefly, discussed of late by distinguished critics, notably Katharine

Eisaman Maus and Debora Shuger, who have located in the inwardness of the mode one important source of changing views of the subject; but *The Challenges of Orpheus* reveals the need for further revising these and similar revisionist analyses. Maus's contrast between the displayed inwardness of theater and the more privatized lyric inwardness with which she implicitly compares it needs to be complicated by all the types of display lyric can involve, not least those emphasized by the versions of framing explored in my book. Shuger's suggestion that lyric offers a private space that contrasts with the social dimensions she traces elsewhere is a useful corrective to the many critics of her—and my—generation who refuse to see lyric or virtually anything else as anything other than social; but I have argued for a middle position where lyric, the genre of turns and twists, moves back and forth between private and social worlds.[8]

Furthermore, references to lyric as a potential breeding ground for the self need to be extended and qualified with an acknowledgment of how the changing positions the speaker may assume, notably the exchange of roles with the auditor and the voicing of fragments from others, can complicate subjectivity. Indeed, in a powerful reading of the *Rime sparse*, Lynn Enterline traces the alienation of lyric speakers from their own voices, and of course certain theorists and experimental poets of our own age have questioned to what extent if at all a putative subject should even be posited and studied.[9] Those changing positions of lyric speakers and audiences also invite reinterpretation of assumptions about subjectivity that extend to areas besides lyric. Although some of the theoretical models behind early modern criticism, notably the work of Althusser and Foucault, do attribute to subject positions types of instability and fluidity cognate to those I have been positing, too often students of the period reduce the complexity of those models in the interests of conforming to current shibboleths. Thus approaches to subjectivity frequently emphasize the creation of a passive static state or position rather than a continuing process that may involve some agency: interpellation is misinterpreted as definitive and unchangeable, the stitches of suture as unalterably binding.

Another approach for future work would be to explore how and why the dialogic and choric propensities of lyric as much as its inwardness are an arena for the development of the subject; Ramie Targoff's argument that social rules formulate the self in devotional situations is not unproblematical, but one could build on her insights by considering the cognate possibility that it is through interaction as much as meditation that the self is defined in lyric.[10] Similarly, future studies could profitably consider whether lyric contributes to the development of subjectivity as much by the positionalities it designs for its audiences as by its speaker's voice. Indeed, despite the widespread demonization of that student and victim of demons Freud, he could be fruitfully adduced in this context: the process of voicing that is critical rather than identificatory, that repeats words in an ironic or twisted form much as the dissonant singer of psalms might do, is strikingly similar to the Freudian theory that the self develops by incorporating but also criticizing a superego.

Although, as I have noted, an extensive discussion of other eras is outside the scope of *The Challenges of Orpheus,* one of its aims has been to develop perspectives from which students of those periods could themselves profitably reconsider fundamental questions about lyric. The following brief samples of and suggestions for that endeavor are among the several reasons the title of this conclusion deploys the plural, "rhetorics." To begin with, adducing some of the analyses from this study could illuminate issues about the relationship of speaker and audience, including their manifestations in cruxes of both canonical and less familiar texts, in periods other than the English Renaissance. Recalling the shifting direction of address and the volatility of the audience's subject position in early modern lyric, consider, for example, the moment in "Lines Written a Few Miles Above Tintern Abbey" when Wordsworth famously turns to direct address to Dorothy.[11] On one level, in so doing he gains sustenance from her and an antidote to the losses the poem elsewhere chronicles: "in thy voice I catch / The language of my former heart" (117–118).[12] On another level, in lines whose speech act swerves among declaration, prophecy, and injunction ("Nor . . . wilt thou then forget" [147–150], "Nor wilt thou then forget" [156]), his brotherly address acquires an avuncular didacticism. But, alerted by the insistence in the copulatio and epizeuxis earlier in the verse stanza ("my dearest Friend, / My dear, dear Friend . . . My dear, dear Sister" [116–117, 122]), as well as by the covert agendas uncovered in my analyses of early modern audiences, readers are likely to note the limitations on the interpersonal intimacy apparently established by the turn to direct address, a pattern we encountered in early modern lyric as well. And just as those lyrics often problematize the relationships established through address, here the interlocking roles of comforted and comforter apparently facilitated by that turn are qualified and questioned in many ways; the verse paragraph is weighted down with apotropaic negatives referring to what must not happen; and, like the opening of the poem, it stresses the losses inherent in passing time. In short, this passage, like so many others we have studied, demonstrates the significance of changes in address—and in so doing demonstrates too how often it is precisely within those changes that we discover the poet's desires in not only the erotic sense relevant to early modern lyric but also the broader sense germane here.

Poetry more recent than Wordsworth's also offers intriguing instances of how both overt meaning and covert agendas emerge when one studies the relationship of speaker and audience from the perspectives employed in Chapter 2. As I demonstrated there, when one recognizes that a coterie of gallants, or of women, or both might overhear within the diegetic world of the poem—a possibility to which early modern readers would be particularly alert because of the nondiegetic lack of privacy to which I referred—such texts as "Blame not my lute" and many sonnets in the *Amoretti* become even nastier. Future readings of the poems in Ted Hughes's *Birthday Letters* might explore how they are mirror images of these early modern practices. As Hughes's title indicates, these lyrics speak to Sylvia Plath—or, more precisely, a representation of her—directly through second person pronouns, whereas many Renaissance love poems ostensibly turn their back on the lady. On the other hand, to the extent that living readers are imagined as bystanders, Hughes's missives, like their early modern counterparts, are involved in the rhetoric of self-justification. Once again, anxieties about judges shape direction of address.

My argument that malleability of size and structure is often a more significant factor in interpreting early modern lyrics than the mode's putative brevity glosses texts by numerous writers of other periods as well. For instance, Robert Lowell's "Quaker Graveyard in Nantucket," a poem that pivots on rupture and return, also enacts those processes in the history of its many versions, and Americanists could fruitfully analyze it from the perspectives developed in Chapter 4. In particular, the stanza about Our Lady of Walsingham appears in the version published in *Lord Weary's Castle* in 1946, while twenty-eight years later, in *Robert Lowell's Poems: A Selection*, edited by Jonathan Raban, it is detached and printed as a separate lyric; in his collected poems, it migrates back to its original home. Thus the spiritual hope that it represents, in however ironized a form, and more specifically the turn to Catholicism, is proffered, rejected, restored.

Medieval literature offers a telling example of how another of the arguments of *The Challenges of Orpheus*, the contention that lyric may impel, not just impede, narrative, could be exported to other fields. Set off from the text in some manuscripts by the title "Canticus Troili" and by one of Chaucer's self-consciously distancing frames ("I dar wel seyn, in al, that Troilus / Seyde in his song" [I.396–397]), Troilus's song in Book I, lines 400–420 might at first appear a textbook instance of the deferrals of narrativity often associated with lyric.[13] But it is succeeded immediately by two stanzas in which Troilus addresses the god of love, beginning, "O lord, now youres is / My spirit" (422–423). The use of the exclamatory "O" here links the rhetoric of this passage to that of the preceding lament. Even more to the point, alerted by the wording of lines 422–423 and two subsequent usages of "lord" (424, 430), a medieval audience would have interpreted these stanzas as a pledge of fealty to the lover's equivalent of a feudal lord—in other words, as an action carrying with it the obligation to perform many future actions. Hence here, as in many other instances, lyric recalls the workings of that often misunderstood strategy, so-called comic relief. Much as lyric reflections are conventionally read as an interruption to narrative, so those comic episodes have often been interpreted as a temporary blockage in the dramatic and narrative action; and, much as that "relief" in fact frequently comments on the main action in a way that complicates and intensifies it, so Chaucer's passage intensifies and in so doing instigates narrative. Thus the turning to the god of love is the product of the lament; thus an indisputably lyric passage advances, not interrupts, the progress of the story.

The arguments made in this book have implications not only for specific texts but also for broader literary and cultural inquiries. Witness, for example, debates about the dramatic monologue, a form as slippery as some of the characters who deliver it. The object of a number of subtle studies, this genre has proved the arena for highly contested debates, with students of Victorian literature parting company on subjects that include its sources, its relationship to modern literature, and its central characteristics. Many of their analyses, however, are based on neglecting or misreading the early modern lyric, especially the work of Donne and Marvell, in order to establish differences between it and the dramatic monologue. (This desire to locate the exceptional, especially the harbinger or prototype of change, in the period in which one specializes has all too many analogues in the criticism of early modern texts.)[14] In fact, we have already seen that the identificatory voicing used by some critics to distinguish lyric from various other forms, including the dramatic monologue, is not a consistent characteristic of early modern lyric and perhaps less common in its counterparts in other eras. Indeed, Marshall Brown argues that all poems are to some extent dramatic monologues.[15]

Similarly, among the most contested subjects in the study of the dramatic monologue is to what extent, if at all, the nondiegetic audience experiences sympathy for the main figure and to what extent instead passes judgment; and here too critics have often gone astray by addressing lyric in general baldly and early modern lyric not at all.[16] To be sure, John Maynard's work on the dramatic monologue does dovetail with my arguments about lyric by emphasizing how the reader's shifting positions complicate judgment and so much else.[17] But many other students of the dramatic monologue accept without qualification the commonplace that lyric does not encourage judgment, thus facilitating an overly neat contrast between the forms.

Also relevant to that putatively nineteenth-century type the dramatic monologue is how I have here anatomized the motives—often dubious—that inform
definitions and descriptions of literary types. Teleological approaches risk misreading literary forms in the interest of establishing them as an improvement
over a demonized predecessor or an anticipation of a privileged successor. Thus
students of Victorian poetry sometimes create a chronology that turns a statement like "The dramatic monologue is a character study with a listener present"
into "The dramatic monologue is what reacted against and ensued from the
Romantic lyric" or "The dramatic monologue prefigures modern poetry." Such
analyses are not without truth, but they carry with them the customary dangers of
progress models and of Oedipal scenarios, as well as the risk I just identified of
ignoring similar patterns in Renaissance lyrics.

Recognizing such dangers also alerts us to how an examination of Renaissance lyric from the vantage points of this book could provide a useful matrix
for some future studies of contemporary verse, including experimental poetry
(though, given the range and complexity within that category, these suggestions
are necessarily even more preliminary than the examples that precede them).
The absence in early modern texts of qualities that many Language poets attribute to lyric in their dismissive commentaries on it, such as a solipsistic focus on
the individual, calls some of their analyses into question, reminding us yet again
of the subterranean agendas that so often distort the study of lyric. At the same
time, early modern antecedents to characteristics frequently and sometimes exclusively associated with the experimental writing of our own age, such as an emphasis on the visual appearance of the poem, could help us better understand the
poetry of both periods. Similarly, tracing parallels between the seriality often attributed to postmodern poetry and the early modern sonnet cycle might well be
productive. Although certain sequences do achieve the sort of decisive closure
that distinguishes them from serial forms, most do not; and they share with such
forms a predilection for the disjunctive and the labile. The methodological
agenda of this comparison should not be to substitute for the celebration of the
postmodern period as the originary moment of seriality a comparable privileging
of the early modern, but rather to recall yet again the dubious investments that
often impel such acclaim and the selective reading of texts outside one's own spe-
cialty that facilitates it.

Many examples above focus on similarities between early modern and other
poems, but of course extending the arguments of *The Challenges of Orpheus* to
other eras uncovers no less significant differences, and both are apparent in the
arenas of gender. For example, in asserting that poetry should be like granite,

Ezra Pound contrasts that ideal with the putative practices of his Victorian predecessors, thus implicitly effeminizing them while asserting the masculinity of his
own verse; arguably experimental poets craft verse that is hard in more senses
than one in reaction against the flaccidity they attribute to that contemned category lyric.[18] Future studies might usefully compare these recent practices of gendering to the ways Sidney re-genders lyric, beginning with the observation that
the military ideal and the public celebratory stance of poetry of praise are more
accessible to him as an alternative realm for a masculinized lyric than they were
to many subsequent writers.

In addition, transhistorical comparisons could fruitfully encompass the conditions of production. For example, participating as it does in the current challenges to the binary contrast of scribal *versus* print culture, *The Challenges of
Orpheus* invites one to observe parallels between modes of writing often categorized as scribal in early modern England and their analogues in our own culture.
Interactions among writers today permit and even facilitate many characteristics
associated with scribal transmission. Poets in the twenty-first century share their
work informally with each other all the time; in one common version of this, the
round robin, a poem will be passed around among a circle of writers, each of
whom will comment on it, often adding a poem of her or his own. Lines suggested by another poet may well be incorporated into a later version of the text.
Writing workshops, an activity in which not only novice but established writers
often participate, involve a similar circulation of manuscripts. In both instances,
having in effect shared authorship with those making suggestions, the original
poet will reassert agency and control over the text by winnowing the recom-
mended revisions. The striking similarities between early modern coterie circulation and twenty-first century practices like the round robin are, then, yet another
reason to reject a historical trajectory that positions characteristics putatively associated with scribal culture, such as coterie exchange, in the distant past. This is
not to deny that contemporary practices also differ from their early modern analogues in significant respects; for example, the exchange of poetry was but one of
many social and socializing activities within early modern coteries, while it is
generally the primary focus of modern workshops. And whereas poets in our own
day do still transmit their texts by hand or by traditional mail, one might explore
how the potentialities of electronic mail have reshaped such exchanges.

In addition to suggesting new directions like these for critics of early modern
literature and their counterparts in other fields, *The Challenges of Orpheus* has
implications for certain professional procedures. Like virtually all my previous
books, this study has attempted to foster a more capacious and generous ap-

proach to critical methodologies. Whereas some of them are obviously incompatible with each other in their practices and assumptions, many apparent incompatabilities are posited to fulfill political agendas, notably the drive to establish one's own cohort as the victors over the forces of darkness. In demonizing New Criticism, many assume it necessarily and inevitably mandated an ahistorical focus on deracinated texts; that perspective was certainly normative in the movement, yet the writings of one of its deans, William Empson, exemplify the need to challenge a totalizing representation of New Criticism on this and other issues.[19] Indeed, comparing its English and American versions and even distinctions within America might tempt us to refer to it as a series of related movements. More to the point now, close attention to the text should not be seen as synonymous with New Criticism in any of its versions, and many techniques of close reading can and should be deployed today to further historicized analysis.

The same is true of the recuperation of form. Having demonstrated and defended what I termed the "new formalism" for about twenty years in a professional climate less hospitable to such arguments than the current one, it is a pleasure to be preaching, if not to the choir, at least to committed and potential converts.[20] The goals of the recent drive to develop a redefined formalism are supported and exemplified by this book. My exploration of stanzas, for example, demonstrates the connections among form, cultural history, and materialist analysis. Perhaps it is not wholly coincidental that my enjoinders to trace cooperation and collaboration, not just warfare, in the relationship between narrative and lyric, as well as that among authors, readers, printers, and publishers, trope these recommendations about critical approaches. In particular, to dismiss the study of form as old-fashioned is to cast as a demonic siren what is in fact a far more protean and promising member of our professional choruses. More specifically, as I have argued at length elsewhere when demonstrating and defending this new formalism, to see the aesthetic, whether manifested through form or other strategies, as an Enlightenment construct inimical to progressive political analysis is to reduce complexities to another either/or binary.[21] My analysis of stanzas also indicates how questions about subjectivity and agency that preoccupy so many critics today are, so to speak, informed by aesthetic issues; my emphasis on the solitary work involved in producing an elaborate metrical or stanzaic pattern complicates common presuppositions about the relationship of the individual writer to an audience, coterie or otherwise. As this book has pointed out on more than one occasion, Adorno reminds us that the apparently asocial aesthetic space of literature can enable experiments that have not only social but profoundly political consequences.[22] But I am not advocating the recuperation of the study of form solely on the grounds that it can help us understand materiality and other recent critical concerns. *Techne* is worth exploring in its own right; and surely, as I have attempted to demonstrate, one can not only analyze but also delight in the resulting accomplishments without reverting to belles-lettristic platitudes or to the uncritical acclamation of an autonomous author.

The preceding analysis exemplifies some interrelated types of argumentation with wider ramifications: my emphasis throughout this study has been on the multiple over the monolithic, the inclusive over the rigidly hierarchical or exclusionary. I have tried to attribute a series of qualities and practices to lyric without privileging a signature trope or mechanism and to pursue a number of interlocking arguments without focusing on a single central assertion. Similarly, in several instances this book has proffered both/and analyses of the texts in its era—the speech of lyric is both internalized and social, it juxtaposes effects of immediacy and distance, it sometimes impedes and sometimes impels narrative—rather than bestowing dominance on one side or another. The variability and range of English early modern lyric, as well as its predilection for process and movement, encourages such approaches.

Crafting interlocking arguments rather than a single overarching thesis and adopting both/and approaches would benefit critical analyses of many subjects besides early modern lyric. To be sure, I hardly suggest that these perspectives should become norms for all literary and cultural analysis: numerous subjects demand and numerous monographs have benefited from more unidirectional approaches. Conversely, at their weakest the models I advocate can slide into fruitless indeterminacy. But, that risk averted, those paradigms would prove valuable for many subjects besides lyric. Should further material evidence (so to speak) of their value be needed, witness the practices of land ownership outlined in the conclusion of Chapter 4. More generally, such approaches allow a writer to avoid a clear and present danger, the central assertion designed to unite an entire book, which, though not perilous in its own right, so readily morphs into its hyperbolically insistent cousin. As a result, too much scholarly writing values the audacious at the expense of the judicious, striving to create a tidal wave itself rather than navigating smoothly through storms.

The alternative forms of argumentation advocated here offer more positive benefits as well, a contention adumbrated in Chapter 4 in particular. In terms of their intellectual potentialities, far from instantiating indecisiveness, they can initiate powerful and forceful insights, for often it is precisely in the dialogue between apparent opposites that important truths about both of them are spoken. Thus the relationship between internalized and socially oriented speech illuminates issues ranging from the relationship of ecclesiastical practices and secular poetry to gendered combat. And in terms of their contributions to collegiality, inclusive arguments model cooperation and reconciliation, behaviors too often lacking in our profession. Conversely, frequently (though certainly not invariably) the blanket dismissal rather than incorporation or negotiation of rival arguments encourages and is encouraged by the winner-take-all competitiveness that too often structures professional relationships on so many levels. An Australian scholar, Liam Semler, ruefully observed that the struggles to obtain one of the very few faculty positions available there frequently inducts scholars into a model of competitiveness that shapes the rest of their careers, and the same danger is clearly present in the United States.[23] Having herself forcefully and influentially advocated both/and approaches elsewhere in her writing, Linda Hutcheon also comments cogently on the price paid for such rivalries: "despite our ideological protests against the commercialization and corporatization of the academy (and the attendant rhetoric), we [may] have somehow absorbed the business model of competition along with the individualist model of looking out only for ourselves. . . . the opposition must be removed or destroyed; our intellectual profits must be maximized by minimizing the intellectual profits of others."[24] Do we not need to reconsider the intellectual presuppositions and the rewards systems that too often privilege such habits, thus undermining collegiality in the many positive senses of that contested term?[25]

By celebrating the achievements of Orpheus, the eponymous myth of this book also invites us to address another threat to collegiality: the gap between critics and creative writers (a term rejected by some sailing under its flag). The fact that many writers still attribute that fissure to the dominance of theory in the academy, years after that critical approach has lost much of its status, is a symptom and source of, not a justification for, the rupture. Similarly, literary and cultural critics too often regard the more pragmatic responses that writers of poetry, prose, and creative nonfiction typically bring to literature as not a different language but an unsophisticated version of their own tongue. One solution would be to build more experiences with creative writing into literature courses; students studying sonnets, for example, can be encouraged to create them or required to compose at least a quatrain or couplet. Likewise, another remedy would be to include more courses in literary criticism in those graduate writing programs that scant them. And if critics of literature celebrate Orpheus, the more established members of the profession should also encourage and support graduate students and younger colleagues who wish to wear hats as both poets and critics—in part by reevaluating reward systems, pecuniary and otherwise, which too often discourage that type of cross-dressing.

But, as I noted at the beginning of this book, Orpheus, though the keynote speaker in so many analyses of lyric, is by no means its only mythological exemplar. Orpheus kept singing until the Maenads tore him apart. His colleague Arion, a lesser but wiser poet, jumped ship at a more opportune moment—hoping that alert copyeditors and beneficent book reviewers, not sharks, waited in the waters below, having enjoyed his song enough to waft him to shore.

# Notes

INTRODUCTION

1. Northrop Frye, "Approaching the Lyric," in *Lyric Poetry: Beyond New Criticism*, ed. Chaviva Hošek and Patricia Parker (Ithaca: Cornell University Press, 1985), 31.

2. See P. Adams Sitney, *Visionary Film: The American Avant-Garde, 1943–2000*, 3rd ed. (1974; rpt., Oxford: Oxford University Press, 2002), Chapter 6.

3. Maristalla Casciato, *The Amsterdam School* (Rotterdam: 010 Publishers, 1996), 66.

4. On the writings of Adorno and Mill on this issue, see below, Chapter 2.

5. Crate and Barrel holiday catalogue, 2003.

6. All citations are to *The Poetical Works of Robert Herrick*, ed. L. C. Martin (Oxford: Clarendon Press, 1956).

7. Eavan Boland, *An Origin Like Water: Collected Poems 1967–1987* (New York: W. W. Norton, 1996).

8. Gwen Harwood, *Selected Poems*, ed. Gregory Kratzmann (London: Penguin, 2001).

9. *The Collected Poems of Langston Hughes*, ed. Arnold Rampersad and David Roessel (New York: Alfred A. Knopf, 1995).

10. Heather Dubrow, "Remission and Revision," *Journal of the American Medical Association* 291 (January 14, 2004), 160.

11. See, e.g., Marjorie Perloff, *The Dance of the Intellect: Studies in the Poetry of the Pound Tradition* (Cambridge: Cambridge University Press, 1985), esp. 172–181.

12. Earl Miner, "Why Lyric?" in *The Renewal of Song: Renovation in Lyric Conception and Practice*, ed. Earl Miner and Amiya Dev (Calcutta: Seagull Books, 2000).

13. I quote Harold Fisch, *Poetry with a Purpose: Biblical Poetics and Interpretation* (Bloomington: Indiana University Press, 1988), 104.

14. W. R. Johnson, *The Idea of Lyric: Lyric Modes in Ancient and Modern Poetry* (Berkeley: University of California Press, 1982), 16.

15. Daniel Albright, *Lyricality in English Literature* (Lincoln: University of Nebraska Press, 1985), 1.

16. René Wellek, "Genre Theory, the Lyric, and *Erlebnis*," in *Discriminations: Further Concepts of Criticism* (New Haven: Yale University Press, 1970), 252. Also compare the observations of Paul Hernadi, who, after proposing some paradigms for distinguishing lyric, epic, and narrative, cautions that several principles, including ones customarily associated

with the other two modes, coexist in each text (*Beyond Genre: New Directions in Literary Classification* [Ithaca: Cornell University Press, 1972], 166).

17. Helen Vendler, *The Art of Shakespeare's Sonnets* (Cambridge: Harvard University Press, 1997), 1–2.

18. Emil Staiger, *Basic Concepts of Poetics*, trans. Janette C. Hudson and Luanne T. Frank, ed. Marianne Burkhard and Luanne T. Frank (University Park: Pennsylvania State University Press, 1991), esp. 43–96.

19. On that putatively undue emphasis on subjectivity, see, e.g., Jonathan Culler, "Changes in the Study of the Lyric," esp. 38–41, in *Lyric Poetry*, ed. Hošek and Parker.

20. A more recent challenge to these questions appears in the important work of Roland Greene: he has diagrammed lyric in terms of two principal drives, the ritualistic, which he associates with a communal, often aurally focused activity that coerces participation and identification, and the fictive, in many versions of which a clearly defined speaker emerges (*Post-Petrarchism: Origins and Innovations of the Western Lyric Sequence* [Princeton: Princeton University Press, 1991], esp. Introduction).

21. Anne Ferry, *The Title to the Poem* (Stanford: Stanford University Press, 1996), esp. Chapters 1–4.

22. Sharon Cameron, *Lyric Time: Dickinson and the Limits of Genre* (Baltimore: Johns Hopkins University Press, 1979); see esp. the useful overview of her position on 212–213.

23. In a thoughtful comparatist analysis that unfortunately appeared after I had written my manuscript, Lisa Lai-ming Wong observes, as I do, that lyric operates in both interior and social arenas; she argues that repetitive performativity bridges them ("A Promise [Over] Heard in Lyric," *New Literary History* 37 [2006], 271–284).

24. C. Day Lewis, *The Lyric Impulse* (Cambridge: Harvard University Press, 1965), 3.

25. Marshall Brown, "Negative Poetics: On Skepticism and the Lyric Voice," *Representations*, no. 86 (Spring 2004), 127.

26. Paul de Man argues that lyric's claim to be song, directly asserted in Charles Baudelaire's "Correspondances," is compromised in that and other of his poems, thus complicating the very conception of lyric (*The Rhetoric of Romanticism* [New York: Columbia University Press, 1984], 254); but applying the concept of family resemblances and acknowledging that certain periods are more prone to produce songlike lyrics than others preserves some options for classification. For a debatable but provocative argument about the differences between lyric and song, also see John T. Shawcross, *Intentionality and the New Traditionalism: Some Liminal Means to Literary Revisionism* (University Park: Pennsylvania State University Press, 1991), 79–80.

27. Mark W. Booth, *The Experience of Songs* (New Haven: Yale University Press, 1981), 23–26; this assertion is, however, rendered problematical by the study's equation of song with a communal expression of predictable sentiments, a definition often but not invariably valid.

28. I am indebted to conversations with David Lindley for useful comments on this and many other issues about the relationship of music and lyric.

29. Northrop Frye, *Anatomy of Criticism: Four Essays* (Princeton: Princeton University Press, 1957), 273. On the significance of chant, also see Andrew Welsh, *Roots of Lyric: Primitive Poetry and Modern Poetics* (Princeton: Princeton University Press, 1978), Chapter 7.

30. I cite *Zepheria* (London, 1594).

31. See Alastair Fowler, *Kinds of Literature: An Introduction to the Theory of Genres and Modes* (Cambridge: Harvard University Press, 1982), 40–41; the passage I quote appears on 41. Also cf. the application of the theory in Robert C. Elliott, "The Definition of Satire: A Note on Method," *Yearbook of Comparative and General Literature* 11 (1962), 22–23; and the challenge to it in Maurice Mandelbaum, "Family Resemblances and Generalization Concerning the Arts," *American Philosophical Quarterly* 2 (1965), 219–228.

32. Paul Alpers, *What Is Pastoral?* (Chicago: University of Chicago Press, 1996); Michael McKeon, *The Origins of the English Novel, 1600–1740* (Baltimore: Johns Hopkins University Press, 1987).

33. Timothy Bahti, *Ends of the Lyric: Direction and Consequence in Western Poetry* (Baltimore: Johns Hopkins University Press, 1996); Susan Stewart, *Poetry and the Fate of the Senses* (Chicago: University of Chicago Press, 2002); William Waters, *Poetry's Touch: On Lyric Address* (Ithaca: Cornell University Press, 2003).

34. See the discussion of the transgressiveness of the *ghinnāwa* in Lila Abu-Lughod, *Veiled Sentiments: Honor and Poetry in a Bedouin Society* (Berkeley: University of California Press, 1986), esp. 243–244, 251.

35. William Fitzgerald, *Catullan Provocations: Lyric Poetry and the Drama of Position* (Berkeley: University of California Press, 1995), 5.

36. Nigel Smith, *Literature and Revolution in England, 1640–1660* (New Haven: Yale University Press, 1994), Chapter 8.

37. Charles Bernstein, *A Poetics* (Cambridge: Harvard University Press, 1992), 1.

38. J. W. Lever, *The Elizabethan Love Sonnet*, 2nd ed. (London: Methuen, 1966), 9, 13.

39. William Preston, *Thoughts on Lyric Poetry* (Transactions of the Royal Irish Academy, 1787), 60–61.

40. Newberry Library Case MS A.15.179, 24.

41. Paul H. Fry, *The Poet's Calling in the English Ode* (New Haven: Yale University Press, 1980).

42. David Lindley, *Lyric* (London: Methuen, 1985), 23–24.

43. On critical investments in subjects other than lyric, see Gerald Graff, *Professing Literature: An Institutional History* (Chicago: University of Chicago Press, 1987).

44. George T. Wright, *Hearing the Measures: Shakespearean and Other Inflections* (Madison: University of Wisconsin Press, 2001), 57, 58.

45. Wright, *Hearing the Measures*, 56.

46. See, e.g., my essay, "Guess Who's Coming to Dinner? Reevaluating Formalism and the Country House Poem," *MLQ* 61 (2000), 59–77.

47. The turns in this legend are explored as well in Melissa F. Zeiger, *Beyond Consolation: Death, Sexuality, and the Changing Shapes of Elegy* (Ithaca: Cornell University Press, 1997), esp. 50.

48. As noted above, one of the best discussions of temporality in lyric is Cameron, *Lyric Time*.

CHAPTER 1: THE RHETORIC OF LYRIC

1. Roland Greene, "The Lyric," in *The Cambridge History of Literary Criticism*, Vol. III, *The Renaissance*, ed. Glyn P. Norton (Cambridge: Cambridge University Press, 1999), 216.

2. Compare Paul H. Fry's trenchant demonstration of the failures and tensions in early modern odes in particular (*The Poet's Calling in the English Ode* [New Haven: Yale University Press, 1980], Chapters 1 and 2).

3. These and many other modern poems on Orpheus appear in Deborah DeNicola, ed., *Orpheus and Company: Contemporary Poems on Greek Mythology* (Hanover, NH: University Press of New England, 1999).

4. For the theory, posited by Spenser's editors, that this allusion is present, see *The Yale Edition of the Shorter Poems of Edmund Spenser*, ed. William A. Oram et al. (New Haven: Yale University Press, 1989), 67. I cite this edition throughout this chapter.

5. For a more detailed treatment of these issues, see the source on which my overview is largely based, John Block Friedman's comprehensive study, *Orpheus in the Middle Ages* (Cambridge: Harvard University Press, 1970).

6. Anthony Cope, *A Godly Meditacion upon .xx. Select Psalmes of David* (London, 1547), sig. ii^v.

7. Compare Melissa F. Zeiger's reminder that in both the classical and the Christian retellings of this myth, Orpheus is associated with failure (*Beyond Consolation: Death, Sexuality, and the Changing Shapes of Elegy* [Ithaca: Cornell University Press, 1997], esp. 27).

8. Frye discusses blocking throughout "Approaching the Lyric," in *Lyric Poetry: Beyond New Criticism*, ed. Chaviva Hošek and Patricia Parker (Ithaca: Cornell University Press, 1985); see esp. 32–33.

9. Judith Wright, *Collected Poems, 1942–1985* (Sydney: Angus and Robertson, 1994).

10. Mario DiGangi, *The Homoerotics of Modern Drama* (Cambridge: Cambridge University Press, 1997), 44–47. Also cf. Lynn Enterline, *The Rhetoric of the Body from Ovid to Shakespeare* (Cambridge: Cambridge University Press, 2000), 86–87; Maria Teresa Micaela Prendergast, *Renaissance Fantasies: The Gendering of Aesthetics in Early Modern Fiction* (Kent, OH: Kent State University Press, 1999), esp. 69.

11. Jonathan Bate, *Shakespeare and Ovid* (Oxford: Clarendon Press, 1993), 51.

12. George Sandys, *Ovid's Metamorphosis Englished* (London, 1632), 339.

13. See Scott Newstok's as yet unpublished manuscript, "How to Do Things with Renaissance Epitaphs." I thank the author for making his work available to me.

14. On Arion, see Linda Phyllis Austern, "The Siren, The Muse, and The God of Love: Music and Gender in Seventeenth-Century Emblem Books," *Journal of Musicological Research* 18 (1999), 125–128; C. M. Bowra, "Arion and the Dolphin," *Museum Helveticum* 20 (1963), 121–134; A. W. Pickard-Cambridge, *Dithyramb: Tragedy and Comedy* (Oxford: Clarendon Press, 1927), 19–22.

15. In *Will in the World: How Shakespeare Became Shakespeare* (New York: W. W. Norton, 2004), 46–47, Stephen Greenblatt suggests that the Kenilworth production may lie behind Shakespeare's reference to Arion in *Twelfth Night*.

16. For a transcription and discussion of Ramsey's poem, see Arthur F. Marotti, *Manuscript, Print, and the English Renaissance Lyric* (Ithaca: Cornell University Press, 1995), 193–194.

17. On Whitney's emblem see Linda Phyllis Austern, "The Siren," 123–125; the essay also comments usefully on broader questions about the gendering of music.

18. Leslie C. Dunn, whose work I encountered only after drafting this chapter, also observes that singing women are often represented as sirens and associated with effeminizing seduction ("The Lady Sings in Welsh: Women's Song as Marginal Discourse on the Shakespearean Stage," in *Place and Displacement in the Renaissance*, ed. Alvin Vos, Medieval and Renaissance Texts and Studies [Binghamton: Center for Medieval and Early Renaissance Studies, State University of New York, 1995], esp. 60–64).

19. Stephen Owen, *Mi-Lou: Poetry and the Labyrinth of Desire* (Cambridge: Harvard University Press, 1989), 134.

20. Northrop Frye, *Anatomy of Criticism: Four Essays* (Princeton: Princeton University Press, 1957), 272.

21. Frye, *Anatomy of Criticism*, 271.

22. Barbara Johnson, "Poetry and Syntax: What the Gypsy Knew," in her collection, *The Critical Difference: Essays in the Contemporary Rhetoric of Reading* (Baltimore: Johns Hopkins University Press, 1980), 69.

23. A. R. Ammons, "A Poem Is a Walk," in *Set in Motion: Essays, Interviews, and Dialogues*, ed. Zofia Burr (Ann Arbor: University of Michigan Press, 1996), 17.

24. Heather McHugh, "Naked Numbers: A Curve from Wyatt to Rochester," in *Green Thoughts, Green Shades: Essays by Contemporary Poets on the Early Modern Lyric*, ed. Jonathan F. S. Post (Berkeley: University of California Press, 2002), 67.

25. Marvin Spevack, ed., *The Harvard Concordance to Shakespeare* (Cambridge: Harvard University Press, 1973), s.v. "poesy," "poem," "verse."

26. Throughout this chapter I cite *The Poetical Works of Robert Herrick*, ed. L. C. Martin (Oxford: Clarendon Press, 1956).

27. I cite *Ben Jonson*, ed. C. H. Herford, Percy Simpson, and Evelyn Simpson, 11 vols. (Oxford: Clarendon Press, 1925–1952).

28. Ovid, *Metamorphoses*, 2nd ed., ed. and trans. Frank Justus Miller, rev. G. P. Goold, Vol. 2 (Cambridge and London: Harvard University Press and William Heinemann, 1984).

29. I cite Edmund Spenser, *The Faerie Queene*, ed. A. C. Hamilton (London: Longman, 1977).

30. Although she does not explore the relevance to lyric, Patricia Parker's brief comments on the connection between turning and translation uncover a number of germanely pejorative associations (*Shakespeare from the Margins: Language, Culture, Context* [Chicago: University of Chicago Press, 1996], esp. 121–122, 140–141). While her examination of "joining" (see esp. 76–115), which focuses on linguistic and marital unions, is also cognate to my discussion inasmuch as both are types of artisanal shaping, the distinctions between the turning I discuss and the joining on which she concentrates are as suggestive as the similarities.

31. *OED*, s.v. "turn." Throughout this book I cite the first edition of the *Oxford English Dictionary* (changes in subsequent editions are not significant for my purposes here).

32. See Henry S. Turner, *The English Renaissance Stage: Geometry, Poetics, and the Practical Spatial Arts, 1580–1630* (Oxford: Oxford University Press, 2006). I thank the author for sharing his work prior to publication.

33. Mary Thomas Crane, "What Was Performance?" *Criticism* 43 (2001), 41–59.

34. On the musical influences on "Lycidas," see esp. Louise Schleiner, *The Living Lyre in English Verse from Elizabeth through the Restoration* (Columbia: University of Missouri Press, 1984), 102–112; the hypothesis about Herbert appears in Diane Kelsey McColley, *Poetry and Music in Seventeenth-Century England* (Cambridge: Cambridge University Press, 1997), 161; the suggestion about these psalms appears in Anthony Low, *Love's Architecture: Devotional Modes in Seventeenth-Century English Poetry* (New York: New York University Press, 1978), 29.

35. One of the most balanced discussions of this subject is the cautious analysis in David Lindley, *Thomas Campion* (Leiden: E. J. Brill, 1986), Chapter 3.

36. The influence of Petrarchism is traced in James Anderson Winn, *Unsuspected Eloquence: A History of the Relations between Poetry and Music* (New Haven: Yale University Press, 1981), 138–149; that of metaphysical poetry in Elise Bickford Jorgens, *The Well-Tun'd Word: Musical Interpretations of English Poetry, 1597–1651* (Minneapolis: University of Minnesota Press, 1982), esp. 220–221, 225, 240. The quotation is from Lindley, *Thomas Campion*, 143. Historical changes in the relationship of the arts are the principal focus of John Hollander's important study, *The Untuning of the Sky: Ideas of Music in English Poetry, 1500–1700* (1961; rpt., New York: W. W. Norton, 1970); Paula Johnson (*Form and Transformation in Music and Poetry of the English Renaissance* [New Haven: Yale University Press, 1972]) argues, sometimes problematically, for historical shifts based on patterns of recurrence and progression in the two arts.

37. John Stevens, *Music and Poetry in the Early Tudor Court* (London: Methuen, 1961), 27–31.

38. Hollander, *Untuning of the Sky*, 288; Patrick Cheney, *Shakespeare, National Poet-Playwright* (Cambridge: Cambridge University Press, 2004), esp. 32–34.

39. Thomas Ravenscroft, *A Briefe Discourse . . . Measurable Music* (London, 1614), sig. A3ᵛ.

40. On the gendered seductiveness of music, see, e.g., two essays by Linda Phyllis Austern: "The Siren" and " 'No women are indeed': The Boy Actor as Vocal Seductress in Late Sixteenth- and Early Seventeenth-century English Drama," in *Embodied Voices: Representing Female Vocality in Western Culture*, ed. Leslie C. Dunn and Nancy A. Jones (Cambridge: Cambridge University Press, 1994). The gendering of music is also cogently discussed in Hollander, *Untuning of the Sky*, 107–108, 337; Carla Zecher, "The Gendering of the Lute in Sixteenth-Century French Love Poetry," *Renaissance Quarterly* 53 (2000), 769–791, and Zecher's *Sounding Objects: Musical Instruments, Poetry, and Art in Renaissance France* (Toronto: University of Toronto Press, 2006), Chapter 1. I am grateful to Zecher for sharing her work with me before its publication.

41. Austern, "The Siren," 107.

42. Hollander, *Untuning of the Sky*, 35.

43. I thank my colleague Patricia Rosenmeyer for valuable information on this subject.

44. Matthew Spring, *The Lute in Britain: A History of the Instrument and Its Music* (Oxford: Oxford University Press, 2001), 49, 255–256; Zecher, *Sounding Objects*, 139–146.

45. William Fitzgerald, *Catullan Provocations: Lyric Poetry and the Drama of Position* (Berkeley: University of California Press, 1995), 10–11.

46. *The Collected Poems of Wallace Stevens* (New York: Alfred A. Knopf, 1967).

47. Daniel Tiffany, *Toy Medium: Materialism and Modern Lyric* (Berkeley: University of California Press, 2000), esp. Chapter 4.

48. Susan Stewart, *Poetry and the Fate of the Senses* (Chicago: University of Chicago Press, 2002), 211.

49. John Makluire, *The Buckler of Bodilie Health* (Edinburgh, 1630), 64–66.

50. John Donne, *Letters to Severall Persons of Honour* (London, 1651), 31.

51. Wallace Stevens, "Adagia," in *Opus Posthumous*, rev. ed., ed. Milton J. Bates (New York: Alfred A. Knopf, 1989), 185. Future citations appear in parentheses within my text.

52. On the history of this movement, see John Rogers, *The Matter of Revolution: Science, Poetry, and Politics in the Age of Milton* (Ithaca: Cornell University Press, 1996).

53. Gina Bloom, *Voice in Motion: Staging Gender, Shaping Sound in Early Modern England* (Philadelphia: University of Pennsylvania Press, 2007).

54. Joseph Trapp, *Lectures on Poetry* (London, 1742), 6; Margaret Atwood, *Negotiating with the Dead: A Writer on Writing* (Cambridge: Cambridge University Press, 2002), 16.

55. Citations are to John Donne, *The Elegies and The Songs and Sonnets*, ed. Helen Gardner (Oxford: Clarendon Press, 1965).

56. Yeats, *The Poems*, 2nd ed., ed. Richard J. Finneran (New York: Scribner, 1997).

57. See Zecher, "Gendering of the Lute," 769–791.

58. Hollander, *Untuning of the Sky*, esp. Chapter 2.

59. Henry S. Turner, "Plotting Early Modernity," in *The Culture of Capital: Property, Cities, and Knowledge in Early Modern England*, ed. Henry S. Turner (London: Routledge, 2002).

60. Paula Blank, *Shakespeare and the Mismeasure of Renaissance Man* (Ithaca: Cornell University Press, 2006).

61. *Englands Helicon* (London, 1600), sig. A3.

62. See Mary Thomas Crane, *Framing Authority: Sayings, Self, and Society in Sixteenth-Century England* (Princeton: Princeton University Press, 1993), 177.

63. I thank Wendy Hyman for this insight, as well as a number of other useful suggestions about this book.

64. Rachel Blau DuPlessis, "'Corpses of Poesy': Some Modern Poets and Some Gender Ideologies of Lyric," in *Feminist Measures: Soundings in Poetry and Theory*, ed. Lynn Keller and Cristanne Miller (Ann Arbor: University of Michigan Press, 1994).

65. All citations are to *The Riverside Shakespeare*, ed. G. Blakemore Evans, 2nd ed. (Boston: Houghton Mifflin, 1997).

66. Thomas Palmer, *The Emblems of Thomas Palmer: Two Hundred Poosees: Sloane Ms. 3794*, ed. John Manning (New York: AMS Press, 1988).

67. Throughout this discussion of Greek lyric I am indebted to Bruno Gentili, *Poetry and Its Public in Ancient Greece: From Homer to the Fifth Century*, trans. A. Thomas Cole

(Baltimore: Johns Hopkins University Press, 1988) and to valuable conversations with Patricia Rosenmeyer.

68. Gentili, *Poetry and Its Public*, 32–35, argues it was not.

69. On these usages, see Winn, *Unsuspected Eloquence*, 3. I am also indebted to Patricia Rosenmeyer for information on this issue.

70. Greene, "The Lyric," 219–220.

71. George Puttenham, *The Arte of English Poesie*, ed. Baxter Hathaway (1906; rpt., Kent, OH: Kent State University Press), 40, 77. Subsequent references will appear in parentheses within my text.

72. The citation is to Roger Ascham, *English Works: "Toxophilus," "Report of the Affaires and State of Germany," "The Scholemaster,"* ed. William Aldis Wright (1904; rpt., Cambridge: Cambridge University Press, 1970), 283–284. Subsequent citations from this book will appear in my text.

73. Michael Drayton, *Poems* (London, 1619), "To the Reader," 279.

74. Although he does not address the issue of gender in this passage, David Lindley comments trenchantly on the hierarchies implicit in Drayton's passage and on his emphasis on social function (*Lyric* [London: Methuen, 1985], 6–7).

75. I cite John Milton, *Complete Poems and Major Prose*, ed. Merritt Y. Hughes (Indianapolis: Odyssey Press, Bobbs-Merrill, 1957), 669–670.

76. Greene, "The Lyric," 217.

77. On this use of love poetry, see Ilona Bell, *Elizabethan Women and the Poetry of Courtship* (Cambridge: Cambridge University Press, 1998); Marotti, *Manuscript*, esp. 2–10.

78. Stevens, *Music and Poetry*, esp. Chapter 9. Although this study anticipates Marotti's, Bell's, and others in situating the lyrics in social interactions, it differs in emphasizing that the poems in question might well evoke fictive situations rather than participating more directly and straightforwardly in "real" events (see esp. 154–155).

79. Marotti, *Manuscript*, 76–82.

80. All citations are to *The Poems of Sir Philip Sidney*, ed. William A. Ringler, Jr. (Oxford: Clarendon Press, 1962).

81. Among the many studies discussing the gendering of lyric in other periods is Rachel Blau DuPlessis, " 'Corpses of Poetry.' " This otherwise valuable study replicates an error common to students of poetry written after the early modern period: it assumes that a celebration of male power is not only normative but also virtually unchallenged in Petrarchism and other movements of its era.

82. Herodotus, *The Famous Hystory of Herodotus*, trans. Barnabe Riche (London and New York: Constable and Alfred A. Knopf, 1924), 100.

83. I am indebted to my colleague Patricia Rosenmeyer for this translation and for many other helpful suggestions about this section of the book.

84. *OED*, s.v. "minikin."

85. See esp. three essays by Linda Phyllis Austern: "The Siren"; " 'No women are indeed' "; and " 'Alluring the Auditorie to Effeminacie': Music and the Idea of the Feminine in Early Modern England," *Music and Letters*, 74 (1993), 343–354. Also see Zecher's "Gendering of the Lute" and *Sounding Objects*, esp. Chapter 1. Although Zecher chooses most of her examples from France, many of the texts in question were certainly

familiar to English poets and arguably influenced their own genderings of song and of lyric.

86. Roland Greene, *Post-Petrarchism: Origins and Innovations of the Western Lyric Sequence* (Princeton: Princeton University Press, 1991), esp. 5–6.

87. *The Poems of Robert Sidney*, ed. P. J. Croft (Oxford: Clarendon Press, 1984).

88. Philip Stubbes, *The Anatomie of Abuses* (London, 1583), sig. O4ᵛ, O5.

89. George Gascoigne, *A Hundreth Sundrie Flowres*, ed. G. W. Pigman III (Oxford: Clarendon Press, 2000).

90. For the argument that the poem alludes to the speaker's penis and other useful commentary, see Douglas L. Peterson, *The English Lyric from Wyatt to Donne: A History of the Plain and Eloquent Styles*, 2nd ed. (East Lansing, MI: Colleagues Press, 1990), 160–162, 267.

91. The connection between lyric and toys is discussed throughout Tiffany, *Toy Medium*. On the linguistic usage, see *OED*, s.v. "toy."

92. See, e.g., Stephen Orgel, *Impersonations: The Performance of Gender in Shakespeare's England* (Cambridge: Cambridge University Press, 1996), Chapter 4.

93. Austern, " 'Alluring,' " esp. 347–348.

94. Hollander, *Untuning of the Sky*, esp. 11–12.

95. Zeiger, *Beyond Consolation*, esp. 2; she does not, however, pursue the relevance of her insight to the maenads.

96. Peter J. Manning, "Wordsworth in the *Keepsake, 1829*," in *Literature in the Marketplace: Nineteenth-century British Publishing and Reading Practices*, ed. John O. Jordan and Robert L. Patten (Cambridge: Cambridge University Press, 1995), 68–69.

97. For the information about "lispt" I am indebted to private correspondence with Stephen Orgel.

98. The edition that Herrick probably used is valuably discussed by Gordon Braden in the Appendix of *The Classics in English Renaissance Poetry: Three Case Studies* (New Haven: Yale University Press, 1978). His comparison of Herrick's "Vision" with its source focuses on the similarities rather than the differences (206–208).

99. Comparing Herrick's text with a version of the same Anacreontic poem by the Civil War writer Thomas Stanley underscores how much Herrick revises Anacreon and how profoundly he destabilizes his poem as a consequence:

As on Purple carpets I
Charm'd by wine in slumber ly,
With a troop of Maids (resorted
There to play) me thought I sported:
Whose companions, lovely Boies,
Interrupt me with rude noise:
Yet I offer made to kisse them.
But o'th'sudden wake and misse them:
Vext to see them thus forsake me,
I to sleep again betake me.
        (Thomas Stanley, *Poems* [1651])

Notice that this text is on the whole far more simple and straightforward in its approach to gender. Admittedly, the unclear referent of the pronoun "them" in line 7 arguably at least gestures, however briefly and ambiguously, towards same-sex desire. But whereas the enchantress in Herrick's poem is threatening, the cognate figures in Stanley's version are responsible for nothing more aggressive than playing and making noise. Similarly, in contrast to Herrick's: anticlosural ending, Stanley's speaker, though "Vext" (9), seems to go back to sleep without much trouble, with the happy implication that the maids might return. (An interpretation of this poem from a different perspective may be found in Nigel Smith, *Literature and Revolution in England, 1640–1669* [New Haven: Yale University Press, 1994], 255–256; although it does not comment on the connection with Herrick, I am indebted to this book for drawing Stanley's poem to my attention.)

## CHAPTER 2: THE DOMAIN OF ECHO

1. These are not Piano's first work in the United States; in particular, he designed the Menil Collection and the neighboring gallery of Cy Twombly's work in Houston.

2. Renzo Piano, *Logbook*, trans. Huw Evans (New York: Monacelli Press, 1997), 253.

3. Piano, *Logbook*, 253.

4. Dan Graham, *Works, 1965–2000*, ed. Marianne Brouwer (Düsseldorf: Richter Verlag, 2001), 77. Subsequent quotations from this book are identified parenthetically within my text.

5. Wendy Wall, *The Imprint of Gender: Authorship and Publication in the English Renaissance* (Ithaca: Cornell University Press, 1993), 33.

6. Three studies that appeared after I completed this chapter all reconsider the model of a solitary speaker merely addressing himself or vainly attempting through apostrophe to evoke an absent listener; in one, Anne Keniston demonstrates how the losses associated with apostrophe produce fruitful commentaries on poetry (*Overheard Voices: Address and Subjectivity in Postmodern American Poetry* [Routledge: London, 2006]). Virginia Jackson posits "an intersubjective space" in which the writer may be "alone with" (*Dickinson's Misery: A Theory of Lyric Reading* [Princeton: Princeton University Press, 2005], esp. Chapter 3; the passage cited appears on 133). Helen Vendler argues that addresses to invisible listeners may build, not frustrate, intimacy (*Invisible Listeners: Lyric Intimacy in Herbert, Whitman, and Ashbery* [Princeton: Princeton University Press, 2005]). My work participates in the project of rethinking direction of address but approaches that agenda differently from these and other studies; for example, I stress lability more than most other critics do and demonstrate how conditions distinctive to early modern England contribute to that instability. Also see William Fitzgerald, *Catullan Provocations: Lyric Poetry and the Drama of Position* (Berkeley: University of California Press, 1995). This acute study also stresses that the audience assumes a range of subject positions, relating the interplay between audience and speaker to conditions in Roman culture, and Fitzgerald comments with particular acuity on overhearing; but his work differs from mine in a number of ways, such as his recurrent emphasis on the empowerment of Catullus and his greater emphasis on the speaker.

7. Throughout this chapter, references to Spenser's minor poetry are to *The Yale Edition of the Shorter Poems of Edmund Spenser*, ed. William A. Oram et al. (New Haven: Yale University Press, 1989).

8. On Spenser's involvement with the woodcuts, see Ruth Samson Luborsky, "The Allusive Presentation of *The Shepheardes Calender*," *Spenser Studies* 1 (1980), esp. 29, 41–43.

9. *OED*, s.v. "record."

10. On writing for a future audience, cf. the comparatist study of Lisa Lai-ming Wong, "A Promise (Over) Heard in Lyric," *New Literary History* 37 (2006), 271–284.

11. Roland Greene, "*The Shepheardes Calender*, Dialogue, and Periphrasis," *Spenser Studies* 8 (1987), 10–12. Also cf. Ilona Bell's arguments about the dialogic propensities of early modern love poetry, which are explored throughout *Elizabethan Women and the Poetry of Courtship* (Cambridge: Cambridge University Press, 1998).

12. Carla Zecher, "The Gendering of the Lute in Sixteenth-Century French Love Poetry," *Renaissance Quarterly* 53 (2000), 771.

13. Readers, if any, who have not thrown down the book in response to that pun may wish to consult the development of the argument about coteries in two studies by Arthur F. Marotti: *John Donne, Coterie Poet* (Madison: University of Wisconsin Press, 1986); *Manuscript, Print, and the English Renaissance Lyric* (Ithaca: Cornell University Press, 1995). Among the many other important discussions of the effects of circulation within a coterie is Wall, *Imprint of Gender*, esp. 34–50.

14. I am indebted to Ernest Gilman for drawing this figure and its relevance to Spenser to my attention and to Kimberly Huth for a number of useful observations.

15. Leon Battista Alberti, *On Painting*, trans. John R. Spencer (London: Routledge and Kegan Paul, 1956), 78.

16. Michael Baxandall, *Painting and Experience in Fifteenth-Century Italy: A Primer in the Social History of Pictorial Style*, 2nd ed. (Oxford: Oxford University Press, 1988), 71–81.

17. On this dilemma within narrative, see, e.g., Gérard Genette, *Narrative Discourse: An Essay in Method*, trans. Jane E. Lewin (Ithaca: Cornell University Press, 1980), 228–231.

18. Marotti, *Manuscript*, esp. 141–142, 159–171. Also see Cristina Malcolmson, *Heart-Work: George Herbert and the Protestant Ethic* (Stanford: Stanford University Press, 1999), 114–119, on Herbert's unusual approach to answer poems; her argument that many of these texts in fact eschew responses is cognate to my suggestion below about blocked direction of address in "Windows."

19. Throughout this chapter, citations of Ben Jonson are to *Ben Jonson*, ed. C. H. Herford, Percy Simpson, and Evelyn Simpson, 11 vols. (Oxford: Clarendon Press, 1925–1952).

20. All citations are to *The Poems of Sir Philip Sidney*, ed. William A. Ringler, Jr. (Oxford: Clarendon Press, 1962).

21. George T. Wright, *Hearing the Measures: Shakespearean and Other Inflections* (Madison: University of Wisconsin Press, 2001), 267.

22. Committed to maintaining the solitude of the lyric speaker, Helen Vendler instead maintains that these poems by Herbert introduce God's voice through the assumption that the Lord is omnipresent (*The Art of Shakespeare's Sonnets* [Cambridge: Harvard University Press, 1997], 19).

23. Gémino H. Abad, *A Formal Approach to Lyric Poetry* (Quezon City: University of the Philippines Press, 1978), esp. Chapter 4.

24. See the discussions of repetition and reenactment in my book *Echoes of Desire: English Petrarchism and Its Counterdiscourses* (Ithaca: Cornell University Press, 1995), esp. 35–39.

25. Pamela S. Hammons, *Poetic Resistance: English Women Writers and the Early Modern Lyric* (Aldershot, England: Ashgate, 2002), esp. 168. As noted later in the paragraph, however, the primacy she and many other critics attribute to the social is problematical.

26. David Schalkwyk, *Speech and Performance in Shakespeare's Sonnets and Plays* (Cambridge: Cambridge University Press, 2002), 14.

27. Charlton T. Lewis and Charles Short, eds., *A New Latin Dictionary* (New York: American Book Company, 1907), s.v. "meditor."

28. *The Works of John Milton*, ed. Frank Allen Patterson et al. (New York: Columbia University Press, 1936), Vol. 12, 26–27; *Complete Prose Works of John Milton*, ed. Don M. Wolfe et al. (New Haven and London: Yale University Press and Oxford University Press, 1953), Vol. 1, 327.

29. I cite *The Prose Works of William Wordsworth*, ed. W. J. B. Owen and Jane Worthington Smyser (Oxford: Clarendon Press, 1974), Vol. I, 138. Frye refers to a chorus in *Anatomy of Criticism: Four Essays* (Princeton: Princeton University Press, 1957), 249. All subsequent references to both books appear in parentheses within my text.

30. Textual problems potentially complicate the discussion of this and other issues. Initially planned as a preface to Mill's work on Tennyson, "Thoughts on Poetry and its Varieties" appeared first in the *Monthly Repository* and subsequently in his collection *Dissertations and Discussions*, sustaining a number of revisions in the process, including the addition of some qualifications. I rely on the latest version, and none of my principal points is significantly altered by the changes. On the versions of this and related essays, see Introduction in John Stuart Mill, *Autobiography and Literary Essays*, ed. John M. Robson and Jack Stillinger (1981), esp. xxx–xxxvi, which is Volume 1 of *The Collected Works of John Stuart Mill*, ed. John M. Robson et al., 33 vols. (Toronto and London: University of Toronto Press and Routledge and Kegan Paul, 1963–1991). All citations of Mill are to this edition and appear in parentheses within my text.

31. After completing this chapter, I read the section on Mill in Jackson, *Dickinson's Misery*, esp. 130–133, and discovered that we had arrived independently at a couple of similar observations. Jackson acutely traces contradictions in Mill's distinction between lyric and eloquence, and she relates them to his insistence on the significance of address.

32. See Jackson, *Dickinson's Misery*, 130–133, for a different but compatible discussion of that figure.

33. I am indebted to the revisionist reading of Adorno's "On Lyric Poetry and Society" in a number of essays by Robert Kaufman and to the author's willingness to share his work prior to publication. See, e.g., "Adorno's Social Lyric, and Literary Criticism Today: Poetics, Aesthetics, Modernity," in *The Cambridge Companion to Adorno*, ed. Tom Huhn (Cambridge: Cambridge University Press, 2004); and "Negatively Capable Dialectics: Keats, Vendler, Adorno, and the Theory of Avant-Garde," *Critical Inquiry* 27 (2001), 354–384.

34. T. S. Eliot, "The Three Voices of Poetry," in *On Poetry and Poets* (New York: Noonday Press, 1961), 102–103.

35. W. R. Johnson, *The Idea of Lyric: Lyric Modes in Ancient and Modern Poetry* (Berkeley: University of California Press, 1982), 1.

36. Eliot, "The Three Voices of Poetry," 111.

37. Eliot, "The Three Voices of Poetry," 112.

38. Northrop Frye, "Approaching the Lyric," in *Lyric Poetry: Beyond New Criticism*, ed. Chaviva Hošek and Patricia Parker (Ithaca: Cornell University Press, 1985).

39. On Frye's relationship to history, see Jonathan Hart, *Northrop Frye: The Theoretical Imagination* (Routledge: London, 1994), esp. 90–95.

40. For the argument that Frye is merely adapting Mill, see, e.g., Allen Grossman with Mark Halliday, *The Sighted Singer: Two Works on Poetry for Readers and Writers* (Baltimore: Johns Hopkins University Press, 1992), 212.

41. See esp. Don H. Bialostosky, *Wordsworth, Dialogics, and the Practice of Criticism* (Cambridge: Cambridge University Press, 1992); Michael Macovski, *Dialogue and Literature: Apostrophe, Auditors, and the Collapse of Romantic Discourse* (New York: Oxford University Press, 1994); also cf. Schalkwyk, *Speech and Performance.*

42. I cite M. M. Bakhtin, *The Dialogic Imagination: Four Essays*, ed. Michael Holquist, trans. Caryl Emerson and Michael Holquist (Austin: University of Texas Press, 1981), 280.

43. Bakhtin, *Dialogic Imagination*, 285, 286.

44. V. N. Voloshinov, "Literary Stylistics," trans. Noel Owen and Joe Andrew, in *Bakhtin School Papers*, ed. Ann Shukman, Russian Poetics in Translation 1983, No. 10. (Oxford: RPT Publications and Holdan Books, 1983), 112.

45. V. N. Voloshinov [M. M. Bakhtin?] "Discourse in Life and Discourse in Poetry: Questions of Sociological Poetics," trans. John Richmond, in *Bakhtin School Papers*, esp. 25.

46. Marianne Shapiro and Michael Shapiro, "Dialogism and the Addressee in Lyric Poetry," *University of Toronto Quarterly* 61 (1992), 392–413.

47. Sara Guyer, "Wordsworthian Wakefulness," *Yale Journal of Criticism* 16 (2003), 93–111.

48. On the "what-sayer," see Ellen B. Basso, *A Musical View of the Universe* (Philadelphia: University of Pennsylvania Press, 1985), 15–18.

49. Erving Goffman, *Forms of Talk* (Philadelphia: University of Pennsylvania Press, 1981), Chapter 3.

50. I cite *The Poems of Andrew Marvell*, ed. Nigel Smith (Harlow and London: Pearson Education, 2003).

51. Throughout this chapter I cite *The Riverside Shakespeare*, ed. G. Blakemore Evans, 2nd ed. (Boston: Houghton Mifflin, 1997).

52. On the concept of side participants see Herbert H. Clark and Thomas B. Carlson, "Hearers and Speech Acts," *Language* 58 (1982), 332–373.

53. Clark and Carlson, "Hearers and Speech Acts."

54. William Waters, *Poetry's Touch: On Lyric Address* (Ithaca: Cornell University Press, 2003). Compare, from Fitzgerald, *Catullan Provocations*, "overhearing is not only an illusion, it is also a relation" (4). Another useful perspective on shifts in audiences

appears in an as yet unpublished text by Elizabeth Sagaser, "Elegaic Intimacy"; I thank the author for sharing it prior to publication.

55. Bell, *Elizabethan Women.*

56. Revisionist studies have challenged earlier assertions that Jonson pioneered a radically new conception of authorship. See, e.g., Joseph Loewenstein, *Ben Jonson and Possessive Authorship* (Cambridge: Cambridge University Press, 2002); James Mardock, "Spatial Practice and the Theatrical Authoring of Jacobean London" (unpublished doctoral dissertation, University of Wisconsin-Madison, August 2004).

57. For an overview of the roles of the psalms in England, see Hannibal Hamlin, *Psalm Culture and Early Modern English Literature* (Cambridge: Cambridge University Press, 2004). I thank the author for making his work available to me before publication; although he does not address the impact of the psalms on secular lyric from my perspectives, I gratefully draw on other aspects of his research throughout the ensuing argument.

58. One of the few exceptions to this point about the neglected influence of the psalms on secular poetry is Roland Greene, "Sir Philip Sidney's *Psalms*, the Sixteenth-Century Psalter, and the Nature of Lyric," *SEL* 30 (1990), 19–40; his approach is very different from mine, however, focusing as it does on the psalms in relation to Greene's divide between fictional and ritualistic potentialities for lyric. Among the numerous other studies of versions of the psalms by and the influence of the psalms on particular poets are Carol Kaske, "Spenser's *Amoretti and Epithalamion*: A Psalter of Love," in *Centered on the Word: Literature, Scripture, and the Tudor-Stuart Middle Way*, ed. Daniel W. Doerksen and Christopher Hodgkins (Cranbury, NJ: Associated University Presses, 2004); Annabel Patterson, "*Bermudas* and *The Coronet*: Marvell's Protestant Poetics," *ELH* 44 (1977), 478–499; Mary Ann Radzinowicz, *Milton's Epics and the Book of Psalms* (Princeton: Princeton University Press, 1989); Nigel Smith, *Literature and Revolution in England, 1640–1669* (New Haven: Yale University Press, 1994), 260–276. Extensive discussions of the psalms also appear throughout Barbara Kiefer Lewalski, *Protestant Poetics and the Seventeenth-Century Religious Lyric* (Princeton: Princeton University Press, 1979); see esp. 39–53 on the psalms as a compendium.

59. Hamlin, *Psalm Culture*, 38.

60. On these and other debates about polyphony, see esp. John Hollander, *The Untuning of the Sky: Ideas of Music in English Poetry, 1500–1700* (1961; rpt., New York: W. W. Norton, 1970), esp. 186–191.

61. *The Psalmes of David and Others With M. John Calvins Commentaries* (London, 1571), 158. Also see John Calvin, *Institutes of the Christian Religion*, ed. John T. McNeill, trans. Ford Lewis Battles (Philadelphia: Westminster Press, 1960), Vol. 2, 894–896. For a useful summary of Luther's attitudes to the psalms, see Lily B. Campbell, *Divine Poetry and Drama in Sixteenth-Century England* (Berkeley: University of California Press, 1961), 29–30.

62. Miles Coverdale, *Goostly Psalmes* (London, 1539?), sig. iii–iii$^v$.

63. On this anxiety, compare Patterson, "*Bermudas.*"

64. Miles Coverdale, *The Order that the Churche in Denmarke doth Use* (London, 1550?).

65. *The Psalter or Psalmes of David* (London, 1566), title page.

66. This rubric appears repeatedly. See, e.g., the title page of *The Whole Booke of Psalmes* (London, 1576).

67. On the meditative elements in the psalms, see James Limburg, "Psalms," in *The Anchor Bible Dictionary*, ed. David Noel Freedman et al. (New York: Doubleday, 1992), Vol.5, 525, 526.

68. Hammons, *Poetic Resistance*, 1–2, Chapter 3.

69. See, e.g., the title page of *The Whole Booke of Psalmes* (London, 1576).

70. Limburg, "Psalms," 525.

71. For a different but not incompatible interpretation of such titles, see Anne Ferry, *The Title to the Poem* (Stanford: Stanford University Press, 1996), 258–259.

72. Kenneth M. Kensinger, *How Real People Ought to Live: The Cashinahua of Eastern Peru* (Prospect Heights, IL: Waveland Press, 1995), Chapter 4.

73. That coerciveness is a central thesis of Ramie Targoff's important revisionist study, *Common Prayer: The Language of Public Devotion in Early Modern England* (Chicago: University of Chicago Press, 2001). For Roland Greene's argument about the interplay between "fictive" and "ritualistic" elements in psalm-singing, see his essay, "Sir Philip Sidney's *Psalms*"; although he does not discuss the issue of multiple audiences, his model has many implications for it.

74. Richard Rogers, *Seven Treatises, Containing Such Direction as is Gathered out of the Holie Scriptures* (London, 1603), 224.

75. Louis L. Martz, *The Poetry of Meditation: A Study in English Religious Literature of the Seventeenth Century*, rev. ed. (New Haven: Yale University Press, 1962), 32–43.

76. Susan Stewart, *Poetry and the Fate of the Senses* (Chicago: University of Chicago Press, 2002), 147–149.

77. A. D. Nuttall, *Overheard by God: Fiction and Prayer in Herbert, Milton, Dante and St John* (London: Methuen, 1980), esp. 1–21.

78. John Donne, *Letters to Severall Persons of Honour* (London, 1651), 110–111.

79. I cite *Complete Prose Works of John Milton* (ed. Wolfe et al.), Vol. III, 1648–1649, ed. Merritt Y. Hughes (1962). For a useful commentary on this and related passages, see Achsah Guibbory, "Charles's Prayers, Idolatrous Images, and True Creation in Milton's *Eikonoklastes*," in *Of Poetry and Politics: New Essays on Milton and His World*, ed. P. G. Stanwood (Binghamton, NY: Medieval and Renaissance Texts and Studies, 1995), esp. 286–292.

80. Richard Baxter, *The Saints Everlasting Rest* (London, 1650), 750.

81. On connections between preaching and meditation, see, e.g., Walter R. Davis, "Meditation, Typology, and the Structure of John Donne's Sermons," in *The Eagle and the Dove: Reassessing John Donne*, ed. Claude Summers and Ted-Larry Pebworth (Columbia: University of Missouri Press, 1986), esp. 167–168, 183–188. The subtitles I cite occur in two books by Thomas Gataker: *A Mariage Praier, or Succinct Meditations* (London, 1624) and *Abrahams Decease; A Meditation on Genesis 25.8* (London, 1627).

82. Michael C. Schoenfeldt, *Prayer and Power: George Herbert and Renaissance Courtship* (Chicago: University of Chicago Press, 1991), 188; because of the conditional, however, I find the relationship of the poem to mortal readers less "coercive" than Schoenfeldt does in this analysis. On how this lyric relates to its divine audience, also see

Richard Strier, *Love Known: Theology and Experience in George Herbert's Poetry* (Chicago: University of Chicago Press, 1983), 91–96.

83. *The Works of George Herbert*, ed. F. E. Hutchinson (Oxford: Clarendon Press, 1941); I cite this edition throughout the chapter.

84. For an overview of these architectural changes, see William Alexander Mc-Clung, *The Country House in English Renaissance Poetry* (Berkeley: University of California Press, 1977), 46–61; Patricia Fumerton traces how the development of the banqueting house permitted increased privacy for the aristocracy (*Cultural Aesthetics: Renaissance Literature and the Practice of Social Ornament* [Chicago: University of Chicago Press, 1991]), 113–128. The broader issue of secrecy is discussed in John Stevens, *Music and Poetry in the Early Tudor Court* (London: Methuen, 1961), esp. 190–192.

85. George Wright, *Hearing the Measures*, Chapter 13.

86. Wendy Wall, *Imprint of Gender*, 38–50, argues for that encoding, a move that not coincidentally establishes the primacy of the materialist implications of a text at the expense of other valences rather than focusing on their coexistence. As influential as it is problematical, Arthur F. Marotti's "'Love is not love': Elizabethan Sonnet Sequences and the Social Order," *ELH* 49 (1982), 396–428, makes the same move.

87. Malcolmson, *Heart-Work*, 56–59.

88. Quintilian, *Institutio Oratoria*, 4 vols., trans. H. E. Butler (Cambridge: Harvard University Press, 1920–1924), Vol. 3, *Books VII–IX* (1921), IX.ii.38–39. I replicate the italics from the translation in this edition.

89. Christina Luckyj, *"A moving Rhetoricke": Gender and Silence in Early Modern England* (Manchester: Manchester University Press, 2002).

90. On the pairing of lute poems, see Carla Zecher, *Sounding Objects: Musical Instruments, Poetry, and Art in Renaissance France* (Toronto: University of Toronto Press, 2006), 136–138. Approaching polyphony from a different but compatible perspective, Diane Kelsey McColley relates the preservation of individual voices in polyphony to the individuation of seventeenth-century poetic speakers (*Poetry and Music in Seventeenth-Century England* [Cambridge: Cambridge University Press, 1997], 77–78).

91. James Anderson Winn, *Unsuspected Eloquence: A History of the Relations between Poetry and Music* (New Haven: Yale University Press, 1981), 174.

92. Raymond Williams, "Monologue in *Macbeth*," in *Teaching the Text*, ed. Susanne Kappeler and Norman Bryson (London: Routledge and Kegan Paul, 1983). The critical literature on soliloquy and the specific issue of to whom it is addressed is of course vast. In addition to the Williams essay cited here, see, e.g., Wolfgang Clemen's emphasis on the frequency of direct address to an audience (*Shakespeare's Soliloquies*, trans. Charity Scott Stokes [London: Methuen, 1987], esp. 4–5); in contrast, James Hirsch distinguishes soliloquies addressed to the audience, spoken ones addressed to the self, and internalized ones, arguing that the first category essentially disappeared after the sixteenth century (*Shakespeare and the History of Soliloquies* [Madison, NJ, and London: Fairleigh Dickinson University Press and Associated University Presses, 2003]). A transhistorical discussion appears in Ken Frieden, *Genius and Monologue* (Ithaca: Cornell University Press, 1985); his argument in Chapter 5 about the introjection of divine or demonic interlocutors exaggerates

an occasional occurrence into a norm but does indicate one way soliloquies sometimes evoke an audience (see esp. 130).

93. Wall, *Imprint of Gender*, 50. She too observes that the reader, like the lady, holds the book. As noted above, however, I take issue with her observation that the lady primarily serves to figure coterie exchange.

94. I quote *The Works of Michael Drayton,* ed. J. William Hebel, Bernard H. Newdigate, Kathleen Tillotson, 5 vols. (Oxford: Basil Blackwell, 1931–1941).

95. Devotional poetry of the period does, of course, assume many other forms as well. Some texts represent a generalized speaker participating in communal devotion or marking an event widely celebrated by others; such as Jonson's "Hymne on the Nativitie of my Saviour"; others substitute for a single voice a dialogue, a chorus, or both, such as Marvell's "Dialogue Between the Resolved Soul, and Created Pleasure."

96. For a useful summary of the debate about Donne's poem and the case that the speaker's role is priestly, see Theresa M. DiPasquale, *Literature and Sacrament: The Sacred and the Secular in John Donne* (Pittsburgh: Duquesne University Press, 1999), 90–96.

97. Schoenfeldt, *Prayer and Power*, 104–110.

98. This interplay is a central argument throughout Bell, *Elizabethan Women;* although she sometimes posits a closer connection between diegetic and nondiegetic readers than I would, her study offers valuable evidence of the social interactions I, too, associate with the audiences of early modern lyric.

99. Gémino Abad, *A Formal Approach to Lyric Poetry*, 73–93; as I indicate elsewhere, although its reliance on the methods of categorization of the Chicago School sometimes limits the value of this study, in other passages its capacious approach to lyric is a useful corrective.

100. See, e.g., Terry G. Sherwood, *Herbert's Prayerful Art* (Toronto: University of Toronto Press, 1989), 67–69; Strier, *Love Known*, 127–133.

101. Targoff, *Common Prayer*, esp. Introduction and Chapters 1 and 2.

102. The issue of penitence is, of course, complicated by how we read the final two lines; it is an issue tangential to my argument here but discussed acutely in, e.g., Helen Vendler, *The Poetry of George Herbert* (Cambridge: Harvard University Press, 1975), 132. Vendler's distinctions on the same page among what she terms judgmental, narrative, and spoken times also support the distinction for which I am arguing.

103. John Carey, *John Donne: Life, Mind and Art* (London: Faber and Faber, 1981), 51; John Donne, *The Divine Poems*, ed. Helen Gardner (Oxford: Clarendon Press, 1952), xxvi; this edition is cited whenever I quote Donne's religious poetry.

104. The shift in these pronouns is also discussed in Anthony Low, *Love's Architecture: Devotional Modes in Seventeenth-Century English Poetry* (New York: New York University Press, 1978), 53–54.

105. On the amalgamation of personal and more general concerns here, see esp. A. B. Chambers, *Transfigured Rites in Seventeenth-Century English Poetry* (Columbia: University of Missouri Press, 1992), 10–11.

106. Donne, *Letters,* 32–33.

107. Donne, *Divine Poems*, xxviii.

108. Chambers, *Transfigured Rites*, 5–11. Similarly, a central argument throughout Part II of R. V. Young's *Doctrine and Devotion in Seventeenth-Century Poetry: Studies in*

*Donne, Herbert, Crashaw, and Vaughan* (Woodbridge, England: D. S. Brewer, 2000) is that private devotion and public worship are linked in many ways. The relationship between meditative poems and public worship in Herbert's poetry is analyzed in McColley, *Poetry and Music*, esp. 149–153.

109. Paul Alpers, *What Is Pastoral?* (Chicago: University of Chicago Press, 1996), esp. 80–81.

110. Paul Alpers, "Pastoral and the Domain of Lyric in Spenser's *Shepheardes Calender*," *Representations*, no. 12 (Fall 1985), 94–95.

111. I cite *The Poems of Aemilia Lanyer: "Salve Deus Rex Judaeorum,"* ed. Susanne Woods (Oxford: Oxford University Press, 1993). Woods's decision to gloss the pronoun in 207 as "the Countess of Cumberland's" (138), though an understandable response to the expository needs of a reader, risks directing attention away from the implications of the confusion.

112. Compare William Waters's acute demonstrations throughout *Poetry's Touch* of how direction of address in lyrics relates to the thematization of address.

113. See, e.g., Jonathan Culler, *The Pursuit of Signs: Semiotics, Literature, Deconstruction* (Ithaca: Cornell University Press, 1981), Chapter 7; Paul de Man, "Lyrical Voice in Contemporary Theory: Riffaterre and Jauss," in *Lyric Poetry*, ed. Hošek and Parker.

114. Steven Winspur, "The Pragmatic Force of Lyric," *Yearbook of Comparative and General Literature* 42 (1994), 143; also see two essays by Ralph W. Rader, "The Dramatic Monologue and Related Lyric Forms," *Critical Inquiry* 3 (1976), 131–151; "Notes on Some Structural Varieties and Variations in Dramatic 'I' Poems and Their Theoretical Implications," *Victorian Poetry* 22 (1984), 103–104.

115. Vendler, *Art of Shakespeare's Sonnets*, 2, 18.

116. On recent discoveries about mirror neurons, see "Cells That Read Minds," *New York Times*, first page of *Science Times*, national edition, January 10, 2006.

117. Marotti, *Manuscript*.

118. Bell, *Elizabethan Women*. Wendy Wall (*Imprint of Gender*, esp. 38–50) also acutely traces interactions with the mistress, who, she argues, tropes the active reader; unlike Bell, however, Wall positions these exchanges as counters for homosocial coterie relationships.

119. David Schalkwyk, *Speech and Performance*.

120. Lynne Magnusson, *Shakespeare and Social Dialogue: Dramatic Language and Elizabethan Letters* (Cambridge: Cambridge University Press, 1999).

121. Andrew Welsh, *Roots of Lyric: Primitive Poetry and Modern Poetics* (Princeton: Princeton University Press, 1978), Chapter 7; Richard Schechner, "Magnitudes of Performance" in *By Means of Performance: Intercultural Studies of Theatre and Ritual*, ed. Richard Schechner and Willa Appel (Cambridge: Cambridge University Press, 1990), 38–41.

122. Mark W. Booth, *The Experience of Songs* (New Haven: Yale University Press, 1981), esp. 14–17; yet Booth's admission on page 17 that disapproval of the song interferes with that identification could also be adduced to support my point about the limits on identificatory voicing.

123. Harold Love, *Scribal Publication in Seventeenth-Century England* (Oxford: Clarendon Press, 1993), 219.

124. Stephen Owen, *Mi-Lou: Poetry and the Labyrinth of Desire* (Cambridge: Harvard University Press, 1989), 15.

125. Bell, *Elizabethan Women*, 59–60.

126. Roland Greene, *Post-Petrarchism: Origins and Innovations of the Western Lyric Sequence* (Princeton: Princeton University Press, 1991), 5–14.

127. I thank Patricia Rosenmeyer for useful comments on this and many other issues connected to classical lyric.

128. Frye, *Anatomy of Criticism*, 271.

129. Marshall Brown, "Negative Poetics: On Skepticism and the Lyric Voice," *Representations*, no. 86 (Spring 2004), 120–140.

130. On *fort-da*, see esp. Chapter 2 of Sigmund Freud, *Beyond the Pleasure Principle*, cited here from *The Standard Edition of the Complete Psychological Works of Sigmund Freud*, trans. James Strachey et al., Vol. XVIII (London: Hogarth Press and Institute of Psycho-Analysis, 1955).

131. Wall, *Imprint of Gender*, esp. 42–50. Wall also notes the effects of holding the book (46–47), though her analysis primarily stresses the power of the reader.

132. John Donne, *The Elegies and The Songs and Sonnets*, ed. Helen Gardner (Oxford: Clarendon Press, 1965).

133. For a different but compatible analysis of Herrick's responses to rebirth through nature, see Achsah Guibbory, *The Map of Time: Seventeenth-Century English Literature and Ideas of Pattern in History* (Urbana: University of Illinois Press, 1986), 152–159.

134. Throughout this chapter all citations are to *The Poetical Works of Robert Herrick*, ed. L. C. Martin (Oxford: Clarendon Press, 1956).

135. Jonson's titles are acutely discussed a number of times in Ferry, *Title*, though she primarily focuses on the self-assertion involved in his first-person titles (see esp. 46–49).

136. *Collected Poems of Sir Thomas Wyatt*, ed. Kenneth Muir and Patricia Thomson (Liverpool: Liverpool University Press, 1969).

137. William Shakespeare, *Complete Sonnets and Poems*, ed. Colin Burrow (Oxford: Oxford University Press, 2002), 450.

138. Paul Alpers, "Learning from the New Criticism: The Example of Shakespeare's Sonnets," in *Renaissance Literature and Its Formal Engagements*, ed. Mark David Rasmussen (New York: Palgrave, 2002), 132.

139. Helen Vendler, *Art of Shakespeare's Sonnets*, 188, suggests that the poem implies two lawsuits, with the speaker as plaintiff in the first and as both defendant and plaintiff in the second; but it is at least as likely that the poem implies that positions change within the same legal action.

## CHAPTER 3: THE CRAFT OF PYGMALION

1. Paul Celan, *Collected Prose*, trans. Rosemarie Waldrop (Riverdale-on-Hudson, NY: Sheep Meadow Press, 1986), 25–26.

2. William Waters, *Poetry's Touch: On Lyric Address* (Ithaca: Cornell University Press, 2003), 159–161.

3. On touch in lyric, see esp. Susan Stewart, *Poetry and the Fate of the Senses* (Chicago: University of Chicago Press, 2002), Chapter 4.

4. Throughout this chapter I cite John Donne, *The Elegies and The Songs and Sonnets*, ed. Helen Gardner (Oxford: Clarendon Press, 1965).

5. In *The English Lyric from Wyatt to Donne: A History of the Plain and Eloquent Styles*, 2nd ed. (1967; rpt., East Lansing, MI: Colleagues Press, 1990), 301, Douglas L. Peterson cites the poem as an instance of its author's practice of presenting, then undercutting, fashionable attitudes; his approach is a valuable corrective to the still-widespread practice of adducing biographical explanations for changes and contradictions in Donne's stance towards love.

6. John Carey, *John Donne: Life, Mind and Art* (London: Faber and Faber, 1981), 180.

7. Also telling is the way "sigh" (19) relocates what had seemed to be anti-Petrarchism on the borders of Petrarchism, demonstrating the contiguity of those movements.

8. Nor, for that matter, should we see as normative the skeptical distancing that Marshall Brown's revisionist argument posits; his argument, though acute and powerful, is an overcorrection ("Negative Poetics: On Skepticism and the Lyric Voice," *Representations*, no. 86 [Spring 2004], 120–140).

9. Jonathan Bate, *Shakespeare and Ovid* (Oxford: Clarendon Press, 1993), 200.

10. Deixis is discussed in ways germane to this chapter at several points in Jane Hedley's *Power in Verse: Metaphor and Metonymy in the Renaissance Lyric* (University Park: Pennsylvania State University Press, 1988); see esp. 31–34.

11. *The Poems of John Keats*, ed. Jack Stillinger (Cambridge: Harvard University Press, 1978).

12. Lawrence Lipking, *The Life of the Poet: Beginning and Ending Poetic Careers* (Chicago: University of Chicago Press, 1981), 181.

13. For fine readings of the poem which include these and other debates, see Timothy Bahti, *Ends of the Lyric: Direction and Consequence in Western Poetry* (Baltimore: Johns Hopkins University Press, 1996), 89–94; Jonathan Culler, *The Pursuit of Signs: Semiotics, Literature, Deconstruction* (Ithaca: Cornell University Press, 1981), 153–154; Lipking, *Life of the Poet*, 180–184.

14. Brooke Hopkins, "Keats and the Uncanny: 'This living hand,'" *Kenyon Review* 11 (1989), 28–40. On this response, cf. Susan J. Wolfson, *The Questioning Presence: Wordsworth, Keats, and the Interrogative Mode in Romantic Poetry* (Ithaca: Cornell University Press, 1986), 368.

15. On the range of paratexts, see Gérard Genette, *Paratexts: Thresholds of Interpretation*, trans. Jane E. Lewin (Cambridge: Cambridge University Press, 1997).

16. I cite Quintilian, *Institutio Oratoria, Books VII–IX*, 4 vols., trans. H. E. Butler (Cambridge: Harvard University Press, 1920–1924), Vol. 3 (1921), VIII.iii.61–62. Future references appear in my text. For a useful overview of the concept of *energia* and Sidney's use of it, see Neil L. Rudenstine, *Sidney's Poetic Development* (Cambridge: Harvard University Press, 1967), Chapter 10.

17. George Puttenham, *The Arte of English Poesie*, ed. Baxter Hathaway (1906; rpt., Kent, OH: Kent State University Press, 1970), 155.

18. Sir Philip Sidney, *An Apology for Poetry*, ed. Geoffrey Shepherd (London: Nelson, 1965), 137.

19. *OED*, s.v. "betray."

20. See, e.g., Emil Staiger, *Basic Concepts of Poetics*, trans. Janette C. Hudson and Luanne T. Frank, ed. Marianne Burkhard and Luanne T. Frank (University Park: Pennsylvania State University Press, 1991), esp. 68. In apparent reaction against models of *Erlebnis*, Käte Hamburger insists on the immediacy of this form—but attributes it to her contention that lyric, unlike the other two modes, is experienced as a direct statement made by a real subject, not as fictive (*The Logic of Literature*, rev. ed., trans. Marilynn J. Rose [Bloomington: University of Indiana Press, 1973], 271).

21. Culler, *Pursuit of Signs*, 149.

22. On deixis, see Stewart, *Poetry and the Senses*, esp. 154–156, 221–222; Roland Greene, *Post-Petrarchism: Origins and Innovations of the Western Lyric Sequence* (Princeton: Princeton University Press, 1991), esp. Chapter 1.

23. Sidney, *Apology for Poetry*, 100.

24. I cite *The Complete Works of Percy Bysshe Shelley*, ed. Roger Ingpen and Walter E. Peck, Vol. 7 (New York: Gordian Press, 1965), 117, 136.

25. For one of the most influential statements of this position, see Paul de Man, "Lyrical Voice in Contemporary Theory: Riffaterre and Jauss," in *Lyric Poetry: Beyond New Criticism*, ed. Chaviva Hošek and Patricia Parker (Ithaca: Cornell University Press, 1985). Also cf. Karen Mills-Courts's deconstructionist analysis of the interplay between incarnation and representation in poetry (*Poetry as Epitaph: Representation and Poetic Language* [Baton Rouge: Louisiana State University Press, 1990]).

26. W. R. Johnson, *The Idea of Lyric: Lyric Modes in Ancient and Modern Poetry* (Berkeley: University of California Press, 1982), 31.

27. See, e.g., Sharon Cameron, *Lyric Time: Dickinson and the Limits of Genre* (Baltimore: Johns Hopkins University Press, 1979).

28. See esp. Anne Ferry, *The Title to the Poem* (Stanford: Stanford University Press, 1996); William W. E. Slights, *Managing Readers: Printed Marginalia in English Renaissance Books* (Ann Arbor: University of Michigan Press, 2001); Evelyn B. Tribble, *Margins and Marginality: The Printed Page in Early Modern England* (Charlottesville: University Press of Virginia, 1993).

29. Compare Culler's observation that "This living hand, now warm and capable" acknowledges the fictiveness of its own claims; his use of the term "mystification" for its workings is, however, revealing (*Pursuit of Signs*, 154).

30. Stewart, *Poetry and the Senses*, 309.

31. Allen Grossman with Mark Halliday, *The Sighted Singer: Two Works on Poetry for Readers and Writers* (Baltimore: Johns Hopkins University Press, 1992), ix.

32. Theodor W. Adorno, "Lyric Poetry and Society," *Telos* 20 (1974), 56–71.

33. Mary Thomas Crane, "What Was Performance?" *Criticism* 43 (2001), 43.

34. Joel C. Kuipers, *Power in Performance: The Creation of Textual Authority in Weyewa Ritual Speech* (Philadelphia: University of Pennsylvania Press, 1990), 2.

35. [Cicero], *Ad C. Herennium*, trans. Harry Caplan (London and Cambridge: William Heinemann and Harvard University Press, 1954), 405.

36. George Gascoigne, *A Hundreth Sundrie Flowres*, ed. G. W. Pigman III (Oxford: Clarendon Press, 2000), 216. Subsequent references to this volume appear within my text.

37. Ferry, *Title*, esp. 11–19.

38. On Renaissance practices of framing, see Rayna Kalas's unpublished doctoral dissertation, "Frames, Glass, and the Technology of Poetic Invention" and an essay by the same author, "The Language of Framing," *Shakespeare Studies* 28 (2000), 240–247. These arguments appear in revised form in Kalas's book, *Frame, Glass, Verse: The Technology of Poetic Invention in the English Renaissance* (Ithaca: Cornell University Press, 2007).

39. For this reading of the opening psalms, see James Limburg, "Psalms," in *The Anchor Bible Dictionary*, ed. David Noel Freedman et al. (New York: Doubleday, 1992), Vol. 5, 524. Also compare John Hollander's related but different point that emblem books prefigure titles (*Vision and Resonance: Two Senses of Poetic Form*, 2nd ed. [New Haven: Yale University Press, 1975], 221–222).

40. On the reflexiveness of the psalms, cf. Harold Fisch, *Poetry with a Purpose: Biblical Poetics and Interpretation* (Bloomington: Indiana University Press, 1988), 118–120.

41. For a useful discussion of this and related beliefs, see A[lex] B. Chambers, " 'Goodfriday, 1613. Riding Westward': Looking Back," *John Donne Journal* 6 (1987), 193–194.

42. On this type of framing and its implications, see Rayna Kalas's. "Frames."

43. Augustine, *St. Augustine on the Psalms*, trans. and ed. Dame Scholastica Hebgin and Dame Felicitas Corrigan, Vol 1 (London and Westminster, MD: Longmans, Green, and The Newman Press, 1960), 207. Subsequent page references appear in parentheses in my text.

44. See Louis Martz's influential study of the Ignatian meditative tradition, *The Poetry of Meditation: A Study in English Religious Literature of the Seventeenth Century*, rev. ed. (New Haven: Yale University Press, 1962). Also see A. D. Cousins, *The Catholic Religious Poets from Southwell to Crashaw: A Critical History* (London: Sheed and Ward, 1991); the issue of immediacy is discussed on 32.

45. Barbara Kiefer Lewalski, *Protestant Poetics and the Seventeenth-Century Religious Lyric* (Princeton: Princeton University Press, 1979), Chapter 5.

46. Joseph Hall, *The Arte of Divine Meditation* (London, 1605), 3.

47. I am indebted to Alexandra Block for many useful insights into the eucharistic debates.

48. Debora Kuller Shuger, *Habits of Thought in the English Renaissance: Religion, Politics, and the Dominant Culture* (1990; rpt., Toronto: University of Toronto Press, 1997), esp. 90.

49. Jonathan Culler, "Apostrophe Revisited," paper delivered at the 2001 Modern Language Association convention in New Orleans. I am grateful to the author for making his work available to me prior to publication.

50. Richard Todd, "In What Sense Is John Donne the Author of the 'Songs and Sonnets'?" in *La Poésie Métaphysique de John Donne*, ed. Claudine Raynaud (Tours: Groupe des Recherches Anglo-Américaines de l'Université de Tours, 2002), 111.

51. Michael Archer, Guy Brett, Catherine de Zegher, *Mona Hatoum* (London: Phaidon, 1997), 25.

52. See, e.g., Michel de Certeau, *The Practice of Everyday Life,* trans. Steven Rendell (Berkeley: University of California Press, 1984), esp. 117–118; Henri Lefebvre, *The Production of Space,* trans. Donald Nicholson-Smith (Oxford: Blackwell, 1991).

53. As the title suggests, the education of the audience is a central focus throughout Slights, *Managing Readers;* it is also a recurrent point in Tribble, *Margins,* though at several points, especially Chapter 3, she concentrates instead on the undermining of authority.

54. Throughout this chapter references are to Thomas Watson, *The Hecatompathia or Passionate Centurie of Love* (London, 1582).

55. Arthur F. Marotti, *Manuscript, Print, and the English Renaissance Lyric* (Ithaca: Cornell University Press, 1995), 219–220.

56. On historicized formalism and the general advantages of dovetailing more traditional and recent critical methods, see, e.g., my study *Echoes of Desire: English Petrarchism and Its Counterdiscourses* (Ithaca: Cornell University Press, 1995), 278–284.

57. I cite Giles Fletcher, *The English Works of Giles Fletcher, the Elder,* ed. Lloyd E. Berry (Madison: University of Wisconsin Press, 1964).

58. Here and throughout this chapter I cite Samuel Daniel, *"Poems" and "A Defence of Ryme,"* ed. Arthur Colby Sprague (Chicago: University of Chicago Press, 1930).

59. John Donne, *The Epithalamions, Anniversaries, and Epicedes,* ed. W[esley] Milgate (Oxford: Clarendon Press, 1978).

60. *The Poems of Sir Philip Sidney,* ed. W. A. Ringler, Jr. (Oxford: Clarendon Press, 1962).

61. I cite *The Poems of Robert Sidney,* ed. P. J. Croft (Oxford: Clarendon Press, 1984).

62. See, e.g., John T. Shawcross, *Intentionality and the New Traditionalism: Some Liminal Means to Literary Revisionism* (University Park: Pennsylvania State University Press, 1991), 79. Helen Vendler, though conservative in many of her assumptions about the mode, argues that Shakespeare, eschewing the option of representing experience in the form in which it happens, writes about it in his sonnets "analytically and retrospectively" (*The Art of Shakespeare's Sonnets* [Cambridge: Harvard University Press, 1997], 550).

63. Andrew Welsh, *Roots of Lyric: Primitive Poetry and Modern Poetics* (Princeton: Princeton University Press, 1978), Chapter 6.

64. Yi-Fu Tuan, *Space and Place: The Perspective of Experience* (Minneapolis: University of Minnesota Press, 1977), 6.

65. On this and other issues, see John Hollander's important studies of refrains in the sixth and eighth chapters of *Melodious Guile: Fictive Pattern in Poetic Language* (New Haven: Yale University Press, 1988). The comment on remembering appears on 135.

66. Vendler, *Art of Shakespeare's Sonnets;* the comment on "morning-after" reflections appears on 550, the observation about judgment on 551–554.

67. Renzo Piano, *Logbook,* trans. Huw Evans (New York: Monacelli Press, 1997), 251.

68. Genette, *Paratexts,* esp. 1–2.

69. Throughout this chapter I cite Andrew Marvell, *The Poems of Andrew Marvell,* ed. Nigel Smith (London: Longman, 2003).

70. See the texts by Kalas cited in n. 38.

71. George T. Wright, *Hearing the Measures: Shakespearean and Other Inflections* (Madison: University of Wisconsin Press, 2001), Chapter 2.

72. Herbert Blau, "Universals of Performance," in *By Means of Performance: Intercultural Studies of Theatre and Ritual*, ed. Richard Schechner and Willa Appel (Cambridge: Cambridge University Press, 1990), esp. 250.

73. See Richard Schechner and Willa Appel, Introduction, in *By Means of Performance*, 4–5. Also see Schnechner's essay "Magnitudes of Performance," 45, in the same volume.

74. Erving Goffman, *Frame Analysis: An Essay on the Organization of Experience* (Boston: Northeastern University Press, 1986), esp. 43–44.

75. Ferry, *Title*, esp. 2, 6–7, 12; Hollander, *Vision and Resonance*, 214.

76. Compare Marcy L. North, *The Anonymous Renaissance: Cultures of Discretion in Tudor-Stuart England* (Chicago: University of Chicago Press, 2003).

77. On these types of invocation, see Stewart, *Poetry and the Senses*, esp. 146–150; Grossman and Halliday, *The Sighted Singer*, 20–21.

78. Ernst Häublein, *The Stanza* (London: Methuen, 1978), 59–71.

79. Greene, *Post-Petrarchism*, 5–6.

80. On how recognizing formal patterns creates detachment, cf. Paula Johnson, *Form and Transformation in Music and Poetry of the English Renaissance* (New Haven: Yale University Press, 1972), 55.

81. Schechner, "Magnitudes of Performance," 25–26.

82. Schechner and Appel, Introduction, 4.

83. John Milton, *Complete Poems and Major Prose*, ed. Merritt Y. Hughes (Indianapolis: Odyssey Press, Bobbs-Merrill, 1957). This edition will be cited throughout the chapter.

84. All citations are to Richard Crashaw, *The Complete Poetry of Richard Crashaw*, ed. George Walton Williams (New York: W. W. Norton, 1970). I quote the later version of the poem, but the original is similar in the relevant ways.

85. Throughout this chapter I cite *The Yale Edition of the Shorter Poems of Edmund Spenser*, ed. William A. Oram et al. (New Haven: Yale University Press, 1989).

86. Mary Oates O'Reilly, "A New Song: Singing Space in Milton's Nativity Ode," *John Donne Journal* 22 (1998), 95–115.

87. I cite *The Poems of Lady Mary Wroth*, ed. Josephine A. Roberts (Baton Rouge: Louisiana State University Press, 1983).

88. Christina Luckyj has acutely traced the positive valences within the paradoxical treatment of silence in Wroth's poetry, demonstrating its association with female agency; although these associations are not immediately present in the text at hand, their presence elsewhere in the sequence further complicates the categories of speech and writing ("*A moving Rhetoricke*": *Gender and Silence in Early Modern England* [Manchester: Manchester University Press, 2002], 140–146).

89. Waters, *Poetry's Touch*, 112.

90. Jeff Masten, "'Shall I turne blabb?': Circulation, Gender, and Subjectivity in Mary Wroth's Sonnets," in *Reading Mary Wroth: Representing Alternatives in Early Modern England*, ed. Naomi J. Miller and Gary Waller (Knoxville: University of Tennessee Press, 1991), 67–87.

91. Annabel Patterson, "*Bermudas* and *The Coronet*: Marvell's Protestant Poetics," *ELH* 44 (1977), 478–499.

92. Although he does not comment on the specific techniques I cite, Jonathan F. S. Post also notes that the poem moves from a telescopic to a close-up view (*English Lyric Poetry: The Early Seventeenth Century* [London: Routledge, 1999], 259–260).

93. Rosalie L. Colie, *"My Ecchoing Song": Andrew Marvell's Poetry of Criticism* (Princeton: Princeton University Press, 1970), 18.

94. On that detachment, see Colie, *"My Ecchoing Song,"* 129–130.

95. Compare John Klause's brief but suggestive observation that the tone of this poem is "knowing and regretful" and that Marvell has some reservations about the paradise portrayed in it (*The Unfortunate Fall: Theodicy and the Moral Imagination of Andrew Marvell* [Hamden, CT: Archon Books, 1983], 92).

96. See, e.g., Arthur Barker, "The Pattern of Milton's *Nativity Ode,*" *University of Toronto Quarterly* 10 (1941), 167–181; Richard Halpern, "The Great Instauration: Imaginary Narratives in Milton's 'Nativity Ode,'" in *Re-membering Milton: Essays on the Texts and Traditions,* ed. Mary Nyquist and Margaret W. Ferguson (London: Methuen, 1987); Stella P. Revard, *Milton and the Tangles of Neaera's Hair: The Making of the 1645 "Poems"* (Columbia: University of Missouri Press, 1997), Chapter 3.

97. J. Martin Evans, *The Miltonic Moment* (Lexington: University Press of Kentucky, 1998), Chapter 1; Hugh MacCallum, "The Narrator of Milton's 'On the Morning of Christ's Nativity,'" in *Familiar Colloquy: Essays Presented to Arthur Edward Barker,* ed. Patricia Bruckmann (n.p.: Oberon Press, 1978).

98. David Quint, "Expectation and Prematurity in Milton's *Nativity Ode,*" *Modern Philology* 97 (1999), 195–219. Also see Gregory F. Goekjian's analysis of the limitations of human authority and the emphasis on silence in the poem ("Deference and Silence: Milton's Nativity Ode," in *Milton Studies* 21 [1985], 119–135).

99. For an opposing reading of that question, see Goekjian, "Deference and Silence," 127.

100. Several other critics have noted the shifts in time sequence, though they have not focused on the implications for the interplay of immediacy and mediation in lyric; see, e.g., Lowry Nelson, Jr., *Baroque Lyric Poetry* (New Haven: Yale University Press, 1961), Chapter 3.

101. For a different interpretation of the Alexandrines in this poem, see Balachandra Rajan, *The Lofty Rhyme: A Study of Milton's Major Poetry* (London: Routledge and Kegan Paul, 1970), 11–12, 16–17.

102. Halpern, "The Great Instauration," esp. 4–10.

103. Heather Dubrow, "The Masquing of Genre in *Comus,*" *Milton Studies* 44 (2005), 62–83.

104. Paul H. Fry, *The Poet's Calling in the English Ode* (New Haven: Yale University Press, 1980), 2; Fry's own analysis of the poem focuses primarily on vocational issues, though he does briefly acknowledge its doubts about the accessibility of scriptural events (see esp. 44).

105. David Schalkwyk, *Speech and Performance in Shakespeare's Sonnets and Plays* (Cambridge: Cambridge University Press, 2002).

106. Blau, "Universals of performance," 258.

107. Crane, "What Was Performance?"

108. Greene, *Post-Petrarchism*, esp. 14–16.

109. Shawcross, *Intentionality*, esp. 86.

110. Stewart, *Poetry and the Senses*, 166.

111. On the aphoristic sayings of the humanists, see Mary Thomas Crane, *Framing Authority: Sayings, Self, and Society in Sixteenth-Century England* (Princeton: Princeton University Press, 1993).

### CHAPTER 4: THE PREDILECTIONS OF PROTEUS

1. Seth Lerer, "Medieval English Literature and the Idea of the Anthology," *PMLA* 118 (2003), 1251–1267.

2. Peter J. Manning, "Wordsworth in the *Keepsake, 1829,*" in *Literature in the Marketplace: Nineteenth-century British Publishing and Reading Practices*, ed. John O. Jordan and Robert L. Patten (Cambridge: Cambridge University Press, 1995), 45.

3. Harold Love, *Scribal Publication in Seventeenth-Century England* (Oxford: Clarendon Press, 1993), 230.

4. See Arthur F. Marotti, *Manuscript, Print, and the English Renaissance Lyric* (Ithaca: Cornell University Press, 1995), esp. Chapter 3, which is entitled "Social Textuality in the Manuscript System."

5. Elizabeth L. Eisenstein, *The Printing Press as an Agent of Change*, 2 vols. (Cambridge: Cambridge University Press, 1979).

6. Adrian Johns, *The Nature of the Book: Print and Knowledge in the Making* (Chicago: University of Chicago Press, 1998); the line I cite appears on page 36.

7. Roger Chartier, *The Order of Books: Readers, Authors, and Libraries in Europe between the Fourteenth and Eighteenth Centuries*, trans. Lydia G. Cochrane (Cambridge: Polity Press, 1994), 25–59.

8. On critical attitudes to the aesthetic, see, e.g., essays on the subject in two collections: *Aesthetics and Ideology*, ed. George Levine (New Brunswick, NJ: Rutgers University Press, 1994); and *Modern Language Quarterly* 61 (2000), a special issue on the aesthetic. An expanded collection of the essays from the *MLQ* special issue may be found in *Reading for Form*, ed. Susan J. Wolfson and Marshall Brown (Seattle: University of Washington Press, 2006).

9. Arthur F. Marotti, "Shakespeare's Sonnets as Literary Property," in *Soliciting Interpretation: Literary Theory and Seventeenth-Century English Poetry*, ed. Elizabeth D. Harvey and Katharine Eisaman Maus (Chicago: University of Chicago Press, 1990), 143; Wendy Wall, *The Imprint of Gender: Authorship and Publication in the English Renaissance* (Ithaca: Cornell University Press, 1993), 34.

10. See two important studies by Joseph Loewenstein: *Ben Jonson and Possessive Authorship* (Cambridge: Cambridge University Press, 2002) and *The Author's Due: Printing and the Prehistory of Copyright* (Chicago: University of Chicago Press, 2002). On the significance of copyright, see Mark Rose, *Authors and Owners: The Invention of Copyright* (Cambridge: Harvard University Press, 1993).

11. Marotti, *Manuscript*, 135.

12. See, e.g., Love, *Scribal Publication*, 287.

13. Important examples of these revisionist approaches include David Scott Kastan, *Shakespeare and the Book* (Cambridge: Cambridge University Press, 2001); and Marcy L. North, *The Anonymous Renaissance: Cultures of Discretion in Tudor-Stuart England* (Chicago: University of Chicago Press, 2003).

14. See Jennifer Summit, *Lost Property; The Woman Writer and English Literary History, 1380–1589* (Chicago: University of Chicago Press, 2000), esp. 49–59, 76–77. Also see the study cited above, Chartier, *The Order of Books*, esp. 30–32.

15. Zara Bruzzi, "'I find myself unparadis'd': The Integrity of Daniel's *Delia*," *Cahiers Élisabéthains* 48 (1995), 12.

16. For a commentary on these poems, see *Liber Lilliati: Elizabethan Verse and Song (Bodleian Ms Rawlison Poetry 148)*, ed. Edward Doughtie (Newark and London: University of Delaware Press and Associated University Presses, 1985), 138–139. They appear as Numbers 11 and 12 in the collection.

17. See the paper Marcy North delivered at the 2000 Modern Language Association meeting in Washington, DC, "Finis: Manuscript Lyrics and the Problem of Endings." I am grateful to the author for making her work available to me before publication.

18. Doughtie, *Liber Lilliati*, 108–109.

19. *Henry Stanford's Anthology: An Edition of Cambridge University Library Manuscript Dd.5.75*, ed. Steven V. May (New York: Garland, 1988), Items 284–289, 291–293.

20. On the editorial history of these texts, see Doughtie, *Liber Lilliati*, 165 and 178–179 respectively.

21. Compare Nancy J. Vickers, "Diana Described: Scattered Women and Scattered Rhyme," *Critical Inquiry* 8 (1981), 265–279. Vickers, however, reads the fear of dismemberment as Oedipal, while I am arguing that the poet fears the dismemberment of his poem.

22. Mary Thomas Crane, *Framing Authority: Sayings, Self, and Society in Sixteenth-Century England* (Princeton: Princeton University Press, 1993).

23. Yopie Prins, *Victorian Sappho* (Princeton: Princeton University Press, 1999).

24. I cite Ovid, *Metamorphoses*, 2nd ed., ed. and trans. Frank Justus Miller, rev. G. P. Goold, Vol. 2 (Cambridge and London: Harvard University Press and William Heinemann, 1984).

25. Chartier, *The Order of Books*, esp. 59.

26. Marotti, *Manuscript*, 141–142, 169.

27. Ernst Häublein, *The Stanza* (London: Methuen, 1978), 5.

28. I cite George Puttenham, *The Arte of English Poesie* (Kent, OH: Kent State University Press, 1970), 102. Subsequent references appear in parentheses within my text.

29. All citations are to George Gascoigne, *A Hundreth Sundrie Flowres*, ed. G. W. Pigman III (Oxford: Clarendon Press, 2000), 460. Future references to this edition will be included parenthetically in my text.

30. Michael Drayton, *The Barrons Wars* (London, 1603), sig. A3.

31. *OED*, s.v. "stave."

32. *OED*, s.v. "staff."

33. Paul Scarron, *The Whole Comical Works of Monsr. Scarron*, trans. Thomas Brown et al. (London, 1700), 60.

34. See Henry S. Turner, *The English Renaissance Stage: Geometry, Poetics, and the Practical Spatial Arts* (Oxford: Clarendon Press, 2006).

35. Thomas Palmer, *The Emblems of Thomas Palmer: Two Hundred Poosees: Sloane Ms. 3794*, ed. John Manning (New York, AMS Press, 1988).

36. Häublein, *The Stanza*, 78.

37. Marotti, *Manuscript*, 141–142, 169

38. On fires and other threats to buildings, see my book *Shakespeare and Domestic Loss: Forms of Deprivation, Mourning, and Recuperation* (Cambridge: Cambridge University Press, 1999), Chapter 3.

39. Throughout this chapter I cite *Ben Jonson*, ed. C. H. Herford, Percy Simpson, and Evelyn Simpson, 11 vols. (Oxford: Clarendon Press, 1925–1952).

40. Jonathan Tuck, " 'Thou Fall'st, My Tongue': Success and Failure in the Cary-Morison Ode," *George Herbert Journal* 22 (1998), 86. Also see Jonathan F. S. Post's persuasive suggestion that the self-division enacts Jonson's responses to the fraught issue of his own advancement and authority, *English Lyric Poetry: The Early Seventeenth Century* (London: Routledge, 1999), 48, 50–52.

41. For a different reading of the poem, see Paul H. Fry, *The Poet's Calling in the English Ode* (New Haven: Yale University Press, 1980), 15–26; he finds "self-deformation" (17) throughout and argues that Jonson chose the Pindaric ode in part because it lends itself to "strain[ing] against the very idea" of regular form (17).

42. John Donne, *The Elegies and The Songs and Sonnets*, ed. Helen Gardner (Oxford: Clarendon Press, 1965). I cite this edition throughout the chapter.

43. R[obert] L[ynche], *Diella, Certaine Sonnets* (London, 1596).

44. [Thomas Lodge], *Phillis* (London, 1593).

45. Jorge de Montemayor, *Diana*, trans. Bartholomew Young (London, 1598), 15.

46. Crane, *Framing Authority*.

47. John Hollander, *Melodious Guile: Fictive Pattern in Poetic Language* (New Haven: Yale University Press, 1988), Chapter 7.

48. Susan Stewart, *Poetry and the Fate of the Senses* (Chicago: University of Chicago Press, 2002), 229.

49. Helen Vendler, *The Art of Shakespeare's Sonnets* (Cambridge: Harvard University Press, 1997), 21.

50. Marotti, *Manuscript*, esp. Chapter 1.

51. Herrick's orderings of the poems is discussed extensively by Ann Baynes Coiro in *Robert Herrick's "Hesperides" and the Epigram Book Tradition* (Baltimore: Johns Hopkins University Press, 1988); see, e.g., 11–12.

52. For an instance of the disagreements about the order, see the conflict among: Arthur Barker's claim that the placement of the Nativity Ode reflects its status as a confident announcement of Milton's role as poet-prophet ("The Pattern of Milton's *Nativity Ode*," *University of Toronto Quarterly*, 10 [1941], 170); Stella P. Revard's reinterpretation of that claim (*Milton and the Tangles of Neaera's Hair: The Making of the 1645 Poems* [Columbia: University of Missouri Press, 1997], 64–90); and the darker reading of the poem that David Quint, like a number of other critics, has developed ("Expectation and Prematurity in Milton's *Nativity Ode*," *Modern Philology* 97 [1999], 195–219).

53. Wall, *Imprint of Gender*, 93–95.

54. Neil L. Rudenstine, *Sidney's Poetic Development* (Cambridge: Harvard University Press, 1967), Chapters 14–16.

55. David Kalstone, *Sidney's Poetry: Contexts and Interpretations* (Cambridge: Harvard University Press, 1965), 133.

56. Dubrow, "'Uncertainties now crown themselves assured': The Politics of Plotting Shakespeare's Sonnets," *Shakespeare Quarterly* 47 (1996), 291–305.

57. For brief but useful comments on the problems in the term "sonnet sequence," also see Kalstone, *Sidney's Poetry*, 133.

58. Gérard Genette, *Narrative Discourse: An Essay in Method*, trans. Jane E. Lewin (Ithaca: Cornell University Press, 1980), 161; Gerald Prince, "The Disnarrated," *Style* 22 (1988), 4. Some critics have, of course, offered an alternative version of the relationship of narrative to certainty; see, e.g., Uri Margolin, "Of What Is Past, Is Passing, or to Come: Temporality, Aspectuality, Modality, and the Nature of Literary Narrative," in *Narratologies: New Perspectives on Narrative Analysis*, ed. David Herman (Columbus: Ohio State University Press, 1999).

59. Vendler, *Art of Shakespeare's Sonnets*, 3.

60. Dubrow, "'Dressing old words new'?: Shakespeare's 1609 Volume and the 'Delian Structure,'" in *A Companion to Shakespeare's Sonnets*, ed. Michael Schoenfeldt (Oxford: Blackwell, 2007).

61. Colin Burrow, Introduction, in William Shakespeare, *Complete Sonnets and Poems*, ed. Burrow (Oxford: Oxford University Press, 2002), 95.

62. I cite Edmund Spenser, *The Yale Edition of the Shorter Works of Edmund Spenser*, ed. William A. Oram et al. (New Haven: Yale University Press, 1989).

63. Anne Lake Prescott, "The Thirsty Deer and the Lord of Life: Some Contexts for *Amoretti* 67–70," *Spenser Studies* 6 (1985), 33–76.

64. See Marotti, *Manuscript*; Wall, *Imprint of Gender*.

65. Among the many instances of this work is Charles Cathcart, "Authorship, Indebtedness, and the Children of the King's Revels," *Studies in English Literature* 45 (2005), 357–374; Cathcart reasserts the possibility of authorship within theatrical collaboration. In her recent study *Collaborations with the Past: Reshaping Shakespeare across Time and Media*, Diana E. Henderson develops a model of collaboration, primarily, though not exclusively, tailored to later writers and filmmakers adapting an earlier text; throughout the book she acknowledges the complex and often negative political valences of "collaboration" but also the opportunities for resistance, ambivalence, and authorial agency (Ithaca: Cornell University Press, 2006).

66. Stephen B. Dobranski, *Milton, Authorship, and the Book Trade* (Cambridge: Cambridge University Press, 1999).

67. On the theory of a "Delian tradition," see esp. William Shakespeare, *The Sonnets and A Lover's Complaint*, ed. John Kerrigan (Harmondsworth: Penguin, 1986), 13–15; *Shakespeare's Sonnets*, ed. Katherine Duncan-Jones, The Arden Shakespeare (London: Thomas Nelson, 1997), 88–95; Thomas P. Roche, Jr., *Petrarch and the English Sonnet Sequences* (New York: AMS Press, 1989), 343–344, 440–461. I challenge many assumptions in these studies in my essay "'Dressing old words new'?"

68. Also see the expanded discussion of this issue about Daniel in my essay, "'Lending soft audience to my sweet design': Shifting Roles and Shifting Readings of Shakespeare's 'A Lover's Complaint,'" *Shakespeare Survey* 58 (2005), 26. John Roe also draws attention to Daniel's title page, but rather than comparing different versions of it, he focuses on the contrast between the 1592 title page and its counterpart in Thorpe's edition of Shakespeare, arguing that Daniel's paratextual material offers an encouragement to connect the ensuing texts that is absent in the Shakespearean edition (*The Poems* [Cambridge: Cambridge University Press, 1992], 63).

69. Love, *Scribal Publication*, esp. 52–54, 180–181; North, "Finis."

70. *Stanford's Anthology*, 269–275.

71. Love, *Scribal Publication*, 52–54, also notes that scribal practices encouraged continuing editing, though Love's argument, unlike mine, focuses on not the resulting assertion of authorial agency but rather how such revisions complicate the ideal of final intention.

72. Marotti, *Manuscript*, 22–23.

73. *The Variorum Edition of the Poetry of John Donne: The Holy Sonnets*, ed. Paul A. Parrish et al. (Bloomington: Indiana University Press, 2005), lx–lxxi.

74. For a more detailed exposition of this argument, see my essay "'And Thus Leave Off': Reevaluating Mary Wroth's Folger Manuscript, V.a.104," *Tulsa Studies in Women's Literature* 23 (2003), 273–291.

75. A few critics anticipated my challenge to Roberts's reading of the manuscript, although they adduced evidence different from mine. See Gavin Alexander, "Constant Works: A Framework for Reading Mary Wroth," *Sidney Newsletter and Journal* 14 (1996), 5–32; Jeff Masten, "'Shall I turne blabb?': Circulation, Gender, and Subjectivity in Mary Wroth's Sonnets," in *Reading Mary Wroth: Representing Alternatives in Early Modern England*, ed. Naomi J. Miller and Gary Waller (Knoxville: University of Tennessee Press, 1991); Elizabeth Hanson, "Boredom and Whoredom: Reading Renaissance Women's Sonnet Sequences," *Yale Journal of Criticism* 10 (1997), 165–191.

76. See *The Poems of Lady Mary Wroth*, ed. Josephine A. Roberts (Baton Rouge: Louisiana State University Press, 1983), 61–65. All citations of Wroth are from this edition. Roberts also discusses V.a.104 as a unified collection in an article anticipating many arguments in her edition, "The Biographical Problem of *Pamphilia to Amphilanthus*," *Tulsa Studies in Women's Literature* 1 (1982), esp. 43–44.

77. Compare Love, *Scribal Publication*, 53–54, on how editing made scribes feel more attached to the text; below I will make the different but complementary argument that it had a comparable and too often neglected impact on writers.

78. On the possibility that the manuscript was shared with others, see, e.g., Michael G. Brennan, "Creating Female Authorship in the Early Seventeenth Century: Ben Jonson and Lady Mary Wroth," in *Women's Writing and the Circulation of Ideas: Manuscript Publication in England, 1550–1800*, ed. George L. Justice and Nathan Tinker (Cambridge: Cambridge University Press, 2002), esp. 75, 79–81.

79. I am indebted to Donald Rowe for valuable observations on this subject.

80. Rose, *Authors*, 8; Chartier, *Order of Books*, 34.

81. Throughout this chapter, all citations from Shakespeare are to *The Riverside Shakespeare*, ed. G. Blakemore Evans, 2nd ed. (Boston: Houghton Mifflin, 1997).

82. See, e.g., Robert Kaufman, "Aura, Still," *October* 99 (Winter 2002), esp. 48–49; his essay "Negatively Capable Dialectics: Keats, Vendler, Adorno, and the Theory of Avant-Garde," *Critical Inquiry* 27 (2001), 354–384; and my essay "The Politics of Aesthetics: Recuperating Formalism and the Country House Poem," in *Renaissance Literature and Its Formal Engagements*, ed. Mark David Rasmussen (New York: Palgrave Press, 2002). My essay is an expanded version of one that appeared in a special issue of *Modern Language Quarterly* 61 (2000) devoted to form; that issue includes a number of valuable contributions to this debate.

### CHAPTER 5: THE MYTH OF JANUS

1. See Jonathan Culler, *The Pursuit of Signs: Semiotics, Literature, Deconstruction* (Ithaca: Cornell University Press, 1981), esp. 149–152. The phrase I quote appears on 149.

2. Throughout this chapter I cite *Collected Poems of Sir Thomas Wyatt*, ed. Kenneth Muir and Patricia Thomson (Liverpool: Liverpool University Press, 1969).

3. Roland Greene, *Post-Petrarchism: Origins and Innovations of the Western Lyric Sequence* (Princeton: Princeton University Press, 1991), esp. 19–20, 22–62.

4. Gerald Prince, "The Disnarrated," *Style* 22 (1988), 1–8.

5. On time in Wyatt's poetry, see Jane Hedley, *Power in Verse: Metaphor and Metonymy in the Renaissance Lyric* (University Park: Pennsylvania State University Press, 1988), 37–48.

6. On the relationship of verse forms to content in Herbert, see, e.g., Achsah Guibbory, *Ceremony and Community from Herbert to Milton: Literature, Religion, and Cultural Conflict in Seventeenth-century England* (Cambridge: Cambridge University Press, 1998), 65–67; Joseph H. Summers, *George Herbert: His Religion and Art* (Cambridge: Harvard University Press, 1954), in which the discussion of the verse of "The Collar" appears on 90–92; and Helen Vendler, *The Poetry of George Herbert* (Cambridge: Harvard University Press, 1975), 131.

7. *The Works of George Herbert*, ed. F. E. Hutchinson (Oxford: Clarendon Press, 1941).

8. Michael C. Schoenfeldt, *Prayer and Power: George Herbert and Renaissance Courtship* (Chicago: University of Chicago Press, 1991), esp. 105–106.

9. Richard Strier, *Love Known: Theology and Experience in George Herbert's Poetry* (Chicago: University of Chicago Press, 1983), 219.

10. Alternatively, this divide can be discussed in terms of a split between speaker and author; see, e.g., A. D. Nuttall, *Overheard by God: Fiction and Prayer in Herbert, Milton, Dante and St John* (London: Methuen, 1980), 3.

11. Although the destabilizing force of the conclusion is more subterranean and delimited than Barbara Leah Harman suggests, her reading offers a useful corrective to the critical move of finding comprehensive spiritual resolution in the concluding lines (*Costly Monuments: Representations of the Self in George Herbert's Poetry* [Cambridge: Harvard University Press, 1982], 76–88).

12. Indeed, tracing the interplay of narrative and lyric in these and many other poems can be a particularly fruitful way of teaching students the value of both learning and challenging traditional categories of literary analysis, such as generic definitions.

13. Heather McHugh, "Moving Means, Meaning Moves: Notes on Lyric Destination," in *Poets Teaching Poets: Self and the World*, ed. Gregory Orr and Ellen Bryant Voigt (Ann Arbor: University of Michigan Press, 1996), 208.

14. Maria Teresa Micaela Prendergast, "Philoclea Parsed: Prose, Verse, and Femininity in Sidney's *Old Arcadia*," in *Framing Elizabethan Fictions: Contemporary Approaches to Early Modern Narrative Prose*, ed. Constance C. Relihan (Kent, OH: Kent State University Press, 1996), 109, 115.

15. The several essays in which Kaufman develops his argument for distinguishing the aesthetic and aestheticization include "Red Kant, or The Persistence of the Third *Critique* in Adorno and Jameson," *Critical Inquiry* 26 (2000), 682–724; and "Negatively Capable Dialectics: Keats, Vendler, Adorno, and the Theory of Avant-Garde," *Critical Inquiry* 27 (2001), 354–384. Many other critics have also demonstrated the relevance of formal and aesthetic issues to Marxism and other forms of materialism; see, e.g., Anthony Easthope, *Poetry as Discourse* (London: Methuen, 1983), esp. 22–24 and Chapter 4.

16. Susan Stanford Friedman, "Lyric Subversions of Narrative in Women's Writing: Virginia Woolf and the Tyranny of Plot," in *Reading Narrative: Form, Ethics, Ideology*, ed. James Phelan (Columbus: Ohio State University Press, 1989), 180.

17. *The Complete Works of Percy Bysshe Shelley*, ed. Roger Ingpen and Walter E. Peck, Vol. 7 (New York: Gordion Press, 1965), 115.

18. John Stuart Mill, "Thoughts on Poetry and Its Varieties," in *Autobiography and Literary Essays*, ed. John M. Robson and Jack Stillinger (Toronto and London: University of Toronto Press and Routledge and Kegan Paul, 1981), 345 (Vol. 1 of *The Collected Works of John Stuart Mill*, ed. John M. Robson et al., 33 vols. [1963–1991]).

19. Robert E. Stillman, *Sidney's Poetic Justice: "The Old Arcadia," Its Eclogues, and Renaissance Pastoral Traditions* (Lewisburg, PA, and London: Bucknell University Press and Associated University Presses, 1986); the passages cited appear on 86, 86, 88, and 88 respectively.

20. Jay Clayton, *Romantic Vision and the Novel* (Cambridge: Cambridge University Press, 1987).

21. Mary Thomas Crane, *Framing Authority: Sayings, Self, and Society in Sixteenth-Century England* (Princeton: Princeton University Press, 1993), 163.

22. Timothy Bahti, *Ends of the Lyric: Direction and Consequence in Western Poetry* (Baltimore: Johns Hopkins University Press, 1996), esp. 21–23.

23. Susan Stanford Friedman, "Craving Stories: Narrative and Lyric in Contemporary Theory and Women's Long Poems," in *Feminist Measures: Soundings in Poetry and Theory*, ed. Lynn Keller and Cristanne Miller (Ann Arbor: University of Michigan Press, 1994), 15–42.

24. See Susan Stanford Friedman, "Lyric Subversions of Narrative," and her more persuasive modification of that argument in "Craving Stories." See also James Phelan, *Narrative as Rhetoric: Technique, Audiences, Ethics, Ideology* (Columbus: Ohio State University Press, 1996).

25. James Phelan, "Rhetorical Ethics and Lyric Narrative: Robert Frost's 'Home Burial,'" *Poetics Today* 25 (2004), 627–651; and "Toward a Rhetoric and Ethics of Lyric Narrative: The Case of 'A Clean, Well-Lighted Place,'" *Frame* 17 (2004), 27–43. I thank the author for making this work available to me prior to publication.

26. Clayton, *Romantic Vision*.

27. Theodor W. Adorno, "Lyric Poetry and Society," trans. Bruce Mayo, *Telos* 20 (1974), 56–71.

28. *The Poems of Richard Lovelace*, ed. C. H. Wilkinson (Oxford: Clarendon Press, 1930).

29. Susan Stewart, *Poetry and the Fate of the Senses* (Chicago: University of Chicago Press, 2002), 203–207.

30. Northrop Frye, "Approaching the Lyric," in *Lyric Poetry: Beyond New Criticism*, ed. Chaviva Hošek and Patricia Parker (Ithaca: Cornell University Press, 1985), 32.

31. John Donne, *The Divine Poems*, ed. Helen Gardner (Oxford: Clarendon Press, 1952).

32. Jonathan F. S. Post, *English Lyric Poetry: The Early Seventeenth Century* (London: Routledge, 1999), 19.

33. See, e.g., A. B. Chambers, *Transfigured Rites in Seventeenth-Century English Poetry* (Columbia: University of Missouri Press, 1992), 203–204.

34. Donne, *The Elegies and The Songs and Sonnets*, ed. Helen Gardner (Oxford: Clarendon Press, 1965). I cite this edition throughout this chapter.

35. Although this potentiality has been largely neglected by critics, Earl Miner has commented briefly but cogently on it in "Why Lyric?" in Earl Miner and Amiya Dev, eds. *The Renewal of Song: Renovation in Lyric Conception and Practice* (Calcutta: Seagull Books, 2000), 13, 15; his claim that in such passages that lyric may not be interrupted by narrative or drama is, however, problematical.

36. Peter Brooks, *Reading for the Plot: Design and Intention in Narrative* (New York: Random House, 1984), Chapter 2.

37. See, e.g., two essays by Kaufman: "Negatively Capable Dialectics," esp. 362; and "Aura, Still," *October* 99 (Winter 2002), esp. 46–52.

38. I cite *The Yale Edition of the Shorter Poems of Edmund Spenser*, ed. William A. Oram et al. (New Haven: Yale University Press, 1989).

39. Frye, "Approaching the Lyric," 32–33.

40. Charlton T. Lewis and Charles Short, eds., *A New Latin Dictionary* (New York: American Book Company, 1907), s.v. "meditor"; David Noel Freedman et al., eds. *The Anchor Bible Dictionary* (New York: Doubleday, 1912), 525.

41. All citations are to *The Poetical Works of Robert Herrick*, ed. L. C. Martin (Oxford: Clarendon Press, 1956).

42. James Schiffer, "The Sonnets as Anti-Narrative," paper presented at conference "The New Formalism and the Lyric in History," University of Michigan, January 2001. I thank the author for making his work available to me prior to publication.

43. For an intriguing analogue, compare Clayton, *Romantic Vision and the Novel*, 148–150. In the course of analyzing how Wordsworth moves from an emphasis on consequences to a focus on human feeling, Jay Clayton examines visionary moments and images in George Eliot's *Adam Bede*. He demonstrates that, inasmuch as Dinah is part of the narrative order as well as the "higher" order, she bridges the two; but Clayton, like many other critics, primarily emphasizes instead the propensity of the modes to rupture each other.

44. *Ben Jonson*, ed. C. H. Herford, Percy Simpson, and Evelyn Simpson, 11 vols. (Oxford: Clarendon Press, 1925–1952).

45. Herrick, *Poetical Works*.

46. The text appears in *Henry Stanford's Anthology: An Edition of Cambridge University Library Manuscript Dd.5.75*, ed. Steven V. May (New York: Garland, 1988).

47. Sharon Cameron, *Lyric Time: Dickinson and the Limits of Genre* (Baltimore: Johns Hopkins University Press, 1979).

48. David Herman, *Story Logic: Problems and Possibilities of Narrative* (Lincoln: University of Nebraska Press, 2002), Chapter 6.

49. Prince, "The Disnarrated," 2.

50. Uri Margolin, "Of What Is Past, Is Passing, or to Come: Temporality, Aspectuality, Modality, and the Nature of Literary Narrative," in *Narratologies: New Perspectives on Narrative Analysis*, ed. David Herman (Columbus: Ohio State University Press, 1999), 153–159. Structuralist narratologists have also commented on the use of the future tense, though typically in passing. See, e.g., the discussion of optatives, conditions, and predictives in Tzvetan Todorov, *The Poetics of Prose*, trans. Richard Howard (Ithaca: Cornell University Press, 1977), 114–116.

51. Michael Riffaterre, *Semiotics of Poetry* (Bloomington: Indiana University Press, 1978), 12.

52. George T. Wright, *Hearing the Measures: Shakespearean and Other Inflections* (Madison: University of Wisconsin Press, 2001), 56.

53. I thank Jennifer Lewin for suggesting to me the parallel between this poem and "My lute, awake!"

54. See two essays by James Phelan, "Rhetorical Ethics and Lyric Narrative" and "Toward a Rhetoric and Ethics of Lyric Narrative."

55. For one version of this common position, see William Waters, *Poetry's Touch: On Lyric Address* (Ithaca: Cornell University Press, 2003), 8–9.

56. Catherine Bates, *The Rhetoric of Courtship in Elizabethan Language and Literature* (Cambridge: Cambridge University Press, 1992); Ilona Bell, *Elizabethan Women and the Poetry of Courtship* (Cambridge: Cambridge University Press, 1998).

57. Mary Ann Radzinowicz, *Milton's Epics and the Book of Psalms* (Princeton: Princeton University Press, 1989), 1.

58. Henry Ainsworth, *Annotations Upon the Book of Psalmes*, 2nd ed. (London, 1617), A2–A2ᵛ.

59. Robert Scholes, "Language, Narrative, and Anti-Narrative," *Critical Inquiry* 7 (1980), 210.

60. Greene, *Post-Petrarchism*, esp. 34–35, 42.

61. On the relationship between achieved seduction and temporality, see Claudine Raynaud, "Naked Words: Figures of Seduction in Donne's Poetry," in *La Poésie Métaphysique de John Donne*, ed. Claudine Raynaud (Tours: Groupe de Recherches Anglo-Américaines de l'Université François Rabelais de Tours, 2002), 35.

62. Because of the popularity and influence of this text in England during the early modern period, instances from it can usefully be juxtaposed with those from romances by English authors.

63. *The First Part of the Countess of Montgomery's Urania*, ed. Josephine A. Roberts (Binghamton, NY: Medieval and Renaissance Texts and Studies, 1995), 254. Future references to this edition appear within my text.

64. Stillman, *Sidney's Poetic Justice*, 85.

65. Citations from the *Old Arcadia* are to Sir Philip Sidney, *The Countess of Pembroke's Arcadia (The Old Arcadia)*, ed. Jean Robertson (Oxford: Clarendon Press, 1973). The quotation in question appears on 55.

66. Sir Philip Sidney, *The Countess of Pembroke's Arcadia*, ed. Maurice Evans (Harmondsworth, England: Penguin, 1977), 773. Subsequent page references are to this edition and will appear in parentheses within my text. When discussing both versions of the *Arcadia*, I follow its author's practice in referring to characters in terms of the name and gender associated with them at that point in the text, since this practice is so significant in the text.

67. David Kalstone, *Sidney's Poetry: Contexts and Interpretations* (Cambridge: Harvard University Press, 1965), 71–72.

68. Blair Worden, *The Sound of Virtue: Philip Sidney's "Arcadia" and Elizabethan Politics* (New Haven: Yale University Press, 1996), 11.

69. On these aspects of Antissia, see, e.g., Sheila T. Cavanagh, *Cherished Torment: The Emotional Geography of Lady Mary Wroth's "Urania"* (Pittsburgh: Duquesne University Press, 2001), 73–77; Naomi J. Miller, *Changing the Subject: Mary Wroth and Figurations of Gender in Early Modern England* (Lexington: University of Kentucky Press, 1996), 174–176.

70. Although Robert F. Stillman's analysis differs from mine in emphasizing the dangers of solipsism and of persuasion rather than gender, in "The Perils of Fancy: Poetry and Self-Love in *The Old Arcadia*" (*TSLL* 26 [1984], 1–17) he comments usefully on what their lyrics show about the princes. Maria Teresa Micaela Prendergast demonstrates persuasively that the *Old Arcadia* connects femininity and poesy in the broad sense of the latter, but, as my earlier comment on her essay indicates, her assertions about how and why Sidney distinguishes verse and prose in this text are not convincing ("Philoclea Parsed").

71. For an analysis of one exception, see R. S. White, "Functions of Poems and Songs in Elizabethan Romance and Romantic Comedy," *English Studies* 5 (1987), 399–400. This essay also provides a useful overview of its subject.

72. On the association of songs with marginalized characters, see esp. two studies by Leslie C. Dunn: "The Lady Sings in Welsh: Women's Song as Marginal Discourse on the Shakespearean Stage" in *Place and Displacement in the Renaissance*, ed. Alvin Vos, Medieval and Renaissance Texts and Studies (Binghamton: State University of New York, 1995); and "Ophelia's Songs in *Hamlet*: Music, Madness, and the Feminine," in *Embodied Voices: Representing Female Vocality in Western Culture*, ed. Leslie C. Dunn and Nancy A. Jones (Cambridge: Cambridge University Press, 1994). Also see John H. Long, *Shakespeare's Use of Music: A Study of the Music and Its Performance in the Original Production of Seven Comedies* (1955; rpt., Gainesville: University of Florida Press, 1961), esp. 3. These critics' analyses differ from mine in a number of ways, however. For example, Dunn also observes the containment of the threat represented by singing women, but she attributes it largely to the framing devices used by men (64–66), and she argues throughout that the contrast between song and other discursive registers primarily intensifies the prior marginalization of these characters. Though he also notes the power of song in performance (66–67), Long unpersuasively attributes the association of song with marginal characters to mores forbidding gentlemen to perform publicly (3).

73. William R. Bowden, *The English Dramatic Lyric, 1603–42: A Study in Stuart Dramatic Technique* (New Haven and London: Yale University Press and Oxford University Press, 1951), v–vi; Diana E. Henderson, *Passion Made Public: Elizabethan Lyric, Gender, and Performance* (Urbana: University of Illinois Press, 1995). Citations from these books appear in parentheses within my text.

74. Jonathan Culler, "Apostrophe Revisited," paper delivered at the 2001 Modern Language Association convention in New Orleans. I am grateful to the author for making his work available to me prior to publication.

75. Andrew Welsh, *Roots of Lyric: Primitive Poetry and Modern Poetics* (Princeton: Princeton University Press, 1978), Chapters 6, 7.

76. I am indebted to Dunn for drawing my attention to this comment and for a useful analysis of the passage in which it appears ("The Lady Sings in Welsh," 58–60).

77. Welsh, *Roots of Lyric*, esp. 162–166.

78. Wolfgang Clemen, *Shakespeare's Soliloquies*, trans. Charity Scott Stokes (London: Methuen, 1987); James Hirsh, *Shakespeare and the History of Soliloquies* (Madison, NJ, and London: Fairleigh Dickinson University Press and Associated University Presses, 2003).

79. Henderson, *Passion Made Public*, 169.

80. Paul Alpers, "Pastoral and the Domain of Lyric in Spenser's *Shepheardes Calender*," *Representations*, no. 12 (Fall 1985), 83–100.

81. On the relationship of singing to social status, see esp. Dunn, "The Lady Sings in Welsh" and "Ophelia's Songs in *Hamlet*." Also see John H. Long, *Shakespeare's Use of Music*.

82. Nona Paula Fienberg, "'She Chanted Snatches of Old Tunes': Ophelia's Songs in a Polyphonic *Hamlet*," in *Approaches to Teaching Shakespeare's* Hamlet, ed. Bernice W. Kliman (New York: Modern Language Association of America, 2002), 154–155.

83. In "Functions of Poems and Songs" (404–405), R. S. White notes a different but related form of transgression, the use of songs to call into question the celebration of marriage on which Shakespearean comedies typically end.

84. William C. Carroll, "Songs of Madness: The Lyric Afterlife of Shakespeare's Poor Tom," *Shakespeare Survey* 55 (2002), 82–95.

85. On the sources of Ophelia's songs, see Ross W. Duffin, *Shakespeare's Songbook* (New York: W. W. Norton, 2004), esp. 52–53, 72–74, 407–408.

86. Greene, *Post-Petrarchism*, esp. 5–13, 109–152; Welsh, *Roots of Lyric*, esp. Chapter 6.

87. On the putative coerciveness of lyric, see Greene, *Post-Petrarchism*, esp. 5–6; Ramie Targoff, *Common Prayer: The Language of Public Devotion in Early Modern England* (Chicago: University of Chicago Press, 2001).

88. Mark W. Booth, *The Experience of Songs* (New Haven: Yale University Press, 1981), esp. 14–17.

89. See Maurice Bloch's discussion of song as one type of formalized language, "Symbols, Song, Dance and Features of Articulation: Is Religion an Extreme Form of Traditional Authority?" in *Archives Européennes de Sociologie* 15 (1974), 55–81.

90. White, "Functions of Poems and Songs," 392–405.

91. See Sigmund Freud, The Standard Edition, VIII, 88–89 on connections between dreamwork and jokework.

92. For a valuable discussion of Feste's final song, see Booth, *Experience of Songs*, 1–5, 26–28.

93. J. L. Austin, *How to Do Things with Words*, ed. J. O. Urmson and Marina Sbisà (Cambridge: Harvard University Press, 1962), 22.

94. The central argument of Dunn's "Ophelia's Songs" is that the play links song to madness, irrationality, and the feminine. See also Sophie Tomlinson, *Women on Stage in Stuart Drama* (Cambridge: Cambridge University Press, 2005), 129–155.

95. My interpretations differ significantly from Dunn's, however, inasmuch as I emphasize the significant, though limited, communicative potential of Ophelia's words.

96. For a more detailed discussion of authorizers, see my essay "'The tip of his seducing tongue': Authorizers in *Henry V*, 'A Lover's Complaint,' and *Othello*," in *Critical Essays on Shakespeare's "A Lover's Complaint": Suffering Ecstasy*, ed. Shirley Sharon-Zisser (Burlington, VT: Ashgate, 2006). I am indebted to Linda Woodbridge for some useful comments in personal correspondence on the issue of authorizers. Citing Desdemona's song as an instance of authorizers, the essay also includes an early version of the argument about Desdemona that I lay out in this chapter.

97. On this and other issues about the passage, see Emily C. Bartels, "Strategies of Submission: Desdemona, the Duchess, and the Assertion of Desire," *Studies in English Literature* 36 (1996), 417–433; Bartels and I agree that the song empowers Desdemona, though Bartels traces that effect to its content rather than to its status as a song (see esp. 429–431).

98. On the addition of Barbary and other changes in the text, see Ernest Brennecke, "'Nay, That's Not Next!': The Significance of Desdemona's 'Willow Song,'" *Shakespeare Quarterly* 4 (1953), 35–38.

99. Sources of the willow song are analyzed in Duffin, *Shakespeare's Songbook*, 467–470.

100. My argument thus differs from that of Brennecke, who sees the song as a product of "her subconscious awareness" ("'Nay, That's Not Next!'" 37).

101. Lloyd Davis, "The Plots of *Othello*: Narrative, Desire, Selfhood," *Sydney Studies in English* 25 (1999), esp. 17.

102. Other analyses of the power of song include Roland Barthes's theory of what he terms the "grain" in the singing voice: identified in his essay with a bodily materiality, the grain plays down the literal meaning of the song and instead conveys the authority of the Father. One might question that argument in some respects (e.g., Do not certain voices, notably sopranos, seem to escape materiality? Do not many songs with "grain" in Barthes's sense lack authority?), and in this instance Desdemona's authority is closely related to her ability to create meaning. But his argument does remind us how intense the impact of the singing voice can be, thus, from a different perspective, implicitly questioning the critical interpretations that focus on Desdemona's impotence ("The Grain of the Voice," in *Image, Music, Text*, trans. Stephen Heath [New York: Hill and Wang, 1977]).

103. Henderson, *Passion Made Public*, esp. 169.

## CHAPTER 6: THE RHETORICS OF LYRIC

1. In contrast to my point about borders, Philip Schwyzer, in an astute article, argues that Milton associates Sabrina with the purity of boundaries, which, he maintains, the text contrasts with the impurity and hybridity of the region's borderlands ("Purity and Danger on the West Bank of the Severn: The Cultural Geography of *A Masque Presented at Ludlow Castle*, 1634," *Representations*, no. 60 [Fall 1997], 22–48).

2. All citations from Milton are to *Complete Poems and Major Prose*, ed. Merritt Y. Hughes (Indianapolis: Odyssey Press, Bobbs-Merrill, 1957); translations of his Latin and Italian poems are also from this volume.

3. Louis L. Martz, "The Music of *Comus*," in *Illustrious Evidence*, ed. Earl Miner (Berkeley: University of California Press, 1975), 106–107. The shift from Martz's assertion that the text valorizes and celebrates poesy to my emphasis on Milton's anxieties about lyric aptly marks a shift in critical paradigms.

4. Stella P. Revard, *Milton and the Tangles of Neaera's Hair: The Making of the 1645 "Poems"* (Columbia: University of Missouri Press, 1997), 131. Also see 140–146 for her argument that the positive associations of the sirens dominate here.

5. S. E. Sprott, *John Milton, "A Maske": The Earlier Versions* (Toronto: University of Toronto Press, 1973), 8.

6. *A Variorum Commentary on the Poems of John Milton*, ed. A. S. P. Woodhouse and Douglas Bush, Vol. 2, Pt. 3 (London: Routledge and Kegan Paul, 1972), 965; John Guillory, *Poetic Authority: Spenser, Milton, and Literary History* (New York: Columbia University Press, 1983), 90.

7. See Nancy Lindheim, "Pastoral and Masque at Ludlow, *University of Toronto Quarterly* 67 (1998), 654–655, 659–660; the phrase cited appears on 655.

8. Katharine Eisaman Maus, *Inwardness and Theater in the English Renaissance* (Chicago: University of Chicago Press, 1995), esp. 32. Debora Kuller Shuger, *Habits of Thought in the English Renaissance: Religion, Politics, and the Dominant Culture* (1990; rpt., Toronto: University of Toronto Press, 1997), 257.

9. Lynn Enterline, *The Rhetoric of the Body from Ovid to Shakespeare* (Cambridge: Cambridge University Press, 2000), Chapter 3.

10. Ramie Targoff, *Common Prayer: The Language of Public Devotion in Early Modern England* (Chicago: University of Chicago Press, 2001), esp. Chapters 1 and 2.

11. Compare Michael Macovski's Bakhtinian analysis of the passage, which stresses that the poet is also addressing former selves, *Dialogue and Literature: Apostrophe, Auditors, and the Collapse of Romantic Discourse* [New York: Oxford University Press, 1994], 56–66.

12. Wordsworth, *"Lyrical Ballads" and Other Poems, 1797–1800*, ed. James Butler and Karen Green (Ithaca: Cornell University Press, 1992).

13. I cite *The Riverside Chaucer*, 3rd ed., ed. Larry D. Benson and F. N. Robinson (Boston: Houghton Mifflin, 1987).

14. Two important exceptions do trace connections between Renaissance literature and the dramatic monologue: John Maynard, "Speaker, Listener, and Overhearer: The Reader in the Dramatic Poem," *Browning Institute Studies* 15 (1987), 105–112; Alan Sinfield, *Dramatic Monologue* (London: Methuen, 1977), Chapter 5.

15. Marshall Brown, "Negative Poetics: On Skepticism and the Lyric Voice," *Representations*, no. 86 (Spring 2004), 131.

16. In addition to Maynard's "Speaker, Listener, and Overhearer" and Sinfield's *Dramatic Monologue*, among the most influential treatments of these and related issues are Carol Christ, *Victorian and Modern Poetics* (Chicago: University of Chicago Press, 1984), Chapter 2; Robert Langbaum, *The Poetry of Experience: The Dramatic Monologue in Modern Literary Tradition* (London: Chatto and Windus, 1957); and two essays by Ralph W. Rader, "The Dramatic Monologue and Related Lyric Forms," *Critical Inquiry* 3 (1976), 131–151; and "Notes on Some Structural Varieties and Variations in Dramatic 'I' Poems and Their Theoretical Implications," *Victorian Poetry* 22 (1984), 103–120. In Chapter 2 Langbaum argues that the reader's predominant response to the dramatic monologue's speaker is sympathy, though he acknowledges the presence of judgment as well. For the argument that we judge the speaker in dramatic monologue in ways we do not use to evaluate his counterpart in lyric, see, e.g., Rader, "Notes," esp. 103–104.

17. Maynard, "Speaker, Listener, and Overhearer."

18. Ezra Pound, "A Retrospect," in *Literary Essays of Ezra Pound*, ed. T. S. Eliot (New York: New Directions, 1918), 11–12.

19. See, e.g., William Empson, *Some Versions of Pastoral* (London: Chatto and Windus, 1935).

20. For earlier versions of this argument, see, e.g., Chapter 6 of my study, *A Happier Eden: The Politics of Marriage in the Stuart Epithalamium* (Ithaca: Cornell University Press, 1990).

21. See esp. my essay "Guess Who's Coming to Dinner? Reevaluating Formalism and the Country House Poem," *Modern Language Quarterly* 61 (2000), 59–77; reprinted in revised and expanded form as "The Politics of Aesthetics: Recuperating Formalism and the Country House Poem," in *Renaissance Literature and Its Formal Engagements*, ed. Mark Rasmussen (New York: Palgrave Press, 2002).

22. Theodor W. Adorno, "Lyric Poetry and Society," *Telos* 20 (1974), 56–71.

23. Semler's observation was made at a meeting of the Macquarie University (Australia) Department of English Early Modern Group, July 2006.

24. Hutcheon has written frequently and powerfully on replacing combative exchanges with collaborative "both/and" models. See, e.g., "Presidential Address," *Publications of the Modern Language Association* 116 (2001), 518–530. The citation is from Linda Hutcheon, "Saving Collegiality," *Profession 2006* (New York: Modern Language Association of America, 2006), 62.

25. For a fuller discussion of this and other issues in collegiality, see Dubrow, Introduction, in *Profession 2006*, as well as other articles and features in the section on collegiality in the journal.

# Index

Halpern, Richard, 149, 267n96
Hamburger, Käte, 263n20
Hamlin, Hannibal, 256n57
Hammons, Pamela S., 63, 254n25
handshake metaphor, 5, 106
Hanson, Elizabeth, 272n75
Harman, Barbara Leah, 273n11
harmony, celestial, 36, 169–71
Hart, Jonathan, 67, 255n39
Harwood, Gwen, "Fido's Paw is Bleeding," 2
Hatoum, Mona, 124
Häublein, Ernst, 135, 166, 170, 266n78
headnotes, 124–26, 131, 137. *See also* Watson,
    Thomas
Heaney, Seamus, *Electric Light*, 128
Hedley, Jane, 191, 262n10, 273n5
heightening, 200–202, 207–8, 212–13
Henderson, Diana E., 216–19, 271n65, 278n73
Herbert, George, 88–89, 118; "Aaron," 89;
    "Church-floore, The," 89; "Collar, The," 90,
    94, 165, 189, 191–93, 199; "Dialogue," 88;
    "Easter," 31; "Obedience," 81; *Priest to the
    Temple*, 89
Herman, David, 205, 276n48
Hernadi, Paul, 243n16
Herodotus, 47
Herrick, Robert: "Argument of his Book," 33;
    "Fresh Cheese and Cream," 88; *Hesperides*,
    41, 177–78; "Lyrick for Legacies," 41; "Ode of
    the Birth of our Saviour," 36, 148–49; "Ode
    to Sir Clipsebie Crew," 2; "To his Verses,"
    93–94; "To Musick, A Song," 25; "To Robin
    Red-brest," 100; "To the King," 28; "Vision,"
    12, 51–53, 203
Hirsch, Edward, 19
Hirsch, James, 217, 258n92, 278n78
historicizing of lyric, 210
Hollander, John, 31–32, 36, 50, 130, 134, 175–76,
    248n36, 248n40, 256n60, 264n39, 265n65,
    270n47
homoeroticism, in Orpheus myth, 22–23
Hooker, Richard, 121
Hopkins, Brooke, 111, 262n14
Hughes, Langston, "Little Lyric (Of Great
    Importance)," 2
Hughes, Ted, *Birthday Letters*, 235
Hutcheon, Linda, 241, 281n24
Huth, Kimberly, 253n14

hybridity, 109, 194
Hyman, Wendy, 249n63
Hymen, 22
hymn, 32; in Marvell's "Bermudas," 142–43. *See
    also* psalms

identificatory voiceability, 94–102, 236; and
    Shakespeare's Sonnet 35, 103–5
immediacy: and distance, 139, 150–55; in
    Donne's "The Indifferent," 106–9; in
    Marvell's "Bermudas," 142–45;
    methodological problems, 109–17; in
    Milton's Nativity Ode, 145–50; in Wroth's
    *Pamphilia*, 141–42
immortalization, promise of, 38
infant mortality, 35
inscription, 38, 58; as ending, 100–101; and
    permanence, 139–41, 165; as product, 153–55
interaction, lyric of, 89
interplay: of narrative and lyric, 189–94,
    196–215; of songs and plays, 215–27
interruption, of solitary speech, 82
introductory poem, as mediating device, 126
irony, 28, 97–98

Jackson, Virginia, 65, 252n6, 254n31, 254n32
Johns, Adrian, 158, 268n6
Johnson, Barbara, 28, 247n22
Johnson, Paula, 248n36, 266n80
Johnson, W. R., 4, 66, 115, 243n14, 255n35,
    263n26
Jonson, Ben, 118, 131; "Celebration of Charis in
    Ten Lyrick Peeces," 41, 61, 72–74, 86, 101,
    203; *Forest*, 178; *Irish Masque*, 210; "To the
    Immortall Memorie, and Friendship . . . ,"
    28, 171–72
Jorgens, Elise Bickford, 248n36
judgment, and distance, 131–32

Kalas, Rayna, 118, 133, 264n38, 264n42
Kalstone, David, 179, 214, 271n55, 277n67
Kaske, Carol, 256n58
Kastan, David, 161, 269n13
Kaufman, Robert, 188, 196, 201, 254n33, 273n82,
    274n15, 275n37
Keats, John, "This living hand, now warm and
    capable," 110–11
"keepsakes," 157